# Anglais



## texts & methods

## BTS

Béatrice Firobind
*Professeur agrégé au lycée Claude Monet (Paris 13e)*

Marie-Hélène Fougeron
*Professeur certifié au lycée Jean Lurçat (Paris 13e)*

Les auteurs et l'éditeur tiennent à remercier :

- Claude Renucci, pour ses nombreuses suggestions, son aide indéfectible et ses relectures attentives,

- Alan Geary, Jodie Mitchell, Rob Mitchell, Sébastien Slisse et Keith Wycherley, pour leurs relectures de qualité.

Nathan
TECHNIQUE

# Votre manuel

Destiné à être utilisé sur les 2 années de BTS, ce manuel a pour ambition de vous aider à préparer les examens des différents BTS et à acquérir une utilisation fluide de l'anglais en vue de votre future situation professionnelle.

Il comprend :

- **1 chapitre pour faire la transition Lycée-BTS**, *The rules of the game*, qui commente les différentes typologies d'activités et de compétences attendues en sections de techniciens supérieurs ;
- **14 chapitres thématiques** à exploiter sur les 2 années de BTS ;
- **19 fiches méthode** réunies à la fin de l'ouvrage.

## Ouverture

Encourager la prise de parole sur le thème du chapitre par des activités d'anticipation variées

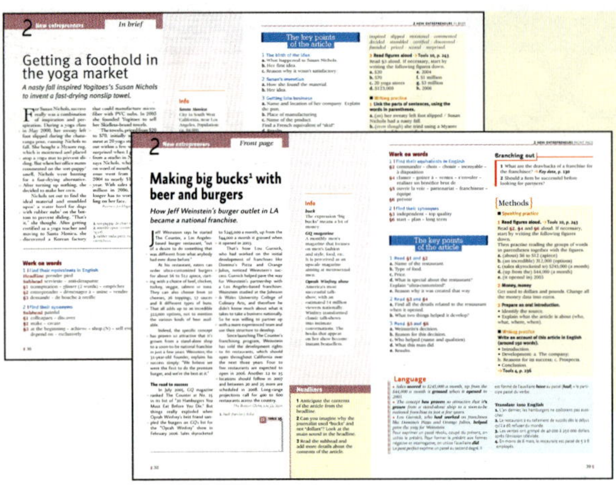


## In brief, Front page

Travailler à partir d'articles de presse et d'enregistrements authentiques, acquérir une méthode de compréhension et d'expression

- **In brief** : deux supports courts (un article de presse et un enregistrement)
- **Front page** : un article de presse plus long (type examen)

## Key data, Landmark

Acquérir des connaissances générales

- **Key data** : 3 pages de cours pour se forger une culture du monde de l'entreprise
- **Landmark** : zoom sur une entreprise ou un mouvement incontournable dans son domaine

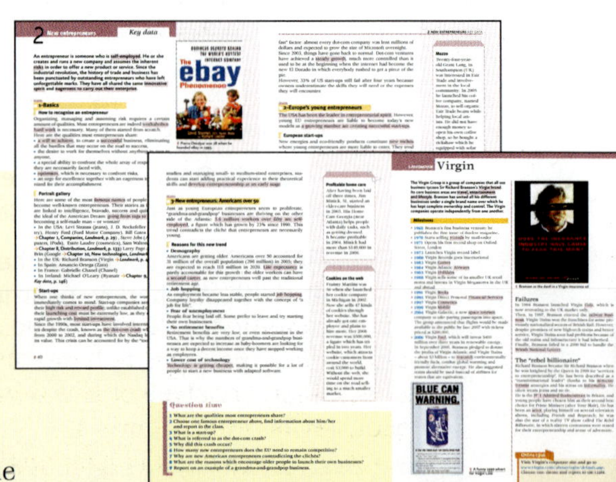

Les compétences d'expression mises en œuvre dans votre manuel sont identifiées par des pictogrammes :

Interaction orale

Prise de parole en continu

Expression écrite

(cf. *Cadre européen commun de référence pour les langues*)

## Vocabulary, CD

Apprendre du lexique de spécialité

■ **Vocabulary** : lexique essentiel du thème

■ **CD fourni avec le manuel** : un logiciel d'auto-apprentissage pour assimiler plus facilement le vocabulaire (lexique du manuel + mots supplémentaires)

→ **page 8**

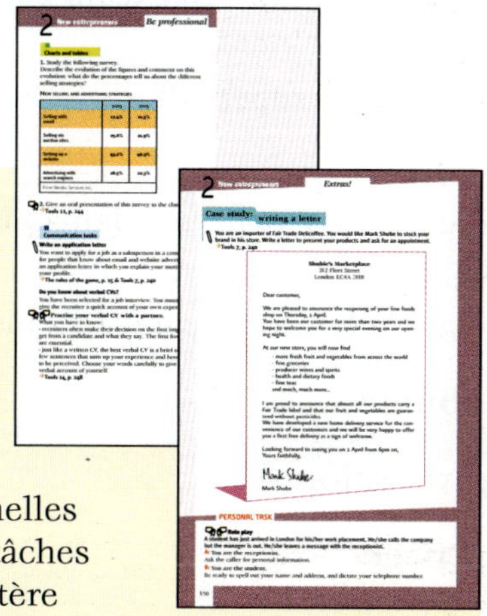

## Be Professional, Extras!

S'approprier la langue à partir d'activités de communication basées sur des situations professionnelles

■ **Be Professional** : tâches de production à caractère professionnel (supports : graphiques, recherches en ligne, jeux de rôle)

■ **Extras!** : études de cas à partir de documents professionnels, tâches personnelles

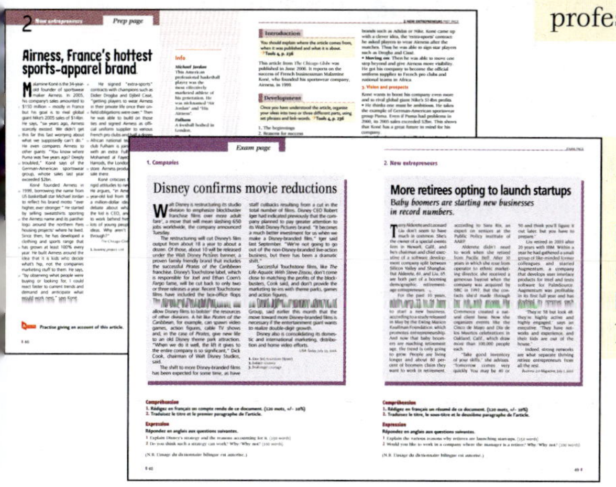
Airness, France's hottest sports-apparel brand

Disney confirms movie reductions

More retirees opting to launch startups

## Prep page, Exam page

Se préparer à l'examen

■ **Prep page** : compte rendu corrigé d'un article de presse pour s'entraîner

■ **Exam page** : un sujet conforme à l'examen écrit par chapitre

3. Rédiger un résumé

11. Utiliser des graphiques, diagrammes ou tableaux

## Tools

Des fiches méthode à lire sans modération pour :

- maîtriser les épreuves de l'examen
- mener à bien l'analyse et la production de documents professionnels
- réviser les bases de la langue anglaise

## 0 The rules of the game



## 1 Companies



## 2 New entrepreneurs



## 3 Work

## 8 Distribution



## 9 Transport



## 10 New technologies



## 11 Sustainable development

Tous les textes des articles des pages *In brief*, *Front page*, ainsi que les *Listening Practice* des ouvertures et des pages *In brief*, sont enregistrés sur les CD professeurs.
Les enregistrements sont signalés par la mention CD suivi du numéro de la ou des pistes concernées.

En complément de son manuel, **Nathan Technique** vous propose un logiciel d'aide à l'apprentissage et aux révisions, Woonoz. Cet outil original va vous aider à mémoriser le vocabulaire des différents thèmes de votre manuel d'anglais BTS et à gagner en efficacité.

## Qu'y a-t-il dans ce logiciel ?

Ce logiciel contient les **listes de vocabulaire de votre manuel d'anglais BTS enrichies de mots supplémentaires** (termes anglais et traductions en français). Elles sont classées en trois niveaux de difficulté. Dans chaque niveau, vous retrouvez les différents thèmes de votre manuel : *Companies, New entrepreneurs*, etc.

## Quelles sont les fonctionnalités possibles de ce logiciel ?

Le logiciel propose deux fonctionnalités.

- **Consulter** : vous voyez simultanément les mots anglais et leur traduction. Cela vous aide à mémoriser les différents termes.
- **Apprendre** : le logiciel vous présente les mots en anglais ou en français et vous devez penser à leur traduction, ou, si vous le souhaitez, saisir les termes demandés pour travailler votre orthographe. Vous configurez vous-même les différents paramètres de l'apprentissage. C'est la fonctionnalité phare du logiciel.

## Quelle est l'originalité de ce logiciel ?

Le moteur d'apprentissage du logiciel Woonoz est **basé sur des travaux de recherche sur la mémoire** et conçu pour **s'adapter automatiquement à vous** : plus vous avez de difficultés sur certains mots, plus il vous les présente. Cet outil ne se contente pas de vous évaluer : vous bénéficiez de toute la puissance du moteur d'apprentissage pour mémoriser toutes les bonnes réponses.

**Configuration minimale :** Mac/PC : 500 Mhz (1500 Mhz conseillé) - 128 Mo de RAM (256 Mo conseillé) - 80 Mo d'espace disque disponible pour l'installation
Carte graphique et moniteur ayant une résolution minimum de 1024x768
Systèmes d'exploitation : WindowsTM 98, 2000 ou XP; Mac OS 10.4 Tiger (avec Java 1.5)

**Procédure d'installation**

**Sous Windows**

1. Insérez le CD-ROM dans le lecteur prévu à cet effet.
2. Attendez le lancement automatique du programme d'installation. Si le programme se lance automatiquement, allez au point 4.
3. Si au bout d'1 minute le programme d'installation ne s'est pas lancé automatiquement, effectuez les opérations suivantes :
   - Cliquez sur le bouton [Démarrer] et sélectionnez la commande Exécuter.
   - Saisissez le nom du lecteur CD-ROM, suivi de la commande \Install.exe (par exemple si le lecteur se nomme D:, saisissez D:\Install.exe)
4. Suivez ensuite les instructions s'affichant à l'écran.

**Sous Mac**

1. Insérez le CD-ROM dans le lecteur prévu à cet effet.
2. Double Cliquez sur l'icône représentant votre CD-ROM.
3. Double cliquez sur le programme « install.dmg ».
4. Double cliquez sur le programme « Woonoz Installer ».
5. Suivez ensuite les instructions s'affichant à l'écran.
6. Pour éjecter le CD, éjectez d'abord le volume « NATHAN001_WOONOZ » puis éjectez le CD « NATHAN Bloz 001 ».

Une fois l'installation effectuée, retirez le CD-ROM du lecteur et utilisez l'icône pour lancer le logiciel.
**Pour toute question relative à l'installation et au fonctionnement du CD-ROM, contacter le support Woonoz par e-mail à support@woonoz.com.**

# IN THIS UNIT...

- ▶ Discover your book & learn how to use it
- ▶ Choose an ad & a company to work in
- ▶ Write your CV & a letter

# 0

## The rules of the game

**→ Before you START**

*In brief:* **Qualities for your CV**
*Front page:* **Working alone or in a team**

**Do you think your English lessons will be different, as a business student?**

## Words

- **Nouns:** business, student, grades, skills
- **Adjectives:** independent, organised, anxious, specialized, interesting

### LISTENING PRACTICE

CD TRACK 1

Listen to the recording.
**1.** What are the people talking about?
**2.** Explain their opinions.

*In brief*

**Tâche :** Entrer dans le chapitre avec un article court.
**Objectifs :** Vous familiariser avec le thème ; développer des stratégies de lecture rapide.

# *Dealing with the arrogance of youth*

## Employers are finding that many new graduates still have much to learn.

Young people, especially new graduates, believe they are fully qualified to leap up the corporate ladder immediately, while their bosses see them as lacking the social and communications skills to organise a coffee rota.

Experts believe the problem is serious enough to warrant inclusion of social and communications skills in the school curriculum. One of them says: "Young people do not realise they do not have the communications skills needed in the corporate world. We want to integrate communications skills rather than put them in a separate subject. We need to teach the ability to work with others." This could be done by introducing a "skills portfolio" that every school student would build up.

Kim Collins, a manager at Manpower, advises students to work during holidays to build the inter-personal and communications skills employers need. A variety of experiences is desirable, including jobs that demonstrate reliability and team working. "Employers like work experience that involves work with customers, where punctuality and reliability shine through[1]. I advise temporary work with different roles. It is a great way to broaden your horizons and gives you a reality check[2]."

The traditional gap year is now more often combined with work rather than simply travelling. This can include valuable items on a student's CV.

*The Times*, June 27, 2006

1. *shine through*: transparaître
2. *give a reality check*: permettre d'être réaliste

CD TRACK 2

**Tâche :** Repérer le contexte.
**Objectifs :** Mieux comprendre l'article grâce à des repères (mots en gras) sur la société anglo-saxonne, des infos sur les entreprises, etc.

### Info

***graduate***
Someone who has completed his/her university education.

***gap year***
A prolonged period – usually a year – when a student has finished secondary school and before he/she goes on to study at university. Some people travel, others work. It is a very common practice in English-speaking countries.

**Tâche :** Décrypter les titres.
**Objectifs :** Trouver les échos du titre dans le reste de l'article, le plus souvent dans le sous-titre ou le premier paragraphe ; anticiper sur la lecture.

### Headlines

Headlines can be difficult to understand. The subhead can help you: it usually explains and says the same thing in different words. Use the headline and the subhead to answer the following questions.

**1** Which youths is the article about?

**2** Why are they arrogant?

**3** What is the problem for employers?

## Work on words

**Tâche :** Rechercher du lexique (équivalents et synonymes) dans l'ordre de l'article.
**Objectifs :** Mieux comprendre l'article et avoir du lexique à utiliser pour résumer ou rendre compte du contenu de l'article.

### 1 | Find their equivalents in English

§1 d'entreprise – manquer de – compétence
§2 programme scolaire
§3 client – fiabilité – équipe – travail temporaire
§4 de valeur – article

### 2 | Find their synonyms

§1 climb quickly – rotation order
§2 justify
§3 become more open-minded

## The key points of the article

**Tâche :** Lire l'article en suivant les guides.
**Objectifs :** Repérer l'essentiel ; analyser et hiérarchiser pour pouvoir synthétiser.

### 1 Graduates
**a.** What they want.
**b.** Reason for their arrogance.
**c.** What they lack. Give a precise example.

### 2 Possible improvements
**a.** How school could help.
**b.** How personal experience could help.
**c.** Important qualities that can be gained.

## {Methods}

### Speaking practice

**Tâche :** S'entraîner à des activités de prononciation et de lecture.
**Objectifs :** Améliorer vos compétences à l'oral.

**Practise your pronunciation**
Some words in this article are understood easily but their English pronunciation is different from the French one. Which words correspond to the following phonetic symbols?

**a.** ['ærəgəns]
**b.** ['səʊʃl]
**c.** [kəˌmjuːnɪ'keɪʃn]
**d.** ['prɒbləm]
**e.** [rəʊlz]
**f.** [hə'raɪznz]

### Writing practice

**Tâche :** S'entraîner à des activités écrites ; étudier des faits de langue isolés.
**Objectifs :** Améliorer vos compétences à l'écrit, pour être capable de construire des paragraphes.

**1 Using "enough"**
• *The problem is serious enough to warrant inclusion of social and communications skills in the school curriculum.*
Mind the word order: adjective + *enough* – *enough* + noun!
Rewrite the sentences, including "enough" to qualify the underlined word.
**a.** Young graduates believe / qualified / leap up the corporate ladder immediately.
**b.** They don't have / communications skills / be efficient in a company.
**c.** Employers like students / with experience.

**2 Prepare a short account in English.**
Use the sentences you built in part **1** to sum up the article. Add an introduction to sentence **a**. Add "yet" to sentence **b** and an expression to conclude with sentence **c**.
→Tools 4, p. 236

## Branching out

**Tâche :** Réfléchir à partir de questions.
**Objectifs :** Être capable d'élargir une discussion à partir de l'article.

What assets may early work experience emphasize on your CV?

## LISTENING PRACTICE

*Young adults are talking to Emma Tippins.*

CD TRACK 3-4

### 1. Comprehension

**Tâche :** Comprendre une conversation, une interview, etc.
**Objectif :** Développer une stratégie d'écoute efficace ; repérer les mots-clés et les idées essentielles.
Les repères ci-dessous doivent vous servir de guides.

Listen to the recording to find the following information.

**Part 1**
**a.** Type of conversation.
**b.** Details about the 3 young people (names, age).
**c.** The woman's experience (place, activities) and benefits.

**Part 2**
**a.** The first man's experience.
**b.** Reasons he gives.
**c.** What he found difficult. Positive aspects.
**d.** The second man's experience.
**e.** What he found difficult. Positive aspects.

### 2. Expression

**Tâche :** Mettre vos notes en ordre, hiérarchiser les informations.
**Objectif :** Savoir faire le compte rendu d'une conversation ou d'une réunion en anglais.

Give an oral account, or write a 100-word paragraph, summing up what you have heard.

**Tâches :** Repérer les mots-clés et les idées d'un article de presse ; enrichir son vocabulaire par la lecture de documents authentiques.
**Objectif :** Développer des stratégies de lecture efficaces pour traiter l'information.

# Tune up your skills as a team player – and emerge a winner

A famous cartoon drawing published some years ago depicted a small dog standing beneath[1] a tall kitchen cupboard. High on a shelf above his head – and out of his reach – stood a delicious packet of biscuits. However, balancing precariously[2] on the dog's back stood a long-legged cat – and the cat fetched them both down the biscuits they wanted. The caption read: "Teamwork makes the impossible simple."

In business, too, working closely with colleagues often brings out the best in people and breathes[3] truth into the old adage that the sum of the parts is greater than the whole.

Rather than working in isolation, you can tap into software that helps you to share your research, your report's findings, or your first draft of a memorandum with other people – and the pooled results of your colleagues' feedback may well be to your, and their, advantage. Teaming up with fellow members of your team can often lead to a valuable cross-fertilisation of ideas. Close collaboration with team colleagues isn't always possible over tea and biscuits in the canteen or conference room, of course, especially when you're linking with a colleague in another country. New technology allows you to do this.

Everyone has a part to play in team working. Technology, which can streamline interactions between colleagues, is important, of course, but often, shifts in behaviour and attitudes towards teamwork can also be important. There are probably occasions when you will feel that doing a job yourself is the quickest and most effective way of getting it done. But this should not lead you to believe that working on your own is always best. Collaboration and consultation with colleagues is productive in most cases.

So whether you are sailing round the world, rowing to Olympic glory, chasing a gold medal in the downhill skiing, winning The Ashes or the World Cup, now is the time to tune up your skills as a team player – and emerge a winner.

*The Telegraph*, 21 March 2006

CD TRACK 5

1. *beneath*: sous
2. *precariously*: dangereusement
3. *breathe* (ici): insuffler

## Info

**Tâche :** Voir *In brief*, p. 10.

***The Ashes***
One of cricket's most celebrated contests, played between England and Australia, dating back to 1882. It is played every two years, alternately in England and Australia.

## Work on words

**Tâche :** Voir *In brief*, p. 10.

### 1 | Find their equivalents in English

**Headline** mettre au point – compétence – équipe
**§1** représenter – légende
**§3** exploiter – logiciel – partager – un brouillon – circulaire – mis en commun – réaction, retour
**§4** rationaliser – changement
**§5** faire de la voile – ramer – poursuivre

### 2 | Find their synonyms

**§1** get
**§2** co-worker – develop
**§3** on your own – get connected with – enable

## Headlines

**Tâche :** Voir *In brief*, p. 10.

**1** Find the paragraph in which the headline is mentioned.

**2** The article is not about sports but about life in a company. Explain why the journalist uses the comparison.

## The key points of the article

**Tâche :** Lire un article long en suivant les guides.
**Objectifs :** Lire progressivement à l'aide de guides ; repérer l'organisation de l'article et les liens logiques entre les paragraphes ; aller rapidement à l'essentiel.

### 1 Read §1 and §2
**a.** Explain the meaning of the cartoon which is described in §1.
**b.** Explain the link between §1 and §2: what is similar in the cartoon and in business?
**c.** Why did the journalist use a cartoon in §1?

### 2 Read §3
**a.** Explain where and how people can work together.
**b.** List the advantages of team-working.

### 3 Read §4
**a.** Some people think the best way to work is on their own. Does the journalist agree? Explain.
**b.** What is essential for teamwork to be most effective?

## Branching out

**Tâche :** Voir *In brief*, p. 11.

**1** Working together is encouraged in companies. Is it the same at school? Sum up the differences and give your own point of view.

**2** To what extent can new technologies help people work together?

## {Methods}

### ■ Speaking practice

**Tâche :** Voir *In brief*, p. 11.

**1 Cognates**
The following words are all cognates (transparent words): they look just like French words. However, their English pronunciation is different! Practise their pronunciation, paying attention to the stress.

**a.** [ɑisɔ'leiʃən] **b.** [fɜːtɪlɑi'zeiʃən] **c.** [kəˌlæbə'reiʃən] **d.** [kɔnsə'teiʃən]

**2 Prepare an oral introduction.**

**Tâche :** Proposer une introduction à un compte rendu de l'article.
**Objectifs :** Identifier rapidement les sources de l'article et savoir répondre aux questions essentielles (qui, quoi, où, quand).

- Identify the source.
- Explain what the article is about (who, what, where, when).

### ■ Writing practice

**Tâche :** S'entraîner aux différents exercices écrits à partir d'un article.
**Objectif :** Être capable de rédiger un compte rendu ou un résumé à l'aide de guides.

**Write an account of this article in English (around 150 words).**
- Introduction
- Development: a. Definition of team working; b. Advantages; c. Necessary conditions
- Conclusion

→ Tools 4, p. 236

**Tâche :** Revoir les faits de langue fondamentaux en contexte.
**Objectifs :** Améliorer vos compétences pour être capable d'exprimer ce que vous voulez dire dans un anglais correct.

## Language

- *Working closely with colleagues often brings out **the best** in people.*
- *Doing a job yourself is **the quickest** and **most effective** way of getting it done.*

Le superlatif se forme en ajoutant le déterminant ***the*** + ***most*** devant les adjectifs longs et ***the*** **+ le suffixe *-est*** pour les adjectifs courts (une syllabe ou deux syllabes terminé en *-y*).
Trois superlatifs sont irréguliers : *good* > *the best* ; *bad* > *the worst* ; *far* > *the furthest/farthest.*

**Translate into English**
**1.** De nos jours, le travail en équipe est l'activité la plus enrichissante.
**2.** Le meilleur vendeur (*salesperson*) ne peut se passer de (*do without*) ses collègues pour atteindre ses objectifs.
**3.** Il faut que notre circulaire soit la plus détaillée à la réunion de ce soir.
**4.** La pire méthode est de travailler seul. Il faut faire équipe avec plusieurs techniciens.

# Rédiger un CV (pour une demande de stage)

**CURRICULUM VITAE**

Karine CHAN
19, rue Bottero
06000 Nice
Tel : (00 33) (0)7 93 12 54 89
Mobile phone: (00 33) (0)7 23 58 96 47
email: kchan@club-internet.fr
Date of birth: 25 June 19..... Age: 19
Sex: female
Nationality: French
Marital status: single

> Il est fréquent de préciser si on est une femme ou un homme (*female/male*) mais ce n'est plus obligatoire (lutte contre la discrimination à l'embauche).

> Donnez les informations dans l'ordre rétrochronologique, de la date la plus récente à la plus ancienne.

**Education**
**200_ to now**: Attending the first year of a two-year post-A-level course in (*name of the speciality*) at (*name and address of the school*). My BTS exam is scheduled for June 200_.
**200_ 200_**: Graduated from secondary school in June 200_ with the French Baccalaureate specialised in Accountancy. (A-Level equivalent)

**Work experience**
**August 200_**: Summer job as a shop assistant in ZARA (Nice) – customer advice at the point of sale and cashier
**July 200_**: Summer job at a call centre (200 phone calls a day)
**Other jobs**: Baby sitting, school children tutoring

> Vos expériences professionnelles, même limitées, montrent que le monde du travail ne vous est pas totalement étranger.

**Languages**
French
English: working knowledge, written and oral
Chinese: mother tongue

> Mentionnez vos compétences en matière de langue(s) vivante(s), très importantes aujourd'hui.

**Computer literacy**
Good working knowledge of computers
Regular use of Word, Excel and Power Point

**Interests and hobbies**
- Volunteer work for the Restaurants du Cœur in Nice (3 nights a week from November to March)
- Going to the cinema, concerts and theatre
- Travelling

> Vos intérêts aident l'employeur à mieux cerner votre personnalité.

**Additional information**
- Clean driving licence
- First aid certificate

**References**
Upon request

> *References* vous permet de fournir les coordonnées de personnes susceptibles de vous recommander.

## Lexique utile

### a. Votre diplôme

• Le baccalauréat : *A-levels* (GB), *High School Graduation* (US).
• Les filières : *maths/physics/biology* (S) ; *Arts /literature/languages* (L) ; *Economics, History, Languages* (ES) ; *accountancy, marketing, management* (STG).

### b. Votre section

• Les BTS n'existent pas au Royaume-Uni ni aux États-Unis. Dire *a two-year post-A-level course.*
• Les différents BTS tertiaires : Assistant de Direction : *Personal Assistant (PA)* – Assurance : *Insurance* – Commerce International : *International Trade* – Comptabilité gestion des entreprises : *Accountancy and Management* – Communication des Entreprises : *Communication and Advertising* – Management des Unités Commerciales : *Marketing and Management* – Négociation Relations Client : *Sales and Marketing* – Assistant PME PMI : *Small and Medium Size Firms* – Profession immobilière : *Real Estate* – Tourisme : *Tourism.*

### c. Le stage

stage : *work placement, internship, training period*
stagiaire : *trainee, intern (US)*
formation en alternance : *sandwich course*

# Rédiger la lettre d'accompagnement

L'objectif de cette lettre, qui accompagne votre CV, est d'obtenir un stage dans une entreprise anglophone. (Attention, si vous écrivez aux États-Unis, CV se dit *résumé*). Elle doit être correctement rédigée et mise en page : relisez-vous attentivement.

## La méthode

• Présentez votre lettre comme dans le modèle : votre adresse, la date, l'adresse de l'entreprise, puis le corps de la lettre.
• Entrez directement dans le vif du sujet. Il faut expliquer vos besoins qui sont motivés par :
- les études que vous poursuivez (le stage doit correspondre au référentiel de votre BTS),
- la durée du stage (selon votre section),
- le caractère obligatoire de ce stage,
- son caractère non rémunéré (*unpaid*), ce qui peut faciliter la décision positive de l'entreprise.
• Donnez les dates de votre stage, dites comment vous avez connu l'entreprise et pourquoi la ville où elle est située vous plaît particulièrement.
• Vous pouvez faire brièvement allusion à vos qualités personnelles de motivation, autonomie, facilité d'adaptation, etc., à l'aide d'adjectifs (*autonomous, dynamic,* etc.).
• La formule finale, convenue, vous permet de remercier par avance l'entreprise de prendre le temps de se pencher sur votre demande.
• Signez à la main, puis ajoutez votre nom complet sous votre signature.

Karine Chan
19, rue Bottero
06000 Nice
France

Human Resources Manager
Kraft Foods
54 Charlton Street
Manchester
M3 7DB
Grande Bretagne

4 January 200-

Dear Mrs Baxter,

I am currently doing a two-year post-A-level course in Sales and Management in Nice, France. A 13-week unpaid work placement is a compulsory part of the course and I would be most grateful if you would consider my application for a placement in your company.

As part of the final exam, I have to give a detailed oral report on the tasks and activities I carry out during the work placement. I also have to provide a well-documented written report, of which you would receive a copy.

Your firm has been highly recommended to me by a former student who had the opportunity to do his work placement with you. Also, Manchester has the reputation of being a dynamic business centre, and I would consider it a great opportunity to work there.

I'm sure I would learn a lot from this experience. What's more my strong motivation and ability to learn quickly mean I could easily adapt to your company.

Due to the demands of my course, the placement would have to take place from March $5^{th}$ to June $4^{th}$.

Please find enclosed a copy of my CV. Thank you for considering my application and I look forward to hearing from you.

Yours sincerely,

Karine Chan

Karine Chan

**Tâche :** Apprendre du lexique spécialisé.
**Objectifs :** Enrichir vos connaissances lexicales, revoir des termes oubliés, vérifier l'accentuation des mots.
Certains mots composés sont parfois regroupés au début autour d'un ou de plusieurs mots racine.

**account:** compte en banque
**achievement:** réalisation
**advertising campaign:** campagne de publicité
**advice:** conseils
**advise:** conseiller (V)
**A-levels:** équivalent britannique du baccalauréat
**allowance:** indemnité
**apply for:** poser sa candidature
**business:** entreprise
**cash :** argent liquide
**corporate:** d'entreprise
**corporate world:** le monde de l'entreprise
**customer:** client
**deal with:** traiter
**delivery:** livraison
**demanding:** exigeant
**draft:** brouillon
**employer:** employeur
**face *(V)*:** faire face à
**failure:** échec
**fear:** craindre
**feedback:** retour, réaction
**firm:** entreprise
**franchise:** franchise
**franchisee:** franchisé
**full-time job:** travail à plein temps
**gap year:** année sabbatique
**graduate:** jeune diplômé
**grant:** accorder
**guideline:** conseil
**hands-on experience:** expérience pratique
**job applicant:** candidat
**job interview:** entretien d'embauche
**lack:** manquer de
**living costs:** coût de la vie
**manager:** directeur
**operate:** exploiter, gérer
**operation:** entreprise
**outlet:** magasin
**own:** posséder
**part time:** temps partiel
**pay off:** rapporter
**pie-chart:** camembert
**placement:** stage
**pooled:** en équipe
**portfolio:** portefeuille
**profitable:** rentable
**punctuality:** ponctualité
**recruiter:** recruteur
**reliability:** fiabilité
**report:** rapport
**resources:** ressources
**résumé (= CV):** curriculum vitae
**run a business:** gérer une entreprise
**sales:** ventes
**school curriculum:** programme scolaire
**shift:** modification
**skill:** compétence
**small business:** petite entreprise
**staff:** personnel
**store:** magasin
**streamline:** rationaliser
**tap into:** exploiter
**team working:** travail en équipe
**teamwork:** travail d'équipe
**temporary work:** travail intérimaire
**trainer:** formateur
**training:** formation
**travel expenses:** frais de voyage
**tune up:** mettre au point
**valuable:** de valeur
**warrant:** garantir

"This company needs young brains like yours."

## Charts and tables

**Tâche :** Analyser des tableaux et graphiques.
**Objectif :** Consulter les pages de méthode et de lexique pour apprendre les termes appropriés ; vous familiariser avec le monde de l'entreprise.

**1.** Study the following pie chart about communication in job interviews. →Tools 11, p. 244

**2.** Give an oral presentation of this pie chart to explain what recruiters take into account during a job interview.

WHAT JOB APPLICANTS ARE JUDGED ON DURING A JOB INTERVIEW

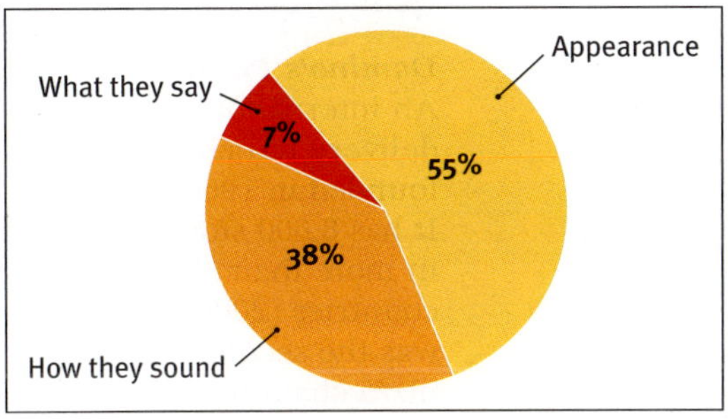


## Online tasks

**Tâche :** Faire des recherches sur internet.
**Objectif :** Trouver, classer et hiérarchiser l'information pour en rendre compte.

### Verbal communication

**1.** Explain what verbal communication is.

**2.** Give examples of positive and negative gestures, movements or attitudes that may influence the recruiter.

**3.** Test yourself online and report on your personal answers and the comments at the bottom of the page.
Visit the website of the University of Kent and discover the page about body language during job interviews:
**www.kent.ac.uk/careers/interviews/nvc.htm**

## Communication tasks

**Tâche :** S'entraîner à des activités de communication.
**Objectif :** Vous mettre en situation pour écrire ou parler.

### Roleplay: Verbal communication

**A: You know about verbal communication.**
Explain the advantages of mastering the techniques.
**B: You've never heard about verbal communication.**
You are a bit sceptical about the meaning of gestures and attitudes.

Tâche : Rendre compte de l'article.
**Objectifs :** Utiliser des stratégies de lecture rapide et de compréhension ; développer des stratégies d'organisation et de présentation.

# Pizza franchises

*Want your own business but can't take the plunge? A franchise could be the first step.*

If you like the idea of running your own business but fear failure or are lacking in skills and resources, then buying your own franchise might be the answer. It certainly was for Lisa Tobias, one of eight female Domino's Pizza franchisees in the UK, who, at just 25, already owns two outlets in Scotland.

Tobias started working part time at the pizza delivery company when she was 17. She then went to university but, six months later, decided that it wasn't for her, so she returned to Domino's and worked her way up to be manager. Two years ago, she decided that she wanted to run a business for herself, so she raised the necessary cash – "The banks are very helpful!" – and now has stores in Kilmarnock and Ayr.

She says that Domino's looks for people who are hands-on[1], and if you follow the training and marketing guidelines, you'll do well. Franchising, says Tobias, is a safer option for people who want to have their own business but are afraid of taking the plunge alone.

The British Franchise Association (BFA) says that franchises appear less likely to fail than other types of small business organisations. Ninety-six per cent of franchised units still operate profitable businesses after five years, whereas only 66 per cent of small firms survive their first three years. But franchising still means a lot of hard work and money, particularly in the early stages.

In simple terms, franchising means that a company grants a licence that enables someone else to sell its product or service. The advantages include the fact that you are selling an idea that has already been tested, and well-established franchise operations have national advertising campaigns and a solid trading name, as well as offering training in sales and business skills.

*The Independent*, 3 August 2006

1. *hands-on*: doué d'un sens pratique

## Info

**Tâche :** Voir *In brief*, p. 10.

***Domino's Pizza***
An international pizza delivery franchise founded in 1960. It has 8,000 stores in more than 55 countries (2006). It was the second-largest pizza chain in the US when it went public in 2004.

**Tâche :** Chercher davantage d'informations.
**Objectifs :** Élargir votre connaissance du monde de l'entreprise en vous référant aux pages de cours.

## References

You can find relevant information by reading various pages in your book and memorising a few facts and ideas.

→ **Distribution, p. 125**

**ACTIVITY** **Practise giving an account of this article.**

**Tâche :** Introduire le compte rendu.
**Objectifs :** Situer l'article (date, titre) et donner l'idée générale.

## Introduction

You should explain where the article comes from, when it was published and what it is about. →**Tools 4, p. 236**

This article, which was published in *The Independent*, a British daily, in August 2006, reports on people who start a new business. Starting with a franchise has various advantages and is less risky.

**Tâche :** Rendre compte du contenu.
**Objectifs :** Structurer le compte rendu en plusieurs parties (plan) qui ne répètent pas l'article mot pour mot mais le reformulent ; articuler ces parties entre elles.

## Development

Once you have understood the article, organize your ideas into two or three different parts, using set phrases and link-words. →**Tools 4, p. 236**

1. An example: a self-made business woman
2. Definition of franchising
3. A safe option

You should also use the information given in *Info* and what you have learnt, for example by referring to the various pages indicated in *References*.

### 1. An example: a self-made business woman

A young Scottish woman (25) is given as an example of a successful franchisee of Domino's Pizza, the second-largest pizza chain in the US, with 8,000 stores in more than 55 countries (2006). Lisa Tobias already owns two stores in Scotland, in Kilmarnock and Ayr. She's also given as an example because she went from part-time worker to manager: in 2004, she borrowed money from the bank and started as a franchisee.

### 2. Definition of franchising

Companies give people a licence that enables them to sell their products or services. Many fast food chains or clothes companies such as Gap operate as franchises.

Franchising has various advantages for a new entrepreneur: for instance, you sell a famous brand and can profit from advertising campaigns, which enables you to save a lot of money. Many companies also provide training in sales and business skills.

### 3. A safe option

Therefore, running a franchise is much safer than starting on one's own, and borrowing money is easier as the risk is lower. As a matter of fact, according to the British Franchise Association, almost all (96%) of franchises remain profitable after five years, whereas only two-thirds of small firms survive after three years. Franchising can also be the first step for future entrepreneurs before they start on their own.

**Tâche :** Conclure le compte rendu.
**Objectifs :** Reprendre les idées clés de l'article ; ouvrir des pistes plus générales.

## Conclusion

You should sum up the main ideas and try to open out in a new direction.

This article explains that franchisees can profit from the franchiser's name, know-how and advertising campaigns, and also get help as far as business skills are concerned. In addition, they may find it easier to borrow from a bank. In today's competitive business world, fewer risks are certainly worth it. However, one should not underestimate the fact that you need hard work if you want to succeed, especially at the beginning.

**Tâche :** Ouvrir une discussion.
**Objectifs :** Utiliser le compte rendu comme tremplin pour développer une ou deux idées.

## Branching out

Now, you should move away from the article and develop more ideas. The following questions can help you.

**1** What famous franchises do you know?

**2** Would you like to run a franchised business? Why/Why not?

*Extras!*

**Tâche :** S'entraîner à des activités de communication.
**Objectif :** Vous mettre en situation pour écrire ou parler.

## Case study: job ads

**1.** Read the three job ads. Choose one. Explain your choice to the class.

### SALES ASSISTANT

Our client, based in Byfleet, is seeking a Sales Assistant to join their friendly team. The role involves serving customers both face to face and over the phone. You will also be showing customers around, selling merchandise and helping keep a clean store. Candidates need to be confident on the telephone, have excellent customer services skills and a flexible attitude. Hours are between 8am and 6pm Monday to Saturday and 10-2.00 on a Sunday. It will normally be a Tuesday to Saturday week. Immediate start available.

Start date: ASAP
Duration: N/A
Salary: £14,400 pa + bonus
Ref No: 113004-GU001TF

@ Apply on http://www.gojobsite.uk with reference number.

### JUNIOR HELPDESK TECHNICIANS

➤ Want a hand-on role in a fast paced environment? Leading law firm based in the city are currently seeking to employ Junior IT Technicians to work on contract/permanent basis. Your role will be to provide high level IT support.

➤ The main focus of the role will be to provide 1st line support for all system users within the law firm. This will be roughly 60% of your daily duties. The platforms you will be supporting will be varied and include: Windows NT4/XP, Office 97-2003, DMS, Call logging systems, Printers, Time recording and Digital Dictation.

➤ You will also be involved in the preparation, basic repair and replacement of computers (which involves lifting), maintaining inventories of PCs, laptops, networks, other equipment and checking and maintaining the backup/server logs.

➤ The candidate should have excellent knowledge of Microsoft Office applications / Windows-based O/S systems coupled with Exchange, SQL, Active Directory, and Hummingbird Document Management.
The ability to work within a team and one's own initiative is a must as is the willingness to work on a shift system.

Start date: ASAP
Duration: 3 months to perm
Salary: 21,000-22,000 Per Annum
Ref No: 141799-JSITSA
Apply on http://www.gojobsite.uk with reference number.

### PERSONAL ASSISTANT

An experienced PA is currently required by this reputable company in Central Bromley.
The role will integrate into the current team assisting Senior Management. Main duties will be audio typing, fielding phone calls and some data entry.
The successful candidate will have good grammar and the ability to accurately proof read all documents.

Start date: ASAP
Duration: Permanent
Salary: £17,500
Ref No: 139704-KW2891
Apply on http://www.gojobsite.uk with reference number.

**2.** Write an e-mail applying for the job and attach your CV.

Organise your message: Reason for writing; background and experience; the job; mention your CV; final comment.
→ Tools 7, p. 241

## PERSONAL TASK

What type of company would you like for your work placement? Why? Report to the class.

# IN THIS UNIT...

- Companies: Heinz, Toyota, Microsoft...
- Learn about organization charts
- Study a website
- Identify the sales manager in a company
- Give an oral presentation of a company
- Turn a headline into a paragraph

# 1 Companies

## → Before you START

*In brief:* What can a company bring to a city?
*Front page:* Cars and the environment

### Would you like to work in a similar environment? Why/Why not?

## Words

- **Nouns:** open plan environment, individual offices, team, barrier, privacy
- **Adjectives:** distracting, noisy, personal, collective, stressful

## LISTENING PRACTICE

CD TRACK 6

Listen to the recording.
**1.** What are the people talking about?
**2.** Explain their opinions.

# Heinz means friends

## A bid by an outsider to take over the Heinz board has made the ketchup maker's hometown see red.

The world's biggest ketchup maker, Heinz, has delivered a lesson this week on why a multinational company should bother to keep in touch with its local community.

For 137 years, Heinz has been based in Pittsburgh and its imprint is everywhere in the Pennsylvania city: the local concert hall is the Heinz Hall and the Pittsburgh Steelers play at the Heinz Field. Heinz has supported local charities and doled out[1] annual gifts to pensioners. This week, local people repaid Heinz's loyalty with a crucial vote of confidence.

Heinz has been under attack from a hedge fund manager[2], Nelson Peltz, who put himself and four colleagues up for election to replace Heinz directors. Mr Peltz told Wall Street that he would slash brands and jobs, possibly including factories in Britain, to save $575m (£302.2m) annually. Several influential New York advisers urged fund managers to support Mr Peltz to improve Heinz's dismal[3] recent share price.

However, the Pennsylvania Treasury voted its substantial stock[4] in favour of Heinz's board. Some 150 local Heinz employees volunteered to spend time lobbying investors. Pennsylvania's unions urged their members to support the company.

How many British companies could count on such a wave of local sympathy? Heinz has shown that even multinationals need help once in a while from their local friends and neighbours.

Andrew Clark, *The Guardian*, August 17, 2006

1. *dole out:* distribuer
2. *hedge fund manager:* spéculateur
3. *dismal:* (ici) épouvantable
4. *stock:* actions, titres

CD TRACK 7

## Info

***Heinz***
Food processing company, founded in 1869 by Henry John Heinz. A famous slogan is "Beanz Meanz Heinz", used in the 1960s and beyond to advertise their baked beans in the U Today, Heinz sells more th 1,300 products worldwide ranging from ketchup to baby food.

***Pittsburgh Steelers***
Professional football team based in Pittsburgh, often champions. They won the 2006 Super Bowl.

***Wall Street***
A narrow street in lower Manhattan (New York City considered the historical heart of the Financial District. It was the home of the New York Stock Exchange. The phrase "Wa Street" is also used to refer American financial marke like London's "Square Mile the financial heart of the U

## Work on words

### 1 | Find their equivalents in English

**Subhead** offre – prendre le pouvoir
**§2** empreinte – salle de concert – soutenir – organisation caritative – retraité – confiance
**§3** marque – usine – économiser – conseiller (N) – presser quelqu'un de – améliorer – action
**§4** exercer une pression – syndicat

### 2 | Find their synonyms

**Subhead** people who control a company
**§1** take the trouble – keep contact
**§3** reduce
**§4** someone working for a company

## Headlines

**1** Which sound is repeated three times in this headlin

**2** Read **Info** on the compan and find a famous slogan that is similar to this headline.

**3** Read the subhead and explain why the word "friends" is used in the headline.

**4** Find humour in the subtitle.

## The key points of the article

### 1 The company
**a.** Identity (name, age).
**b.** The company's local commitment.

### 2 The attack
**a.** Who launched it and what he wanted to do.
**b.** Peltz's support.

### 3 An unexpected outcome
**a.** Different reactions of the locals.
**b.** Lesson to be taken.

## {Methods}

### ■ Speaking practice
**Read figures aloud** →Tools 10, p. 243
137 years – $575m – £302.2m – 150 employees

### ■ Writing practice
**1 Verb structures**

**Compare the following examples:**
- *A bid by an outsider to take over the Heinz board* ***has made*** *the ketchup maker's hometown* ***see*** *red.*
- *Several influential New York advisers* ***urged*** *fund managers* ***to support*** *Mr Peltz.*

*Make, let and help* are followed by bare infinitives whereas *urge* is followed by a full infinitive (with *to*), like many other verbs.

The most important of these are:
*advise – allow – command – compel – convince – enable – encourage – entitle – forbid – force – invite – oblige – order – persuade – request – train – warn.*

**Complete the following sentences with the right verb structure.**
**a.** Several fund managers were (to advise) / support Nelson Peltz.
**b.** Heinz has (*encourage*) several local charities / work in Pittsburgh, PA.
**c.** Nelson Petz (*persuade*) Wall Street / support him.
**d.** Many Heinz employees (*convince*) investors / vote against Peltz.
**e.** Pennsylvania's unions (*invite*) their members / support the company.
**f.** Heinz (*let*) its employees / lobby investors.

**2 Prepare a short account in English.**
Use the sentences you made in part 1 to explain what happened to Heinz and how the local community reacted. Use the appropriate link-words to show the contrast between the two events.
→Tools 4, p. 236

## Branching out

Do you think it is important for companies to get involved and committed in local communities? Why/why not? → *Key data*, p. 27

## LISTENING PRACTICE

CD TRACK 8-9

*George Dompton and Cliff Pinkhurst are talking money.*

**1 Comprehension**
Listen to the recording to find the following information.

**Part 1**
**a.** Topic of conversation.
**b.** Reason for this conversation.
**c.** Cliff's reaction to the news.
**d.** Amount of money Cliff spent.

**Part 2**
**a.** Name of the two companies.
**b.** Give details about the buyer.
**c.** Consequences of the deal.
**d.** Cliff's reaction.

**2 Expression**
Give an oral account, or write a 100-word paragraph, summing up what you have heard.

# Leading role for hybrids in 21st century

Hybrid power for vehicles is here to stay, Jim Press, president of Toyota Motor North America, said.

Press declared that hybrids "will play a starring role in the automotive industry during the 21st century," adding that they are "absolutely essential to the future success of this industry." He explained that Toyota is working on a plug-in hybrid which will use batteries that can be recharged without drawing on the gasoline engine. However plug-ins could take ages to develop, depending on the progress in battery technology.

Another project Toyota is "strongly considering" is selling flexible-fuel cars and trucks on the US market, Press said. Flex-fuel vehicles can burn gasoline or a blend with up to 85% ethanol, called E85. However E85 can be bought at only about 800 of the nation's 170,000 petrol stations.

Honda was actually first in the USA to market hybrids, with the Insight hybrid in December 1998. It now sells three. Ford Motor, General Motors and Ford affiliate Mazda all sell hybrid SUVs[1]. But Toyota sells the most models now, seven hybrid models in all, two of them under its Lexus brand. It sells more gasoline-electric hybrids in the USA than any other automaker – 350,000 since introducing Prius in 1999, according to Press.

Hybrids use up less fuel thanks to their electric motor which does part of the work. In June, PricewaterhouseCoopers forecast global hybrid sales would quadruple in five years, to more than 1.3 million in 2010.

Eric Antebi, spokesman for environmental group Sierra Club, says hybrids will be around for a long time: "The single biggest step America can take to reduce global warming, reduce dependence on oil and save consumers money is to make cars go much farther on a gallon of gas. There's no reason (hybrid) technology couldn't be used to go much farther on a gallon of ethanol or a gallon of diesel."

*The Detroit News*, July 19, 2006

1. SUV: *Sport Utility Vehicle*

CD TRACK 10

## Info

***gallon***
The word *gallon* exists in French but people rarely know how much liquid it means. In Britain (or Canada), the Imperial gallon equals 4.546 litres. In the US – which is the case here – one American gallon equals 3.785 litres.
→Tools 10, p. 243

## Work on words

### 1 I Find their equivalents in English

**§1** énergie –véhicule
**§2** secteur – ajouter – pile – moteur
**§3** carburant – camion
**§5** mondial
**§6** porte-parole – écologiste – prendre une mesure – économiser

### 2 I Find their synonyms

**§3** think about – combination
**§4** car manufacturer
**§5** consume – predict
**§6** limit (V)

## Headlines

**1** Find an equivalent of "leading role" in the first two paragraphs.

**2** Look for a repetition of the headline in the first two paragraphs.

**3** Explain and develop the headline of the article.

## The key points of the article

### 1 Read §1 and §2
**a.** Complete name of the company.
**b.** President.
**c.** What the company makes.
**d.** What the company considers essential.
**e.** Definition of a plug-in hybrid.
**f.** Jim Press thinks plug-ins will be ready in the near future. Yes ❑ No ❑ Explain.

### 2 Read §3 and §4
**a.** What other type of vehicle is Toyota considering?
**b.** Characteristic of such vehicles.
**c.** Problem in the USA for this type of vehicle.
**d.** First company to sell hybrids on the US market and name of the car.
**e.** Which car makers sell hybrids in the USA?
**f.** Who is the market leader?

### 3 Read §5 and §6
**a.** Reason why hybrids are more economical.
**b.** Estimated number of hybrids by the end of the decade.
**c.** Three advantages in the long term.

## Branching out

**1** What are the advantages of developing cars that consume less petrol? →*Key data*, p. 176

**2** Why is it essential for companies to develop new products? →*Key data*, p. 28

## {Methods}

### ■ Speaking practice

**1 Read figures aloud.** →Tools 10, p. 243

Read §3 and §4 aloud. If necessary, start by writing the following figures down.
**a.** 85%
**b.** E85
**c.** 800
**d.** 170,000
**e.** 1998
**f.** 350,000

**2 Prepare an oral introduction.**
• Identify the source.
• Explain what the article is about (who, what, where, when).

### ■ Writing practice

**Write a summary of this article in English (around 110 words).**
• Read the article again and list the key idea of each paragraph following the order of the article.
• Introduce link words between the various ideas.
→Tools 3, p. 234

## Language

• *Toyota* ***is considering*** *selling flexible-fuel cars and trucks on the US market.*
• *Toyota* ***sells*** *more gasoline-electric hybrids in the USA than any other automaker.*
Les deux présents – présent en ***be*** **+V-*ing*** et présent simple avec l'auxiliaire ***do*** pour former questions et négations – ne sont pas utilisés de la même manière. Pour exprimer une action en cours au moment où l'on parle/écrit, on utilise le présent en *be* +V-*ing*. Pour exprimer une généralité, on utilise le présent simple.

**Translate into English**
**1.** Les fabricants automobiles développent toujours de nouveaux modèles.
**2.** L'entreprise réfléchit à un nouveau moteur électrique.
**3.** Les consommateurs économisent de l'argent et leurs voitures vont plus loin avec la même quantité d'essence.
**4.** Le secteur automobile essaie de trouver des solutions pour consommer moins d'énergie.

**Whether they are called companies, firms or corporations corporations, they can all be referred to as businesses.**

## 1-Definitions

### The different types of companies

There are four different types of companies.

- Private Limited Companies (Ltd), which are not quoted on the Stock Exchange,
- Public Limited Companies (PLC), quoted on the Stock Exchange,
- Partnerships are run by more than one person,
- Single Proprietorships are companies owned by one person who can work on their own or with employees.

Multinational firms as well as small-and-medium-sized firms (SMFs) can belong to any of the four categories.

→**Chapter 14, Globalisation**

In order to fight competition, companies sometimes choose to merge. This is what happened between the French giant retailer Carrefour which merged with Promodès in 2000 in order to keep the American super giant Wal-Mart at bay.

### Organization

Independently from their size, category, or business, firms are organized in departments : Management, Finance and Accounting, Human Resources, Marketing and Sales, Production, Customer Service, Research and Development, Information Technology, Purchasing.

Here is an organization chart.

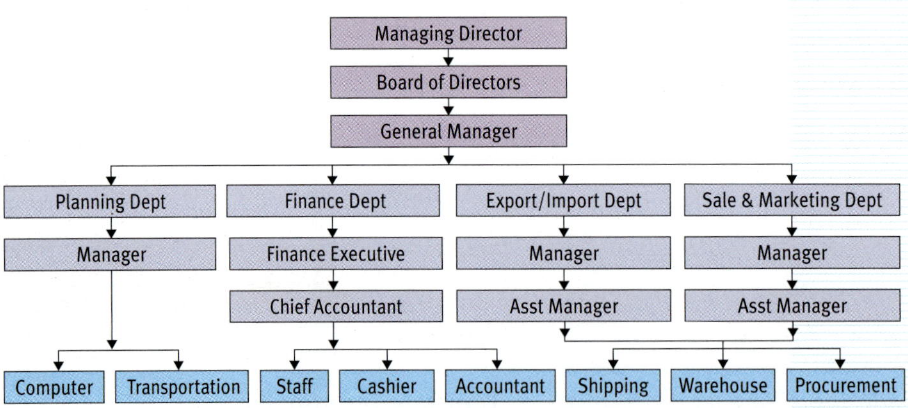


### How to succeed

Offering a good product or service is a must. A good marketing mix is essential. →**Chapter 5, Marketing**

Efficient management is also essential. A good manager should be creative, innovative, have a good know-how in his/her sector and adequate interpersonal skills.

Many big French companies have a workers' council, partly subsidized by the company. It implements perks, and social and cultural benefits for the company's employees and their families.

**A company's ID: HP**

Facts and Figures in 2006

**Type:** Company (Co.), quoted on the NYSE (New York City Stock Exchange)

**Founded:** 1939 by Bill Hewlett and Dave Packard

**Headquarters:** Palo Alto, California

**Industry:** information technology

**Products:** printers, computers

**Annual revenue:** $91.7 billion

**Market:** over 1bn customers in more than 170 countries on 6 continents

**Employees:** approximately 150,000 employees worldwide

**R&D budget:** $3.5 billion

## 2-Corporate citizens

Today, companies care more and more about their image and compete to be recognized as corporate citizens.

### How to be a good corporate citizen

Traditionally, companies were rated according to the satisfaction of their shareholders. But, since the beginning of the 21st century, ethical limits have been set. Companies have to show responsible attitudes towards current issues, such as the environment, working conditions, sustainable development, etc.

### Listings

The American publication, *Business Ethics*, rates American companies according to a various number of areas with the following categories:

- environment: pollution reduction programmes, energy saving measures, recycling projects
- community relations: involvement in NGOs, charities, programmes of culture and sport sponsoring
- employee relations: wages, perks, benefits, vocational training and career opportunities offered to the staff
- diversity: staff's gender and ethnic diversity
- customer relations: customer satisfaction, law suits, quality standards.

Among the top hundred corporate citizen companies in 2006: Green Mountain Coffee Roasters (1), Hewlett Packard (2), Motorola (4), Timberland (6), Dell (9), Texas Instrument (10), Nike (14), Starbucks (17), Gap (21) and Apple Computers (25).

**A code of business**

Motorola's code of business conduct: "These principles guide our actions:
- Innovative products, customer delight and quality
- Ethics and transparency
- Environmental quality: use of the earth's resources in our products and operations
- Shareholder value"

## 3-Company problems

### Internal problems

Internal problems concern the company itself.

- Poor management: Franco-German company Airbus will have lost €2bn by 2010 because of delivery delays due to problems of mismanagement. →**Chapter 9, Transport, *Landmark,* p. 149**
- Financial problems: companies can find themselves in the red due to high overheads and distrust from shareholders.
- Social unrest can also affect a company when its workforce goes on strike.
- Faulty products. This has been the case with Perrier and Wal-Mart (→**Chapter 7, Brands**), Danone and Nike (→**Chapter 3, Work**), among many others.
- An ill-adapted marketing strategy: for example, a company should pay attention to cultural differences when it launches a product in a foreign country where a brand/product name might be rejected by consumers. →**Chapters 5, Marketing & 6, Communication**

### External problems

A company cannot ignore competition. Today's global market is often saturated and companies have to work hard to succeed or simply to remain competitive. →**Chapter 14, Globalisation**.
Loss of sales due to a tough challenger or changing buying

Why are they Good Samaritans?

habits among consumers can lead a company into decline. This was the case for Levi's which had to close down all its US factories and only kept its San Francisco headquarters. The Big Three American automakers – General Motors Corporation, Ford Motor Company and DaimlerChrysler – are having a hard time competing with Japanese Toyota. →*Front Page*, p. 24
Companies' external problems can be aggravated by deregulation, which means opening a whole sector to competition, such as airline deregulation. →**Chapter 9, Transport**

### How to react

The companies faced with problems above, must, of course, react. If their overheads are too high, they can streamline, restructure, close the unprofitable sectors or relocate.

- Restructuring

It often means drastic cuts in the workforce. To avoid social unrest, companies try to encourage early retirements by offering incentives to the employees willing to retire. They can stop hiring, or make some of their employees redundant.

- Relocating

An even less popular measure is to relocate or outsource production to countries with cheap labour costs. →**Chapters 3, Work & 14, Globalisation**

- Updating

Companies can choose to re-train their staff, to increase the Research and Development (R&D) department, and to update their tools and equipments.

- Adopting new strategies or launching new products
- Adopting new forms of business

Companies can merge or develop a franchising system, try to tap new markets or refocus on their core market. Marks & Spencer, the great British retailer, decided to leave France in 2001. Although its French outlets were profitable, M&S was losing market share at home and felt refocusing on its home market was an emergency. →**Chapter 14, Globalisation**, *In Brief*

**Ford: on the road to new success?**

Ford's restructuring innovation plan will force the company to close down 14 of its 43 plants by 2012, resulting in 30,000 jobs being slashed out of a total 123,000 in North America.
A more optimistic perspective lies in the fact that the new CEO wants to adopt a risk-taking policy. He is ready to pour billions of dollars in eco-friendly plants and cars. The company will increase its production of hybrid gas electric models to 250,000 units a year by 2010.
Ford has also decided to focus on design. Ford's design team has won praise for the Reflex, featuring solar panels, butterfly doors and internal insulation made of recycled Nike shoes.

## Question time

**1** What are the different types of companies?
**2** Define a good manager.
**3** What are the internal problems a company may face?
**4** Where can most of a firm's external problems originate from?
**5** What measures can a company take to solve its problems?
**6** Which measures are considered the most unpopular?
**7** What is a corporate citizen company?
**8** According to what criteria are companies rated as corporate citizens?
**9** Why did Marks & Spencer leave France in 2001?
**10** Why do some companies merge?

# Microsoft

## Facts and figures

Microsoft is a computer technology multinational corporation with global annual sales of $44.28bn and more than 70,000 employees in more than 100 countries. It develops, manufactures, licenses and supports software products for computing devices. Its best selling products are the Microsoft Windows operating system and the Microsoft Office software, which are used by almost every computer on earth. Microsoft has footholds in other markets, such as the MSNBC cable TV network, the MSN portal and the Encarta encyclopedia. The company also markets computer hardware products, such as the Microsoft mouse, and home entertainment products such as the Xbox.

## The beginnings

Microsoft's name is a portmanteau word ("micro-computer" + "software") and is often abbreviated as *MS*. The company was founded in Albuquerque, New Mexico in April 1975 by Bill Gates and Paul Allen. In the mid 1980s, Microsoft gained a contract with IBM, which it used to dominate the home computer operating system market with MS-DOS.

**1985** Windows 1.0 was launched. It was sold as an extension of MS-DOS. Its original name was "Interface Manager" but the head of marketing at Microsoft convinced the company that "Windows" would be more appealing to consumers.

## Corporate culture

Microsoft has become famous for its codes of conduct for employees. It spends a lot of time and money each year on recruiting young university-trained software developers, who are the stars of the company. Every developer has a private or semiprivate closed office as soon as she/he enters the company, instead of being entitled only to a cubicle desk within a large office space filled with other cubicles. The company is known for its hiring interviews: candidates are asked questions to determine whether they are creative thinkers who can adapt solutions to changing, dynamic scenarios, such as "I am your grandmother. Describe what MatLab is."

Employees use the latest Microsoft products inside the company in order to test them before they are put on the market.

Lastly, Microsoft is the top company in the world for donations per employee: not including Bill Gates, Microsoft employees have given over $2.5bn dollars to non-profit organizations worldwide in 2006.

A 2006 magazine advert

## Diversity and discrimination

Microsoft hires many foreign workers and opposes the H1B visas, which say foreigners can remain in the US for a maximum period of six years at a time, after which they must live outside the country for one year before they can be issued a new visa. Bill Gates claims H1B visas make it difficult to hire employees for the company, whose policy is to keep employees at the company.

Partly through the work of the Gay and Lesbian Employees at Microsoft (GLEAM) group, Microsoft added gender expression to its antidiscrimination policies in April 2005. This put Microsoft among the most progressive companies in the world, according to the Human Rights Campaign.

## Criticism

- Unfair and anticompetitive business tactics

Microsoft has been convicted of monopolistic business practices. Advocates of free software are opposing Microsoft's tactics.

- Too much work

Microsoft has been called a "velvet sweatshop" because its employees work too much.

- Insecurity of software

Many Microsoft products have been described unstable. The "Blue Screen of Death", when Windows abruptly terminates an application, still happens with Windows 2000 and XP.

- Complexity

It has been said that the user interface has been designed for computer geeks rather than normal people.

- Insecurity

Numerous Microsoft products, most notably Internet Explorer, are insecure to viruses and worms.

**Online t@sk**

**Visit Microsoft's corporate site and go to www.microsoft.com/about/default.mspx. Choose "corporate campaigns" or "corporate citizenship" and report to the class.**

# Vocabulary

**accounting:** comptabilité
**advertise:** faire de la publicité
**amount to:** se monter à
**bankrupt (to go ...):** (faire) banqueroute / faillite
**based:** qui se trouve à
**benefit:** avantage
**bid:** offre
**board:** conseil d'administration
**brand:** marque
**business:** affaire, entreprise
**buying habits:** habitudes d'achat
**career:** carrière
**CEO (chief executive officer):** PDG
**charity:** organisation caritative
**close down:** fermer
**code of business:** déontologie des entreprises
**colleague:** collègue
**company:** entreprise
**compete:** être en concurrence
**competition:** concurrence
**competitive:** concurrentiel
**consumer:** consommateur
**core market:** marché principal
**corporate:** d'entreprise
**corporation:** entreprise
**customer service:** service client
**deal:** accord
**delivery:** livraison
**department:** service, département
**drop:** chuter
**eco-friendly:** respectueux de l'environnement
**employee:** employé
**environmental:** écologiste
**factory:** usine
**fair trade:** commerce équitable
**faulty:** défectueux
**firm:** entreprise
**focus:** se concentrer sur
**forecast:** prévoir
**found** ***(V)*****:** fonder
**franchising:** système de franchise
**funds:** fonds
**global:** mondial
**growth:** croissance
**headquarters:** siège social
**hire:** embaucher
**human resources:** ressources humaines
**implement:** mettre en œuvre
**incentive:** prime
**industry:** industrie, secteur
**Information Technology (IT):** informatique
**investment:** investissement
**investor:** investisseur
**involvement:** implication
**issue:** problème, question
**job losses:** pertes d'emplois
**know-how:** savoir-faire
**law:** loi
**lawsuit:** procès
**make someone redundant:** licencier économiquement
**maker:** fabricant
**management:** direction, gestion
**manager:** directeur
**market share:** part de marché
**marketing mix:** plan de marchéage
**merge:** fusionner
**merger:** fusion
**multinational:** multinationale
**net income:** revenu net
**NGO (non-governmental organisation):** organisation non gouvernementale
**operate:** (faire) fonctionner
**operating income:** compte d'exploitation
**organization chart:** organigramme
**outsource:** externaliser, sous-traiter
**overheads:** frais généraux
**own:** posséder
**partnership:** partenariat
**pensioner:** retraité
**perk:** avantage en nature
**plant:** usine
**policy:** stratégie
**power:** énergie
**premium:** bonus, prime
**Private Limited Company (Ltd):** société à responsabilité limitée (SARL)
**product:** produit
**profitability:** rentabilité
**profitable:** rentable
**Public Limited Company (PLC):** société anonyme (SA)
**purchasing department:** service des achats
**quality standard:** norme de qualité
**quoted:** (bourse) coté
**range from... to...:** aller de... à
**recycling:** recyclage
**red (in the):** dans le rouge
**relocate:** délocaliser

*"Due to corporate cutbacks, we'll all have to sacrifice, which is why my company car will be a Mercedes, instead of the Jaguar I normally drive."*

**Research and Development (R&D):** recherche & développement
**restructure:** restructurer
**retirement:** retraite
**revenue:** recettes
**rise:** augmenter, augmentation
**sales:** ventes
**save:** économiser
**sell:** vendre
**share:** action
**shareholder:** actionnaire
**single proprietorship:** entreprise en nom propre
**small-and-medium-sized companies/enterprises (SMEs):** petites et moyennes entreprises (PME)
**spokesman:** porte-parole
**staff:** personnel
**standards:** normes
**stock:** actions, titres
**stock exchange:** bourse
**streamline:** dégraisser
**strike (on):** grève (en)
**subsidiary:** filiale
**subsidize:** subventionner
**supplier:** fournisseur
**sustainable development:** développement durable
**tool:** outil
**union:** syndicat
**update:** mettre à jour
**vocational training:** formation professionnelle
**wages:** salaires
**workers' council:** comité d'entreprise
**workforce:** main-d'œuvre
**working conditions:** conditions de travail

## Charts and tables

**1.** Study the following organisational chart to learn more about the way companies are structured. Identify the different departments and the person at the head of each department, then determine who has the power in this organisation.

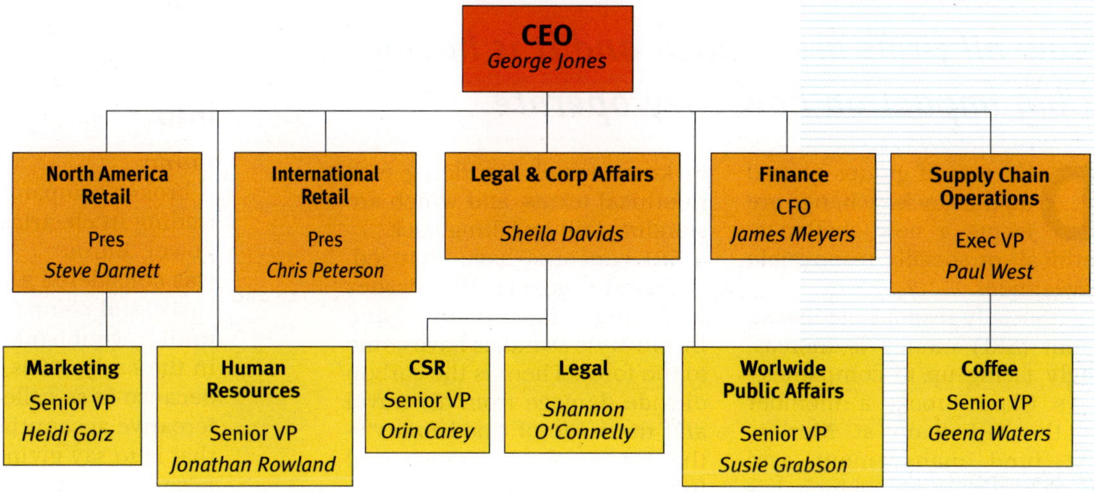


**2.** Give an oral presentation of the company. Don't forget to explain its industry.

## Communication tasks

### Roleplay: A phone call

**A: You are a salesperson.**
You need to identify the sales manager in the company you want to sell your goods to. You phone the marketing assistant and try to talk him/her into giving you the organisation chart of the company. Be persuasive, remain polite and nice!

**B: You are the marketing assistant.**
Someone calls you on the phone to get the name and as much information as possible on the sales manager. You are not supposed to give him/her this kind of information. Be determined, but remain polite!

→Tools 9, p. 242

## Online tasks

### Do you know about the WTO?

Visit the World Trade Organization website to see a different organisation chart:
**www.wto.org/english/thewto_e/whatis_e/tif_e/org2_e.htm**
Compare the two organisation charts and report to the class.

# Socially responsible investment

## *Now all firms are graded and it is having a big impact on how they operate.*

Directors of groups quoted on the stock exchange are facing a new challenge: "ethical" or socially responsible investment.

"Socially responsible investment (SRI) money is increasingly facing up to companies," says Clare Brook, a member of the SRI team at Morley, the fund management arm of Norwich Union, which has £150bn under its control.

Morley has a regularly updated list so consumers and investors can see how companies are meeting the challenge of sustainability.

Firms are listed A to E, according to their basic business. A is the highest. Out of the 100 biggest quoted companies in the UK and those of the Eurotop 50 index of leading European firms, just four make the top echelon: pharmaceuticals GlaxoSmithKline and Smith & Nephew and two publishers, Pearson and Reed Elsevier.

At the other end, there are six companies in the E category, three tobacco companies, one armaments group and two electricity generators.

Morley and many other SRI managers no longer divide companies into saints or sinners[1]. Here's why:

- Consumers and others affected by companies' decisions need to know which are doing well in ethical terms, and which are standing still or falling back.
- SRI concerns have changed. Corporate governance issues including "fat-cattism"[2] and Enron-style scandals have come to the fore[3]. There is the carbon dioxide damage from air travel and the issue of "food miles" – the distance food is transported from source to store shelf.
- SRI now recognises that some companies will never be approved by ethical purists but that these organisations can become aware of what they are doing to the world and make amends.

"We would rather call it 'progressive' as we are trying to change companies. It's not white lists, black lists or grey lists, but how companies are moving towards a future of sustainability," Ms Brook says. "We focus more on whether companies are getting better or worse in understanding and dealing with the impact of their activities and their vision for sustainable development."

Tony Levene, *The Guardian*, April 22, 2006

1. *sinner*: pécheur (par opposition à *saint*)
2. *fat-cattism*: le fait de s'enrichir pour ceux qui sont déjà riches. *A fat cat* = un gros richard
3. *come to the fore*: se manifester

## Info

***Enron***
A broker company trading in electrical power, Enron was considered a successful company until it went bankrupt in the early 2000s because of so-called "creative accounting", that is to say giving false information to investors and the public about the actual situation of the company.

## References

You can find relevant information by reading various pages in your book and memorising a few facts and ideas.

→ **Companies, p. 27**
→ **Consumers, p. 70**
→ **Sustainable development, p. 178**

ACTIVITY **Practise giving an account of this article.**

## Introduction

You should explain where the article comes from, when it was published and what it is about. →Tools 4, p. 236

This article, published in *The Guardian*, a British daily, in April 2006, reports on "socially responsible investment", or SRI, a new issue companies have to consider.

## Development

Once you have understood the article, organise your ideas into two or three different parts, using set phrases and link-words. →Tools 4, p. 236

1. Definition of SRI
2. Reasons for developing SRI
3. Neither saints nor sinners

You should also use the information given in *Info* and what you have learnt, for example by referring to the various pages indicated in *References*.

### 1. Definition of SRI

Socially responsible investment is when companies show that they have become aware that they have a responsibility towards the rest of the world, when they manufacture products and produce waste, for instance. Companies have to prove that they are environment-conscious, and that they are working towards developing less polluting activities: they may invest in recycling, in less polluting materials, in machines that cut polluting emissions, etc.

### 2. Reasons for developing SRI

If they want investors and customers to have a positive opinion of the company, firms have to show they are socially responsible. It is not enough any more for companies to just say they care. They have to prove it to the investors, or their value on the stock exchange might drop. More generally, they have to meet sustainable development targets to project a positive image in the eyes of the public.
Fund management companies help potential investors and the public find out which companies can be considered ethical. For instance, Morley offers a list where investors can choose between five grades, A to E. Companies listed A meet the challenge of sustainability. Only four British companies have been listed A, two pharmaceuticals, GlaxoSmithKline and Smith & Nephew, and two publishers, Pearson and Reed Elsevier. More have been listed in the E category, three tobacco companies, one armaments group and two electricity generators.

### 3. Neither saints nor sinners

It is not possible to have a fixed list.
- First of all, some companies may be socially responsible one year and fall back the following year. A company may invest in a sustainable development project to gain investors one year and go back to its polluting practices afterwards.
- New issues appear. For example, no one had heard of food miles a few years ago, but people are now aware that transporting fruit and vegetables or other food products generates pollution.
- Finally, some industries such as tobacco, armaments or oil can never be considered positive. However, they can show that they try to compensate for what wrong they are doing. Therefore, public lists can help investors and consumers but they can also push companies to keep sustainability in mind and set targets to improve all the time.

## Conclusion

You should sum up the main ideas and try to open out in a new direction.

This article shows that companies can no longer ignore the community as they used to. Being profitable is not enough: firms also have to show that they behave responsibly and that they are thinking about sustainability. They have to project a positive image or investors may wish to put their money elsewhere and consumers may wish to take action against the company.

## Branching out

Now, you should move away from the article and develop more ideas. The following questions can help you.

**1** How can firms project a positive image of themselves?

**2** How can consumers influence companies and the way they behave?

## Case study: a new service

Study smile's web site and report to the class about the online bank services for students.

.co .uk

welcome to **smile** the internet bank

account login | bank | invest | why smile | talk to us | help | security

### student account

bank

bank
- student account
- £2,000 free overdraft
- 3.04% AER interest
- getting money in and out
- 24/7 control
- where does your money go?
- faqs
- tariffs, t&cs

**WEALTH WARNING:**
**smiling is good for your heart and your wallet, start**

**smile** has just scooped best online student account provider at the Your Money 2006 awards, so what's all the fuss about?

On top of a free overdraft of up to £2,000 we'll give you things you might not get from other high street banks:

- around 30 times more interest than some other banks when you're in credit, that's 3.04% AER interest
- we calculate interest daily and pay it to you every month
- you can move your money from one **smile** account to another at the click of a mouse - "Eek!"
- we'll switch your existing account to **smile** for you - no hassle.

Plus the stuff you'd expect:

- a **smile** debit and cashpoint card which you can use at over 32,000 Link machines
- a **smile** chequebook
- if we change our interest rates we'll let you know.

All we ask is that you are at least 17 and a half, a UK citizen, UK resident, in full time higher education at degree level or equivalent with full time student status (with more than 6 months left on your course) and you deposit:

- at least £300, or
- an LEA grant cheque, or
- a student loan (you'll need to provide proof that you have funding of £2,500 or more).

From www.**smile**.co.uk

## PERSONAL TASK

Here are two headlines. Choose one and turn it into a 30-word paragraph. Use the information given in brackets.

- Hamleys to expand into Middle East (*famous, Regent Street, toys, franchise, Middle East, also India and China*).
- Firms find it pays to relax dress code (*formal business wear, past, nowadays, allow, casual, every day*).

# IN THIS UNIT...

- Companies: Virgin, Yogitoes, Airness, ...
- Learn about start-ups and verbal CVs
- Phone to obtain a work placement
- Present a survey
- Write an application letter

# 2
## New entrepreneurs

**→ Before you START**

*In brief:* **Can you start a company with a funny idea?**
*Front page:* **Original hamburgers**

## Would you say launching a new business is risky? Why/Why not?

### Words

- **Nouns:** independence, employer, risk, investment, loan, results
- **Adjectives:** own, independent, organised, overworked, risky
- **Expressions:** get a foothold in

### LISTENING PRACTICE

CD TRACK 11

Listen to the recording.
1. What are the people talking about?
2. Explain their opinions.

# Making big bucks[1] with beer and burgers

*How Jeff Weinstein's burger outlet in LA became a national franchise.*

Jeff Weinstein says he started The Counter, a Los Angeles-based burger restaurant, "out of a desire to do something that was different from what anybody had ever done before."

At his restaurant, eaters can order ultra-customized burgers for about $6 to $12 apiece, starting with a choice of beef, chicken, turkey, veggie, salmon or tuna. They can also choose from 10 cheeses, 26 toppings, 17 sauces and 8 different types of buns. That all adds up to an incredible 312,000 options, not to mention the various kinds of beer available.

Indeed, the specific concept has proven so attractive that it's grown from a stand-alone shop to a soon-to-be national franchise in just a few years. Weinstein, the 31-year-old founder, explains his success simply: "We believe we were the first to do the premium burger, and we're the best at it."

**The road to success**

In July 2005, *GQ magazine* ranked The Counter at No. 15 in its list of "20 Hamburgers You Must Eat Before You Die." But things really exploded when Oprah Winfrey's best friend sampled the burgers on *GQ*'s list for the "Oprah Winfrey" show in February 2006. Sales skyrocketed to $245,000 a month, up from the $44,000 a month it grossed when it opened in 2003.

That's how Lou Gurnick, who had worked on the initial development of franchises like Domino's Pizza and Orange Julius, noticed Weinstein's success. Gurnick helped pave the way for Weinstein's partnership with a Los Angeles-based franchiser. Weinstein studied at the Johnson & Wales University College of Culinary Arts, and therefore he didn't know much about what it takes to take a business nationally. So he was willing to partner up with a more experienced team and use their structure to develop.

Since launching The Counter's franchising program, Weinstein has sold the development rights to 60 restaurants, which should open throughout California over the next three years. Four to five restaurants are expected to open in 2006. Another 12 to 15 locations should follow in 2007 and between 20 and 25 more are scheduled in 2008. Long-range projections call for 400 to 600 restaurants across the country.

*The Boston Globe*, July 22, 2006

1. *buck* (familier): dollar

CD TRACK 15

## Info

***buck***
The expression "big bucks" means a lot of money.

***GQ magazine***
A monthly men's magazine that focuses on men's fashion and style, food, etc. It is perceived as an upscale magazine aiming at metrosexual men.

***Oprah Winfrey show***
America's most successful talk-show, with an estimated 14 million viewers nationally. Winfrey transformed classic talk-shows into intimate conversations. The books that appear on her show become instant bestsellers.

## Headlines

**1** Anticipate the contents of the article from the headline.

**2** Can you imagine why the journalist used "bucks" and not "dollars"? Look at the main sound in the headline.

**3** Read the subhead and add more details about the contents of the article.

## Work on words

### 1 I Find their equivalents in English

§2 commander – choix – choisir – incroyable – à disposition
§4 classer – goûter à – ventes – s'envoler – réaliser un bénéfice brut de
§5 ouvrir la voie – partenariat – franchiseur – équipe
§6 prévoir

### 2 I Find their synonyms

§3 independent – top quality
§6 start – plan – long term

## The key points of the article

### 1 Read §1 and §2

**a.** Name of the restaurant.
**b.** Type of food.
**c.** Price.
**d.** What is special about the restaurant? Explain "ultra-customized".
**e.** Reason why it was created that way.

### 2 Read §3 and §4

**a.** Find all the details related to the restaurant when it opened.
**b.** What two things helped it develop?

### 3 Read §5 and §6

**a.** Weinstein's decision.
**b.** Reason for this decision.
**c.** Who helped (name and qualities).
**d.** What this man did.
**e.** Results.

## Branching out

**1** What are the drawbacks of a franchise for the franchisee? →*Key data*, p. 130
**2** Should a firm be successful before looking for partners?

## {Methods}

### ■ Speaking practice

**1 Read figures aloud.** →Tools 10, p. 243
Read §2, §4 and §6 aloud. If necessary, start by writing the following figures down.
Then practise reading the groups of words in parentheses together with the figures.
**a.** (about) $6 to $12 (apiece)
**b.** (an incredible) 312,000 (options)
**c.** (sales skyrocketed to) $245,000 (a month)
**d.** (up from the) $44,000 (a month)
**e.** (it opened in) 2003

**2 Money, money**
Get used to dollars and pounds. Change all the money data into euros.

**3 Prepare an oral introduction.**
• Identify the source.
• Explain what the article is about (who, what, where, when).

### ■ Writing practice

**Write an account of this article in English (around 150 words).**
• Introduction.
• Development. a. The company; b. Reasons for its success; c. Prospects.
• Conclusion.
→Tools 4, p. 236

## Language

• *Sales **skyrocketed** to $245,000 a month, up from the $44,000 a month it **grossed** when it **opened** in 2003.*
• *The concept **has proven** so attractive that it**'s grown** from a stand-alone shop to a soon-to-be national franchise in just a few years.*
• *Lou Gurnick, who **had worked** on franchises like Domino's Pizza and Orange Julius, **helped** pave the way for Weinstein.*

Pour exprimer un passé révolu, coupé du présent, on utilise le prétérit. Pour former le prétérit aux formes négative et interrogative, on utilise l'auxiliaire ***did***.
Le *past perfect* exprime un passé au second degré. Il est formé de l'auxiliaire ***have*** au passé (***had***) + le participe passé du verbe.

**Translate into English**
**1.** L'an dernier, les hamburgers ne coûtaient pas aussi cher.
**2.** Le restaurant a eu tellement de succès dès le début qu'il a dû refuser du monde.
**3.** Les ventes ont grimpé de 40 000 à 250 000 dollars après l'émission télévisée.
**4.** En moins de 6 mois, le restaurant est passé de 5 à 8 employés.

**An entrepreneur is someone who is self-employed. He or she creates and runs a new company and assumes the inherent risks in order to offer a new product or service. Since the industrial revolution, the history of trade and business has been punctuated by outstanding entrepreneurs who have left unforgettable marks. They have all shared the same innovative spirit and eagerness to carry out their enterprise.**

## 1-Basics

### How to recognise an entrepreneur

Organizing, managing and assuming risk requires a certain amount of qualities. Most entrepreneurs are indeed workaholics: hard work is necessary. Many of them started from scratch. Here are the qualities most entrepreneurs share:

- a will to achieve, to create a successful business, eliminating all the hurdles that may occur on the road to success,
- the desire to work for themselves without anything to owe to anyone,
- a special ability to confront the whole array of responsibilities they are necessarily faced with,
- optimism, which is necessary to confront risks,
- an urge for excellence together with an eagerness to be recognized for their accomplishment.

### Portrait gallery

Here are some of the most famous names of people who have become well-known entrepreneurs. Their stories as individuals are linked to intelligence, bravado, success and quite often to the ideal of the American Dream: going from rags to riches and becoming a self-made man – or woman!

- In the USA: Levi Strauss (jeans), J. D. Rockefeller (oil industry), Henry Ford (Ford Motor Company), Bill Gates (Microsoft →**Chapter 1, Companies, *Landmark*, p. 29**) , Steve Jobs (Apple computers, IPods), Estée Lauder (cosmetics), Sam Walton (Wal Mart →**Chapter 8, Distribution, *Landmark*, p. 133**) Larry Page and Sergey Brin (Google →**Chapter 10, New technologies, *Landmark*, p. 163**)
- In the UK: Richard Branson (Virgin →***Landmark*, p. 43**)
- In Spain: Amancio Ortega (Zara)
- In France: Gabrielle Chanel (Chanel)
- In Ireland: Michael O'Leary (Ryanair →**Chapter 9, Transport, *Key data*, p. 146**)

### Start-ups

When one thinks of new entrepreneurs, the word start-up immediately comes to mind. Start-up companies are noted for their high risk and reward profile; unlike established companies, their launching cost must be extremely low, as they count on a rapid growth with limited investment.

Since the 1990s, most start-ups have involved internet companies despite the crash, known as the dot-com crash which lasted from 2000 to 2002, and during which the Nasdaq lost 78% of its value. This crisis can be accounted for by the "too much too

Pierre Omidyar was 28 when he founded eBay in 1995.

**The history of blue jeans**

In 1853, the California gold rush was in full swing, and everyday items were in short supply. Levi Strauss, a 24-year-old German immigrant, left New York for San Francisco with a small supply of dry goods with the intention of opening a branch of his brother's New York dry goods business. Shortly after his arrival, a prospector wanted to know what Mr. Strauss was selling. When Strauss told him he had rough canvas to use for tents and wagon covers, the prospector said, "You should have brought pants!" saying he couldn't find a pair of pants strong enough to last. That's how it all started, and the rest is history.

fast" factor: almost every dot-com company was lent millions of dollars and expected to grow the size of Microsoft overnight.
Since 2003, things have gone back to normal. Dot-com ventures have achieved a steady growth, much more controlled than it used to be at the beginning when the internet had become the new El Dorado in which everybody rushed to get a piece of the pie.
However, 33% of US start-ups still fail after four years because owners underestimate the skills they will need or the expenses they will encounter.

## 2-Europe's young entrepreneurs

The USA has been the leader in entrepreneurial spirit. However, young EU entrepreneurs are liable to become today's new models as a growing number are creating successful start-ups.

### European start-ups

New energies and eco-friendly products constitute new niches where young entrepreneurs are more liable to enter. They tend to be more involved with sustainable development than their older counterparts.
Start-ups are also made easier by the globalisation process which erases barriers and tariffs and encourages deregulation.
→Chapter 14, Globalisation
Although new entrepreneurship is getting more and more prolific thanks to 20 million small-and-medium-sized companies, experts estimate that the EU needs 5 million new entrepreneurs to remain competitive in the long term. New entrepreneurship is encouraged by the EU authorities who are aware that better education and better training will represent the backbone of new entrepreneurship in Europe. The challenge is big as new countries are joining the EU, some of them reputed to be extremely poor.

### New technology-based firms

NTBFs, as they are called, are well-established at EU level. Thanks to new technologies and the rise in the demand of services, it has become much easier to create a start-up from scratch: a computer and internet broadband access can be enough to create a small company. In spite of the many obstacles to overcome, new firms emerge every day and form a new business generation sharing the same values and goals. The majority of those firms address the EU, or the EU and the US markets. They are unevenly distributed across the EU and are still rare or non-existent in some of the EU new member countries. The major problem they have to face is the skills shortage, which makes some of them relocate to the US.

### Junior enterprises

Europe favours the development of junior enterprises, that is to say local non-profit organisations where students work as young entrepreneurs. The idea is to promote entrepreneurship among students. For instance, JADE is a student-run, pan-European network representing more than 20,000 young entrepreneurs in 225 Junior Enterprises. By running professional consulting

**Mozzo**

Twenty-four-year-old Grant Lang, in Southampton (UK) was interested in Fair Trade and involvement in the local community. In 2005 he launched his coffee company, named Mozzo, to sell organic Fair Trade beans while helping local artists. He did not have enough money to open his own coffee shop, so he bought a rickshaw which he equipped with solar panels and a wind turbine. Local painters decorated the sides of the cart to make it more eye-catching, while local bands played on a portable stereo. The first year, Mozzo's sales reached $225,000. Lang donates 5% of profits to community causes.

**Jobetudiant**

Julien Genestoux (23) created an on-line company, Jobetudiant, in 2003. This site is a job service aimed at students. In 2005, 200,000 jobseekers were registered, with 10,000 open job postings every day. His revenues reached over $100,000 in 2006.

studies and managing small- to medium-sized enterprises, students can start adding practical experience to their theoretical skills and develop entrepreneurship at an early stage.

## 3-New entrepreneurs: Americans over 50

Just as young European entrepreneurs seem to proliferate, "grandma-and-grandpop" businesses are thriving on the other side of the Atlantic: 5.6 million workers over fifty are self-employed, a figure which has grown by 23% since 1990. This trend contradicts the cliché that entrepreneurs are necessarily young.

### Reasons for this new trend

- **Demography**

Americans are getting older. Americans over 50 accounted for 31 million of the overall population (296 million) in 2005; they are expected to reach 118 million in 2020. Life expectancy is partly accountable for this growth : the older workers can have a second career, as new entrepreneurs well past the traditional retirement age.

- **Job hopping**

As employment became less stable, people started job hopping. Company loyalty disappeared together with the concept of "a job for life".

- **Fear of unemployment**

People fear being laid off. Some prefer to leave and try starting their own businesses.

- **No retirement benefits**

Retirement benefits are very low, or even non-existent in the USA. That is why the numbers of grandma-and-grandpop businesses are expected to increase as baby-boomers are looking for a way to keep a decent income once they have stopped working as employees.

- **Lower cost of technology**

Technology is getting cheaper, making it possible for a lot of people to start a new business with adapted software.

**Profitable home care**

After having been laid off three times, Jim Minick, 51, started an elder-care business in 2003. His Home Care Georgia (near Atlanta) helps people with daily tasks, such as getting dressed. It became profitable in 2004. Minick had more than $140,000 in revenue in 2006.

**Cookies on the web**

Franny Martins was 56 when she launched her cookie company in Michigan in 2002. Now she sells 47 kinds of cookies through her website. She has already got one employee and plans to hire more. Her 2006 revenue was $500,000, a figure which has tripled in two years. Her website, which attracts cookie customers from around the world, cost $3,000 to build. Without the web, she would spend more time on the road selling to a much smaller market.

## Question time

1 What are the qualities most entrepreneurs share?
2 Choose one famous entrepreneur above, find information about him/her and report to the class.
3 What is a start-up?
4 What is referred to as the dot-com crash?
5 Why did this crash occur?
6 How many new entrepreneurs does the EU need to remain competitive?
7 Why are new American entrepreneurs contradicting the clichés?
8 What are the reasons which encourage older people to launch their own businesses?
9 Report on an example of a grandma-and-grandpop business.

# Virgin

**The Virgin Group is a group of companies that all use business tycoon Sir Richard Branson's Virgin brand. Its core business areas are travel, entertainment and lifestyle. Branson has united all his different businesses under a single brand name over which he has kept complete ownership and control. The Virgin companies operate independently from one another.**

## Milestones

- **1968** Branson's first business venture: he publishes the first issue of *Student* magazine.
- **1970** Starts selling records by mail-order
- **1971** Opens his first record shop on Oxford Street, London
- **1973** Launches Virgin record label
- **1980** Virgin Records goes international
- **1983** Virgin Games
- **1984** Virgin Atlantic Airways
- **1985** Virgin Holidays
- **1988** Virgin sells some of its smaller UK retail stores and invests in Virgin Megastores in the UK and abroad
- **1991** Virgin Books
- **1995** Virgin Direct Personal Financial Services
- **1997** Virgin Cosmetics
- **1999** Virgin Mobile
- **2004** Virgin Galactic, a new space tourism company to take paying passengers into space. The group announced that flights would be made available to the public by late 2007 with tickets priced at $200,000.
- **2006** Virgin Fuel, which will invest $400 million over three years in renewable energy. In September 2006, Branson pledged to donate the profits of Virgin Atlantic and Virgin Trains – about $3 billion – to research environmentally friendly fuels, combat global warming and promote alternative energy. He also suggested trains should be used instead of airlines for routes that are equivalent.

A funny 1990 advert for Virgin Cola

Branson as the devil in a Virgin insurance ad

## Failures

In 1994 Branson launched Virgin Cola, which is now retreating to the UK market only.
Then, in 1997, Branson entered the railway business. Virgin Trains won the franchises for some previously nationalized sectors of British Rail. However, despite promises of new high-tech trains and better service, Virgin Trains soon had problems because of the old trains and infrastructure it had inherited.
Finally, Branson failed in a 2000 bid to handle the British National Lottery.

## The "rebel billionaire"

Richard Branson became Sir Richard Branson when he was knighted by the Queen in 1999 for "services to entrepreneurship". He has been described as a "transformational leader" thanks to his non-conformist strategies and his stress on informality. He often wears jeans and no tie.
He is the N° 1 Admired Businessman in Britain, and young people have chosen him as their second best choice for Prime Minister (after Tony Blair). He has been an actor, playing himself on several television shows, including *Friends* and *Baywatch*; he was also the star of a reality TV show called *The Rebel Billionaire*, in which sixteen contestants were tested for their entrepreneurship and sense of adventure.

**Online t@sk**

Visit Virgin's corporate site and go to www.virgin.com/aboutvirgin/default.asp. Choose one theme and report to the class.

# Vocabulary

**achieve:** réussir
**ads:** pubs, publicités
**advertising:** la publicité
**advise:** conseiller
**aim at:** cibler
**asset:** actif, avantage
**available:** disponible
**be worth:** valoir
**bid:** offre
**boost:** renforcer, accroître
**bottom line:** résultat financier
**brand:** marque
**business (a –):** entreprise
**business venture:** entreprise
**businessman:** homme d'affaires
**candidate:** candidat
**career:** carrière
**chief executive officer (CEO):** président directeur général
**choice:** choix
**choose:** choisir
**core:** essentiel/central
**cosmetics:** produits de beauté
**cost:** coûter
**crash:** effondrement (boursier)
**customer:** client
**customized:** sur mesure
**deli (delicatessen):** épicerie fine
**department store:** grand magasin
**donate:** donner, faire don de
**employee:** employé
**entertainment:** loisir
**entrepreneur:** entrepreneur
**entrepreneurship:** esprit d'entreprise
**estimated:** estimé
**exceed:** dépasser
**expenses:** frais
**factory:** usine
**fail:** échouer
**failure:** échec
**fair trade:** commerce équitable
**fashion:** mode
**feature:** caractéristique
**figure:** chiffre
**flight:** vol
**focus:** (V) (se) concentrer sur ; (N) priorité, centre d'intérêt
**found *(V)*:** fonder, créer
**founder:** créateur
**franchise:** franchise
**franchiser:** franchiseur
**free of charge:** gratuit
**from scratch:** à partir de rien
**fuel:** carburant
**global:** mondial
**global warming:** réchauffement de la planète
**goal:** but, objectif
**graduate:** diplômé
**grocery store:** épicerie
**gross *(V)*:** dégager un bénéfice brut
**grow:** grandir, croître
**growth:** croissance
**hire:** recruter, engager
**hurdle:** obstacle
**income:** revenu
**increase:** augmenter
**independent:** indépendant
**instant:** immédiat
**invent:** inventer
**invest:** investir
**investment:** investissement
**item:** produit, article
**job interview:** entretien d'embauche
**jobseeker:** demandeur d'emploi
**launch:** lancer
**lay off:** licencier
**leader:** dirigeant
**lend:** prêter
**life expectancy:** espérance de vie
**location:** emplacement
**long-range:** à long terme
**mail order:** vente par correspondance
**maker:** fabricant
**manufacture:** fabriquer
**marketed:** commercialisé
**milestone:** moment clé, jalon
**motto:** devise
**office mate:** collègue
**old-fashioned:** démodé
**operate:** gérer, exploiter
**order:** commander
**owe:** devoir
**own:** posséder
**owner:** propriétaire
**ownership:** propriété
**partner:** partenaire
**partnership:** partenariat
**pave the way:** ouvrir la voie
**premium:** de grande qualité
**profit:** bénéfice
**profitable:** rentable, bénéficiaire
**promote:** promouvoir
**rank:** classer
**recruiter:** recruteur
**rely on:** s'appuyer sur

*"I wanna own a Ferrari by the time I'm 16."*

**retail store:** magasin de détail
**retirement age:** âge de la retraite
**retirement benefits:** pension (argent perçu par les retraités)
**revenue:** recettes
**rival:** concurrencer
**run:** gérer
**sales:** ventes
**sample:** goûter, tester
**schedule *(V)*:** prévoir
**self-employed:** indépendant, qui travaille à son compte
**sell (out):** vendre (tout le stock)
**share *(V)*:** partager
**single:** unique
**skill:** compétence, savoir-faire
**soar:** s'envoler, prendre son essor
**software:** logiciel
**sports apparel:** vêtements de sport
**stand-alone:** seul
**start-up:** jeune entreprise
**stock:** approvisionner
**store:** magasin
**succeed:** réussir
**success:** succès
**successful:** qui a du succès
**supplier:** fournisseur
**supply *(N)*:** stock
**team:** équipe
**tool:** outil
**trade:** échanges, commerce
**trend:** tendance
**tycoon:** magnat
**unemployment:** chômage
**upmarket:** haut de gamme
**upscale:** haut de gamme
**website:** site internet
**workaholic:** accro du travail
**worldwide:** dans le monde entier

## Charts and tables

**1.** Study the following survey.
Describe the evolution of the figures and comment on this evolution: what do the percentages tell us about the different selling strategies?

New selling and advertising strategies

| | 2003 | 2005 |
|---|---|---|
| Selling with email | **12.4%** | **10.3%** |
| Selling via auction sites | **25.6%** | **21.9%** |
| Setting up a website | **43.2%** | **46.3%** |
| Advertising with search engines | **18.5%** | **22.3%** |
| From Vendio Services Inc. | | |

**2.** Give an oral presentation of this survey to the class.
→**Tools 11, p. 244**

## Communication tasks

### Write an application letter

You want to apply for a job as a salesperson in a company looking for people that know about email and website advertising. Write an application letter in which you explain your motivation and your profile.
→**The rules of the game, p. 15 & Tools 7, p. 240**

### Do you know about verbal CVs?

You have been selected for a job interview. You must be able to give the recruiter a quick account of your own experience.

**Practise your verbal CV with a partner.**
What you have to know:
- recruiters often make their decision on the first impression they get from a candidate and what they say. The first five minutes are essential.
- just like a written CV, the best verbal CV is a brief one – just a few sentences that sum up your experience and how you want to be perceived. Choose your words carefully to give a positive verbal account of yourself.
→**Tools 14, p. 248**

# Airness, France's hottest sports-apparel brand

Malamine Koné is the 34-year-old founder of sportswear maker Airness. In 2005, his company's sales amounted to $150 million – mostly in France but his goal is to rival global giant Nike's 2005 sales of $14bn. He says, "six years ago, Airness scarcely existed. We didn't get this far this fast worrying about what we supposedly can't do." He even compares Airness to other giants: "You know where Puma was five years ago? Deeply troubled," Koné says of the German-American sportswear group, whose sales last year exceeded $2bn.

Koné founded Airness in 1999, borrowing the name from US basketball star Michael Jordan to reflect his brand motto "ever higher, ever stronger." He started by selling sweatshirts sporting the Airness name and its panther logo around the northern Paris housing projects[1] where he lived. Since then, he has developed a clothing and sports range that has grown at least 100% every year. He built Airness around the idea that it is kids who decide what's hip, not the companies marketing stuff to them. He says, "by observing what people were buying or looking for, I could react faster to current trends and demand and anticipate what would work next," says Koné.

He signed "extra-sports" contracts with champions such as Didier Drogba and Djibril Cissé, "getting players to wear Airness in their private life once their on-field obligations were over." Then he was able to build on those ties and signed Airness as official uniform supplier to various French pro clubs and half a dozen African national teams. London club Fulham is joining in 2007, with an extra: Fulham's owner, Mohamed al Fayed, also owns Harrods, the London department store. Airness products will be on sale there.

Koné criticizes France for its rigid attitudes to new businesses. He argues, "in America, if a 15-year-old kid from the Bronx has a million-dollar idea, there's no debate about what's possible: the kid is CEO, and people get to work behind him. France has lots of young people with great ideas. Why aren't they getting through?"

*The Chicago Globe*, June 17, 2006

1. *housing project*: cité

## Info

***Michael Jordan***
This American professional basketball player was the most effectively marketed athlete of his generation. He was nicknamed "Air Jordan" and "His Airness".

***Fulham***
A football hotbed in London.

***Harrods***
Upmarket department store, owned by Egyptian billionaire Mohamed al Fayed since 1985.

***Bronx***
One of New York City's five boroughs, it is known as the toughest part of the city. Its population, around 1.3 million, is of diverse ethnic origin.

## References

You can find relevant information by reading various pages in your book and memorising a few facts and ideas.

→ **New entrepreneurs, p. 41**
→ **Marketing, p. 86**
→ **Communication, p. 100**
→ **Brands, p. 117**

ACTIVITY **Practise giving an account of this article.**

## Introduction

You should explain where the article comes from, when it was published and what it is about. →Tools 4, p. 236

This article from *The Chicago Globe* was published in June 2006. It reports on the success of French businessman Malamine Koné, who founded his sportswear company, Airness, in 1999.

## Development

Once you have understood the article, organise your ideas into two or three different parts, using set phrases and link-words. →Tools 4, p. 236

1. The beginnings
2. Reasons for success
3. Vision and prospects

You should also use the information given in *Info* and what you have learnt, for example by referring to the various pages indicated in *References*.

### 1. The beginnings

• Even if its name sounds English, Airness is a French company. Its founder was only 28 when he started his business. Koné comes from a housing project, which makes his success story all the more remarkable.
• He chose a name, Airness, which US basketball star Michael Jordan used, a motto ("ever higher, ever stronger") which shows he wants to succeed, and a panther logo.
• He started off by selling sports sweatshirts in Paris' northern poor suburbs where he lived. This helped him make the name known in the housing projects.
• Since the beginning, Airness products have grown at least 100% every year, meaning a strong success in a short time. In 2005, his company's sales reached $150 million.

### 2. Reasons for success

Since he started, Koné has developed a complete range of clothes and sportswear.
• **Street credibility**: Koné explains that his youth has helped him as he knows the power of the market. He thinks that teenagers are the ones who determine what's in. He looked at people's purchases to react to demand quickly, and even to anticipate.
• **Being smart**: Most great sports players already had contracts with famous sports brands such as Adidas or Nike. Koné came up with a clever idea, the 'extra-sports' contract: he asked players to wear Airness after the matches. Thus he was able to sign star players such as Drogba and Cissé.
• **Moving on**: Then he was able to move one step beyond and give Airness more visibility. He got his company to become the official uniform supplier to French pro clubs and national teams in Africa.

### 3. Vision and prospects

Koné wants to boost his company even more and to rival global giant Nike's $14bn profits.
• He thinks one must be ambitious. He takes the example of German-American sportswear group Puma. Even if Puma had problems in 2000, its 2005 sales exceeded $2bn. This shows that Koné has a great future in mind for his company.
• Koné has become the official supplier of London club Fulham for 2007. This new contract is doubly important. First, it will enable Airness to be visible in Britain. Secondly the club is owned by al Fayed who also owns the upmarket department store Harrods, where he has agreed to sell Airness products. This is likely to help sales a lot since Harrods has a very positive image (even though it doesn't sell the latest fashion).

## Conclusion

You should sum up the main ideas and try to open out in a new direction.

This article relates a French success story in an industry where giants Nike and Adidas do not leave much room to newcomers. Even though Koné is now successful, he is rather negative about business attitudes in France. It is true that success stories are far more common in the US than in France. But whether Airness will last more than a decade remains to be seen...

## Branching out

Now, you should move away from the article and develop more ideas. The following questions can help you.

**1** Do you agree that "if a 15-year-old kid from the Bronx has a million-dollar idea", everything is possible in the US? Why?

**2** To what extent is it important for a sportswear company to develop abroad?

## 1. Companies

# Disney confirms movie reductions

Walt Disney is restructuring its studio division to emphasize blockbuster franchise films over more adult fare[1], a move that will mean slashing 650 jobs worldwide, the company announced Tuesday.

The restructuring will cut Disney's film output from about 18 a year to about a dozen. Of those, about 10 will be released under the Walt Disney Pictures banner, a proven family friendly brand that includes the successful *Pirates of the Caribbean* franchise. Disney's Touchstone label, which is responsible for Joel and Ethan Coen's *Fargo* fame, will be cut back to only two or three releases a year. Recent Touchstone films have included the box-office flops *The Alamo* and *The Ladykillers*.

The shift, the company explained, will allow Disney films to bolster[2] the resources of other divisions. A hit like *Pirates of the Caribbean*, for example, can spawn video games, action figures, cable TV shows and, in the case of *Pirates*, give new life to an old Disney theme park attraction. "When we do it well, the lift it gives to the entire company is so significant," Dick Cook, chairman of Walt Disney Studios, said.

The shift to more Disney-branded films has been expected for some time, as have staff cutbacks resulting from a cut in the total number of films. Disney CEO Robert Iger had indicated previously that the company planned to pay greater attention to its Walt Disney Pictures brand. "It becomes a much better investment for us when we make a Disney-branded film," Iger said last September. "We're not going to go out of the non-Disney-branded live-action business, but there has been a dramatic shift."

Successful Touchstone films, like *The Life Aquatic With Steve Zissou*, don't come close to matching the profits of the blockbusters, Cook said, and don't provide the marketing tie-ins with theme parks, games and action figures.

David Miller, managing director of the brokerage[3] firm Sanders Morris Harris Group, said earlier this month that the move toward more Disney-branded films is necessary if the entertainment giant wants to realize double-digit growth.

Disney also is consolidating its domestic and international marketing, distribution and home video efforts.

*USA Today*, July 19, 2006

1. *fare*: (*ici*) nourriture (*figuré*)
2. *bolster*: soutenir
3. *brokerage*: courtage

### Compréhension

**1. Rédigez en français un compte rendu de ce document. (120 mots, +/– 10%)**
**2. Traduisez le titre et le premier paragraphe de l'article.**

### Expression

**Répondez en anglais aux questions suivantes.**

1 Explain Disney's strategy and the reasons accounting for it. (150 words)
2 Do you think such a strategy can work? Why/Why not? (100 words)

(N.B. L'usage du dictionnaire bilingue est autorisé.)

## 2. New entrepreneurs

# More retirees opting to launch startups

## *Baby boomers are starting new businesses in record numbers.*

Terry Alderete and Leonard Liu don't seem to have much in common. She's the owner of a special events firm in Newark, Calif., and he's chairman and chief executive of a software development company split between Silicon Valley and Shanghai. But Alderete, 61, and Liu, 65, are both part of a booming demographic: retirement-age entrepreneurs.

For the past 10 years, adults ages 55 to 64 have been the group most likely to start a new business, according to a study released in May by the Ewing Marion Kauffman Foundation, which promotes entrepreneurship. And now that baby boomers are reaching retirement age, the trend is only going to grow. People are living longer and about 80 percent of boomers claim they want to work in retirement, according to Sara Rix, an expert on seniors at the Public Policy Institute of AARP.

Alderete didn't need to work when she retired from Pacific Bell. After 30 years in which she rose from operator to ethnic marketing director, she received a generous buyout when the company was acquired by SBC in 1997. But the contacts she'd made through her job with groups like the Hispanic Chamber of Commerce created a natural client base. Now she organizes events like the Cinco de Mayo and Día de los Muertos celebrations in Oakland, Calif., which draw more than 100,000 people each.

"Take good inventory of your skills," she advises. "Tomorrow comes very quickly. You may be 40 or 50 and think you'll figure it out later, but you have to prepare."

Liu retired in 2003 after 20 years with IBM. Within a year he had gathered a small group of like-minded former colleagues and started Augmentum, a company that develops user interface products for Intel and tests software for PalmSource. Augmentum was profitable in its first full year and has doubled its revenue each year since.

"They're 58 but look 48; they're highly active and highly engaged," says an executive. "They have networks and experience, and their kids are out of the house."

Indeed, strong networks are what separate thriving retiree entrepreneurs from all the rest.

*Business 2.0 Magazine*, July 5 2006

### Compréhension

**1.** **Rédigez en français un résumé de ce document. (120 mots, +/– 10%)**

**2.** **Traduisez le titre, le sous-titre et le deuxième paragraphe de l'article.**

### Expression

**Répondez en anglais aux questions suivantes.**

1 Explain the various reasons why retirees are launching start-ups. (150 words)

2 Would you like to work in a company where the manager is a retiree? Why/Why not? (100 words)

(N.B. L'usage du dictionnaire bilingue est autorisé.)

## Case study: writing a letter

You are an importer of Fair Trade Delicoffee. You would like Mark Shube to stock your brand in his store. Write a letter to present your products and ask for an appointment.
→Tools 7, p. 240

**Shubie's Marketplace**
312 Fleet Street
London EC4A 2HR

Dear customer,

We are pleased to announce the reopening of your fine foods shop on Thursday, 1 April.
You have been our customer for more than two years and we hope to welcome you for a very special evening on our opening night.

At our new store, you will now find

- more fresh fruit and vegetables from across the world
- fine groceries
- producer wines and spirits
- health and dietary foods
- fine teas

and much, much more...

I am proud to announce that almost all our products carry a Fair Trade label and that our fruit and vegetables are guaranteed without pesticides.
We have developed a new home delivery service for the convenience of our customers and we will be very happy to offer you a first free delivery as a sign of welcome.

Looking forward to seeing you on 1 April from 6pm on,
Yours faithfully,

*Mark Shube*

Mark Shube

## PERSONAL TASK

**Role play**

A student has just arrived in London for his/her work placement. He/she calls the company but the manager is out. He/she leaves a message with the receptionist.

**A:** You are the receptionist.
Ask the caller for personal information.

**B:** You are the student.
Be ready to spell out your name and address, and dictate your telephone number.

# IN THIS UNIT...

- Companies: McDonald's, Bloomingdale's...
- Learn about teleworking, flexitime & equal opportunities employers
- Present your work placement
- Try a job interview

# 3 Work

## → Before you START

*In brief:* **Working mothers**
*Front page:* **Profits: cutting jobs**

## What comparison is made on this 1934 poster?

### Words

- **Nouns:** worker, union, player, match, team, employer, results
- **Adjectives:** strong, organised, aggressive, attractive

### LISTENING PRACTICE

CD TRACK 16

Listen to the recording.
**1.** What are the people talking about?
**2.** Explain their opinions.

# Working mothers denied right to flexible hours

*More women than men are being denied the chance to work from home because of sexist bosses.*

Figures published this weekend reveal that more than two-thirds of working mothers – 10 per cent more than men – complain that employers will not let them work flexibly.

Almost half of women also report a culture of rigid attitudes towards working hours. Campaigners are warning that the findings show a huge gender gap in the workplace which penalises women who want children and a career.

Working Families, the charity which campaigns for a better work/life balance for parents, blames employers for failing in their legal responsibilities to working parents.

"Women who opt for a flexible plan are seen as less committed," said Jonathan Swan, head of policy and research. "Likewise, men are expected to fit into a 'long hours' culture."

Under EU laws, parents can ask to work flexible hours. But the research, based on a survey of more than 1,500 adults across the UK, found that nearly two-thirds of parents were ignorant of their rights.

The Equal Opportunities Commission (EOC) is also calling on ministers to widen access to parental leave for low-income fathers. Research published by the EOC reveals that men on lower wages still face barriers in taking time off around the birth of their child.

Sophie Goodchild, *The Independent*, 18 June 2006

CD TRACK 17

## Info

***Equal Opportunities Commission (EOC)***
This statutory British body was created in 1975 to promote equality between men and women in education and employment, especially regarding the gap in wages for the same job depending on one's gender.

## Headlines

**1** Compare the headline and the subhead. What new information do you have in the subhead?

**2** Rewrite the headline using the same structure as in the subhead.

## Work on words

### 1 | Find their equivalents in English

**Headline** refuser – horaires flexibles
**Subhead** possibilité – patron
**§1** chiffres – se plaindre
**§2** militants – alerter – résultat – énorme – différence hommes-femmes – carrière
**§3** organisation caritative – équilibre – reprocher – ne pas réussir à
**§4** choisir – être impliqué – politique générale – sondage
**§5** élargir

### 2 | Find their synonyms

**Headline** a mother who keeps on working
**§1** the person who hires you – allow
**§2** where work is done
**§4** similarly – adapt
**§5** period of time when you don't work in order to raise your kid – who don't make a lot of money – amount of money you get from working – period of time when you don't work

## The key points of the article

### 1 Working mothers

**a.** Their main problem.
**b.** Who should be blamed.

### 2 Results of the survey

**a.** Prejudice about working parents.
**b.** The EU law.
**c.** Problems for low-income fathers.

## {Methods}

### ■ Speaking practice

**Read the following acronyms aloud. Watch out for the right pronunciation of letters.**

EU laws: European Union laws
The UK: the United Kingdom
The EOC: the Equal Opportunities Commission

### ■ Writing practice

**1 Use the proper verb in the passive to complete the following sentences: *allow, blame, deny, see*.**

**a.** According to EU laws, parents ... ... to work flexible hours.
**b.** But a recent survey has shown that women ... ... chances when they have a child.
**c.** They ... ... as less committed in their work than men.
**d.** Employers ... ... for failing in their responsibilities to working parents.

**2 Prepare a short account in English.**

Mix the four sentences in part 1 together, using the following link words: *actually, in a word, moreover, however.*
→**Tools 4, p. 236**

## Branching out

**1** How could companies make the life of working parents easier? →***Key data*, p. 58**
**2** Do you think employees would be more committed if their private lives were made easier?

## LISTENING PRACTICE

CD **TRACK 18-19**

*Bob Manning is interviewing Frances Barton.*

**1 Comprehension**

Listen to the recording to find the following information.

**Part 1**

**a.** The type of work mentioned in this conversation.
**b.** The two different types of workers.
**c.** The three steps Frances Barton followed.

**Part 2**

**a.** Main benefit.
**b.** Two drawbacks she mentions.
**c.** The importance of new technologies.
**d.** Guest on the following day.

**2 Expression**

Give an oral account, or write a 100-word paragraph, summing up what you have heard.

# Tech giant angers union with plan to slash 1,200 UK jobs

Computer Sciences Corporation, which signed an employment agreement with unions last summer pledging to avoid making compulsory redundancies in the UK, plans to cut 1,200 British jobs. The move comes as the California computer services firm tries to slash costs before a possible sale of the company.

Amicus, the union which negotiated the employment deal with CSC, called the redundancies "the unacceptable face of rampant US corporatism". The job cuts are part of a company-wide plan to lay off 5,000 workers – 4,300 this year and 700 in 2007.

A CSC spokesman would not confirm the number of UK lay-offs, pointing instead to the company's statement on the number of staff to be made redundant globally.

Peter Skyte, Amicus's national officer, said the British workforce was being pillaged[1] to plump up[2] CSC's share price in advance of the sale of the company. CSC, which has its UK base in Aldershot, Hampshire, unveiled its restructuring plans on Tuesday in response to "recent expressions of interest" by unidentified bidders.

The deal that CSC signed with the unions last August stipulated that money saved from sending jobs overseas would be used to retrain displaced UK workers. The agreement, which also said that the company would consult the union before making any decision regarding its globalisation strategy, was heralded[3] by the union, the company, and by the Secretary of State for Trade and Industry, Alan Johnson. Mr Johnson praised both parties for "showing the way ahead" and "[ensuring] that a share of any savings made [by offshoring] are reinvested in skills for the benefit of the workforce." CSC plans to carry out the lay-offs through voluntary redundancies, according to Mr Skyte.

CSC's income has nearly doubled in the past two years. It had \$14.6bn (£8.4bn) in turnover last year but its growth still lagged behind the industry average. Its chief executive, Van Honeycutt, told investors last week that he expects the workforce reshuffle to cut \$150m in costs this year and \$300m the next.

Danny Forston, *The Independent*, 9 April 2006

1. *pillage*: piller
2. *plump up*: gonfler
3. *herald*: annoncer

CD TRACK 20

## Work on words

### 1 | Find their equivalents in English

**§1** accord – syndicat – éviter – licenciement – vente
**§2** licencier
**§3** porte-parole – déclaration – dans le monde entier
**§4** main-d'œuvre – action – enchérisseur, offrant
**§5** économiser – former à nouveau – employé – féliciter – compétence – mettre en œuvre
**§6** revenu – chiffre d'affaires – croissance – être à la traîne – moyenne – directeur général – remaniement

### 2 | Find their synonyms

**Headline** cut (V)
**§1** promise (V) – project (V)
**§2** agreement
**§4** reveal
**§5** abroad – advantage

## Info

***Secretary of State***
In Britain, equivalent of "ministre". For instance, the Secretary of State for Education and Employment is the "ministre de l'Éducation et de l'Emploi".

## Headlines

**1** Make a full sentence to express the meaning of the headline. Use *Work on words* if necessary.

**2** Do you think the company is British? Explain.

## The key points of the article

### 1 Read §1 and §2

**a.** The company (name, place, industry).
**b.** Name of the union.
**c.** Promise the company made in 2005.
**d.** What the company wants to do in 2006.
**e.** Total number of jobs concerned.
**f.** Reason for this plan.

■ Complete this summary of **§1** with: *avoid – computer – costs – redundancies – sold – cut – unions.*
Computer Sciences Corporation, a Californian **...** services firm, had promised **...** it would **...** making compulsory **...** in the UK. However, it has announced it would **...** British jobs to reduce **...** as it may be **....**

### 2 Read §3 and §4

**a.** The company confirmed the number of lay-offs. Yes ❑ No ❑ Explain.
**b.** Why did the company announce its restructuring plan?
**c.** The union's reaction.

### 3 Read §5 and §6

**a.** The 2005 promise regarding the workers.
**b.** The 2005 promise regarding the union.
**c.** What does the company say about the future lay-offs?
**d.** The company's positive result.
**e.** The company's negative result.
**f.** Expected results of the lay-offs.

## Branching out

**1** What else could the company do to reduce its costs? → *Key data*, p. 28
**2** Why do some companies relocate their workforce abroad? → *Key data*, p. 56

## {Methods}

### ■ Speaking practice

**1 Read figures aloud.** → Tools 10, p. 243
Read **§2** and **§6** aloud. If necessary, start by writing the following figures down.

| | |
|---|---|
| **a.** 5,000 workers | **e.** \$14.6bn |
| **b.** 4,300 | **f.** £8.4bn |
| **c.** 700 | **g.** \$150m |
| **d.** 2007 | **h.** \$300m |

**2 Money, money**
Get used to dollars and pounds. Change all the money data into euros.

**3 Prepare an oral introduction.**
• Identify the source.
• Explain what the article is about (who, what, where, when).

### ■ Writing practice

**1 Present the company.**
Group all the information you have about the company and write an organised paragraph.

**2 Explain the lay-offs.**
Group all the information you have about the lay-offs and write an organised paragraph.

**3 Write a summary of this article in French (around 120 words).**
• Read the article again and list the key idea of each paragraph following the order of the article.
• Introduce link words between the various ideas.
› Tools 3, p. 234

## Language

• *The agreement **said** that the company **would** consult the union before making any decision.*
Pour rapporter des paroles, on peut utiliser le discours indirect : les guillemets disparaissent, et on applique la concordance des temps.
Si le verbe qui introduit le discours indirect (« dire » ou « penser », « stipuler », « regretter que », etc.) est au prétérit, le verbe rapporté passe au prétérit s'il était au présent, le modal *will* devient *would*, etc.
Si on transforme l'exemple au discours direct : *The company **will** consult the union...*

**Translate into English**
**1.** Le syndicat a dit que l'entreprise n'a pas respecté leur accord de 2005.
**2.** Le directeur général a expliqué que tous les employés bénéficieraient d'une nouvelle formation.
**3.** Les enchérisseurs ont répondu que cela coûterait trop cher et qu'il y avait trop d'employés.
**4.** L'entreprise avait promis qu'elle ne licencierait pas de main-d'œuvre et que le syndicat serait consulté avant toute décision.

## 1-A brief history of work after WW2

### The Post-war Years: booming employment

After the Second World War, unemployment was not on the agenda of developed countries. After 1945, an amazing growth in all sectors created a great number of jobs.
Most countries were governed by Welfare State policies which improved workers' conditions and allowed them to be defended by trade unions. Employees were guaranteed benefits from "the cradle to the grave", including paid holidays, sick leave, maternity leave, free health care, subsidized day-care, school lunches, retirement benefits, unemployment benefits, subsidized housing and transports, as well as retraining schemes.
People did not often switch from one job to another; it was the job-for-life era.

### The 1980s: unemployment strikes

All the industrialized countries except Japan were struck by high unemployment rates, exceeding 10% among the active population. Only the US and the UK saw their unemployment rate drop in the mid 80s: the rest of Europe had to wait until the 1990s to reduce unemployment thanks to new sectors creating new jobs and new forms of work.
Since the turn of the 21st century, unemployment rates have seen ups and downs. These fluctuations in joblessness are due to global political and economic events, as well as basic internal economic issues involving distribution, production and consumption.

### From Welfare State to Workfare state

Today, the Welfare State concept is swiftly losing ground: employees have lost on most fronts, profitability and cost effectiveness being the most important features in a global world. In the UK, Tony Blair's Labour government (May 1997-2006) explicitly called for a Workfare State to replace the Welfare State. Its aim: to put people back to work instead of paying them unemployment benefits.

## 2-Fighting unemployment

### Two reasons for unemployment: relocation and outsourcing

Because of competition, companies tend to relocate whenever they find their labour costs are too high in their home country. They go to countries with cheaper labour force (Asia, South America) or less strict work regulations (Great Britain, Ireland). For example, because of relocation, 40,000 jobs have been lost in Europe since 2001 in the footwear industry.
Outsourcing consists in employing people in foreign countries; this trend is on the rise and concerns services such as call centres and customer services around the world. Some high tech companies outsource their computer engineering to India.

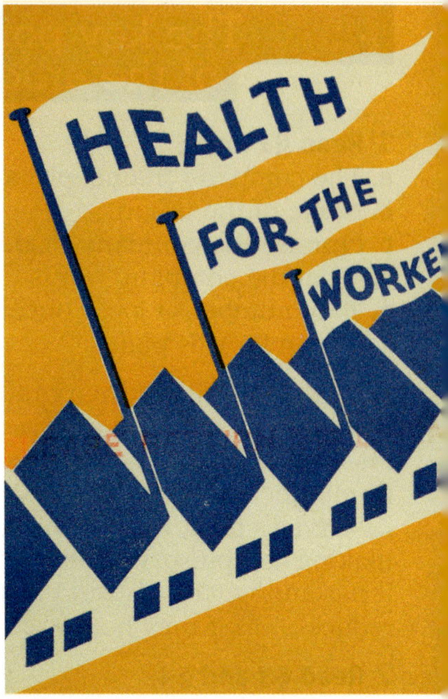

A 1942 booklet providing basic advice on health in the workplace

**The Nike case**

Nike was one of the first companies to manufacture its goods in Asia. For more than ten years activists campaigned against Nike's labour practices. The intensity of the pressure on Nike had positive effects: in 1998, Philip Knight, the firm's chairman at the time, promised to improve workers conditions. He was the first to organize social hearings, that is to say sending watchdogs to check whether the firm's overseas subcontractors follow the international guidelines regulating work worldwide.

### The role of governments

Governments try to play a role in curbing unemployment. However their range of action is more and more limited. Before, they could protect domestic firms with taxes on foreign exports but the WTO (World Trade Organization) now strongly opposes any kind of barriers. →**Chapter 14, Globalisation**

- Governments can allow companies to recruit employees on fixed term contracts.
- They can cut the amount of red tape, thus helping entrepreneurs to create firms, therefore jobs.
- Encouraging young people to study longer and training a more qualified work force are also essential as most unskilled jobs are now performed by automation (robots and computers) or relocated abroad. Hundreds of thousands of factory jobs are suppressed every year in Europe and the US, with few or no possibilities for the employees to follow a retraining programme. It requires long-term investment governments are more and more reluctant to pay for.
- Through legislation, governments can pass laws reducing the working week. In France the 35-hour week was implemented in 2000. They can also ban overtime, and make it harder for companies to make employees redundant.
- Governments can choose to reduce benefits in order to cut costs, or to increase them so as to boost consumption, which would in turn create activity meaning new jobs. The trend today is rather to reduce benefits, especially retirement benefits and social security, which has stirred public discontent all over Europe.

**Cheap salaries for an expensive ball**

The official ball used in the World Soccer Cup 2006 was marketed by Adidas. The ball sold for $140 a piece whereas the employees who assembled the ball in a Thailand factory were paid $200 a month.

**Revolts overseas**

The number of uprisings among exploited overseas workers is growing fast: in June 2006, riots of angry workers took place in Bangladesh. In China, one thousand workers from factories manufacturing toys for McDonald's rioted for better salaries. They were put down by the authorities.

## 3-New trends today

### Putting the pressure on jobs: mergers and shareholders

The increasing number of mergers puts an additional threat on jobs since merging means restructuring and restructuring means streamlining.
Shareholders expect a profitable return on investment and companies do not hesitate to close down the least profitable sectors or factories in order to please their shareholders.

### Temping and flexibility

The job-for-life era has been replaced by flexible working hours, fixed term contracts and temping. This type of employment allows companies to reduce labour costs drastically.
Flexibility means applying the just-in-time principle to employees: people work only when they are needed, and stay home when they are not required on the job.
Temping allows companies to hire temporary workers for any period of time, under very short notice. Temping agencies have been thriving. For example, in France, two million employees worked as temps in 2005, which represented a 2.6% increase in one year.
However, American companies are starting to realize that too much flexibility is incompatible with corporate culture. Surveys have shown that in the long term, companies relying too much on unstable workforces were more liable to become less profitable.

Looking for someone addicted to work...

### Teleworking and telecommuting

Thanks to new technology, more and more employees can work from their homes. They are called telecommuters or teleworkers. Time saving is one of the main advantages of this type of work: people need not spend long hours in transport to go to work. Another advantage is that family life is made simpler especially for working mothers with small children. The main drawbacks are that employees are cut off from their workmates/colleagues and have trouble making a difference between private life and working life. Teleworking also prevents employees from carrying out effective team work and may hinder their innovative spirit. Moreover, working hours are not the usual 9 to 5 schedule: employees can be lured into working much longer hours for the same wages.

### Hot desking/virtual offices

Hot desking means employees do not have their own permanent office. These temporary work stations are equipped with computers, internet and phone lines; the employee's files are ready to be used when he/she comes to work. Hot desking allows companies to cut costs, especially in big cities where the price of real estate is extremely expensive, but this is done at the expense of the staff's comfort.

### Trade unions: the end of an era? →*Landmark*, p. 59

Various factors account for the decline in unions.
With the decrease in manufacturing jobs, automation, which has replaced most low-skilled staff on the assembly lines, and the relocation to countries where labour costs are lower, workers are not as numerous on the job market as they used to be.
In addition, with the rise of teleworking, nomadic work and temping, employees get fewer opportunities to get organized.
Yet, a few public sectors remain unionized, such as transport (when they are not privatised), education, etc.

**Profitable yogurt**

In 2001 the French firm Danone decided to cut 1,800 jobs although the company's overall profits had never been so high. Unions and consumer activists launched a Danone boycott, which didn't save jobs but resulted in a significant shift in government policy: socialist minister Elisabeth Guigou responded to public concern by proposing new legislation to deter thriving companies from making workers redundant simply to increase profit.

## Question time

**1** Describe the main features of the post-war years.
**2** Give a definition of the Welfare State.
**3** Why is temping on the rise?
**4** What are the advantages and drawbacks of teleworking?
**5** Why do companies relocate?
**6** Why are there fewer and fewer low-skilled jobs?
**7** What does outsourcing consist of?
**8** Why are unions in decline?
**9** What encouraged Nike to change its labour policies?

LANDMARK

# Trade unions

## At the beginning

Although trade unions were illegal for many years in most countries, they began to acquire political power, eventually resulting in labour laws that codified the relationship between employers and employees.

## Unions today

Trade unions campaign with various objectives.

- Benefits to insure members against unemployment, ill health, old age and funeral expenses. In many developed countries, the state assumes these functions; unions can provide benefits such as training, legal advice and representation.
- Collective bargaining: unions may negotiate with employers over wages and working hours.
- Industrial action (strikes or lockouts).
- Political activity: unions may campaign, lobby, or support parties.

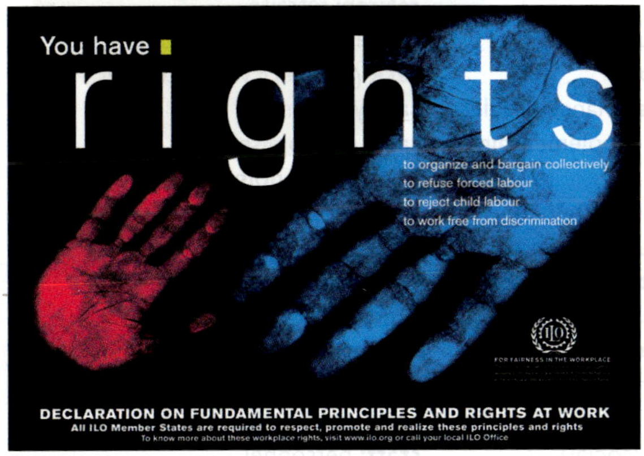


A poster by the International Labour Organization, the UN specialized agency for labour rights

## Structure

Unions are often divided into "locals" and united in national federations. These federations affiliate with Internationals, such as the International Confederation of Free Trade Unions with 231 affiliated organisations in 150 countries and 158 million members. Union leaderships are usually elected democratically.

Research has shown that unionised workers enjoy better conditions and wages than those who are not unionised.

## Early trade unions in the UK

Even though they were severely repressed until 1824, British trade unions were already widespread in cities such as London. From 1830 on, attempts were made to set up national general unions. Their legal status was established in 1867, recognizing that they advantaged both employers and employees. The strongest unions were unions of skilled workers, such as the Amalgamated Society of Engineers.

The Trade Unions Congress (TUC) was founded in 1868. The years 1910-14 witnessed serious industrial unrest and an enormous increase in trade union membership. World War I resulted in a further increase and widespread recognition of unions.

Today, the TUC is a federation of 65 trade unions in the UK, with a total of about 7m members.

## Unions in the USA

In the past, US labour unions were infiltrated by members of organized crime. In the 1920s the Mafia was active in some Teamster locals, particularly in the garment industry in New York City.

American Federation of Labor and Congress of Industrial Organizations, commonly "AFL-CIO", is America's largest federation of unions, with 53 national and international unions and over 9m workers. It was formed in 1955 when the AFL and the CIO merged. From 1955 until 2005, the AFL-CIO's member unions represented almost all unionized workers in the US; however, in 2005, five major unions left the AFL-CIO and went into the Change to Win Federation.

For the last twenty years union growth has been much higher among women and coloured/immigrant workers than among white male workers.

## Diversity of unions worldwide

In many countries unions are linked with a political party. In the US, unions have generally aligned with the Democrats, but International Brotherhood of Teamsters has repeatedly supported Republicans, and the AFL-CIO has been against liberalising abortion so as not to alienate its numerous Catholic members. The TUC's leading member unions formed the British Labour Party and still largely fund it, but there is no formal link between the TUC and the party.

**Online t@sk**

Visit www.unionhistory.info/timeline/timeline.php, a partnership initiative between London Metropolitan University and the Trades Union Congress.

Choose a period in the history of British trade unions and report to the class.

# AFL-CIO *to work with day laborers group*

The nation's largest federation of unions agreed Wednesday to work with a network of immigrant day laborers to improve wages and working conditions for those who solicit work from street corners across America.

The agreement between the AFL-CIO and the National Day Laborer Organizing Network is a sign of day laborers' growing role in the U.S. economy. It does not clear the way for day laborers to become union members, but both sides said it could be a step in that direction. It allows the network's 40 nationwide centers to affiliate with the federation and receive representation on local labor councils. Under the plan, the AFL-CIO and network will pursue minimum wage campaigns, safety at construction sites and legislation to criminalize employers who stiff[1] day laborers.

The agreement comes as day laborers, a majority of whom are Hispanic and undocumented, take steps to become more organized. At a large center in downtown Los Angeles, day laborers said they hoped the agreement would lead to unionization. The center has set the minimum hourly pay for its workers at $8. Skilled workers command up to $15 an hour. "We've all had employers not pay us, and seen workers get hurt at jobs," said Francisco Jimenez, 35, an illegal immigrant from Mexico.

For years, unions have experienced diminishing numbers and clout because of globalization, automation and the transition from an industrial-based economy to one that is service-driven. Some members see undocumented workers as a vast untapped pool of potential new members. Others, however, think they drag down wages and thwart[2] organizing efforts.

The day labor network also has much to gain. Originally a ragtag[3] group in 2001, the network is emerging as a powerful force for organizing day laborers. Its 40 sites are used by thousands of workers each day. Among other things, the sites provide English classes and workshops on labor rights. All laborers and employers are registered in data bases, and workers often vote on center decisions involving wages and operations.

Whether the agreement leads to full unionization will depend on how aggressively the AFL-CIO focuses on day labor issues, and how day laborers respond to organization efforts.

*Business Week*, August 9, 2006

1. *stiff*: refuser de payer
2. *thwart*: contrecarrer, contrarier
3. *ragtag*: disparate

## Info

***AFL-CIO***
→ p. 59

***National Day Laborer Organizing Network***
Some US communities have started supporting day laborers' efforts to organise themselves. Over the past few years, the NDLON has emerged as the immigrant workers' rights movement. The NDLON promotes cooperation between day laborers, local government, police and businesses to avoid unproductive anti-immigrant hysteria and achieve solutions that benefit all involved.

## References

You can find relevant information by reading various pages in your book and memorising a few facts and ideas.

→ **Work, p. 58**
→ **Globalisation, p. 220**

**ACTIVITY** **Practise giving an account of this article.**

## Introduction

You should explain where the article comes from, when it was published and what it is about. →Tools 4, p. 236

This article was published in *Business Week*, an American business weekly magazine, in August 2006. It deals with the issue of day labourers in the USA and the fact that traditional unions, such as the AFL, are now trying to work with their specific organisations.

## Development

Once you have understood the article, organise your ideas into two or three different parts, using set phrases and link-words. →Tools 4, p. 236

1. The day labourers
2. Reasons for the AFL-CIO and the NDLON to work together

You should also use the information given in *Info* and what you have learnt, for example by referring to the various pages indicated in *References*.

### 1. The day labourers

• **Who they are**: Day labourers work on a daily basis, without contracts, by soliciting work from street corners. The majority are Hispanic; they have come from Central or Latin America. And the majority are also undocumented: they are illegal immigrants and therefore have no right to work or stay in the USA.
• **Their numbers**: They have a growing role in the U.S. economy.
• **Their problems**: Some employers take advantage of the fact that they are in a very fragile situation: they can make no legal claims if an employer doesn't pay them, or get compensation if they get hurt while working.
• **Getting more organised**: Illegal day labourers can't be union members, because they are undocumented and also because traditional unions don't take care of them. However, they are getting more organised, with National Day Laborer Organizing Network. Labourers and employers are registered in data bases. This network started in 2001 and now has 40 sites which are used by thousands of workers each day. It has set minimum hourly wages ($8). The sites also help labourers learn English and organise workshops on labour rights.

### 2. The AFL-CIO and the NDLON working together

• **The AFL-CIO** is America's largest federation of unions and as such it is used to working to improve wages and working conditions.
• **The NDLON**: The new network has developed like a union. Workers often vote on decisions involving wages and operations. Just like a union, its various centres are spread across the country.
• **The agreement**: The AFL-CIO should allow the network's 40 centres to affiliate with the federation. The two organisations have the same goals: minimum wage campaigns, safety at construction sites and prosecution of employers who don't pay day labourers.
• **Positive aspects**: The NDLON will be represented on local labour councils.
The AFL-CIO has been declining as the world of work has changed with automation and globalisation which makes companies look for a cheaper labour force in developing countries. Another reason for the decrease in union power is the fact fewer workers are needed in today's service-driven economy than in yesterday's industrial-based economy. Some unionists thus see undocumented workers as a vast untapped pool of potential new members. However, others are hostile to the day labourers who accept cheaper wages.

## Conclusion

You should sum up the main ideas and try to open out in a new direction.

This article shows that the world of work has changed a lot since the first unions were created. Traditional unions need to take the new forms of work into account if they want to remain representative. Similarly, fragile categories of workers need the help of experienced organisations. However, it remains to be seen whether the AFL-CIO is ready to focus on specific day labour issues, and whether day labourers will accept being fully organised in an American union.

## Branching out

Now, you should move away from the article and develop more ideas. The following questions can help you.

**1** What type of jobs do day labourers do?
**2** Where are workers well protected?

## Case study: charts

Study the following bar charts.

THE WAY AMERICANS WORK

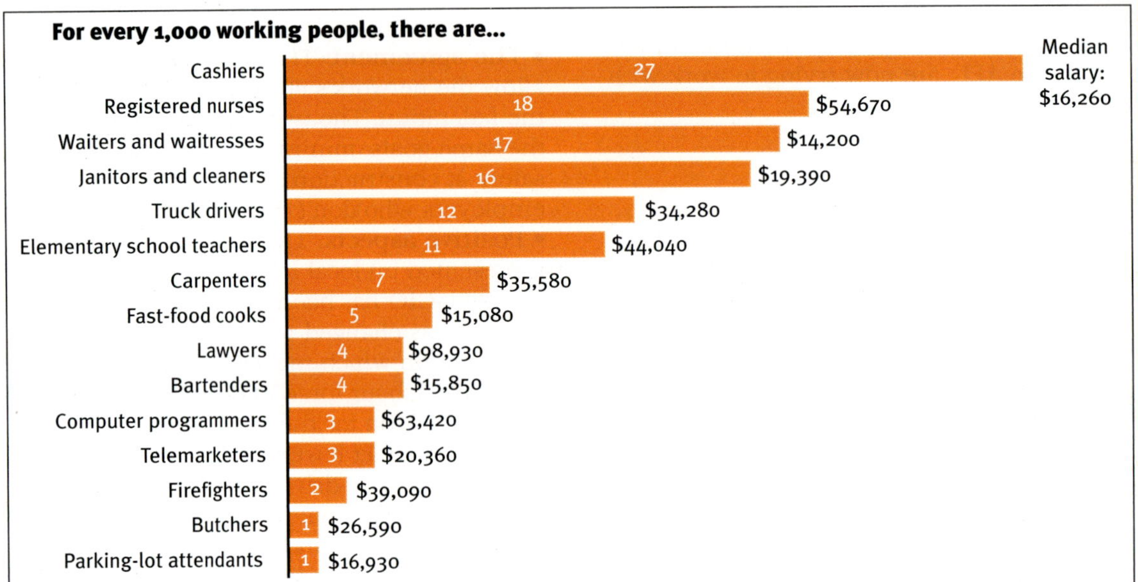

From Bureau of Labor Statistics, 2006.

**1.** Make at least five sentences about the various jobs and report to the class.

• *There are 27 cashiers for every 1,000 people, which is more than all the other jobs in the chart. Cashiers earn $16,260 on average.*

ALL WORK AND NO PLAY

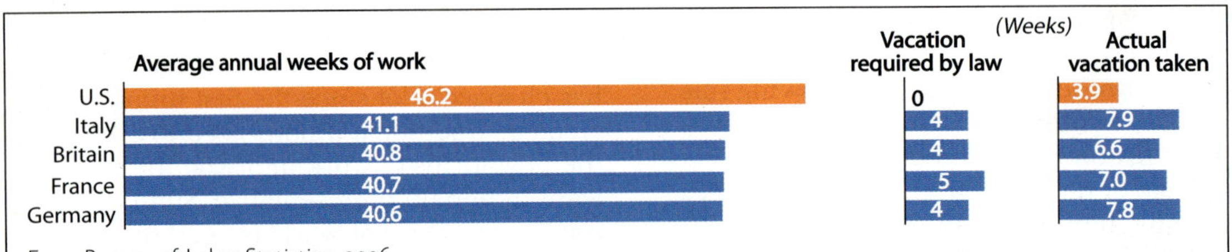

From Bureau of Labor Statistics, 2006.

**2.** Compare the US with the other countries, or the different European countries. Read the example and make at least five more sentences.
Conclude about being French and report to the class.

• *American employees work five more weeks than Italians. In Italy, the law requires four weeks vacation and employees take almost eight weeks on average!*

## PERSONAL TASK

Report to the class about your work placement: present the company, speak about your tasks, what you learnt, what you found interesting/disappointing, etc. Don't forget to talk about the working hours (yours, the staff's, whether employees feel overworked, how many breaks they can take, etc.). →**Tools 8, p. 241**

# IN THIS UNIT...

- Companies: McDonald's, Coca-Cola, Adbusters...
- Learn about Ralph Nader, consumer protection & fair trade
- Report on various consumer complaints
- Write a letter of complaint

# 4
## Consumers

## → Before you START

*In brief:* Happy Meals
*Front page:* Senior consumers

### How do you react to this photo of a little Chinese girl and Ronald McDonald?

### Words

- **Nouns:** fast food, children, trap, attraction, fun, marketing ploy
- **Adjectives:** colourful, bright, gaudy (*voyant*), tricky, funny
- **Verbs:** attract, seduce, lure, entice, trap

### LISTENING PRACTICE

CD TRACK 21

Listen to the recording.
**1.** What are the people talking about?
**2.** Explain their opinions.

# Happy days

Depending on your point of view, the McDonald's "Happy Meal" is either a grossly[1] unethical marketing ploy by giant US corporations to lure children into an early dependency on unhealthy food with the help of small plastic toys, or it is merely a harmless treat. But whichever interpretation you favour, it is the end of an era. Disney has decided that, after this summer, its films will no longer be promoted by the McDonald's Happy Meal tie-in. The world's largest children's entertainment company has made this decision on the grounds that the McDonald's association is damaging its "family-friendly" image.

This is one more sign that the Western love affair with convenience food is waning. It began with Eric Schlosser's ***Fast Food Nation***, which exposed some of the realities behind the fast food industry. Morgan Spurlock's ***Supersize Me*** demonstrated the toll an exclusive diet of fast food takes on health. A junior version of ***Fast Food Nation*** is expected soon.

Some of this is excessive. The company is, after all, merely providing a service that people want. No one is forced through the Golden Arches. Yet it is certainly welcome that the growing recognition of the obesity crisis in our societies is now producing changes at the counter. Let the market decide if people are "lovin' it" or not.

*The Independent,* 10 May 2006

1. *grossly*: nettement

CD TRACK 22

## Info

***Eric Schlosser***
Born in 1959, Schlosser is an American journalist, whose most famous book *Fast Food Nation* (2001) describes the practices of the fast food industry, focusing especially on its sanitary conditions and treatment of workers. The book soon became a bestseller. It was made into a film (November 2006).

***Supersize Me***
To shoot his documentary (2004), Morgan Spurlock ate nothing but McDonald's for 30 days, which made him gain 11kg! →**Chapter 14, *Landmark*, p. 223**

## Work on words

### 1 I Find their equivalents in English

**§1** gâterie – produit dérivé – loisir – à cause de
**§2** plats tout prêts – démontrer (*two words*) – causer des dégâts sur
**§3** au comptoir

### 2 I Find their synonyms

**§1** stratagem – attract – bad – safe – prefer – period – spoil
**§2** decrease (V)
**§3** just – offer (V) – increasing

## Headlines

The headline is very short. What are its two meanings?

## The key points of the article

### 1 Happy Meals

**a.** Find three expressions evoking McDonald's in the article.
**b.** Which company was associated with McDonald's?

### 2 A sociological change

**a.** A two-sided reputation: what are the two opposite opinions about the "Happy Meal"?
**b.** Reason for the split.
**c.** Evidence that convenience food is openly questioned.

## Branching out

**1** "No one is forced through the Golden Arches". What techniques are used to make people go to a McDonald's restaurant?
→ *Landmark*, p. 223

**2** Do you think fast food restaurants will remain profitable?

## {Methods}

### ■ Speaking practice

**Practise your pronunciation of names.**
McDonald's –Happy Meal – Eric Schlosser – Morgan Spurlock – Golden Arches

### ■ Writing practice

**1 Prefixes and suffixes**

- *a grossly **unethical** marketing ploy*
- *an early dependency on **unhealthy** food*

- ethics (noun) → unethical
- health (noun) → unhealthy

To create an adjective from a noun, one adds a suffix: *-y*, *-ish*, *-ful*, *-less*, *-like*, *-ly*, *-en*, *-ic*, *-ical*. To create its opposite, one adds a prefix: *un-*, *in-* or *im-*.
**Create adjectives with the grid below.**
Example: *friend* → *friendly*
There is more than 1 adjective in 2 cases.

| Root | Suffix | | | | | | | | |
|---|---|---|---|---|---|---|---|---|---|
| | *-y* | *-ish* | *-ful* | *-less* | *-like* | *-ly* | *-en* | *-ic* | *-ical* |
| logic | | | | | | | | | |
| harm | | | | | | | | | |
| noise | | | | | | | | | |
| irony | | | | | | | | | |
| child | | | | | | | | | |
| self | | | | | | | | | |
| use | | | | | | | | | |
| gold | | | | | | | | | |

**Now find their opposites.** Fill in the grid below.

| Adjective | Prefix | | | Opposite adjective |
|---|---|---|---|---|
| | *un-* | *in-* | *im-* | |
| friendly | X | | | *unfriendly* |
| dependent | | | | |
| possible | | | | |
| pleasant | | | | |
| mature | | | | |
| experienced | | | | |

**2 Prepare a short account in English.**
Use the adjectives in part 1 to explain what McDonald's position is towards their partners and towards their customers.
→ Tools 4, p. 236

## LISTENING PRACTICE

CD TRACK 23-24

*David Smith is reporting for CNN.*

### 1 Comprehension

Listen to the recording to find the following information.

**Part 1**
**a.** Type of conversation.
**b.** Topic.
**c.** The students' reasons.
**d.** Can students still buy the drink?

**Part 2**
**a.** The analyst doesn't think this could be a problem for the company because...
**b.** The analyst thinks this could be a problem for the company because... (four reasons).

### 2 Expression

Give an oral account, or write a 100-word paragraph, summing up what you have heard.

# Don't be shy about retiring

*More and more pensioners are investing in homes abroad.*

Retirement no longer means having to settle for uncertain British summers and a small flat in the West Country. The Government says 871,000 Britons now draw their state pension while living permanently overseas – and perhaps as many again have retired abroad and are either below[1] pensionable age or choose not to take a pension at all.

Developers are now pitching homes at this growing market, with no better example than the new Santa Pola Life Resort on Spain's Costa Blanca, the most popular non-English-speaking location for British retirees.

Santa Pola is a 450-home version of the retirement communities for 55-plus residents. It looks like a Mediterranean village of bungalows and flats and is 12 kilometres from Alicante and seven from its airport, which has budget flights to and from more than a dozen UK destinations. This scheme offers its own shopping centre, a 24-hour reception and security services, bus shuttles to the beach, buggies to move around the resort, a spa centre, gym and swimming pool, and close proximity to two golf courses. On site there are also consulting rooms, physiotherapy and psychology services, chronic illness assistance and first aid facilities. Properties range from 600 to 1,000 sq ft and prices go from €130,000 (£90,000) to €220,000 in phase 1 of the scheme, which will be completed next year.

Vitalis Park is a similar resort with 150 units at similar costs near Malaga, while there are a dozen more retirement resorts from Barcelona to Spain's southern tip, with more planned.

In many locations you can rent out your property if you do not use it year-round and some resort management schemes such as those at Santa Pola will maintain your home when it is rented out.

In Spain, and most countries popular with older Britons, there are English-speaking communities in popular areas, with good health services which cater for ex-pat residents. If you are brave enough to start a new life abroad, the world is your oyster[2].

Graham Norwood, *The Independent*, July 19, 2006

1. *below*: en-dessous
2. *The world is your oyster*: le monde est à vous

CD TRACK 25

## Info

***The West Country***
The region in the south west of Britain, with mild climate, where many pensioners traditionally settled.

***sq ft***
Abbreviation of "square foot". A foot is the British (imperial) unit of measure, equivalent to 30.48 cm. Although the metric system was officially adopted in 1971 in Britain – and is taught in schools – the imperial system is still used: weights are given in stones and pounds; distances in miles and yards, people's heights in feet and inches. In the US, the imperial system has remained the official one.

→**Tools 10, p. 243**

## Work on words

### 1 | Find their equivalents in English

**Headline** prendre sa retraite
**Subhead** retraité
**§1** s'installer – appartement – à l'étranger (*2 words*) – toucher (argent)
**§3** vol – navette – premier secours – installations – aller de... à
**§5** louer, mettre en location – propriété – entretenir
**§6** région – santé – pourvoir à

### 2 | Find their synonyms

**Headline** timid
**§2** offer (V) – place for holidays – place – someone who has retired
**§3** cheap – project (N) – finish
**§4** identical – end (N)

## Headlines

**1** Which word in the subhead refers to the same idea as "retiring"?

**2** Anticipate the contents of the article from the subhead.

**3** What idea is conveyed by the headline?

## The key points of the article

### 1 Read §1 and §2

**a.** Number of British pensioners who have settled abroad.
**b.** Estimated total number of retirees who have settled abroad.
**c.** Where British pensioners used to settle.
**d.** Their new destination.

■ Complete this summary of §1 with: *Britons – Government – move – overseas – pensioners – settle.*
Although ... used to ... in the West Country, there are now more than one million ..., according to the ..., who have ... to retire ....

### 2 Read §3

**a.** Who lives in Santa Pola?
**b.** Number of homes.
**c.** Precise location.
**d.** What can be found in Santa Pola.
**e.** Size and price of the properties.

### 3 Read §4, §5 and §6

**a.** Is Santa Pola unique?
**b.** Possibilities when retirees aren't in their Spanish homes.
**c.** Is Spain unique?
**d.** Two reassuring aspects for retirees who settle in foreign countries.
**e.** Find an echo of the headline in the last sentence.

## Branching out

**1** Which services are essential if a company targets senior citizens? →*Key data*, p. 71
**2** Give other examples of specific market segments that are targeted nowadays.
→*Key data*, p. 71

## {Methods}

### ■ Speaking practice

**1 Read figures aloud.** →**Tools 10, p. 243**
Read §3 aloud. If necessary, start by writing the following figures down.
Then practise reading the groups of words in parentheses together with the figures.
**a.** (a) 450(-home version)
**b.** 55(-plus residents)
**c.** 12 (kilometres)
**d.** (a) 24(-hour reception)
**e.** (from) 600 (to) 1,000 (sq ft)
**f.** €130,000 (£90,000)
**g.** €220,000

**2 Money, money**
Get used to dollars and pounds. Change all the money data into euros.

**3 Prepare an oral introduction.**
• Identify the source.
• Explain what the article is about (who, what, where, when).

### ■ Writing practice

**1 Translate §3 into French.**

**2 Write an account of this article in French (around 140 words).**
You must insist on the target and the efforts made to reach it. Don't forget to write an introduction and a conclusion.
→**Tools 4, p. 236**

## Language

• *Phase one of the scheme **will be completed** next year.*
• *Some management schemes will maintain your home when it **is rented out**.*
Le passif est formé de l'auxiliaire ***be*** + **participe passé** du verbe. C'est l'auxiliaire qui porte la marque du temps ou de la forme verbale. On utilise le passif quand on ne peut pas (ou qu'on ne veut pas) nommer le sujet de la construction active qui correspondrait. Dans les deux exemples, c'est le fait que le projet soit achevé ou que la maison soit louée qui sont importants. On utilise souvent le passif comme équivalent du « on » français.

**Translate into English**
**1.** Les maisons ont été construites près d'un aéroport.
**2.** Le projet a été conçu pour les retraités anglais qui veulent s'installer à l'étranger.
**3.** Seules les personnes de plus de 55 ans seront autorisées à acheter une propriété.
**4.** On peut trouver davantage de renseignements sur un site internet qui a été mis en route en décembre dernier.

**Mass consumption started in the 1950s in the US and took off in Western Europe in the 1960s. In developed countries, consuming patterns have undergone tremendous changes over the past 50 years.**

## 1-A brief history of consumption

### The rise of consumerism

From the 60s to the 80s, the purchasing power of the average household increased mostly because a lot had to be built or rebuilt in the post World War II society. Women worked more and more, and new products and services appeared on the market. Most people bought a car and household equipment such as white goods (kitchen appliances) and brown goods (TV, hi-fi, etc.).

With the booming of supermarkets people bought FMCGs (fast moving consumer goods). Consuming for the sake of it became a must, although some were already ringing the alarm bell about this new form of addiction. →**Chapter 8, Distribution**

Marketers started launching disposable products such as nappies, razors, pens, etc. →**Chapter 5, Marketing**. They met with tremendous success with a more affluent and more time-pressed audience.

Choosing a basic product, the kettle!

### Today's consuming trends

Several factors can account for the changes in consuming habits.

- Economic recessions made for more cautious consumers who asked for the best quality price ratio: people started adopting price-oriented consuming habits instead of being brand-oriented. They became thriftier and turned to hard discounters. At first, no one believed that store brand products could follow the same quality standards as branded goods. However, many consumers have realized that the premium they paid for branded goods was not always worth it.
- Globalisation has brought changes in the working world with flexibility and the end of the "job for life". →**Chapter 3, Work**
- Consumers have become aware of sustainable development and fair trade. →**Chapter 1, Companies**
- The booming of new technologies has changed consuming patterns. Today's consumers do not need to go the mall or the high streets to do their shopping; they can do it around the clock from their homes, thanks to the internet.

### Getting more and more indebted

Consumer over-indebtedness is a growing issue in developed countries. Spending money has become the easiest thing in the world with easy-to-use terms of payment, plastic money (debit and credit cards), the growing number of ATMs (automatic teller machines, or cash dispensers), plus a wide range of loan offers targeting low-income households. In the UK, 7% of the population is over-indebted.

**Adbusters**

The group is at the origin of "No Buying Day", a day when consumers are encouraged not to buy a single item. Adbusters's ideas have expanded across the Atlantic and No Buying Day is also on the agenda of several European countries (the UK, Germany, France, etc.).

→**Chapter 7, Brands**

### Reactions against consumerism

Many consumer organizations, particularly in the US and the UK, are lobbying to get tougher legislation to protect the consumers from the lure of over consumption and free themselves from the pressure of marketers. →**Chapter 3, *Landmark*, p. 59**

## 2-The new breeds of consumers

### Children, tweenagers and teens

The child and teen markets have been growing fast for the past two decades. They represent a huge market for products such as snacks, sweets, soft drinks (junk food), CDs, DVDs, video games, clothes, mobile phones, MP3 players, etc. In order to reach their target more precisely, marketers have defined a new category of young consumers, the "tweenagers" who belong to the 10-to-12 age group.

Today they are also targeted as purchase influencers for items such as cars, computers, even homes, which used to involve only parents' decision.

### Senior consumers: the grey market

With the ageing of the population in most developed countries, senior citizens have become an important target audience. Thanks to substantial retirement benefits and the significant increase in life expectancy, senior citizens are better off and in better health than they were before.

Sectors such as insurance, health, travel, leisure, or sports are now making profits thanks to senior citizens. Manufacturers make efforts to offer easy-to-use home equipment. Companies also reinforce home deliveries and after-sales services. Advertisers have understood the shift and do not hesitate to feature elderly people in their campaigns. However, senior citizens often remain more reluctant than young people to use new technologies.

### Single people

This category includes divorcees, single parents, widowers and young bachelors.

They represent a profitable market as they often work full time and enjoy more free time than their married counterparts. They are the number one consumers of convenience and take-away food, outings (cinema, theatre, etc.) and travelling.

## 3-The example of food

### Convenience food: a permanent feature in today's world

For a majority of working people it is very difficult not to indulge in convenience food. Frozen and pre-cooked foods have become essential in households thanks to micro-wave ovens.

### Junk food, a health hazard

Time-pressed consumers in a rat-race society have paved the way for the invasion of fast-food restaurants and take-away outlets, encouraging unhealthy food habits worldwide.

Figures in the US are alarming: two thirds of the adult population are overweight or obese, including 17% of children, plus

**Premixed drinks or alcopops**

Premixed drinks are a mixture of sweet-tasting soda and alcohol (vodka, tequila, whisky, gin, etc.). Sold in ready-to-drink packs of 6, they target a young audience and are now considered partly responsible for the dramatic increase in teenage binge drinking.

Targeting children with funny characters

another 15% at risk. The annual increase in the number of obese children in France also stands at 17%, with a 2020 perspective of 65% of the adult population (the current US rate) suffering from obesity.
Being overweight is not a problem of looks; it bears the risk of developing various pathologies such as heart disease and diabetes. Dramatic changes in eating patterns are necessary to reverse the trend. Some measures have been taken to cut down teenage obesity, such as 2005 legislation banning vending machines selling soft drinks and snacks in French schools.

### The marketers' response: low fat, diet products and organic products

Marketers have responded to the challenge by launching diet products, diet sodas, low fat dairy products, etc.
The sales of organic products have been steadily on the rise for the past decade, notably for a more educated, wealthier and more health-oriented part of the population. A lot of people are ready to pay a higher price to be on the safe side (pesticide-free, natural products, etc.).

### Encouraging children to become tomorrow's consumers

Companies now reach children and teens in schools, where they should be protected from marketing. In the USA companies sometimes supply the often under-equipped state schools with equipment, or ready-made educational programs, provided the children watch ads for several minutes every day. Kellogg's (cereal) was one of the first to use this technique.
The trend is catching up on in European countries. In the UK, some food brands offered collectable coupons to give back to the schoolteachers who had to store and collect them in order to exchange them for a computer or books for the class. This process is still very controversial.
In France, the issues of healthy food and the environment are entering the class through brands which have signed a partnership with state-schools: Nestlé campaigns for balanced meals, Colgate campaigns for the prevention of tooth decay and Total campaigns for the environment.

**Satiety foods: just a fad?**

Although several food companies (Nestlé, Unilever which markets Slim Fast, Danone, etc.) have increased their turnovers thanks to the sales of all sorts of diet and slimming products – Americans spend $5bn a year on diet food – they have realized that the worst enemy for people on a diet was hunger. That is why they have decided to launch diet products which will make the consumer feel fuller. With new products such as "Crave Control" yogurt and new companies with paradoxical names such as "LightFull", satiety diet foods may be here to stay.

## Question time

**1** In what ways have consuming trends changed over the past twenty years?
**2** What changes in society encouraged consumers to attend fast-food and take-away outlets?
**3** Do marketers have a responsibility in unhealthy food habits? Quote two examples.
**4** What are the advantages of on line shopping?
**5** How do consumers react towards store brands or home discounters?
**6** What are the targets marketers today covet the most and why?
**7** What are the means used by some companies to attract new customers?
**8** To what extent are school children treated as consumers?
**9** How can you explain the increase in over-indebted consumers?
**10** What does No Buying Day consist of?

LANDMARK

# Consumers everywhere

**Consumerism is a word used to describe the tendency of people to identify with products or services they consume, especially expensive products with famous brand names. Opponents of consumerism argue that many luxuries and consumer products are unnecessary and are used as social signals to identify with a group. They also believe that relationships with a product or brand name are substitutes for healthy human relationships. "Conspicuous consumption" is a phrase that spread to describe consumerism in the US in the 1960s.**

## Ralph Nader, the consumer advocate

Nader (1934-) is an American attorney and political activist who has promoted consumer rights and environmentalism. He is often referred to as a "consumer advocate" because much of his early work involved advocacy to protect consumers (and workers) from unsafe products. He calls for resistance to commercially-driven consumer culture. According to him, mass advertising creates artificial and often harmful desires. In 1965 Nader published a study, *Unsafe at Any Speed*, to show that many American automobiles, especially the Chevrolet Corvair and General Motors, were not safe. GM tried to discredit him, hiring private detectives to tap his phones and investigate his past. Consequently, Nader sued the company for invasion of privacy, forced it to apologize and used the money he won to expand his consumer rights efforts.

## Public Citizen

In 1971, Nader founded the non-governmental organization (NGO) Public Citizen and became famous for his objection to commercialism, the tendency to turn everything into objects and services that are sold to generate profit. Today, Public Citizen has over 140,000 members: its activities range from energy policy to consumer protection and medical malpractice. The organisation represents consumer interests in Congress and the courts. Public Citizen helped create the US Environmental Protection Agency (EPA) and the Consumer Product Safety Commission (CSPC) in 1972.

## Consumer protection

The CPSC aims at protecting consumers "against unreasonable risks of injuries associated with consumer products". It has the authority to regulate the sale and manufacture of more than 15,000 different consumer products, from toys to all-terrain vehicles, barbecue grills and swimming pools. To do so, it develops voluntary and mandatory standards, banning dangerous consumer products and issuing recalls of products already on the market. The CPSC learns about unsafe products through a consumer hotline and website, and the National Electronic Injury Surveillance System, a probability sample of about 100 hospitals. The system collects data on consumer product related injuries treated in emergency rooms and generates national estimates.

Nader promoting honest business in New York (2002)

## Commercial Alert

In 1980, Nader resigned as director of Public Citizen to work on other projects, especially campaigning against the dangers of large multinational corporations. He started several non-profit organizations, among which Commercial Alert, founded in 1999. It is a non-profit organization that opposes advertising to children and the commercialization of culture. It works on issues such as consumerism, product placement and ad-creep (the increase of advertising). It also wants to reduce the negative impacts of advertising on public health, for instance on obesity.

**Online t@sk**

Visit the CPSC's website on www.cpsc.gov/pr/proom.html.
Type "poster" in the search window.
Choose a poster and present it to the class.

### CONSUME, CONSUMERS AND COMPOUNDS

**consume:** consommer
**consumer:** consommateur
**consumer advocacy**: défense des consommateurs
**consumer complaint:** réclamation
**consumer product:** produit/bien de consommation
**consumer spending:** dépenses de consommation
**consumerism:** consumérisme, société de consommation
**consuming habit:** habitude de consommation.
**consuming pattern:** comportement du consommateur
**consumption:** consommation
**FMCGs (fast-moving consumer goods):** biens de consommation à rotation rapide
**mass consumption:** consommation de masse
**over consumption:** surconsommation

**ad:** pub
**ad-creep:** publicité rampante
**addiction:** accoutumance
**affluent:** riche, aisé
**after sales:** après-vente
**ageing:** vieillissement
**around the clock:** 24 heures sur 24
**auction:** vente aux enchères
**automatic teller machine (ATM):** distributeur automatique de billets (DAB)

"Somewhere out there is a credit card company that I don't owe money to."

**bachelor:** célibataire
**ban:** interdire, interdiction
**bank account:** compte en banque
**beverage:** boisson
**binge drinking:** fait de se soûler
**boost:** stimuler
**brand:** marque
**brown goods:** produits bruns
**budget flight:** vol pas cher
**cash dispenser:** distributeur automatique de billets
**cater for:** pourvoir à
**cautious:** qui fait attention
**charge:** (V) faire payer, (N) frais
**commodity:** matière première
**convenience food:** plats préparés
**credit/debit card:** carte de crédit
**customer:** client
**damage:** porter tort à, endommager
**delivery:** livraison
**demand:** exiger
**diet:** régime
**disposable product:** produit jetable
**divorcee:** personne divorcée
**elderly:** âgé
**entertainment:** loisirs
**facilities:** équipements, installations
**fad:** mode, passade, lubie
**fair trade:** commerce équitable
**feature:** (N) caractéristique ; (V) faire figurer
**fee:** droit d'entrée, taxe
**feedback:** retour, réponse
**frozen foods:** surgelés
**harmless:** sans danger
**hazard:** danger
**health:** santé
**high street:** rue commerçante
**home delivery:** livraison à domicile
**homeless:** sans abri
**household:** foyer
**indebted:** endetté
**insurance:** assurance
**item:** article
**kitchen appliance:** appareil ménager
**launch:** lancer
**leisure:** loisir
**life expectancy:** espérance de vie
**loan:** prêt bancaire
**lure:** attirer *(connotation négative)*
**marketing ploy:** stratagème marketing
**micro-wave oven:** four à micro-ondes
**middle-income:** à revenu moyen
**misleading:** trompeur

**nappies:** couches
**organic:** biologique
**over-indebtedness:** surendettement
**overweight:** en surpoids
**pitch:** offrir sur le marché
**plastic money:** cartes de crédit
**pre-cooked meal:** plats pré-cuits
**premixed drink:** boisson prémix
**pre-paid:** pré-payé
**privacy:** vie privée
**property:** propriété
**purchase:** achat, acheter
**purchase influencer:** personne qui influe sur un achat
**purchasing power:** pouvoir d'achat
**quality price ratio:** rapport qualité prix
**quality standard:** norme de qualité
**range:** gamme
**ready-made:** tout prêt
**ready-to-drink (RTD):** prêt à boire
**real estate:** immobilier
**recall:** rappeler, retirer de la vente
**rent:** louer
**resort:** station, lieu de vacances
**sample:** échantillon
**senior citizen:** personne du 3e âge
**shift:** changement
**shopping centre:** centre commercial
**single people:** personnes seules
**slimming product:** produit minceur
**snack:** petit repas, en-cas
**soft drinks:** boissons non alcoolisées
**spend (spent, spent):** dépenser
**store:** magasin
**sue:** faire/intenter un procès
**supply:** fournir
**sustainable development:** développement durable
**take-away:** à emporter
**target:** cibler
**terms of payment:** conditions de paiement
**thrifty:** économe
**tie-in:** produit dérivé
**toll-free number:** numéro vert
**trend:** tendance
**trial offer:** offre d'essai
**vending machine:** distributeur automatique
**wealth:** richesse
**well-off:** riche, à l'aise
**white goods:** produits blancs
**worth (be):** valoir

## Charts and tables

**1.** Study the following pie-chart which gives you information concerning consumer complaints to the Federal Trade Commission (FTC) Bureau of Consumer Protection.
→**Tools 11, p. 244**

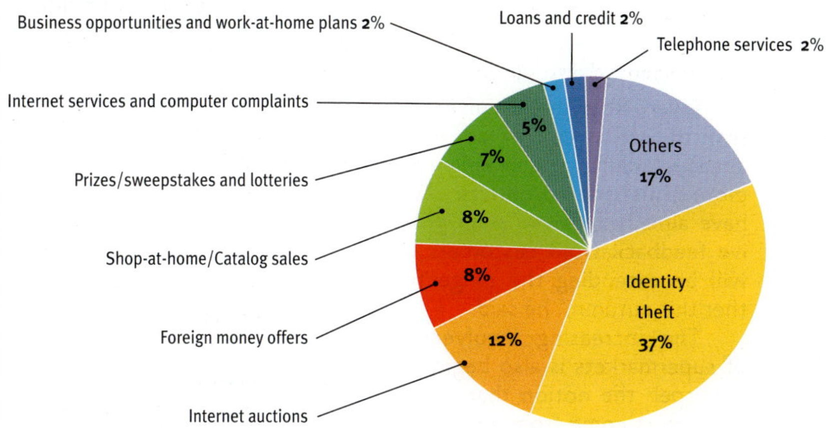


### Complaint Categories

**Loans and credit**: promise of a loan; false credit card loss protection; etc.
**Business opportunities and work-at-home plans**: misleading franchise and business opportunities; etc.
**Foreign money offers**: letters or e-mails offering the "opportunity" to share in a percentage of millions of dollars in exchange for money, bank account numbers, or ID information.
**Identity theft**: when someone appropriates your personal identifying information to commit fraud or theft.
**Internet auctions**: non-delivery of goods; delivery of worthless goods; delays; etc.
**Internet services and computers**: trial offers from Internet Service Provider; difficulty cancelling an ISP account; spy ware.
**Prizes/sweepstakes and lotteries**: promotions for "free" prizes for a fee; foreign lotteries; etc.
**Shop-at-home/catalog sales**: undisclosed costs, delivery delays, non-delivery.
**Telephone services**: charges for calls to "toll-free" numbers for calls consumers didn't make; misleading phone card offers; etc.
**"Others"** include: travel, vacation and timeshare plans; health care; multi-level marketing/pyramids/chain letter, etc.

**2.** Report on the pie-chart. Choose one category of complaints and illustrate with a precise example.

## Online tasks

### Presenting a service

The Federal Trade Commission the FTC enters various fraud-related complaints into Consumer Sentinel®, a secure, online database available to hundreds of civil and criminal law enforcement agencies worldwide.
Visit **www.econsumer.gov/english/**
Report orally: introduce the service. Explain how it works. Give examples of online shopping tips.

### Do you know about consumer protection?

Visit **www.ftc.gov/bcp/menu-tmark.htm** to read advice on telemarketing provided by the Federal Trade Commission. Choose one topic and report to the class.

# How consumer power sparked a Fairtrade revolution on our high streets

A series of deals between the Fairtrade organisation and big-name businesses promises to boost the wealth of some farmers in developing countries.

Among the initiatives launched recently is the announcement from Marks & Spencer that it will switch all its tea and coffee to Fairtrade-certified produce. Meanwhile Virgin Trains is switching to Fairtrade for its hot drinks served on mainline rail services. They join a growing band of more than 200 companies who sell everything from Fairtrade wine, flowers and T-shirts to footballs.

Fourteen years ago Fairtrade was established as a charity which promised to bring a decent deal to isolated coffee and other agricultural producers in the developing world who were faced with a crash in commodity prices.

Its recent success has been dramatic as western consumers demand more information and higher standards from those they buy from. Sales of Fairtrade products rose 40% in 2005 alone and are now worth £195m annually – tiny by total consumer spending, but part of a growing trend.

And the willingness[1] of the big brands to stock ethical products is expected to lead to further success. Said Harriet Lamb, the executive director of Fairtrade, "Thirty-six percent of those surveyed who knew about Fairtrade cited lack of visibility as the biggest barrier to increasing purchases of Fairtrade products."

Stuart Rose, the chief executive of M&S, confirmed he is already looking at stocking even more Fairtrade products. "We have already received such positive feedback from customers we will be extending the range further this autumn," he said.

The increasing involvement of supermarkets is also beginning to dispel[2] the notion that ethical consumers come from a relatively small and affluent group, argues Ms Lamb. "In fact it's often true that people on lower incomes give a higher percentage of income to charity. I visited a homeless project where people have coffee shops on the high street in Edinburgh and they are selling 100% Fairtrade coffee because they say 'we know what it's like for those farmers and we want to play our part in making a difference'. As we see with the incredible success of Fairtrade with the Co-op and Asda it is people across the spectrum[3] who are ready to buy Fairtrade."

Terry Macalister, *The Guardian*, March 8, 2006

1. *willingness*: empressement
2. *dispel*: dissiper
3. *people across the spectrum*: l'ensemble de la population

## Info

***Marks & Spencer***
Also called "Marks and Sparks", or "M&S", the chain is renowned for its clothes and food departments.

***Virgin***
→ *Landmark*, p. 43.

***Ms***
Used by women who don't want their marital status to be indicated by "Miss" or "Mrs".

***Co-op***
A successful chain of supermarkets which runs on a cooperative basis. Customers share profits and can collect stamps which they can exchange for consumer goods.

***Asda***
The largest operator of supermarkets in the UK is now the British subsidiary of US Wal-Mart.

**Activity** Practise giving an account of this article.

## References

You can find relevant information by reading various pages in your book and memorising a few facts and ideas.

→ **Companies, p. 27**
→ **Consumers, p. 70**
→ **Marketing, p. 87**
→ **Sustainable development, p. 176**
→ **Globalisation, p. 222**

## Introduction

You should explain where the article comes from, when it was published and what it is about. →Tools 4, p. 236

This article from *The Guardian*, a British daily, was published in March 2006. It explains the success of Fairtrade products with consumers and the prospects for British supermarkets.

## Development

Once you have understood the article, organise your ideas into two or three different parts, using set phrases and link-words. →Tools 4, p. 236

1. What Fairtrade is
2. The success of Fairtrade
3. Future prospects

You should also use the information given in *Info* and what you have learnt, for example by referring to the various pages indicated in *References*.

### 1. What Fairtrade is

In the early 1990s, Fairtrade was a charity, established to help farm producers in developing countries.

• Then, there was a drop in various commodity prices, such as coffee. Consequently, isolated farmers were faced with tough conditions in their home countries.

• The charity made deals with big supermarket chains on behalf of those farmers.

• In Fairtrade deals, big supermarket chains guarantee farmers a decent price for the produce they buy. Therefore the farmers' revenue has improved.

• Consumers can buy the products with specific labels – such as Max Haavlar in France – in supermarkets.

### 2. The success of Fairtrade

Fairtrade products have been enjoying considerable success and the trend is growing: sales rose 40% in 2005. They are now worth £195m annually.

• Western consumers are more and more concerned with the origin and the quality of the products they buy – whether they have been genetically modified, whether the working conditions were correct, and so on.

• People used to think Fairtrade products were only for affluent consumers. Actually lower income people tend to give more, as the example of homeless people selling Fairtrade coffee in Scotland shows.

• Thanks to Fairtrade's success, more and more companies are offering such products. At the time of publication, more than 200 companies were selling varied products such as wine and T-shirts to footballs. Moreover, as the headline says, it concerns major retailers. A recent example is M&S which has announced that all the tea and coffee it sells will now be Fairtrade-certified produce. Virgin Trains will offer Fairtrade hot drinks on its mainline rail services.

### 3. Future prospects

• **More products**: The big supermarket chains are eager to attract customers as Fairtrade gives a positive image of the company. Therefore, retailers are willing to increase the number of Fairtrade products they stock.

• **More visibility**: A survey of consumers who knew about Fairtrade has shown that the products suffered from a lack of visibility. The products that are successful even though they are not visible enough will be even more so as soon as they are made more visible.

## Conclusion

You should sum up the main ideas and try to open out in a new direction.

This article reports on a trend which started as a charity and has become a profitable business. Fair trade turns out to be a win-win deal for farmers who get a more decent price for their produce, for companies who improve their image of good corporate citizens, and for customers who can purchase good quality products while doing a good deed.
However, do Fairtrade products make a real difference to the farmers? Is this just a new way to attract consumers in a sustainable-development-conscious world?

## Branching out

Now, you should move away from the article and develop more ideas. The following questions can help you.

**1** Is the Fairtrade trend similar in France? Explain and give examples.

**2** Do you think Fairtrade is a serious issue or that it is just a fad? Why/Why not?

## 3. Work

# Chinese Workers Protest at Factory Making Toys for McDonald's

A violent protest erupted last weekend at a factory in southern China that makes toys for McDonald's and other international companies, a rights group said Thursday, and the local police were called to the scene to restore order.

China Labor Watch, a New York-based labor rights group, described a riot by more than 1,000 workers protesting at low pay and poor living conditions at the factory in the industrial city of Dongguan. However, a distributor for the factory said the unrest was not about wages or conditions but was instead prompted by a disgruntled worker who had been laid off.

The factory is owned by the Merton Company, based in Hong Kong, which manufactures promotional toys and other products. Merton's Web site lists Disney and McDonald's among its customers. Workers told China Labor Watch that roughly half of the toys made at the factory were supplied to McDonald's, presumably for Happy Meals.

Lisa Howard, director of corporate communications for McDonald's, said it had purchased toys from the factory through a supplier, Creata Promotion. She said Creata was investigating the matter.

Michael Lillioja, executive director of Creata, confirmed by e-mail that an investigation was under way. He said the factory had won awards for workplace safety and was regularly monitored by outside agencies. In a statement included in his e-mail message, Creata said the episode "was not a wage or hour issue" but quoted factory officials as blaming a "disgruntled employee who was terminated."

In the statement released Thursday, China Labor Watch accused the factory of violating Chinese labor laws, including provisions limiting overtime to 36 hours a month. Instead, the group said, total overtime per worker can reach 70 hours a month, and workers can have their pay deducted if they refuse to work the extra hours. Workers earn $71.75 a month, the minimum wage in Dongguan, but also pay a quarter of their earnings for room and board, the group said.

Jim Yardley, *The New York Times*, 28 July 2006

### Compréhension

**1.** **Rédigez en anglais un résumé de ce document. (110 mots, +/– 10%)**
**2.** **Traduisez le titre, le sous-titre et les deux premiers paragraphes de l'article.**

### Expression

**Répondez en anglais aux questions suivantes.**

1 To what extent are the analysis of Creata and Labor Watch different? (150 words)

2 Is it important for multinationals to make sure their suppliers respect international labour laws? Why/Why not? (100 words)

(N.B. L'usage du dictionnaire bilingue est autorisé.)

## 4. Consumers

# Buy, buy, buy: consumers fuel £1 trillion spending boom

According to a report out today, Britain's thirst for the luxuries of life last year propelled consumer spending to a record £1 trillion.

The research reveals that housing is the country's biggest area of consumer spending. But it is the "big treat" items that have seen the largest growth, up 57% between 1995 and 2005. The amount spent on buying cars, DVD players, luxury furniture and, above all, holidays, is soaring.

The annual British Lifestyles report, by the consumer spending analyst Mintel, calculates that the average household spends £37,000 a year on consumer goods. Britain's total consumer spending has increased 43% over the last 10 years. Mintel's director of research said "Our priorities as consumers appear to reside with fashionable 'must have' products like satellite navigation systems, flat-screen TVs and holidays. Compared to a decade ago, we're living in a society of instant gratification, and more and more of us have the financial means to fund that desire."

Holidays are the favourite non-essential buy. The cost of vacations has reached an average of £790 a year for every adult and child in Britain, largely because of the move towards frequent short breaks.

Spending on motoring has also increased significantly, with drivers paying £65.5bn for their cars last year. Although the new models inspire interest, the report says secondhand cars account for the majority of spending.

Preferences in the home appliances market, another area that has seen big growth, have also shifted. Whereas in 1995 most spending in the sector was on "white goods" such as fridges, dishwashers and freezers, the preference now is for "brown goods" such as TVs, DVD players and stereos, which have seen a growth of 642% since 1995. The home computer has attracted the biggest increase in spending (695%).

Everyday purchases such as food, drink, clothes and toiletries are a decreasing proportion of the consumer market, attracting no more than an 18% increase in spending. Occasional items that are neither essential nor luxury, such as books, gym memberships and visits to the cinema, are more popular, growing by 49% to account for 16% of the consumer market. Particularly popular are hair and beauty treatments (up 56%), household goods and gadgets (62%), and plants and flowers (185%).

Paul Lewis, *The Guardian*, May 12, 2006

### Compréhension

**1.** **Rédigez en anglais un compte rendu de ce document. (150 mots)**
**2.** **Traduisez le titre et le troisième paragraphe de l'article.**

### Expression

**Répondez en anglais aux questions suivantes.**

1 Define the "instant gratification" society. (100 words)

2 Andrew Leicester, of the Institute of Fiscal Studies, thinks that, "as people's incomes increase, their disposable income also goes up, their spending rises, and they end up better off." Do you agree? Why/Why not? (150 words)

(N.B. L'usage du dictionnaire bilingue est autorisé.)

## Case study: recalling a product

Study the following poster and create a new one about air rifles.

Heading: in red

# SAFETY RECALL

Hazard

**SMALL PART CHOKING HAZARD**

**PLAYSKOOL KLACKEROO**

Brand name

Full color photo

Reason of the product recall

**The toy's brightly colored knobs can detach and allow small geometric pieces to come loose, posing a choking hazard to young children.**

Remedy

**Take these toys away from children immediately, and call Playskool toll-free at:**

Toll-free number

**(888) 671-9764**

Web address

**or contact their web site at: www.hasbro.com to arrange for a free, redesigned replacement toy.**

Post until date (at least 120 days)

Post until January 14, 2001

In cooperation with the U.S. Consumer Product Safety Commission

In cooperation with CSPC

GAMO Air Rifles – Distributor: GAMO USA Corp., of Fort Lauderdale, Fla.
Hazard: The scope mount on these rifles can be installed incorrectly, causing the rifle to unexpectedly fire. This poses a serious injury hazard to consumers.
The recalled air rifles are the following GAMO models: Shadow Sport and F1200. These models bear the serial numbers 04-IC-415577-06 through 04-IC-579918-06. The model and serial numbers can be found on the left side of the barrel just above the front left side of the stock. Models look identical.
Remedy: stop using the recalled air rifles immediately and contact the company to receive instructions for returning them and receiving a free repair.
Toll-free number: (877) 246-3831 – company's web site: **www.gamousa.com**

## PERSONAL TASK

**Role play** →Tools 9, p. 242

**A:** You are a customer.
You bought a mobile phone two weeks ago. It doesn't work. Phone the retailer to complain. Describe the problem and ask for a refund or an exchange.

**B:** You are the retailer.
Ask for a description of the problem. Apologise and offer a solution.

# IN THIS UNIT...

- Companies: Ikea, Kleenex...
- Learn about purchase influencers & "affluenza"
- Create a focus group
- Give an oral presentation on where people shop

# 5
## Marketing

**→ Before you START**

*In brief:* **Packaging**
*Front page:* **Hispanics in the USA**

## What information is available on this packaging?

### Words

- **Nouns:** quantity, quality, name, brand, weight, ingredients, information
- **Adjectives:** colourful, attractive, informative

### LISTENING PRACTICE

CD TRACK 26

Listen to the recording.

**1.** What are the people talking about?
**2.** Explain their opinions.

# Product packaging that pays

*How consumer-product companies are revamping their containers to jump-start sales.*

Though it's their first chance to make a good impression, for many companies package design has often been an afterthought[1]. Designers were called in at the last minute, and cost was the deciding factor.

But with more than 30,000 new products expected to hit store shelves this year, creating an innovative exterior has become a crucial way to boost the bottom line.

If packaging is done right, the rewards can be huge. Even a clearer label or a new container shape can lead to double-digit sales growth.

After months of research, Kraft discovered that its customers often transferred Chips Ahoy cookies to jars for easy access and to avoid staleness[2]. The company solved both problems by creating a patented resealable opening on the top of the bag. Since launching in July 2005, it's raked in more than $44 million in sales, nearly doubling sales of the older packaging.

Americans spend more on home decor during the holidays than at any other time, so last season Kimberly-Clark introduced an oval-shaped Kleenex box that was a clear departure from its usual rectangular shapes. The goal was to position the product as a must-have accessory rather than a functional item. It was the company's best-selling holiday line in history, with sales twice those of the 2004 season.

*Business 2.0 Magazine*, July 7 2006

1. *afterthought*: pensée (qui vient) après coup
2. *staleness*: manque de fraîcheur

CD TRACK 27

## Info

***Kraft***
Kraft Foods Inc. is the largest food and beverage company headquartered in the USA and the world's second largest, after Nestlé. A few Kraft brands: Chips Ahoy, Côte d'Or, Kool Aid, Maxwell House, Toblerone, etc.

***Kimberly-Clark***
A Dallas-based corporation with more than 60,000 employees. It produces paper-based consumer products. Kimberly-Clark's famous brands: Kleenex (tissues), Kotex (feminine hygiene products), Huggies (nappies).

## Headlines

**1** What consonant is repeated in this headline? What word is thus emphasized?

**2** What is the use of the subhead?

## Work on words

### 1 I Find their equivalents in English

**Headline** conditionnement
**Subhead** produit de consommation – relancer
**§1** concepteur – coût
**§2** rayonnage(s)
**§3** étiquette
**§4** bocal, pot – breveté – lancement

### 2 I Find their synonyms

**Subhead** renovate – packaging
**§2** increase (V) – essential – financial result
**§3** gain (N) – 10 or more
**§4** that can be opened and closed several times – make money (*col.*)
**§5** aim (N)

## The key points of the article

### 1 Packaging

**a.** Usual tendency about package design.
**b.** Competition: why is packaging important?
**c.** Pick out the words and expressions showing the financial consequences of an efficient packaging.

### 2 Examples

Describe the two examples in your own words (company, customers' needs or desires, strategy).

## {Methods}

### ■ Speaking practice

**Read figures aloud.** →Tools 10, p. 243

**a.** 30,000 **b.** July 2005
**c.** $44 **d.** 2004

### ■ Writing practice

**1 Compound adjectives**

Here are two ways of making a compound adjective:

- adjective or adverb + V-*ing*
→ active adjective > *the company's best-selling holiday line in history*
- adjective or adverb + V-*ed* (past participle)
→ passive adjective > *an oval-shaped Kleenex box*

**Transform the following expressions to get compound adjectives.**

**a.** a box with a rectangular shape
**b.** a product with a clear label
**c.** packaging designers who work hard
**d.** an item with a smart design

**2 Prepare a short account in English.**

Use the expressions in part **1**.

- Make a sentence which explains the benefits of clear product packaging.
- Make a sentence which emphasizes the influence that designers can have on sales.

→Tools 4, p. 236

## Branching out

**1** For what kind of products is the container almost as important as the content?

**2** To what extent can packaging boost sales? →*Key data*, p. 87

## LISTENING PRACTICE

CD TRACK 28-29

*Valerie Bloom and Peter Clapton are discussing a strategy in their shop.*

**1 Comprehension**

Listen to the recording to find the following information.

**Part 1**

**a.** Product concerned (type, company).
**b.** The problem.
**c.** Solution found.

**Part 2**

**a.** How the problem was discovered.
**b.** Solution in the shop.
**c.** Another place where customers can get information.
**d.** Consequences for the brand.
**e.** Peter's conclusion.

**2 Expression**

Give an oral account, or write a 100-word paragraph, summing up what you have heard.

# How To Tap the Hispanic Market

The Hispanic population, currently estimated by the U.S. Census Bureau to be about 39.8 million, is one of the fastest-growing groups in America, making up 13.7% of the population. If current growth rates continue, Hispanics will make up about 25% of the population by 2050. Their buying power tripled between 1990 and 2003 from $222 billion to $653 billion.

*BusinessWeek* spoke with Felipe Korzenny, professor and founding director of the Center for the Study of Hispanic Marketing Communications at Florida State University.

**Although the numbers both in terms of population and revenue are extremely high and robust, the Hispanic market has largely been overlooked. Why?**
I don't believe that marketers have understood how to benefit from targeting Hispanics as separate from the rest of the population. The assumption that most marketers make is that they will catch the Hispanic consumers as they become more acculturated. They do not realize that understanding the culture is part of the way in which you can connect with the consumer.

**What is the biggest mistake companies both big and small make?**
Being stereotypical. They will go with an ad agency that says, "Use some Latin music and a nice family and let's try to lure[1] the consumer." Or there are ones that just don't make an effort. These are the two extremes. In between, there are the ones who just take an ad and translate it and say this is a Hispanic ad. That's the most primitive approach.

**What would you consider a successful approach?**
One of the most successful marketers is Procter & Gamble. They either launch a new product or position it in the Hispanic market by talking to many consumers and finding out how to make the product relevant[2] to them.

**What is the importance of bilingual marketing?**
In the past years there was an emphasis on using the Spanish language. More and more Hispanics are spending a lot of time with both English and Spanish media. And there are families where the kids are bilingual, and family members vary in their linguistic ability. So being bilingual is more effective and it is a way to emphasize culture.

*Business Week*, July 12, 2006

1. *lure*: tromper, attirer par la ruse
2. *relevant*: (ici) dans lequel les gens se reconnaissent

CD TRACK 30

## Info

***Hispanic***
The Hispanics, or "Latinos" (Cubans, Dominicans, Mexicans and Puerto Ricans) accounted for 12% of the total US population in 2000 (census). They are the country's fastest-growing community and are mainly concentrated in California, Florida, Texas and New York.

***Procter & Gamble***
William Procter, a candlemaker, and James Gamble, a soapmaker, formed the company known as Procter & Gamble in 1837. The global company, based in Cincinnati, Ohio, manufactures a wide range of consumer goods such as detergents and cosmetics.

## Headlines

**1** Anticipate the contents of the article from the headline.

**2** Read the last sentence of the introductory paragraph and explain the form of this article.

## Work on words

### 1 I Find their equivalents in English

**Headline** exploiter
**Introduction** recensement – à la croissance la plus rapide – composer – taux de croissance – pouvoir d'achat
**Q&A 1** cibler – hypothèse – se rendre compte
**Q&A 2** agence de publicité – traduire
**Q&A 3** lancer – consommateur
**Q&A 4** passer du temps – efficace

### 2 I Find their synonyms

**Introduction** at the moment
**Q&A 1** neglect (V) – take advantage from – relate to
**Q&A 3** discover

## The key points of the article

### 1 Read the introduction

**a.** Country.
**b.** Number of Hispanics in the country and proportion they represent.
**c.** Estimated proportion by mid-century.
**d.** Buying power in 2003 and in 2006.

### 2 Read question and answer 1 and 2

**a.** Choose an answer and justify your choice using the professor's answer to question 1.
❑ Many marketers have tried to target Hispanics as a specific segment.
❑ Many marketers have waited for Hispanics to lose their Hispanic culture.
**b.** Three examples of mistakes when targeting Hispanics.

### 3 Read question and answer 3 and 4

**a.** Successful company.
**b.** Reason for this success.
**c.** Should English or Spanish be used, and why?

## {Methods}

### ■ Speaking practice

**1 Read figures aloud.** →Tools 10, p. 243
Read the first three sentences of the introduction aloud. If necessary, start by writing the following figures down.
**a.** 39.8 million
**b.** 13.7% (of the population)
**c.** about 25% of the population
**d.** by 2050
**e.** between 1990 and 2003
**f.** $222 billion
**g.** $653 billion
**h.** from $222 billion to $653 billion

**2 Money, money**
Get used to dollars and pounds. Change all the money data into euros.

**3 Prepare an oral introduction.**
• Identify the source.
• Explain what the article is about (who, what, where, when).

### ■ Writing practice

**Write a summary of this article in English (around 130 words).**
• Read the article again and list the key idea of each paragraph following the order of the article.
• Introduce link words between the various ideas.
→Tools 4, p. 236

## Branching out

**1** What are the advantages for American companies to adapt a product to the Hispanic market?

**2** How can companies proceed to target a new market segment? →*Key data*, p. 86-88

## Language

• *What is the biggest mistake companies **both** big and small make?*
• *More and more Hispanics are spending a lot of time with **both** English and Spanish media.*
Quand un ensemble est constitué de deux éléments, on utilise ***both*** pour signifier « les deux (ensemble) ». On ne peut donc pas utiliser *both* si on parle de la différence entre deux éléments.
La construction *both... and...* signifie « à la fois... et ... ».
**Translate the two examples above into French.**

**Translate into English**
**1.** Le marché hispanique grossit à la fois en nombre et en pouvoir d'achat.
**2.** Certaines entreprises ne comprennent pas qu'il faut les cibler en anglais et en espagnol.
**3.** Les Hispaniques ne parlent pas tous la même langue. Les grands-parents parlent espagnol mais la nouvelle génération utilise à la fois l'anglais et l'espagnol.

**Marketing is used to launch a product, keep or increase market share or communicate with customers.**

## 1-The market

### Market research

To study demand and customers' habits, companies resort to market research. This can be done by desk study – official statistics, specialized press, etc. – or field study – establishing direct contact with consumers, through questionnaires and interviews, which can be done face-to-face, on the telephone or the internet. Sales representatives' feedback on trends and preferences can also be collected.

### The target

Thanks to market research, firms can define their targets and establish market segments, i.e. groups of consumers sharing the same needs and desires. These sections or "niches" can be identified according to age-group, gender, income, social background, ethnic group and culture.

**An example of failed market research**

Wal-Mart, the biggest American retailer, has been forced to leave Germany because it failed to take German habits and culture into account; for example, they remained with thousands of unsold pillow cases just because German pillows are not the same size as American ones. →**Chapter 14, Globalisation, *In brief*, p. 216**

## 2-The marketing mix

The marketing mix is the way firms combine the different elements of marketing, usually referred to as the five "Ps": Product, Price, Place, Promotion and Packaging.

### The various types of products

- Fast-moving consumer goods (FMCGs): food, drinks, detergents, toiletries, newspapers, etc. They are called "fast-moving" because they do not remain long on supermarket shelves.
- Durable goods/products: household equipment – electrical/brown goods (TVs, DVD readers, etc.) and kitchen appliances/white goods (refrigerators, etc.) – clothes, books, CDs, phones, etc.
- Disposable products/disposables are thrown away after use (nappies, tissues, plastic bags, pens, razors, contact lenses, etc.).
- Services refer to insurance, financial products, travel, etc.

### The life cycle of a product

The life cycle of a product generally includes five stages:

- Introduction: the product is developed. The marketing and manufacturing costs are high (no or low profit).
- Growth: sales rise. The costs decrease with economies of scale. The company can make profits.
- Maturity: sales continue to grow; profits remain high but competitors appear on the market.
- Saturation: too many suppliers of the same product; the sales start dropping.
- Decline: sales plummet, and the product is withdrawn.

Companies try to delay their products' decline as much as possible by prolonging the maturity stage:

- launching updated versions,
- changing the packaging,

Attracting consumers with low prices

- communicating with advertising campaigns,
→Chapter 6, Communication
- trying to widen their target or tapping foreign countries,
- promoting the products with special offers, reduced prices or free gifts (see "Price" below),
- finding new distributors.

### Price

Price is essential. It must cover manufacturing costs and include the profit margin. It may fluctuate according to competition and demand. It works as an incentive for consumers.
Companies adopt various strategies to find the best price.
- Penetration pricing: entering the market with a low price.
- Skimming pricing: entering the market with a high price because the product is new and has no competitors.
- Critical point, or odd pricing: offering a product for £9.99 instead of £10.
- Premium pricing: offering the product at a high price to add status to the product (luxury/upscale brands).
- Discounting: offering a lower price if payment is cash or if customers buy in bulk.

Lastly, sales are also organized at regular periods, and price cuts are used at the end of a product life cycle to get rid of the stock.

### Place

Products are distributed through different channels.
→Chapter 8, Distribution
There are no middlemen on open markets, through the internet, or through newspaper or magazine advertisements. Since the mid-1990s, online buying has increased dramatically and is still increasing. →Chapter 10, New technologies

### Selling strategies

- Intensive strategy: goods are available in the greatest possible number of stores.
- Selective strategy: only some stores sell the product without having an exclusive agreement.
- Exclusive strategy: store managers must not sell competing brands. These stores are often franchises.

### Promotion

To promote a product or a brand, advertising is the most widely used method. →Chapter 6, Communication

### Packaging

Referred to by experts as "the fifth P of the marketing mix", packaging has become crucial in the building of a product or brand image. It serves as a promotion tool and can boost sales.
→Chapter 6, Communication
For food products, packaging indicates the ingredients used, as well as information required by the law, such as safety warnings, quality labels, instructions for use, etc.
Companies targeting children make a great effort in packaging. This is true for most food products (snacks, sweets, cookies, drinks, etc.). →Chapter 4, Consumers
Yet, packaging can also constitute a threat as it can damage the environment. That is why most packaging is recyclable today.

**The successful updating of beer**

The sales of beer in France have constantly decreased since the 1980s. Brewers have made enormous efforts to appeal to a wider target by changing their packaging and launching new products such as beer blended with vodka, tequila, etc. These efforts are apparently just starting to pay off.

New designs to lure even more consumers?

→Chapter 11, Sustainable development
Packaging has a price, which is taken into account in the retail price.

## 3-Various marketing techniques

### Customer loyalty

Building customer loyalty is a major issue for companies: it is less expensive to keep old customers than to find new ones.
Companies offer loyalty cards which allow the customers to collect points and get free gifts, discounts, air miles (criticised today because of global warming) or vouchers.
→Chapter 11, Sustainable development
Customer loyalty schemes are generally appreciated by the customers. They also allow companies to establish important data on consuming habits and trends. However, customers can get fed up with junk mail, and may feel their privacy threatened by the transmission of personal information.

### Customizing

Products and services are adapted to customers' needs.

### Direct marketing

Customers can be approached directly with:
- direct personalized mail for special offers and promotions,
- e-mails which operate on the same basis as snail mail,
- phone-calls,
- reply coupons found in leaflets or magazines.

### Merchandising, or point of sale (POS) promotion

It aims at encouraging impulse buying. The goods are displayed at eye-level or at strategic places (check-outs, at the end of aisles or end displays) where customers are easily tempted.
Point of sale promotion informs customers through billboards or video screens. Music can create a pleasant atmosphere. Recently, some stores have also added perfume.

### Using information technology →Chapter 10, New technologies

Electronic point-of-sale (EPO) terminals scan bar codes at the check outs, allowing the store to track the best-sellers, and the frequency and quantity of purchases.
Electronic-data interchanges (EDI) allow the stock to be renewed automatically, avoiding shortages.

**Gold for chocolate**

In September 2006 Godiva, the famous Belgian chocolate maker, decided to change its packaging. The firm opted for a new upscale gold box of chocolates. The new box with thick gold paper, looks more luxurious than the old one. In order to prepare consumers for this launch, Teri Hatcher, the star from *Desperate Housewives*, advertised for Godiva during the 2006 Valentine period.

## Question time

1 Explain the difference between a desk market study and a field market study.
2 What risks does a company take if it doesn't make a serious market study?
3 Explain what the marketing mix consists of.
4 Marketers say "place, place, place, place and place" are the 5 Ps of the marketing mix. What do you think they mean by this?
5 What does a product's life cycle consist of?
6 What are the different selling techniques?
7 Do new technologies play an important part in marketing today? Explain how.
8 Describe the advantages and drawbacks of direct marketing.

# Ikea

## Facts and figures

Ikea has become famous for its low cost contemporary furniture. The company was founded in Sweden, in 1943 by Ingvar Kamprad, then 17. "Ikea" is a composite of his initials, plus the first letters of the property and the village in which he grew up. Its pronunciation rhymes with "idea" in English-speaking countries. The chain now has 238 stores in 34 countries, attracting 410 million shoppers a year. Ikea is one of the few store chains to have locations both in Israel and other Middle Eastern nations.

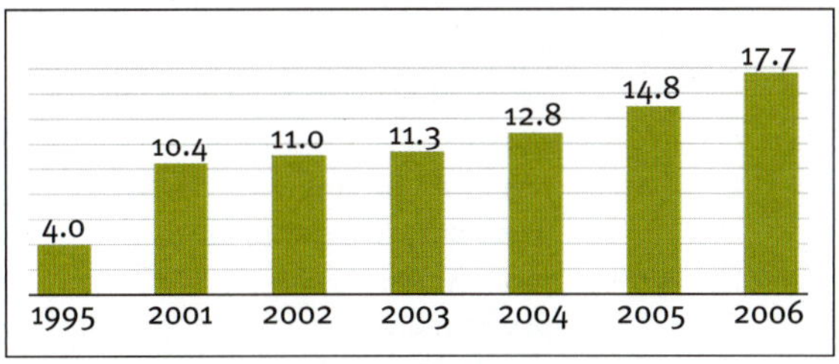


Sales for the Ikea Group rose 15% during the financial year 2005 (1 Sept. 2005 – 31 Aug. 2006) totalling €14.8bn.

## A partner in better living

Ikea claims its vision is "to create a better everyday life", to "offer a wide range of well designed, functional home furnishing products at prices so low that as many people as possible will be able to afford them." Its marketing idea, "We do our part", means that the company focuses on product design and clever solutions so that its customers can benefit from the lowest possible prices. Ikea is always developing new ways to use materials, uses inexpensive materials such as assembled particles and works closely with its factories to streamline manufacturing processes. Although Ikea's products and furniture are Swedish designed, they are produced in developing countries to hold down costs.

## Fun in big, large boxes

The company limits distribution costs thanks to warehouse stores – big, large boxes – which are often located in inexpensive suburbs. The blue-and-yellow buildings average 300,000 square feet, roughly equal to five football fields, selling about 7,000 items, from candlesticks to kitchen cabinets. Customers are encouraged to see everything thanks to the "one-way" store layout: they go through furniture showrooms, housewares ("market halls"), and then the warehouse where they can collect the flat packs for products they have seen before checking out. In market halls, strategically placed bins offer very cheap items. Another key element is surprise: Ikea replaces a third of its product line every year. Many stores include restaurants (serving Swedish food) and play areas for children. Thus Ikea can establish a more meaningful relationship with people who feel connected to a community. The Small Biz Network division accommodates new entrepreneurs; a quarterly electronic newsletter invites them into a store for a networking event.

## Flat packs

Ikea does its part by offering cheap furniture, and customers have to do their part, too. Much of the modern furniture is sold in flat packs, as self-assembly furniture. This allows Ikea to reduce production costs (no assembly costs) and the costs of packaging and volume, when the goods are transported and when they are stored in the shop.

## The main marketing tool

Ikea's catalogue is the key element of its marketing success and can be considered its main marketing tool: 70% of the yearly marketing budget goes into the catalogue. Containing about 12,000 products, the 2006 edition was produced in 38 different editions in 17 languages for 28 countries; 160 million copies were circulated worldwide, and distributed free of charge, through mail and stores.

Products are identified by single word names. Ingvar Kamprad found it easier to remember proper names and words than product codes. For instance, bathroom articles are named after Scandinavian lakes, rivers and bays; dining tables and chairs are Finnish placenames. The Nordic naming has sometimes led to problems: a famous example was the bed frame *Gutvik*, which can be translated as "good performing sex" in German-speaking countries.

One of the basis of Ikea's marketing is that since its products are cheaper, people need less working hours to buy them. There's life outside work!

**Online t@sk**

Visit Ikea's corporate site on www.ikea-group.ikea.com/corporate/.
Choose between the company's organization or code of conduct, and report to the class.

# 5 Marketing

## Vocabulary

### MARKET, MARKETING AND COMPOUNDS

**market:** marché
**market leader:** leader du/sur le marché
**market research:** étude de marché
**market segment:** segment de marché
**market share:** part de marché
**marketer:** responsable de commercialisation
**marketing mix :** plan de marchéage, marketing mix
**mass marketing:** commercialisation de masse
**mass-market:** grand public
**open market:** marché en plein air

**advertisement:** une publicité
**advertising:** la publicité
**advertising campaign:** campagne de publicité
**age-group:** tranche d'âge
**aisle:** allée (dans un supermarché)
**appeal to:** attirer
**bargain:** bonne affaire
**benefit *(V)*:** profiter à
**best-seller:** article très demandé
**best-selling:** qui remporte un grand succès
**billboard:** panneau
**bottom line:** résultat financier
**brown goods:** produits bruns
**buying power:** pouvoir d'achat
**cash:** en liquide
**census:** recensement
**check-out:** caisse de sortie
**competitor:** concurrent
**container:** récipient, barquette, etc.
**cost:** coût
**criteria (*pl.*):** critères
**customer:** client
**customer file:** fichier client
**customer loyalty:** fidélité du client
**customize :** fabriquer sur commande, personnaliser
**data:** données
**decline:** déclin
**design:** conception, graphisme
**designer:** concepteur, graphiste
**desk study:** étude sur documents
**discount price:** prix réduit
**display (V):** mettre à l'étalage
**disposable products/disposables:** produits jetables
**durable goods:** biens de consommation durable
**end display:** tête de gondole
**eye-level:** niveau de l'œil
**fast-moving consumer goods (FMCGs):** biens de consommation à rotation rapide
**field study:** étude sur le terrain
**flavour:** goût
**free:** gratuit
**gender:** sexe
**gift:** cadeau
**hand out:** distribuer
**handle:** manipuler
**hard sell tactics:** stratégie de vente agressive
**high street:** rue commerçante
**household:** foyer
**impulse buying:** achat sur impulsion
**in bulk:** par grande quantité
**incentive *(N)*:** incitation
**income:** revenu
**innovative:** innovant
**instructions for using:** guide d'utilisation
**insurance:** assurance
**item:** article
**jar:** bocal, pot
**jump-start:** relancer
**junk mail:** publicités envoyées par la poste
**just in time:** juste à temps
**know-how:** savoir-faire
**label:** étiquette
**launching:** lancement
**leaflet:** prospectus
**life cycle:** cycle de vie
**location:** emplacement
**loyalty card:** carte de fidélité
**lure :** attirer par la ruse, séduire
**luxury:** de luxe
**mall:** centre commercial
**merchandising :** marchandisage
**middleman:** intermédiaire
**money-conscious:** attentif aux prix
**niche:** créneau
**odd pricing:** prix psychologique
**online buying:** achat en ligne
**outlet:** magasin
**packaging:** conditionnement, emballage
**personalized mail:** courrier personnalisé

"I hate the amount of packaging that food comes wrapped in these days"

**phone-call:** appel téléphonique
**point of sale (POS):** lieu de vente
**position *(V)*:** positionner
**premium pricing:** prix forts
**price cut:** réduction, rabais
**privacy:** vie privée
**profit margin:** marge bénéficiaire
**purchase:** achat
**quality price ratio:** rapport qualité prix
**range:** gamme
**recall:** (V) retirer de la vente ; (N) retour
**reply coupon:** coupon réponse
**research:** recherche
**retail price:** prix de détail
**revamp:** réorganiser
**safety:** sécurité
**sales:** soldes ; ventes
**sales representative *(N)*:** commercial
**shape:** forme
**shelf (*pl.* shelves):** rayonnage
**shortage:** pénurie
**skimming pricing:** prix d'écrémage
**snail mail:** poste
**study *(V)*:** étudier
**succeed:** avoir du succès
**suit *(V)*:** convenir à
**supply:** fournir
**supply and demand:** l'offre et la demande
**tap:** exploiter
**target:** cibler
**toiletries:** articles de toilette
**trend:** tendance
**unsold:** invendu
**updated:** mis à jour
**upscale:** haut de gamme
**voucher:** bon
**warning:** avertissement
**withdraw (withdrew, withdrawn):** retirer
**win-win (situation):** situation où tout le monde est gagnant

## Charts and tables

**1.** Study the following charts which give you information about why people shop the way they do. →Tools 11, p. 244

**2.** Give an oral presentation of each chart. Then give a combined presentation of both.

## Online tasks

### Presenting a service

Visit Commercial Alert on **www.commercialalert.org/**.
Introduce the organisation. Report on its mission.
Give examples of the issues it tackles.

### Do you know about "affluenza"?

Visit **www.pbs.org/kcts/affluenza/** to learn about this disease.
Choose one topic and report to the class.

# A non-taxing way to shop

Saturday through to July 30, shoppers statewide can take advantage of the annual tax break to help cut the cost of clothing, shoes, books, supplies and other items needed for school starting Aug. 14 in Broward and Miami-Dade counties.

Shoppers are drawn in hordes to stores, office supply chains and malls during the nearly week-and-a-half-long event in which retailers, mandated by law, knock off[1] state and local sales tax on school-related purchases. In Miami-Dade the sales tax is 7 percent; in Broward, it's 6 percent.

"It's wonderful," said Lowann Griffith, 31, a parent who lives in Fort Lauderdale. To take advantage of the savings, last year Griffith purchased around $1,200 of both school and non-school-related items for her 11-year-old son. "It's big savings," she said.

**STRICT RULES**

To receive the tax break, school supplies, such as pencils, pens, crayons, notebooks, and paper, etc., must cost less than $10 per item. For clothing, footwear, wallets, book bags and accessories, the price cap is $50 per item. The rules are strict. If you buy a pair of shoes for $50.99, for instance, you'll be taxed on the whole amount.

The state has compiled a detailed list of items that qualify for the exemption that many stores will make available to customers on site. Anyone can reap the savings, too, making the back-to-school event popular among consumers in general.

**WIN-WIN DEAL**

The tax break this year is expected to save consumers $32.1 million in state and $7.2 million in local taxes, which means less is pouring into government coffers.

Bill Herrle, vice president of governmental affairs for the Florida Retail Federation, disagrees the holiday will cost state and local governments. "Even though the state puts a price tag on it as a matter of accounting, we contend[2] that it results in a lot of economic activity where additional money is spent on taxable items. It's a win for consumers, for retailers because if they plan and prepare it can be good business, and we believe it's a windfall[3] for the state."

*Miami Herald*, July 21, 2006

1. *knock off*: faire une remise
2. *contend*: prétendre
3. *windfall*: aubaine, manne

## Info

***Broward county***
A county located in Florida. Its county seat is Fort Lauderdale. It is one of three counties that comprise the South Florida metropolitan area.

***Miami-Dade county***
A county located in the southeastern part of Florida. Its county seat is Miami. It is one of three counties that comprise the South Florida metropolitan area.

## References

You can find relevant information by reading various pages in your book and memorising a few facts and ideas.

→ **Consumers, p. 70**
→ **Marketing, p. 87**
→ **Distribution, p. 130**

ACTIVITY **Practise giving an account of this article.**

## Introduction

You should explain where the article comes from, when it was published and what it is about.
→Tools 4, p. 236

This article comes from the *Miami Herald*, a daily published in Florida, in July 2006, just before an annual tax break on school-related material. It explains how the tax break works in Florida and details the benefits everyone can draw from this operation, whether they are consumers, retailers or the state. The headline of the article plays on "non taxing", which is related to taxes, but also means "not hard".

## Development

Once you have understood the article, organise your ideas into two or three different parts, using set phrases and link-words. →Tools 4, p. 236

1. Definition of the tax break in Florida
2. Strict rules
3. A win-win situation

You should also use the information given in *Info* and what you have learnt, for example by referring to the various pages indicated in *References*.

### 1. Definition of the tax break in Florida

• The tax break occurs every year at the end of July and it lasts a week, right when many people are shopping for their back-to-school supplies as students go back to school in mid-August. It concerns the whole state of Florida.
• The law makes it compulsory for shops to cut the state and local sales tax on all school-related purchases, allowing consumers to enjoy cheaper prices. The tax ranges from 6 to 7%.
• The purchases can be clothing, shoes, books, supplies such as pencils, notebooks, etc.

### 2. Strict rules

The tax break obeys very precise, strict rules.
• **The price of purchases**: The price of each item is limited to a certain amount: $10 per item for cheaper supplies, such as pens, while more expensive items such as clothing or bags can't cost more than $50 per item.
These rules are very strict, meaning that the people who buy a pair of shoes for $50.99 are taxed on the whole amount and not just on the 99 cents over the limit.
• **The items concerned**: Customers know precisely whether what they want to buy is affected or not, since the state has made a list of the items which can be bought with the tax break. The list can be found in stores.
• **The shoppers concerned**: The tax break is not limited to a special category of consumers, such as people with lower incomes or large families.

### 3. A win-win situation

• **For consumers**: This event enables shoppers to profit from special prices at a time when most families are short of money. In 2006, consumers should have saved nearly $40m in taxes – both state and local – and this has made the measures very popular. A parent is quoted as having spent around $1,200 last year for her son, which means she must have saved quite a lot on those items with a 6-7% discount.
• **For retailers**: The tax break makes shopping very attractive for consumers who go shopping in all sorts of outlets, simple shops, shopping centres or office supply chains such as Home Depot. The key element for retailers is they have to plan and stock the items that shoppers will want to buy.
• **For the state**: Of course the tax break means less money goes to the state and some people criticise it.
However, it generates a lot of economic activity. While they are doing their back-to-school shopping, people also buy other items, which are taxable.

## Conclusion

You should sum up the main ideas and try to open out in a new direction.

This article shows how special offers, even when they are generated by the state, can draw customers to the stores and enable all the players – consumers, retailers and the state – to benefit from the situation. At the present time, a lot of consumers have become money-conscious and they often look for a good quality-price ratio.

## Branching out

Now, you should move away from the article and develop more ideas. The following questions can help you.

**1** Are discounts a good way to attract consumers? Why/why not?

**2** What other sort of offers can attract consumers?

## Case study: a focus group

A focus group is a group of 6 to 12 people who are selected to study a product they use (or could use). Companies use this popular tool before launching a new product in order to test attitudes, desires, expectations and reactions. A moderator can help the discussions remain centred on the product.

Work in groups of 6 people plus one moderator.
Task: Analyse your English book, using the following criteria.

1. **Aspect:** colour, size, weight, cover
2. **Convenience:**
   * Table of contents
   * Chapters, different types of pages
   * Finding specific information is rather/very/extremely... easy/difficult
3. **Contents:**
   * Level (quite/very/too... easy/difficult)
   * Presence of vocabulary
   * Not enough... / too much... (articles, recorded material, links to the internet, activities, etc.)
   * Missing elements

Then draw up a synthesis, and report to the class.

## PERSONAL TASK

**Simple tools to boost customer loyalty on a website**

Match the titles and the contents. Then choose which tools you would use and prepare an oral presentation.

**1.** Coupons & Promotions
**2.** Daily Comics & Quotes
**3.** Daily Tips
**4.** Contests
**5.** Weather reports
**6.** Customer testimonials or advice

**a.** They can range from "Name our new product" to "Guess the number of site visitors". Prizes can be used for additional promotion. It's a great way to attract new customers.

**b.** If they appear on the main page of your web site and are updated daily, they make it "fun" to visit.

**c.** Solutions to problems and other kinds of advice related to your product or service area.

**d.** They can be printed and redeemed in person at a shop and are a simple way to increase customer traffic.

**e.** This easily accessible resource is highly popular for small businesses located in a particular area.

**f.** They will make customers feel as if you are giving them free expert "outside world" advice.

Answers: 1d, 2b, 3f, 4a, 5e, 6c

# IN THIS UNIT...

- Companies: US Airways, Benetton...
- Learn about Adbusters, direct marketing & junk food
- Visit an online exhibition
- Compare two advertisements

# 6

## Communication

### → Before you START

*In brief:* **Where to advertise**
*Front page:* **Advertisements for homosexuals**

## What is the hidden message in this advertisement?

### Words

- **Nouns:** brand, advertisement, weight, ingredients, information
- **Adjectives:** colourful, funny, eye-catching, mysterious
- **Phrases:** at first sight

### LISTENING PRACTICE

CD TRACK 31

Listen to the recording.
**1.** What are the people talking about?
**2.** Explain their opinions.

# Same sex ads make sense (and dollars)

There are about 3.6 million gays in Britain: that's around 6% of the population. But they rake in an incredible $130bn per annum, a recent survey claims. Openly gay men in full-time jobs are making $18,000 p.a. above the national average, with lesbians not far behind ($12,000 p.a.). The situation in France is very similar.

Jon Howard, strategy director of London ad agency Quiet Storm, reckons gays are on average "more affluent, more interested in styles and brands, and travel more" than their straight counterparts. So it makes sense for admen to think pink[1]. It makes dollars too. "This is an important market [with] good levels of disposable income," says a British Airways representative whose company has recently placed ads in print and online in the gay media[2].

What's more, more than one-third of British gays and lesbians admit that tailored advertising in gay media will contribute to their loyalty to a brand, the 2006 survey found. According to the commercial director at QSoft Consulting, which operates gay media sites online, gay consumers react kindly to companies "speaking to a part of their identity that is usually ignored."

That advertising in gay-oriented outlets is so widespread is hardly surprising. Beverage companies like Anheuser-Busch, holiday firms including Travelocity and automakers such as Ford helped nudge[3] advertising spend in the US gay and lesbian press to $212 million last year, a 25% rise since 2003. Europe's markets might be more modest, but they are catching up fast.

The risk of alienating other consumers by targeting the same-sex market cannot however be ignored. The American Family Association (AFA) this year reinstated a boycott on Ford cars, protesting against the firm's ads in US gay media. A director at AFA condemns Ford's ads for "giving credit to [homosexuality] as being a normal lifestyle." The UK Advertising Standards Authority (ASA) received 19 complaints that the gay kiss featured in Dolce & Gabbana's TV spot was unacceptable.

*San Francisco Gazette,* August 7, 2006

1. *pink*: (ici) équivalent de *gay*
2. *nudge* : pousser

CD TRACK 35

## Info

***Advertising Standards Authority (ASA)***
The independent British organisation of the advertising industry, the ASA cannot enforce legislation. Its purpose is to ensure that advertising is "legal, decent, honest and truthful". →***Key data*, p. 102**

***American Family Association (AFA)***
Founded by a reverend in 1977. Its purpose is "to promote traditional family values." It publishes articles which oppose abortion, homosexuality and pornography while promoting "clean" entertainment.

## Headlines

**1** What does "same sex" mean? Can you imagine why the journalist used this expression?

**2** Make a hypothesis about the contents of the article.

## Work on words

### 1 | Find their equivalents in English

**§1** empocher – travail à temps plein – moyenne
**§2** riche – marque – homologue – annonceur – revenu – publicité – imprimé – en ligne
**§3** loyauté – consommateur – ne tenir aucun compte de
**§4** débouché – répandu – dépenses – rattraper
**§5** cibler – plainte – figurer

### 2 | Find their synonyms

**§1** per year – study (N) – make money
**§2** heterosexual
**§3** adapt
**§4** drink (N)

## The key points of the article

### 1 Read §1

**a.** Number of British homosexuals and proportion of the population.
**b.** Estimated money they make: what's the difference compared to heterosexual men?
**c.** The situation among women.
**d.** Is Britain alone in this case?

■ Complete this summary of **§1** with: *advertisers – average – earn – target*.
**...** find it profitable to **...** homosexuals as they **...** more money than the national **...**.

### 2 Read §2 and §3

**a.** A company that targeted homosexuals.
**b.** Three differences between the heterosexual and the homosexual markets.
**c.** Advantages for companies to target gays.

### 3 Read §4 and §5

**a.** Examples of US firms targeting homosexuals.
**b.** Money spent on advertising in the gay press in 2005. Compare with 2003.
**c.** Main risk of homosexual advertising.
**d.** Give 2 examples of reactions against gay advertising (one in the US, one in the UK).

## Branching out

**1** Are shocking campaigns good for a brand? Why/Why not? → *Key data*, **p. 102**
**2** Why do companies find it necessary to develop customer loyalty? → *Key data*, **p. 88**

## {Methods}

### ■ Speaking practice

**1 Read figures aloud.** **→ Tools 10, p. 243**
Read **§1** aloud. If necessary, start by writing the following figures down.
**a.** about 3.6 million
**b.** around 6% of the population
**c.** an incredible $130bn per annum
**d.** $18,000 p.a.
**e.** $12,000 p.a.

**2 Money, money**
Get used to dollars and pounds. Change all the money data into euros.

**3 Prepare an oral introduction.**
• Identify the source.
• Explain what the article is about (who, what, where, when).

### ■ Writing practice

**1 Translate §1 into French.**

**2 Write an account of this article in English (around 140 words).**
Group the information you have about the target and the various campaigns mentioned. Don't forget to write an introduction and a conclusion.
**→ Tools 4, p. 236**

## Language

• ... *a British Airways representative* ***whose*** *company has recently placed ads in print and online in the gay media.*
• *This is a part of their identity* ***that*** *is usually ignored.*
• *QSoft Consulting,* ***which*** *operates gay media sites online, has a different opinion.*

Les pronoms relatifs sont ***who, which, whose, that*** et **Ø**. (Le pronom ***whom*** est rare, et on utilise plutôt ***that*** ou **Ø**.)
• Sujet du verbe de la relative : ***who*** (antécédents humains), ***which*** (non humains)
• Complément du verbe de la relative : ***which*** (non humains), ***that*** (humains et non humains)
• Expression de la possession (dont) : ***whose*** (humains ou non)

Il existe également un relatif **Ø** qui peut avoir toutes les fonctions sauf celle de sujet.
Certaines relatives apportent une indication supplémentaire : voir le 3e exemple.

**Translate into English**
**1.** Ce site, qui a été ouvert il y a deux ans, cible les homosexuels qui travaillent à temps plein.
**2.** C'est la publicité la plus choquante que j'ai vue depuis des années.
**3.** Ce sont des consommateurs dont le pouvoir d'achat est plus élevé que la moyenne.
**4.** Les jeunes, qui voyagent davantage que leurs parents, sont aussi plus soucieux des marques.

**Since its birth at the end of the 19th century, advertising has been the main channel for companies to communicate with their customers and to promote their products or brands.**

## 1-Definitions

Since the 1960s (even before in the USA), western societies have been evolving in a mass-market context. Mass marketing resorts to advertising campaigns in order to reach the greatest number of potential customers.
Institutional campaigns are launched by state-owned firms or institutions such as the Army.

### The making of a campaign

Advertising campaigns are designed by advertisers who work in advertising agencies. Some are huge and reputed in the entire advertising world: WPP Group ($48.055bn), Publicis: $34.365bn, Havas ($8.775bn).

### The qualities of an advertising campaign

Advertising campaigns should:
- inform consumers about a new product, or range of products,
- create brand awareness,
- create or improve the companies' image,
- promote the values of the companies,
- convince customers to buy goods or services.

### The rules of visual advertising

- A visual ad must be eye-catching in order to attract attention.
- The bodycopy should be short and easy to read.
- The logo and the slogan should be visible, but not necessarily big or conspicuous.
- The catchphrase should be short, preferably funny or teasing, and immediately visible.

However, advertisers have sometimes turned to much more sophisticated, and sometimes controversial communication techniques. →**Chapter 5, Marketing, *Landmark*, p. 87**

## 2-The various media

### Traditional advertising media

Companies can buy radio or TV time. Peak hours, or prime time, are very expensive. The most expensive TV commercial in history was by Apple computer. Shown during the 1984 Super Bowl it cost $600,000 to produce and $1m to broadcast. As a result, thousands of Americans bought Apple computers. For the 2006 Football World Cup, brands paid €957m to air their ads.

Companies can also:
- buy advertising space in newspapers,
- put up posters and billboards in city streets, on buses, etc.
- send advertising leaflets by mail or hand them out at specific places (outside schools or cinemas, etc.),
- use coupons and vouchers on food products, toiletries, etc.

**Coke and Santa**
When Coca-Cola launched its first advertising campaigns in the 1930s featuring a Santa Claus dressed in red with a white beard, the two colours represented one of the first attempts at creating brand awareness.
→**Chapter 7, Brands, *Landmark*, p. 119**

Coke: the world's largest poster (Poland)

These classical advertising media have advantages and drawbacks.
• They reach a massive audience but are expensive.
• Estimating the response rate is very difficult.
• People have been bombarded with so many advertisements that they tend to ignore, if not "zap" them, especially on TV. Special devices have been created so that programs can be recorded without the ads interrupting them every 15 minutes (in the USA).
• Advertising encourages competition, which should help reduce prices. However, mobile phone providers agree to share the market instead of allowing competition to play its regulating role.
• Most TV channels, radio stations and newspapers around the world are subsidized by advertising which helps them exist.
• Advertising also creates jobs.

### The new advertising media

• Advertisers look for new places to put their ads, for example eggs, or sickness bags in airplanes. →*In brief*, p. 96
• Endorsement. →Chapter 7, Brands
• Internet advertising has seen a tremendous boost over the last decade. Most websites host numerous advertising banners. The money generated by advertising makes the free access of millions of internet surfers possible: this is the case for the most famous Internet search engines such as Google, Yahoo, etc. →Chapter 10, New Technologies, *Landmark*, p. 163
• Pop-up ads: unsolicited ads pop up on some websites. They are so intrusive that they are impossible to ignore, and sometimes difficult to get rid of – this is called "pop-up hell".
• People are bombarded with e-mails, called junk mail or spam, i.e. unsolicited messages that typically advertise medicines and software. A lot of anti-spam software has been generated.
• The rise of the mobile phone generation has pushed marketers to use this new media to target the 15-25 age group, the most liable to respond to customized advertising. Mobile phone providers make enormous profits by encouraging their clients to send SMS, to dial a special number in order to win gifts or to download their favourite games or tunes.
→Chapter 10, New technologies

### Indirect advertising

There are several forms of indirect advertising.
• Targeting an audience that won't buy the goods directly.
Ads may target children who then act as purchase influencers with their parents or other adults. The German upscale car maker BMW launched a campaign featuring children for its 5 Series models, with the following catch phrase: "Just impress his friends". →Chapter 4, Consumers
• Packaging
Packaging can extend brand awareness by being user-friendly and attractive. Special efforts are made for food products targeting children: most cereal brands feature cute animals, or popular children's characters, and sometimes include a freebie.
→Chapter 5, Marketing
• Sponsoring
Sports events, such as the Super Bowl or the World Football Cup can bring added value to a brand by making the compan-

Inflatable Budweiser on a Florida beach

ies' logos always visible. The 2006 Football Cup was sponsored (among others) by Nike, Adidas, Coca Cola, Deutsche Telekom, McDonald's, Philips, Toshiba, Yahoo, Hyundai, Gillette, etc., each paying an average amount of €26m.

• Product placement

It consists of showing a branded product in a movie or TV show and now video games, in order to reinforce brand awareness in the consumers' minds.

## 3-Special issues

### The rules of the game

Laws regulate advertising. They vary according to the country. In France advertising for tobacco has been banned since 1991 with the Loi Evin. Ads for alcohol are banned on TV and on the radio, and must obey strict rules on billboards and in the press, including a warning against the dangers of alcohol.

### Advertising and ethics

Advertising watchdogs – the BVP in France, the ASA (Advertising Standards Authority) in Britain, The Federal Trade Commission (FTC) in the US – can decide whether an ad is ethically correct or not. Ads which are considered sexist, or offensive towards religions, cultures or races are usually withdrawn. Recently, ads targeting gays have upset the American Family Association, which organized a boycott on Ford vehicles. → ***Front page,* p. 98**

Consumer pressure groups have been fighting in various countries to ban advertising targeting children. In Sweden and Greece, laws have been passed banning ads for children on TV.

### Awareness campaigns

Communication techniques are also used to launch awareness campaigns whose goal is to raise people's awareness on topical issues. These campaigns do not sell products and often resort to shock tactics to attract the public's attention.

• Many NGOs (non governmental organizations) try to appeal to public generosity. The most frequently publicised issues are hunger, AIDS, war victims, refugees and natural disasters.

• Other campaigns aim at deterring driving under the influence, smoking, having unsafe sex, etc.

**Unwanted ads**

The French clothes brand "La City" used ads which featured naked women crawling on all fours next to sheep, which was considered degrading for the women. An ad for fashion designers "Marithé et François Girbaud" featured Christ's Last Supper, generating complaints from the Catholic Church.

**A doll with a plastic card**

At the end of the 1990s, American toy giant Mattel launched a shopping Barbie doll which came equipped with a miniature Mastercard. It was eventually withdrawn from the store shelves thanks to consumer pressure groups which considered that the card company was trying to brainwash children into becoming the Mastercard customers of the future.

## Question time

1 Make a brief summary of the role of advertising.
2 List four different advertising media. Which is the most expensive and why?
3 Why are advertisers more and more interested in the Internet?
4 What are the basic rules of advertising?
5 Explain how and why the firm Coca-Cola was successful in creating brand awareness?
6 What is the role played by advertising watchdogs?
7 Why is advertising aimed at children a controversial issue?
8 Give examples of indirect advertising.
9 Explain the difference between an advertising campaign and an awareness campaign.

LANDMARK

# An advertising revolution

**Oliviero Toscani, who became famous for his provocative, controversial Benetton ads, has revolutionized the advertising world.**

## United Colors

The Benettons opened their first store in Italy in 1965 and in France the following year to sell their casual clothing line. What made the company famous is its association with photographer Oliviero Toscani and the Eldorado advertising agency, who used the multi-racial theme before it became fashionable. The agency's director thought that fashion advertising was always the same; so they decided to "start out with the notion of colour. By definition, Benetton means colours. So, we showed a group, made up of people with different coloured skin. It was fantastic to show the products in such a new and simple way."

**1984** Six festive, coloured posters of adults and six of kids were used.

**1985** The only body copy that remained on the posters was "United Colors of Benetton".

## Values instead of products

**1986** Oliviero Toscani declared, "I am not here to sell pullovers, but to promote an image." The pullovers gradually disappeared from the advertisements. The posters played with the idea of the whole world as a globe, for instance two little black boys united by a globe and a chain with the peace symbol. Some pairs attracted more attention, like Israel and Germany, Iran and Iraq, Israelis and Arabs, each time united by a globe. Benetton chose to replace the product with one message: all colours are equal, just as all men are equal. The brand thus addressed individuals rather than customers, with a set of common values.

## Shock tactics

**1989** The "United Colors of Benetton" campaign showed a black hand and a white hand linked by a handcuff, or a black woman breast-feeding a white baby. The pictures symbolised the respect of differences together with a desire for communication. However, the campaigns, which attracted a lot of attention and provoked enormous hype in the press, also started generating negative reactions. Posters then featured multi-coloured condoms, or rows of crosses in an American cemetery, or a newborn baby, still with its umbilical cord and covered in blood, or a priest kissing a nun on the lips... All of them were considered images aiming at nothing but shock.

## Exploiting pain to sell sweaters?

**1992** Toscani went even further and showed difficult, painful subjects, such as an AIDS victim in hospital with his family at his bedside, or Albanian refugees jumping off a sinking ship. The reaction to these real-life photos was sometimes strong. Many publications in several countries refused to print the campaign. Benetton was accused of exploiting pain to get more famous. Angry customers started boycotting the stores.

**1993** A new campaign showed close-ups of various parts of the body tattooed with the abbreviation "H.I.V. positive" The ink evoked stamps on meat about to be commercialised, or worse, numbers tattooed by Nazis on camp prisoners. The general public's impression was that of bodies being marked off and excluded, leading to even more controversy about the company's campaigns.

**2000** Benetton's last campaign with Toscani showed death-sentence prisoners in American jails. Many TV programmes tackled the subject of the death penalty.

Benetton's controversial advertisements and shock tactics have drawn public attention to universal themes, thus focusing on the advertisers' role in our society. Should they restrict themselves to the promotion of a product, or should they address current issues to raise public awareness?

**Online t@sk**

Visit Benetton's website to read their views on their advertising campaigns and look at all the posters on press.benettongroup.com/ben_en/about/campaigns/list/.
Choose one and report to the class.

## ADS, ADVERTISEMENTS, ADVERTISING AND COMPOUNDS

**ad/advert/advertisement:** pub/publicité
**advergaming:** publicité dans les jeux vidéo
**advertainment:** publicité télévisuelle divertissante
**advertise:** faire (de) la publicité
**advertiser:** annonceur
**advertising:** la publicité
**advertising agency:** agence de publicité
**advertising blitz :** matraquage publicitaire
**advertising campaign:** campagne de publicité
**advertising media:** supports de publicité, média
**advertising space:** espace publicitaire
**advertising spend:** dépenses de publicité, budget publicitaire
**advertising watchdog:** organisme de surveillance de la publicité
**customized advertising:** publicité sur mesure
**comparative advertising:** publicité comparative
**indirect advertising:** publicité indirecte
**misleading advertising:** publicité mensongère

**achieve:** réussir à, parvenir à
**affluent:** riche, à l'aise
**aimed at:** en direction de, qui cible
**alienate:** aliéner
**appeal to:** faire appel à, séduire
**attempt:** tentative
**attract:** attirer
**audience:** public
**awareness campaign:** campagne de sensibilisation
**ban:** (V) interdire ; (N) interdiction
**behaviour:** comportement
**billboard:** panneau d'affichage
**body copy:** texte (dans une publicité)
**brainwash:** faire un lavage de cerveau
**catchphrase:** accroche
**channel:** canal
**close-up:** gros plan
**commercial:** spot publicitaire (radio ou télévision)
**compete (with):** concurrencer
**competition:** concurrence ; concours
**complaint:** plainte
**conspicuous:** visible
**content:** contenu
**convince:** convaincre
**coupon:** coupon
**deceive:** tromper
**design:** (V) concevoir ; (N) conception
**deter from:** dissuader, décourager
**device:** dispositif, moyen, procédé
**dial:** composer un numéro (téléphone)
**download:** téléchargement
**efficient:** efficace
**endorsement:** recommandation publicitaire
**endorser:** personne célèbre qui fait de la publicité pour
**ensure:** s'assurer
**ethics:** morale
**exhibition:** exposition, salon
**exploit:** exploiter
**eye-catching:** accrocheur
**fad:** engouement, mode
**feature *(V)*:** figurer, faire figurer
**foster:** générer, engendrer
**free:** gratuit
**gap:** différence, écart
**genuine:** authentique
**gift:** cadeau
**hand out:** distribuer
**host:** accueillir
**hype:** battage médiatique
**infomercial:** publicité informative
**in print:** imprimé
**industry:** secteur
**inform:** informer
**launch:** lancer
**layout:** disposition, maquette
**leaflet:** prospectus, dépliant
**liable to:** susceptible de
**lifestyle:** style de vie
**listener:** auditeur
**logo:** logo
**long-term:** à long terme
**loyalty:** loyauté, fidélité
**mail:** poste
**offensive:** choquant
**online:** en ligne
**pack:** paquet, emballage
**packaging:** emballage
**peak hour:** heure de pointe
**pocket *(V)*:** empocher
**popular:** populaire, qui a du succès
**poster:** affiche
**praise:** louer, féliciter
**pressure group:** groupe de pression
**prime time:** heures de grande écoute
**print:** imprimer
**promote:** promouvoir
**provocative:** provocant
**publicize:** rendre public
**purpose:** objectif
**range:** gamme, variété
**reach:** atteindre
**realise:** se rendre compte
**regulate:** réglementer
**relationship:** relation
**resort to:** recourir à
**response rate:** taux de réponse
**rule:** règle
**search engine:** moteur de recherche
**share:** partager
**shock tactics:** tactique destinée à choquer
**skyrocket:** grimper en flèche
**software:** logiciel
**spam:** courriel indésirable
**sponsor:** sponsoriser
**spread (spread, spread):** répandre
**standard:** norme
**state-owned:** d'état
**straight:** hétérosexuel
**subsidise:** subventionner
**successful:** qui a du succès
**supplier:** fournisseur
**survey:** sondage
**tailored:** sur mesure
**target:** cibler
**teasing:** accrocheur
**trick:** truc, astuce
**turn off:** rebuter
**TV viewer:** téléspectateur
**value:** valeur
**voucher:** bon
**win:** gagner
**withdraw:** retirer

"NOT MUCH · ROGER AND I ARE JUST SITTING AROUND, LETTING OURSELVES BE TARGETED BY ADVERTISERS."

## Advertisements

**1.** Study the two advertisements which were both launched by the clothes company Benetton. Describe each of them as precisely as you can. →**Tools 12, p. 245**

**2.** Compare them in terms of what they show/don't show. You can use ***Landmark*** p. 103 to help.

**3.** Which one is the most successful in your opinion? Explain why.

## Online tasks

### Presenting an organisation: Adbuster

**1.** Go to **adbusters.org/home/**. Introduce Adbusters. Look at their name: what is it made of? What does it stand for?

**2.** Visit the poster shop on **https://secure.adbusters.org/orders/posters/**. Choose one poster from Joe Chemo, the American flag and Prozac. Study it in detail and give a ten-minute oral presentation focusing on the way Adbusters uses traditional advertising methods to make its point. →**Tools 12, p. 245**

### Online advertising exhibitions

Visit **www.eisnermuseum.org/exhibits/online.shtm#** and choose an online exhibition.
Study it in detail and report to the class.

# Football Calls, and Reebok Responds

Reebok is hoping that six top National Football League players will help it regain its footing in the United States sporting goods market.

It will introduce a major branding campaign in September that will feature Peyton Manning, quarterback of the Indianapolis Colts; Vince Young, quarterback of the Tennessee Titans and the hero of the last Rose Bowl, and four more famous players.

The campaign, Reebok's first major marketing push since the Adidas takeover, is an extension of the acclaimed "I Am What I Am" campaign, which was introduced in February 2005 and featured sports and entertainment celebrities like Jay-Z. That campaign helped increase sales by 11 percent during that quarter.

The commercials will be 30 seconds long and were directed by Errol Morris, a long-time maker of commercials and documentaries who has worked previously with Adidas and Nike, and who won an Academy Award for "The Fog of War" in 2004, about Robert McNamara and the Vietnam War.

Reebok has a 10-year contract with the N.F.L., dating from the 2002 football season, to be the exclusive supplier of league-licensed apparel. Howe Burch, Reebok's vice president for marketing for North America, said the company's wants to "re-emphasize its performance heritage and we have an asset in our relationship with the N.F.L." It is the ultimate performance authenticator when you provide uniforms and performance apparel to 1,800 players. We really want to capitalize on our affiliation with the N.F.L. and elevate the entire Reebok brand."

Reebok declined to give the cost of the campaign, saying only that it would be a "very significant investment." According to TNS Media Intelligence, Reebok spent $52 million on advertising last year, the most since 2002, when its spending was $59 million.

A retail analyst praised the new advertising's focus on performance rather than lifestyle to get away from its former emphasis on music-inspired efforts and to emphasize its performance-related products. "Reebok was too susceptible to fashion fads[1]. The popularity of music-inspired endorsers with kids is only good as long as they're publishing songs, and Jay-Z is not recording music anymore."

Jane L. Levere, *The New York Times*, July 24, 2006

1. *fad*: engouement, mode

## Info

***National Football League***
Largest professional US football league.

***Indianapolis Colts, Tennessee Titans***
US football teams

***Rose Bowl***
The American football competition between the two best university teams.

***Jay-Z***
US hip-hop artist who supposedly retired in 2004.

***Academy Award***
The most famous film awards in the US.

***Robert McNamara***
Secretary of Defense during the Vietnam War period (1961-68).

***Adidas takeover***
In 2005, Adidas took over Reebok for $3.8bn. This made Adidas N°2 athletic shoemaker in the world behind Nike.

## References

You can find relevant information by reading various pages in your book and memorising a few facts and ideas.

→ **Companies, p. 28**
→ **Communication, p. 100**
→ **Brands, p. 116**

**ACTIVITY** **Practise giving an account of this article.**

## Introduction

You should explain where the article comes from, when it was published and what it is about. →Tools 4, p. 236

This article appeared in *The New York Times* in July 2006. It tackles a new advertising campaign by Reebok to publicise its brand name, including commercials starring football stars, to come back into the US sporting goods market.

## Development

Once you have understood the article, organise your ideas into two or three different parts, using set phrases and link-words. →Tools 4, p. 236

1. The new campaign
2. Reasons for the new campaign

You should also use the information given in *Info* and what you have learnt, for example by referring to the various pages indicated in *References*.

### 1. The new campaign

• **Timing of the campaign**: It was launched in September 2006, at the beginning of a new season.

• **Type of campaign**: The campaign consists of 30-second commercials. The company has chosen to make quality commercials, directed by a renowned film-maker. The man had already worked with sports companies Adidas and Nike; he also won an Academy Award for "The Fog of War" in 2004, about Robert McNamara and the Vietnam War.
The commercials star 8 famous NFL players, among whom Vince Young, who was the hero of the 2005 Rose Bowl, a major competition for American football.
The campaign is an extension of the famous "I Am What I Am" campaign, which was introduced in February 2005 and featured sports and entertainment celebrities such as Jay-Z, the famous rapper.

• **Cost of campaign**: The company refused to make the cost of the campaign public. However, it declared that it would be a "very significant investment." Reebok spent $52 million on advertising in 2005, the most since 2002, when it had spent $59 million.

### 2. Reasons for the new campaign

• It is the first big campaign since the company was taken over by Adidas in 2005.

• **A foothold on the market**: Reebok is launching the campaign so as to regain a foothold in the US sporting goods market. The previous campaign which started in February 2005 helped increase sales by 11 percent at the time.

• **Back to sports**: The company is moving from entertainment celebrities such as Jay-Z to using sports stars only. In fact, Reebok has had a 10-year contract with the NFL since the 2002 football season. Under the contract, Reebok is the exclusive supplier of league-licensed sportswear. Having a contract with a major sports player such as the NFL with its 1,800 players is an asset for Reebok. Therefore it is only logical for Reebok to go back to basics, so to say, by featuring sports stars, and not singers in its advertising campaigns. Analysts have welcomed the change, since Reebok risked tarnishing its sports brand by associating it with passing fads such as rappers: one year after the previous campaign, Jay-Z had retired.

## Conclusion

You should sum up the main ideas and try to open out in a new direction.

This article describes a new advertising campaign in the very competitive world of sports companies. It explains that choosing the right commercials for the right business is essential. However, it also shows that there may be risks when they choose people to endorse their brand. As a matter of fact, stars can change, and athletes can fail or commit doping offences for example. There have been numerous examples of brands suffering because they had chosen the wrong person who had a negative impact on the brand image. This goes to show that even though choosing someone famous to represent a company is an attractive strategy, it is also a very risky business.

## Branching out

Now, you should move away from the article and develop more ideas. The following questions can help you.

**1** What risks do companies run when they have their brand endorsed by stars or athletes?

**2** How can companies make their brands better known to the public?

## 5. Marketing

# Motorola's new phone models

*The world No. 2 mobile phone maker's latest products, including the KRZR, are smaller than the best-selling RAZR.*

Motorola Inc., the world's second-biggest maker of mobile phones, is launching several new handsets. The new KRZR and the RIZR will be narrower than the popular RAZR.

For the past two years, Motorola has based a range of new mobile phone models around the RAZR, which has helped the company modernise its brand. Motorola has sold about 50 million RAZR phones since they were first launched in late 2004 and the manufacturer hopes the momentum of the RAZR can be kept with new models inspired by its style and four-letter name. Competitors such as Samsung have followed suit with their own small handsets.

Motorola's latest handsets include models designed for high-speed mobile internet browsing and dedicated buttons for cameras and music players as well as a new sliding format. Although the KRZR flips open like the RAZR, it is slightly thicker because it offers a camera and space for storage for up to 500 songs. Motorola's chief executive said Motorola's aim is to sell 500 million RAZR units eventually.

The KRZR is made of magnesium, polished chrome and hardened glass, with a reflective surface that comes in two colours: grey and blue. It should be available worldwide by the end of 2006. Most mobile phone providers around the world have shown interest in the product and China Mobile, the world's number one by subscribers, has already agreed to sell the phone.

The narrower KRZR phone should help the company attract new customers, including women, said an executive in Motorola's handset division, explaining that it fits better than the RAZR for people with smaller hands, especially Asian customers and ladies.

The KRZR should sell at the bottom of the upmarket price range. No specific figures have been revealed so far. Analysts describe phones that sell for more than $250 as top of the range, and $125-to-$250 phones as mid-range. The KRZR will be available for networks running on GSM, the dominant global wireless standard, and CDMA, a popular phone standard in the United States and parts of Asia.

*British News*, July 28, 2006

### Compréhension

**1.** **Rédigez en français un résumé de ce document. (130 mots, +/– 10%)**
**2.** **Traduisez le titre, le sous-titre et le deuxième paragraphe de l'article.**

### Expression

**Répondez en anglais aux questions suivantes.**

1 To what extent can Motorola's new model target new customers? (100 words)

2 Is it necessary for manufacturers to offer – and for customers to buy – new models all the time? Why/Why not? (150 words)

(N.B. L'usage du dictionnaire bilingue est autorisé.)

## 6. Communication

# Pot Noodle ad 'not racist'

An ad for Pot Noodle featuring Welsh "miners" digging for noodles[1] has escaped a ban from the advertising watchdog, despite 81 complaints that it was offensive and racist towards the Welsh.

The £5m "Miners" ad, by agency Mother, pays tongue-in-cheek[2] homage to the tradition of coal mining in Wales. Viewers claim the ad is disrespectful and insensitive to Welsh miners who work in difficult conditions where people have lost their lives.

The ad shows a group of miners walking across a field, while a voiceover says: "This is Crumlin, jewel of the Welsh empire, for beneath[3] these hills lies fuel, not coal or oil, but pure Pot Noodle."

Mother said the ads had been inspired by their local factory in Crumli, which employs a number of former miners. The agency said it had worked with them and the National Coal Mining Museum to create the ad. Welsh people made up 98% of the cast and local reaction to the ad, according to the agency, had been positive.

The Advertising Standards Authority ruled the campaign did not breach its regulations and was not "derogatory", "racist" or "offensive" toward the Welsh.

Mark Sweney, *The Guardian*, July 26, 2006

1. *noodles*: nouilles
2. *tongue-in-cheek*: ironique
3. *beneath*: sous

# Flora ad banned over misleading health claims

A campaign for Flora margarine has been criticised by the advertising watchdog over health claims.

The Unilever-owned product featured in a poster and magazine campaign showing two cobs of corn. Under the first ran the line "Healthy", and under the second, which was covered in Flora, the line "Healthier".

Complainants argued that the ad was misleading because they did not believe adding Flora to a vegetable made it healthier than a plain vegetable. Claims made in the text of the ad that Omega 3 and 6 oils found in the product were "heart healthy" were also questioned.

The Advertising Standards Authority consulted a health expert prior to making its ruling. It ruled that while Flora was a healthier alternative to butter, the use of the word "healthier" under the picture of Flora-smothered corn was misleading, and it ordered Unilever not to repeat the claim.

Mark Sweney, *The Guardian*, November 15, 2006

### Compréhension

**1.** Rédigez en français un compte rendu de ces documents. (110 mots, +/- 10 %)
**2.** Traduisez le titre et le premier paragraphe du second article.

### Expression

**Répondez en anglais aux questions suivantes.**

1 What do people complain about regarding ads? (100 words)
2 To what extent is an advertising watchdog necessary? (150 words)

(N.B. L'usage du dictionnaire bilingue est autorisé.)

## Case study: direct marketing

With a small budget, tradeshows and advertising are completely out of the question. But direct marketing with email and snail mail (i.e. traditional mail) can be one of the cheapest yet effective ways of reaching potential customers.

**Study the advantages and disadvantages of email and snail mail and report to the class orally.**

**Email**
- free
- companies use it too much – challenge: breaking through the clutter
- people hate spam

*Possibility: monthly e-newsletter*
- information that's interesting to the audience
- only one "company offer" per newsletter
- logo at the end
- offered by subscription only

**Snail mail**
- much more expensive (postal costs, design costs)
- needs focus (or will end up in the trash 90% of the time)

*Possibility 1: personalized letters*
- research customers that will be interested
- take more time but better response

*Possibility 2: printed company newsletter*
- a few times a year
- product update article, news on events
- no articles about the company Christmas party or Employee of the Month

## PERSONAL TASK

**Match the following ad words to the corresponding definitions.**

1. banner ad
2. pop-up ad
3. vertical banner
4. trick banner
5. pop-under ad
6. button ad
7. skyscraper ad
8. banner blindness

**a.** A banner ad measuring 120 pixels wide and 240 pixels tall
**b.** An online ad, significantly taller than the 120x240 vertical banner
**c.** An ad that displays itself in a new browser window behind the current browser window
**d.** A graphical web advertising unit, typically measuring 468 pixels wide and 60 pixels tall
**e.** A graphical advertising unit, smaller than a banner ad
**f.** A banner ad that attempts to trick people into clicking, often by imitating a system message
**g.** The tendency of web visitors to ignore banner ads, even when banners contain information visitors are seeking
**h.** An ad that displays itself in a new browser window

Answers: 1d, 2h, 3a, 4f, 5c, 6e, 7b, 8g

# IN THIS UNIT...

- Companies: Coca-Cola, AT&T, Google...
- Learn about brand extensions & spoof brands
- Draw logos from memory
- Report on the 5 "best" and 5 "worst" brands

# 7
## Brands

## → Before you START

*In brief:* **New drinks by Coca-Cola**
*Front page:* **Can a brand name be changed easily?**

## Can you identify with this advertisement for Diesel? Why/Why not?

### Words

- **Nouns:** brand, identity, group, clothes, cloning
- **Adjectives:** famous, bizarre, dangerous, funny

### LISTENING PRACTICE

CD TRACK 36

Listen to the recording.

**1.** What are the people talking about?
**2.** Explain their opinions.

# Coke "has got it wrong"

Coke Zero, the latest offering from US soft-drink giant Coca-Cola, has come under attack for failing to adapt to market trends and for potentially diluting the brand.

The no-sugar fizzy drink goes on sale in Britain tomorrow, backed by a £8m marketing budget. The company is billing[1] Coke Zero as its first brand launch since Diet Coke was introduced 22 years ago. Drinks such as Cherry Coke were not brands in their own right, merely "flavour variants", many of them limited editions, it said.

Experts said Coca-Cola was being "far too optimistic" about its new drink. "They are trying to buck[2] a trend that's moving away from carbonated soft drinks. People want fruit juices, water, natural ingredients. And if it does work, it risks encroaching on Diet Coke. It's also just more confusion for the consumer and I think they have got it wrong."

But a Coca-Cola spokeswoman said the drink had a clear audience as it was aimed at men – it has been dubbed "bloke Coke" – instead of the mostly female Diet Coke drinkers. And unlike Diet Coke, it is supposed to taste like regular Coke. "There's a place for all sorts of products and drinks throughout the day, whether that's juice in the morning, a cup of tea, a carbonated soft drink or an energy drink after the gym," she said.

Abigail Townsend, *The Independent*, 9 July 2006

1. *bill*: annoncer
2. *buck*: contrer, se rebiffer contre, (ici), infléchir

CD TRACK 37

## Work on words

### 1 I Find their equivalents in English

**§1** boisson non alcoolisée – ne pas arriver à – diluer
**§2** gazeux, pétillant – en vente – soutenir – marque – lancement – arôme
**§3** gazeux – empiéter sur
**§4** porte-parole – surnommé

### 2 I Find their synonyms

**§1** product – tendency
**§2** launch (V)
**§4** potential customers – intended for – guy – ordinary

## Headlines

**1** Analyse the different elements of the headline. What does the punctuation indicate?

**2** What effect does the headline produce on the reader?

## The key points of the article

### 1 Argument
Read the first paragraph and write down the key-words that sum up the article and explain the headline.

### 2 Coke Zero
**a.** What does "Zero" stand for?
**b.** Budget intended for the launch.
**c.** Reason why the launch is important.
**d.** Difference with Cherry Coke.

### 3 Marketing strategy
**a.** First flaw in the marketing campaign. Look at §1 and find its explanation in §3.
**b.** Second mistake in Coca-Cola strategy. Look at §1 and find its explanation in §3.

### 4 Reaction of the company
**a.** Target of Coke Zero.
**b.** Reason for launching the product.

## {Methods}

### ■ Speaking practice
• *And if it* ***does*** *work, it risks encroaching on Diet Coke.*
The auxiliary *do* is added in this affirmative sentence to show a contrast between what the journalist thinks (*it won't work*) and what may happen (*it will work*). This is called a "contrastive emphasis". The auxiliary (here, *does*) is stressed.

**1 Add an auxiliary to the underlined verbs. Then read the new sentences, paying attention to the stress.**
**a.** The no-sugar fizzy drink <u>goes</u> on sale in Britain tomorrow.
**b.** Experts <u>said</u> Coca-Cola was being "far too optimistic" about its new drink.
**c.** People <u>want</u> fruit juices, water and natural ingredients.
**d.** I <u>think</u> they have got it wrong.

**2 Read the following names aloud and watch out for your pronunciation.**
• Coca-C<u>o</u>la • Coke Z<u>e</u>ro • Ch<u>e</u>rry Coke • D<u>i</u>et Coke

### ■ Writing practice
**1 Link the following expressions with one of the following prompts expressing difference and contrast: *unlike / contrary to – whereas.***
**a.** ... Diet Coke, Coke Zero is supposed to taste like regular Coca-Cola.
**b.** ... Diet Coke, which is aimed at female drinkers, Coke Zero is intended for men.
**c.** Coke Zero is a brand in its own right, ... Cherry Coke was just a "flavour variant".

**2 Prepare a short account in English.**
Use the article and the sentences in part **1** to relate Coca-Cola's new launch.
→Tools 4, p. 236

## Branching out

**1** What is Coca-Cola's strategy to remain the market leader? What are the risks involved? →*Key data*, p. 26

**2** Do you think innovation is still possible in the soft drinks and carbonated drinks market? Why/Why not? →*Landmark*, p. 119

## LISTENING PRACTICE
CD TRACK 38-39

*Eleanor Rigby and John Marcus are talking about a new brand extension.*

### 1 Comprehension
Listen to the recording to find the following information.

**Part 1**
**a.** Name of company.
**b.** John's idea (object, name of company).
**c.** Reason why the extension is necessary.
**d.** Eleanor's reaction.

**Part 2**
**a.** What Eleanor reminds John.
**b.** She says they have to be careful about...
**c.** What example does she give of a past positive brand extension?
**d.** What example does she give of a future positive brand extension?

### 2 Expression
Give an oral account, or write a 100-word paragraph, summing up what you have heard.

# AT&T Bets Its Brand Is More Than Nostalgia

The venerable AT&T brand was in decline a few years ago. Rivals were outflanking the company in the long-distance market; AT&T Wireless was plagued by service problems; and AT&T had entered and exited the cable television business at great expense. These days, executives at AT&T are betting heavily on a brand resurgence. When SBC Communications bought AT&T last year, it promptly took the AT&T name. And if its purchase of BellSouth is approved by the end of the year, AT&T plans to rename that company as well as Cingular, which they jointly own.

The rebranding campaign is no mere nostalgia trip. Despite its warts[1], AT&T is still the most recognizable name in the phone business. Like other telecommunications companies, AT&T is also selling bundles of services and wants to have a single brand for all its products. "The BellSouth and Cingular names are not just at the iconic level globally," the vice president for advertising at AT&T said. "When you have an integrated solution, you need a single brand. It's about one-stop shopping."

The effort to rebrand Cingular and BellSouth will be extensive, and not without risks. BellSouth operates in nine states in the Southeast, where it has 20 million local phone lines. Cingular has 2,300 stores and an industry-leading 57.3 million subscribers.

For all its success, though, Cingular's name will never have the clout of its parent, AT&T, the Coca-Cola of the telecommunications industry. AT&T has been around for more than a century. Colloquially[2] known as Ma Bell, it reminds many older consumers of the days when AT&T was a government-sanctioned monopoly that provided reliable if bland[3] service.

In an era when electronics have turned into indistinguishable and disposable commodities with spotty service reputations, having a brand that represents stability may not be such a bad thing. "In this category, it's less the name and more the quality of service at the right price," said the chairman of an image management company. "Because grandma had an AT&T phone means it is reliable and the company has proven it."

Ken Belson, *The New York Times,* July 21, 2006

1. *wart*: verrue ; défaut, problème
2. *colloquially*: familièrement
3. *if bland*: bien que terne

CD TRACK 40

## Info

***Ma Bell***
Colloquial nickname for AT&T (set up in 1885). "Bell" comes from Alexander Graham Bell, who invented the telephone. He set up the Bell Telephone Company in 1877 which had a monopoly on the US phone market. "Ma" (or mother) Bell also had babies, the "Baby Bells" (regional Bell operating companies), such as BellSouth in the article.

## Work on words

### 1 | Find their equivalents in English

**Headline** parier - marque
**§1** déborder - sans fil - sortir, quitter - cadre - achat - posséder
**§2** unique - emblématique
**§3** être présent - abonné
**§4** puissance - rappeler - consommateur - fiable
**§5** jetable - président

### 2 | Find their synonyms

**§1** suffer from - having spent a lot of money - nowadays - quickly - together
**§2** a lot of - worldwide
**§5** product - irregular

## Headlines

**1** Anticipate the contents of the article from the headline.

**2** Look for a sentence that repeats the words of the headline and read it carefully.

## The key points of the article

### 1 Read §1
**a.** Name of the company.
**b.** Reputation a few years ago.
**c.** Three reasons for that situation.
**d.** What the company wants to do now.
**e.** What happened in 2005.

■ Complete this summary of **§1** with: *bank - brand - competition - investment - rename*
Even if its **...** name was in decline due to **...**, service problems and wrong **...**, AT&T now wants to **...** on it and **...** two smaller companies.

### 2 Read §2 and §3
**a.** Reason why it is important to have one name for all the products.
**b.** Reason for choosing the AT&T brand, and not Cingular or SouthBell.
**c.** Give information about SouthBell and Cingular.
**d.** Explain what the journalist means by "not without risks" (l. 33).

### 3 Read §4 and §5
**a.** What is AT&T compared with? Explain the comparison.
**b.** Reason why the brand is so famous.
**c.** Reason why stability is important in the phone business.
**d.** Go back to **§1** and find an adjective which expresses the same idea of old age and stability.

## Branching out

**1** How can a company build a positive brand image? →*Key data*, p. 117

**2** Do you think brands are more important for certain types of products? Justify your answer. →*Key data*, p. 118

## {Methods}

### ■ Speaking practice

**1 Read figures aloud.** →Tools 10, p. 243
Read **§3** aloud. If necessary, start by writing the following figures down.
Then practise reading the groups of words in parentheses with the figures.
**a.** (sales of about) $66 billion
**b.** 20 million (local phone lines)
**c.** 2,300 (stores)
**d.** (an industry-leading) 57.3 million (subscribers)

**2 Money, money**
Get used to dollars and pounds. Change all the money data into euros.

**3 Prepare an oral introduction.**
• Identify the source.
• Explain what the article is about (who, what, where, when).

### ■ Writing practice

**1 Write a presentation of AT&T.**
Look on the internet to find more information on the company (150 words).

**2 Translate the first two sentences of the article.**
→Tools 6, p. 239

## Language

• *The venerable AT&T brand was in decline a few years **ago**.*
• *AT&T has been around **for** more than a century.*

La préposition ***ago***, qui se place en fin de complément, sert à exprimer un moment précis dans le passé révolu (= « il y a... ») ; l'action est terminée. On l'utilise donc avec le prétérit.
La préposition ***for*** sert à exprimer une durée. On l'utilise avec toutes les formes exprimant passé et futur.
On peut également situer une action dans le temps avec la préposition ***since***, qui indique le point de départ d'une action dans le passé (souvent une date). On l'utilise donc avec le *present perfect*.
Reformulez le second exemple en utilisant *since*.

**Translate into English**
**1.** SBC Communications a acheté AT&T il y a un an, alors que la marque déclinait.
**2.** AT&T a été un monopole pendant plusieurs décennies.
**3.** AT&T fournit des produits et services dans l'industrie téléphonique depuis plus d'un siècle, depuis 1885 exactement.
**4.** Toutes les entreprises ont fusionné sous la marque AT&T depuis 6 mois.

## 1-Definitions

A brand is the name given to a product or a service by the company which puts it on the market. This is a relatively simple definition. However, brands are automatically associated with a product, a service, a company and branding is the most important aspect of a company's marketing strategy. Companies that take their branding lightly in the beginning may suffer in the long run.

Branding means creating a coherent experience of value for customers who come into contact with a product or a service. The brand of a company must stand for something that customers believe will add value. A successful brand will also be one which knows how to establish and maintain brand loyalty. Some consumers are ready to go out of their way to buy the brand they like. →**Chapter 5, Marketing**

### From the 19th to the 21st century

Brands originated in the 19th century. When shipping their products, the factories "branded" the containers used for transport, that is to say they inscribed their logos on them. Campbell soup, Aunt Jemina and Quaker Oats were among the first mass market products to be branded in an effort to make the brand familiar to the consumers. Gradually, brands came to replace the products themselves in the consumers' minds, and people started to look for brands rather than products.

When the first brands arrived on the market, they corresponded to quality standards which meant guarantees for the customers. Today, however, quality standards are more or less the same for most products and branding has become a much more complex issue: not only should brands convey the values of companies and the quality of its products, but they should also convey the companies' own ethics and philosophy.

### Brand awareness

A company's goal is to create brand awareness. →**Chapter 5, Marketing & Chapter 6, Communication**

Some iconic companies such as McDonald's, Coca-Cola, Nike, Microsoft, etc. are undoubtedly the champions of brand awareness: their brand names are known worldwide even by people who will never buy their products.

Brand image is a symbolic construction created in people's minds, consisting of all the expectations and information associated to the brand. The brand is the major element in an advertising campaign. →**Chapter 6, Communication**

### Brand extension

It consists of giving new names to new products of the same brand: for example, Coca-Cola launched new names associated with its new products such as Diet Coke, Cherry Coke, etc. Each time, the word Coke is repeated. Brand extension is a necessity. However, it can be a risky business, as a brand may lose its "soul" in the process. →***Listening practice*, p. 113**

No brand name is necessary, is it?

**Heinz: ketchup or detergent?**

In 1993, the well-known American food brand **Heinz**, famous for its iconic Ketchup, launched a detergent, the Natural Cleaning Detergent. The consumers were confused as these two widly different products (food and detergent) shared a very similar packaging. Such confusion had a damaging impact on the brand's name, and the detergent was soon withdrawn from the shelves.

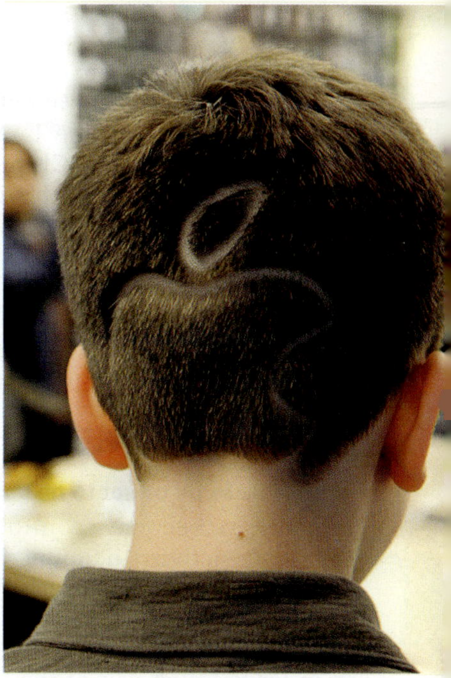

### Co-branding

Co-branding consists of using several brand names together for one product or service. It is cooperation between brands that allows companies to reinforce their marketing strength.
A typical example of co-branding is the iPod, which Apple and Hewlett Packard launched in a co-branded version in 2004.

### Endorsement

Most sportsmen/champions sign endorsement deals with brands. Generally, they endorse sport brands, the most famous ones being Adidas, Nike and Reebok. For example, the French national football team has signed an endorsement deal with Adidas. The amounts of money involved are huge.

### Own brands and generics

Own brands correspond to the retailer's own-branded product or service. When the retailer has a strong identity (for example Marks and Spencer in the UK, Monoprix in France, etc.), they may compete with the brand leaders on the market.
In a brand saturated society, consumers are getting more and more attracted by unbranded goods or generics. They threaten branded fast-moving consumer goods (FMCGs) as they offer the same quality standards for a much cheaper price, sometimes as little as a third of the price of a similar branded item.
On the other hand, some brands have become so famous that their names have entered the dictionary: this has been the case for Kleenex, Hoover, Xerox, etc., and more recently for Google, which has officially entered the dictionary as the verb *to google*.
→*Prep Page*, **p. 122**

## 2-The importance of a logo

Brands are often identified by their names, written in specific fonts. Logos are essential, too. A company may suffer – even if their service or product is great – because its logo is unprofessional, confusing, or offensive.
Logos are the centrepiece of a company's brand image and can tell you a lot about the company. A great logo must:

- follow solid basic design principles,
- be functional,
- represent the company,
- be unique.

→**Chapter 6, Communication**

Another important feature of good logos is their ability to stand out against the crowd. Copycat logos are bound to fail or be confusing to the consumer. Usually they will result in a loss in sales.

**A successful logo: Nike's swoosh**

A design intern at **Nike** named Caroline Davidson came up with the idea of the swoosh in 1971 for $35. The logo started as a simple design idea for a stripe to be placed on a shoe. The result is a universally known logo that is recognized everywhere in the world.

## 3-Maintaining a good brand image

When a consumer has a bad experience with a brand, it is very difficult to recapture his/her loyalty. This bad experience can be due to a failing after-sales service, a lack of availability concerning a product, a delivery delay, or an argument on the phone with the customer service.

• Brands may suffer from much more serious image troubles which may affect their audience worldwide. This was the case for Nike and its unfair labour practice (revealed to the public in the 1990s). Today, Wal-Mart, the biggest American retailer, is facing more than one hundred charges for discrimination, unpaid overtime, etc. →**Chapter 9, Transport, *Landmark*, p. 149**

• A brand image can also be tarnished by an accident occurring in the manufacturing process.

• Major pandemics, such as mad cow disease or bird flu, affect the brands which sell the potentially contaminated products (beef for McDonald's, chicken for KFC, etc.).

• Finally, a failed or misleading advertising campaign can also have damaging consequences and the global market implies that brands should pay attention to the message they convey outside their home market. →**Chapter 6, Communication**

### Brands: to be or not to be a fashion victim

Brands have become a controversial issue in our society; indeed consumer activists denounce the dictatorship of brands which affect people "from the cradle to the grave". The pressure of brands associated with advertising are considered partly responsible for urban violence in underprivileged areas: in a nutshell, in order to buy a pair of the latest branded sneakers, teenagers are encouraged to turn to criminal activities in order to satisfy needs they could not afford otherwise.

The best-known anti-advertising, anti-consumerism organisation is called "Adbusters", whose first magazine was published in Canada in 1989. Adbusters uses real ads and distorts them. →**Chapter 4, Consumers**

### Brand theft or counterfeiting

Before electronic goods became mass consumption products, counterfeiting mostly consisted of copying the logo of a brand, generally a luxury brand (Luis Vuitton, Chanel, Hermès, Lacoste, etc.) and selling it for a fraction of the price.

With the rise of new technologies, copycats have appeared in all sorts of fields: software, CDs, DVDs, everything can now be copied, even by non professionals. Some countries, such as China, are specialized in counterfeiting.

**Coke and Pepsi**

When **Pepsi Cola** used a similar logo to the already established Coca-Cola, it suffered in the competition between the two soft drink companies. Only when Pepsi switched its brand to something unique did it see a major increase in sales.

**Damaged brand image**

• In 1989, French mineral water brand **Perrier** had to retrieve its products after they had been accidentally poisoned with benzene. Perrier made a come back but has never fully recovered.

• In summer 2006, the computer manufacturer **Dell** and the electronics giant **Sony** had to call back 4 million laptops whose flawed Sony batteries could set the computers on fire.

## Question time

1. What is the origin of the word brand?
2. When did brands first appear on the market and why?
3. Give your definition of brand awareness. Give examples.
4. Why is the logo an important part of branding?
5. What can tarnish a brand image?
6. Why is it difficult to crack down on counterfeiters?
7. Why are generics on the rise?
8. What are some consumer groups against brands?
9. Do you agree that brands establish a kind of dictatorship? Explain.

**LANDMARK** # Coca-Cola

**The Coca-Cola Company is the largest manufacturer, distributor and marketer of non-alcoholic beverage concentrates and syrups in the world. Its headquarters are in Altanta, Georgia, where its flagship product, "Coke" was first invented in 1886 by John Pemberton. It is now the world's most popular soft drink.**

**Milestones**

- **1889** First full-page ad for Coca-Cola in *The Atlanta Journal*.
- **1892** Sales multiplied by ten. Coca-Cola Company formed.
- **1899** First bottling plant built in Chanatooga, Tennessee.
- **1916** The famous bottle with its unique contour was born.

## Rivals and other brands

The Coca-Cola Company produces nearly 400 brands in over 200 countries. This includes other varieties of Coca-Cola such as the most famous one, Diet Coke, or others, such as Cherry Coke or Coke with Lemon.

Other soft drinks have been introduced under the Coca-Cola brand name, such as Fanta and Sprite. Since the consumer interest in healthy beverages grew during the 1990s, the company introduced non-carbonated beverage brands such as Minute Maid fruit juice, Powerade sports beverage, flavoured tea Nestea (in a joint venture with Nestlé), Fruitopia fruit drink and Dasani water.

Coca-Cola Company's main rival is PepsiCo and the tension between the two companies peaked during the 1980s, at the height of the Cola Wars.

## Going global

Coca-Cola reached Canada as early as 1906. Today, hundreds of millions of people a day around the world drink Coca-Cola – daily servings are estimated at 1.3bn bottles! – and more than 70% of Coca-Cola's income comes from outside the USA Coca-Cola is the best-selling soft drink in most countries. Nevertheless, Pepsi is the market leader in Quebec, or in the Middle East with 75% market share. Coca-Cola has been having problems in India for several years. →**Chapter 4, Consumers, *In brief*, p. 67**

## Advertising

Coca-Cola's advertising has had a significant impact on American culture and the brand has a high degree of identification with the USA. To promote its drink in the 1930s, the company asked a talented commercial illustrator, Haddon Sundblom, to create a new Santa each Christmas for Coca-Cola advertisements that appeared on the back covers of *Post* and *National Geographic* magazines. The company used Sundblom's Santas until 1966, which helped them increase sales in winter – not the best period for refreshments – and also appealed quite efficiently to children.

In the 1970s, "I'd like to teach the world to sing", a song from a commercial, became a popular hit single, and is considered one of the best advertising campaigns in history, which helped make Coke attractive to young people again. Coca-Cola has gone through a number of different advertising slogans in its long history, including "The pause that refreshes" (1929), "(It's) The Real Thing" (1942), "Things Go Better" (1963), and "Always Coca-Cola" (1993).

Finally the company has a long history of sports marketing relationships, both in the USA and internationally: Coca-Cola sponsors the Olympic Games and was the first-ever sponsor at the 1928 Summer Olympics in Amsterdam; it has also sponsored FIFA since the 1978 FIFA World Cup.

**Online t@sk**

Visit the company's website.
Choose one of the following topics and report.

- The trademark and its evolution at www2.cocacola.com/heritage/cokelore.html
- Milestones in the history of the brand at www.thecocacolacompany.com/heritage/chronicle_global_business.html

## BRANDS AND COMPOUNDS

**brand:** marque
**brand awareness:** notoriété de la marque
**brand extension:** extension de la marque
**brand image:** image de marque
**brand loyalty:** fidélité à la marque
**brand name:** marque (de fabrique)
**branded goods:** produit de marque
**luxury brand:** marque de luxe
**own-brand:** de marque propre
**store brand product:** produit à la marque de l'enseigne
**unbranded:** sans marque

**add:** ajouter
**after-sales:** après-vente
**availability:** disponibilité
**buzz:** (N) murmure, bourdonnement ; (adj.) à la mode, dernier cri
**centrepiece:** pièce maîtresse
**compete:** concurrencer
**confusing:** qui prête à confusion
**consumer:** consommateur
**controversial:** sujet à controverse
**convey:** véhiculer
**copycat:** copieur, copié, d'imitation
**corporate:** d'entreprise
**counterfeiting:** contrefaçon
**customer:** client
**damage:** endommager
**delay:** retard
**delivery:** livraison
**design:** conception
**dilute:** diluer
**dub:** surnommer
**effectiveness:** efficacité
**encroach on:** empiéter sur
**endorsement:** technique publicitaire faisant intervenir une personnalité connue
**ethics:** éthique
**event:** événement
**expectation:** attente
**fail:** échouer
**familiar:** familier, connu
**fast-moving consumer goods (FMCGs):** biens de consommation à rotation rapide
**flavour:** goût, parfum
**flawed:** défectueux
**font:** police (de caractères)
**generic:** générique, produit générique
**guarantee:** garantie
**iconic:** emblématique
**inscribe:** inscrire
**launch:** lancer
**liability:** fiabilité
**logo:** logo
**offensive:** choquant
**outflank:** déborder, dépasser
**owner:** propriétaire
**pressure:** pression
**quality standard:** norme de qualité
**range:** gamme
**recall:** rappeler
**reliable:** fiable
**replace:** remplacer
**retailer:** commerçant, revendeur, détaillant
**retrieve:** retirer, récupérer
**recognizable:** reconnaissable
**rival:** rival, concurrent
**share:** partager
**shelf (*pl.*: shelves):** rayon
**ship:** expédier
**single:** unique
**switch:** changer
**tarnish:** ternir
**theft:** vol
**trademark:** marque de fabrique
**trend:** tendance
**unprofessional:** non professionnel
**value:** valeur
**withdraw (withdrew, withdrawn):** retirer
**worldwide:** dans le monde entier

"I can't identify emotionally with any brand of anything..."

## Charts and tables

**1.** Study the following tables which give you information concerning the five "best" and five "worst" brands for 2006.

**The Big WINNERS**

Google posted the biggest single-year percentage gain of any compagny in the rankings' five-year history. Growth at eBay, the top dog of 2005, slowed from last year.

| BRAND | 2006 BRAND VALUE (BILLIONS) | 2005 BRAND VALUE (BILLIONS) | CHANGE IN BRAND VALUE |
|---|---|---|---|
| GOOGLE | 12.38 | 8.46 | 46% |
| STARBUCKS | 3.10 | 2.58 | 20 |
| EBAY | 6.76 | 5.70 | 18 |
| MOTOROLA | 4.57 | 3.88 | 18 |
| HYUNDAI | 4.08 | 3.48 | 17 |

**The Big LOSERS**

Practically every industry had a loser this year. Gap slipped 12 places in the rankings, and beleaguered Ford made its fifth appearance on this list, falling eight places.

| BRAND | 2006 BRAND VALUE (BILLIONS) | 2005 BRAND VALUE (BILLIONS) | CHANGE IN BRAND VALUE |
|---|---|---|---|
| GAP | 6.42 | 8.19 | -22% |
| FORD | 11.06 | 13.16 | -16 |
| KODAK | 4.41 | 4.98 | -12 |
| HEINZ | 6.22 | 6.93 | -10 |
| INTEL | 32.32 | 35.59 | -9 |

**2.** Sum up the general ideas.

**3.** Choose one brand in each of the two lists and comment on the figures orally. →**Tools 11, p. 244**

## Online tasks

### Presenting a brand

Choose a brand among the following list: Google, Godiva, Gap, Nike, Heinz.
Then go onto the internet to find information and give a ten-minute oral presentation focusing on the brand.

**1.** Introduce the company.

**2.** Explain how the brand name was chosen:
- Is it a famous name?
- What does it stand for?

**3.** Give examples of how the brand is represented visually (show pictures, etc.).

### Do you know your brands?

Try to draw the following eight logos from memory: BP – Adidas – Apple – Lacoste – Maggi – Peugeot – Philips – Iglo.

If you don't want to draw, your task is to describe them as precisely as possible: shape, colour, etc.

Then visit
**www.monochrom.at/markenzeichnen/index-eng.htm**
to see the original brands. By clicking on each logo, you can discover how some people drew them.

# When will Google become generic?

You open your fridge, or use a kleenex, or sit xeroxing or googling on the net. All these names are generic, and their respective owners try very hard to keep them unique by means of graphic logos for better identification.

Currently, the term "to google" is in *Oxford English Dictionary* with a lower case[1] "g". "To google" has entered the English language as a word, making it very difficult for the originators, Google, to keep it exclusive. Today, anyone can manufacture a fridge or a rollerblade, so does this mean that there will be googling software or google kits produced by others?

Now the giant of the search engine universe, Google warns media to back off from using its powerful moniker[2] as a verb. Let's take a closer look.

Netsurfing or E-Mail and many thousands of other brand names became common generic terms. To many, this may sound like free advertising, though in reality, this is a corporate nightmare. A code-red alert strikes the boardroom. Legal SWAT teams swing into action to protect their successful global brand, and an aggressive policing of corporate name usage kicks in.

Normally, lawyers can force people and media to refer to a brand name as a registered trademark of the company. They also instruct their branding agencies to avoid making creative uses on the name. If a name is too playful, it quickly becomes adopted in the language, as rollerblade. On the Google site, the use of the word "goooooooooogle" to represent the number of results pages in more dilution of the mark, and so are the weekly cartooning on its main page. However, in the end, it is the public that decides as to when and how a name will become generic.

Fortunately, studies have shown that, despite their fame and popularity in daily language, certain names remain powerful corporate brands. Some examples are Yahoo, Apple, Microsoft, Sony, Rolex and Nintendo. Have you ever heard, "Leave me alone, I'm Appling" or, "I was depressed and very Microsoftish"?

As a result, finding great corporate names has become a very scientific process. The days of accidental business naming are over.

Naseem Javed, www.bizcommunity.com, 18 August 2006

1. *lower case*: lettre minuscule, bas de casse
2. *moniker*: nom

## Info

***Oxford English Dictionary*** The OED was first issued between 1884 and 1928. It is considered the largest dictionary of the English language.

***SWAT (Special Weapons and Tactics)*** A specialized unit in many US police departments, which is trained to perform dangerous operations, such as performing hostage rescue and preventing terrorist attacks.

## References

You can find relevant information by reading various pages in your book and memorising a few facts and ideas.

→ **Marketing, p. 86**
→ **Communication, p. 100**
→ **Brands, p. 116**

ACTIVITY **Practise giving an account of this article.**

## Introduction

You should explain where the article comes from, when it was published and what it is about. →Tools 4, p. 236

This article, which appeared on www.bizcommunity.com in August 2006, reports on what has happened to the name of the most famous web search engine worldwide, namely Google. The name has entered the OED as a verb, "to google", highlighting the fact that it has turned into everyday language.

## Development

Once you have understood the article, organise your ideas into two or three different parts, using set phrases and link-words. →Tools 4, p. 236

1. Brand names and generic terms
2. Positive and negative aspects

You should also use the information given in *Info* and what you have learnt, for example by referring to the various pages indicated in *References*.

### 1. Brand names and generic terms

• **Generic names**: Many names which were originally brands have become generic and are used in everyday language, as ordinary nouns. Such is the case of fridge (for refrigerator), Kleenex (for tissue) and hundreds of others.
• **Remaining unique**: However, brand owners want to keep their brands unique, so that they can be singled out. Very often, companies work hard to offer a logo which can represent the brand at graphic level. One may mention the Nike swoosh, for instance, which has gone as far as replacing the written name altogether.
• **Google, the new generic term**: The verb "to google" has entered the most famous English dictionary, the *OED*, with a lower case "g".

### 2. Positive and negative aspects

• **A proof of success**: Whenever a brand becomes generic, it shows that the brand is very successful and that it has become identified with the whole category of products or services. The fact that Google has become an ordinary verb shows the popularity of the giant of the search engine industry: everyone knows what Google is, and most people who look for information on the internet do so with Google's help.
• **Risks**: However, brand owners may refuse to see their brands used as a generic name. As a matter of fact, this is the case for Google. If the brand becomes a common term, "googling software" or "google kits" might appear on the market, produced by another firm.
However a brand must actually stand for something that customers believe will add value. Therefore, having one's brand become generic is what the journalist calls "a corporate nightmare" and companies try to protect their global brands when they are that successful.
• **The law**: Normally, lawyers can force people and media to refer to a brand name as a registered trademark of the company, with a circled "r" (®) in written form. However, this may well turn out to be impossible and it is the public who decides to use a brand as a generic term or not.
• **Solutions**: First, branding agencies should be careful when they create a new name: contrary to Google, powerful brands such as Yahoo, Microsoft or Apple have not become verbs or adjectives. Then, companies should avoid offering playful uses of the name. On the Google site, the word has been written out with many "o"s in different colours to show that one can find numerous result pages. Such use has encouraged the public to play with the brand.

## Conclusion

You should sum up the main ideas and try to open out in a new direction.

This article shows that companies have to be very careful when they choose a brand that will represent them in the consumers' eyes. A brand name should be longlasting and easily remembered. However, when a brand name is too easy, or lends itself to easy variation, it may become generic, therefore the company may lose its property of the brand.

## Branching out

Now, you should move away from the article and develop more ideas. The following questions can help you.

**1** Why is it important for brand names to survive the test of time?

**2** How would you differentiate branding from logos and graphic designs?

## Case study: using a brand and a logo

The National Health Service (NHS) redesigned their logo in 1999. Users must adhere to the following key points when using the NHS identity.

NHS

**Match the questions and answers about the NHS logo.**

| | |
|---|---|
| **1.** Am I authorised to use the NHS logo? | **a.** The NHS logo should be printed in NHS Blue (Pantone 300) and black. If this is not possible then it can be printed in black only. |
| **2.** Am I placing the NHS logo in the correct position? | **b.** Use pictures that show we care. Drawings that attempt to show a funny version of a patient's condition risk being disrespectful. Pictures must also be easy to understand. |
| **3.** Am I using the correct colour? | **c.** The NHS official typeface, Frutiger, should be used wherever possible. Alternatively, you can use Arial. |
| **4.** Am I using the correct font? | **d.** The NHS logo should always be positioned in the top right corner. If this is not possible, it may be positioned at the bottom right. |
| **5.** Can I use pictures to convey a message? | **e.** If you are unsure, please see the main identity policy section of this website or call our NHS identity helpline on 020 7972 5250 for clarification. |

Answers: 1e, 2d, 3a, 4c, 5b

## PERSONAL TASK

Choose one of the following spoof ads and explain what is funny about them. Report to the class. Explain whether you find them effective. → **Tools 12, p. 245**

# IN THIS UNIT...

- Companies: Dairy Crest, Avon, Wal-Mart...
- Learn about Macy's & the various means of distribution
- An unattractive shopping experience
- Report on the places where you shop
- Fill in an order form

# 8
## Distribution

## → Before you START

*In brief:* Home delivery
*Front page:* Opening a supermarket at home, or abroad

*The Goose Seller,* aquatint by Rowlandson, 1799

**Do you think door-to-door selling is an easy job? Why/Why not?**

### Words

- **Nouns:** door-to-door selling, intruder, visit, appointment
- **Adjectives:** (un)welcome, disruptive, controversial, difficult, interested, disgusted, funny

### LISTENING PRACTICE

CD TRACK 41

Listen to the recording.
**1.** What are the people talking about?
**2.** Explain their opinions.

# Dairy Crest in £33m doorstep milk deal

Dairy Crest is buying Arla Foods' Express Dairies for £33m to become Britain's biggest milk-delivery service with 2 million customers in an attempt to fight back against the supermarkets.

Dairy Crest, the maker of Clover spread and Cathedral City cheddar, said the acquisition would catapult its doorstep market share from 33 per cent to 49 per cent. It also delivers to retailers, schools, hospitals and restaurants – where its market share moves from 14 per cent to 18 per cent.

Express Dairies currently delivers 690 million pints of milk a year with 77 depots and two dairies in Liverpool and Nottingham. Dairy Crest expects to make savings of £9m by 2008-09 from combining the two milk-delivery businesses. Drummond Hall, the chief executive, said job losses would amount to less than 5 per cent of the combined 6,000-strong workforce.

The milkman has long been losing ground to the supermarkets, where milk is cheaper. Tim Smith, Arla's chief executive, said that the most Dairy Crest could hope for was to stem the 8-9 per cent annual decline in its milk-delivery business. He said the sector's share of the milk market had shrunk from 25 per cent in 2000 to 11 per cent.

Julia Kollewe, *The Independent*, 25 July 2006

CD TRACK 42

## Info

***cheddar***
Cheese which was originally made in England only. Dating back to the Romans, it is now the most widely eaten cheese worldwide.

***Liverpool***
City in North West England. Population: *ca.* 450,000 inhabitants.

***Nottingham***
City in the north of central England. Population: *ca.* 262,000 inhabitants.

***milkman***
Milk has traditionally been delivered at British people's doors every morning, so that they can get fresh milk every day.

***pint***
a measure for liquid (≃ 0.5 l).

## Work on words

### 1 I Find their equivalents in English

**§1** laitier (adj.) – livraison – se défendre
**§2** margarine – part de marché
**§3** laiterie – faire des économies – perte d'emplois – main-d'œuvre
**§4** perdre du terrain – directeur général

### 2 I Find their synonyms

**Headline** business agreement
**§1** purchasing – try (N)
**§2** manufacturer – shops
**§3** at the present time – be equivalent to
**§4** person running the company – stop – decrease (V)

## Headlines

**1** Read the headline aloud: which consonant is repeated three times?

**2** The sentence contains no verb. Use the following words to write a full sentence: *Dairy Crest – £33m – doorstep – milk – deal.*

**3** Which sentence in the article expresses the same idea in more detail?

## The key points of the article

### 1 The topic sentence
**a.** Dairy Crest's two objectives.
**b.** Means used by the company to reach them.

### 2 The two companies
**a.** Dairy Crest's most famous products.
**b.** Customers.
**c.** Dairy Crest's current market share.
**d.** Express Dairies' business.
**e.** Positive consequences of buying out Express Dairies.
**f.** Negative consequence.

### 3 The milk-delivery business
**a.** Situation.
**b.** Reason that accounts for this trend.

## {Methods}

### ■ Speaking practice

**1 Watch out for the right prononciation.**
The following words are close to their French equivalents: *express – service – million – supermarket – cathedral – acquisition – catapult – per cent – hospital – restaurants – depots – decline – sector.*
Read them aloud, paying attention to the pronunciation and the stressed syllable.

**2 Read figures aloud.** →Tools 10, p. 243
Read §3 aloud. If necessary, start by writing the following figures down.
Then practise reading the groups of words in parentheses together with the figures.
**a.** 690 (million pints of milk a year)
**b.** 77 (depots and two dairies)
**c.** (savings of) £9m
**d.** (by) 2008-09
**e.** (less than) 5 (per cent)
**f.** (the combined) 6,000(-strong workforce)

### ■ Writing practice

**1 The present perfect: simple and *-ing* forms; the use of time markers.**
The present perfect shows a strong connection between past and present. When the *-ing* form is added to the verb, the speaker wants to stress the activity. Specific time markers are used with the present perfect: *lately, recently, so far, since* + date, *for* + duration, *all this year, in the past week/month/year/decade.*

**Put the verbs in parentheses in the simple perfect and add the time marker at the right place.**
**a.** (*decline – for years*) The demand for deliveries of milk / as more and more people buy from supermarkets.
**b.** (*decline – for the last decade*) The market / by around 10 per cent per year.
**c.** (*slow – in the last few years*) The rate of decline / and could slow further.
**d.** (*start – lately*) Supermarkets / delivering doorstep groceries again.

**2 Report in English.**
Link the sentences in part **1** using *on the one hand ... on the other hand.* Use other link words as well, such as *yet, but, what is more,* etc.
→Tools 18, p. 253

## Branching out

**1** Can home delivery services benefit from technological advances, such as electronic payment? →*Key data*, p. 132
**2** Do you think the days of home delivery are numbered? Why/Why not?

## LISTENING PRACTICE

CD TRACK 43-44

*Gail Reynolds and Lily Almond are considering a new job.*

**1 Comprehension**
Listen to the recording to find the following information.

**Part 1**
**a.** Gail's job.
**b.** Number of people having the same job.
**c.** Reason why Gail thinks Lily should try.
**d.** Lily's reaction.

**Part 2**
**a.** Is Gail successful at her job? Give details.
**b.** How can reps choose the products?
**c.** The two main drawbacks of the job.
**d.** The main advantages of the job.

**2 Expression**
Give an oral account, or write a 100-word paragraph, summing up what you have heard.

**Retailers sell to the individual customer through various categories of points of sales/outlets. Once a product is manufactured, it is stored in a warehouse, and then sold to retailers or directly to customers. There are five main distribution channels: retailers, mail order, wholesalers, direct selling, and agents.**

## 1-Brick and mortar retailers

### Specialist shops

They specialize in a range of products: kitchen appliances, hi-fi, books, etc. They often belong to a chain and operate through franchising (Zara, Gap, etc.). Franchising has developed on a huge scale: a franchisee buys the right to operate a business and gives back a percentage of his turnover (royalties) to the franchiser. In exchange, the company/franchiser provides its brand name and reputation, training and advertising. Franchised stores are easily recognizable as their store layout is always the same to create a familiar surrounding for the customer. They can be located in the high streets or in shopping centres (UK)/malls (USA).

### Licensed dealers

Some products, such as cars, are sold through licensed dealers, i.e. subcontractors who have the exclusive rights to sell them.

### Corner shops/convenience stores

They are small shops located near people's homes: butcher's, baker's, etc. They are more expensive than supermarkets but they offer shopping at walking distance, longer opening hours and often provide home deliveries, which is a help for senior citizens.

### Department stores

In the 19th century, department stores opened in Europe and the USA. They were the first to offer different categories of products in different departments in one store. Harrods in London, the Galeries Lafayette in France or Macy's in the USA are considered historical and architectural landmarks. After going through a crisis in the past two decades, most have managed to succeed again and target affluent customers with trendy, upscale products.

## 2-The development of superstores

Supermarkets/superstores and hypermarkets appeared in the USA in the 1950s.

### Definition

Superstores are a modern version of department stores: they sell all kinds of products (food, clothing, home appliances, etc.) in one place. They are located in the suburbs, with huge free car parks that encourage one-stop shopping. They offer much cheaper prices than both high-street stores and department stores, with a good quality price ratio and long opening hours. To encourage impulse buying, eye-catching products are stored on the shelves at eye-level. Products targeting children (sweets,

**Dead malls**

Many US malls are considered "dead". A mall can become deserted when the area in which it is located undergoes drastic demographic changes, or when a bigger mall is built close by. One of the most famous dead malls is the Dixie Square Mall in Harvey, Illinois, which was featured in the movie *The Blues Brothers*.

A historical landmark: Macy's in 1920

snacks, chocolate bars, etc.) are on display at the checkouts.

### "Big-box stores"

"Big-box store" is a colloquial term used to describe giant superstores. Located in suburban/rural areas, they look like huge rectangular boxes without windows, surrounded by car parks. They include stores selling several ranges of products, such as Wal-Mart and Target (US), and stores which specialize in a specific range of goods such as Home Depot (furniture), or DIY (Do-It-Yourself) stores. To offer customers cheaper prices, superstores subscribe to central buying offices and have become so powerful that they can impose their prices on suppliers whose margins have dropped. Big-box stores are criticized and regulated because they damage the landscape and endanger high-street businesses.

### Retailtainment or fun-shopping

Apart from offering a wide range of stores and services, malls/shopping centres have become places of "retailtainment", i.e. places where many people also have fun. Some huge US malls have almost been turned into theme parks. Europe is following the lead, with American-size malls such as Val d'Europe near Paris, Bluewater in Kent, England, Kaufhof in Berlin, etc. Malls are also mushrooming in new EU countries.

### Factory outlets

They are located in the suburbs and sell end-of-range products at attractive prices.

### Hard discounters

Hard discounters have conquered the retail market for FMCGs. Their secret: bulk purchase to get the best price from suppliers, no advertising, no aesthetic store layout, zero decoration, the minimum staff who do everything (shelf storage, check out, cleaning, etc.). They sell mainly generics. On the European market, they have been spreading fast over the past decade. Among the most popular discounters: Leader Price, Lidl, Aldi, etc. →Chapter 4, Consumers

## 3-New trends

### Vending machines →Chapter 10, New technologies

Vending machines are now part of the setting in companies, public buildings, stations and airports, i.e. places attended by a lot of customers, travellers or passers-by. They usually sell drinks, snacks, etc. Vending machines need no personnel, which lowers their running cost. Like the internet, they have no opening hours, but they offer on-the-spot delivery.
Some around-the-clock shops are in fact huge vending machines selling anything from food to detergent, available 24 hours a day 7 days a week. Until now, vending machines had been limited to the analogue world. However, they can also sell Wi-Fi access and tickets for airline seats or events, and even downloads of music videos and TV shows in the future.

### Re-focusing on the high streets

High-street malls, which are accessible by public transport and

Always low prices indeed at Wal-Mart!

**A big step for an old technology**

A six-month trial has been carried out in Dublin airport (Ireland), where 30 **Coca-Cola** vending machines connected to the internet have been selling mobile-phone top-ups, ring tones, games and logos – all downloaded from a central database – together with the traditional soft drinks. The operation has been a success since the revenues of the vending machines have already doubled. Coke has 2.8 million machines worldwide, which may be promised a prosperous future!

smaller than their suburban counterparts, attract customers back to deserted city centres. Permits to build new malls in the outskirts are refused if a mall can be built in the centre.

### Charity shops

They are many charity shops in the UK's high streets, selling second-hand goods and sometimes fair trade products. The most famous chain is Oxfam.

### Door-to-door sales

Door-to-door selling is now forbidden in most apartment buildings. However, cosmetics brand Avon has not changed its distribution system since 1959. Services such as insurance can be sold through an agent who visits customers at home after having arranged an appointment. →*In brief*, p. 127

### Home parties

Tupperware initiated this type of distribution. The products are displayed and sold in someone's house for friends and neighbours who meet in a friendly atmosphere.

### Doorstep delivery

In countries, some goods are traditionally delivered on the customers' doorsteps. This is the case for milk in the UK, and for newspapers both in the UK and in the US. →*In brief*, p. 126

### Mail order and online distribution

→Chapter 10, New technologies

The USA first developed mail order as many people who lived far from cities bought their goods from catalogues. Today, the internet is replacing mail order: goods can be bought at "the click of the mouse". Many retailers have become "click and mortar" by developing a website to complete their channels of distribution. Other retailers are strictly online: this is the case for Amazon, which used to specialize in books, CDs and DVDs. →Chapter 10, *In brief*, p. 156. Auction sites such as E-bay have become extremely popular and attract millions of shoppers a day. However, expensive delivery charges can deter customers.

### TV and mobile shopping

Some TV programs are devoted to shopping. Customers can buy the goods via a free number. Buying mobile is the same as TV or computer shopping, except that it is more "mobile".

**Bulky items**

British giant **Tesco** accounted for 66% of online buying in the UK in 2006, the best seller being toilet paper. Marketers have realized that bulky goods are the most liable to be bought online. Other favourites among online shoppers include fresh fruit and vegetables with a relatively long shelf life, such as bananas. Tesco, which accounts for £1 in every £8 spent in the UK, is now the largest online grocer. In 2006, it took around 30,000 orders per day which were collectively worth £2.5m.

## Question time

1 Name three types of stores; for each store give examples of what they sell.
2 Explain why superstores are called big-box stores.
3 Which elements help to make malls places of retailtainment?
4 Which retailers suffer most from supermarkets and malls competition?
5 What are the advantages of home shopping?
6 What can account for the spectacular growth of home shopping in the past decade?
7 Why are consumers more and more attracted by hard discounters?
8 Why are vending machines considered as having a promising future?

# LANDMARK Wal-Mart

**Wal-Mart Stores, Inc. was founded in 1932 by Sam Walton (1918-1992) – hence the "wal" in its name. He said, "The secret of successful retailing is to give your customers what they want. And really, if you think about it from your point of view as a customer, you want everything: a wide assortment of good-quality merchandise; the lowest possible prices; guaranteed satisfaction with what you buy; friendly, knowledgeable service; convenient hours; free parking; a pleasant shopping experience." The company's slogan is "Always Low Prices".**

## The retailing behemoth

In 2006, Wal-Mart was the world's largest retailer and the second largest corporation in the world (behind Exxon). With an estimated 20% of the retail grocery and consumables business, it is also the largest American toy seller in the US, with 22% of the retail toy business.

Wal-Mart operates in Mexico as Walmex, in the UK as Asda and in Japan as The Seiyu Co: its 2006 international operations accounted for 20% of total sales. However, Wal-Mart has had to sell its retail operations in South Korea and Germany.

→**Chapter 14, Globalisation, *In brief*, p. 216**

## Retail formats

Wal-Mart Stores Division U.S. has three retail formats:

- **Wal-Mart Neighborhood Markets**: 108 supermarkets that average 3,900 $m^2$ They offer a variety of groceries, plus pharmaceuticals, health and beauty aids and photo developing services.
- **Wal-Mart Discount Stores**: 1,135 stores from 3,000 $m^2$ to 21,000 $m^2$ (average size: 9,500 $m^2$). They offer general merchandise, with a selection of foods. Many stores also feature a garden centre, a pharmacy, a one-hour photo processing lab, portrait studio and a fast food outlet.
- **Wal-Mart Supercenters**: 2,121 hypermarkets from 9,000 $m^2$ to 24,000 $m^2$ (average size: 17,000 $m^2$). They offer the same as Wal-Mart Discount Stores, plus a food supermarket and numerous alcove shops such as a mobile phone store, hair and nail salons, video rental, a family fun centre and a bank.

Wal-Mart also operates ***walmart.com*** and **Sam's Club**, a chain of warehouse clubs that sells groceries and general merchandise, often in large quantities, to customers who pay an annual fee.

## Criticism

Wal-Mart has been criticised by community groups, trade unions and environmental groups, because of various concerns.

- **Store openings and environmental carelessness**
Wal-Mart often faces traffic and environment problems when planning new store locations. A famous example is the Teotihuacán Superstore that opened in 2004, 1.9 miles from the Pyramid of the Moon (Aztec site, 250 A.D.) north-east of Mexico City.
- **Use of foreign labour and product sourcing**
Unions say Wal-Mart is the largest importer of foreign-produced goods in the US, notably from China. Although Wal-Mart stresses it has US suppliers, 60% of its products were imported in 2004, compared with 6% in 1996.
- **Treatment of employees**
The company has prevented unionization through surveillance and closures of stores or departments who choose to unionize. Only 44% of its 1.3 million US workers are covered by health insurance. Finally, in August 2006, the company announced that it would increase the average pay by 6% for all new employees at 1,200 stores but established pay maximums on veteran workers: critics claim the salary caps are an attempt to push higher-paid, older workers out. A 2005 documentary, *Wal-Mart: The High Cost of Low Price*, presented a negative view of the company. Wal-Mart opened a website at www.walmartfacts.com to answer its critics.

Be a good American with Wal-Mart!

**Online t@sk**

Visit Wal-Mart's sites on walmartstores.com/GlobalWMStoresWeb/navigate.do?catg=217 and www.walmartfacts.com to report on Wal-Mart's sustainability policy.
Choose one theme and report to the class.

## SHOPS, SHOPPING, ETC. AND COMPOUNDS

**around-the-clock shop:** boutique ouverte 24h sur 24
**baker's/ butcher's:** boulanger / boucher
**brick and mortar shop:** boutique en dur (= avec des murs)
**charity shop:** magasin caritatif
**click and mortar:** qui associe vente en magasin et vente en ligne
**convenience shop/store:** magasin de proximité
**corner shop:** magasin/boutique du coin
**grocery shop/store:** épicerie
**home shopping:** achats depuis le domicile
**one-stop shopping:** concentration des achats sur un seul lieu
**shopping centre:** centre commercial
**specialist shop:** boutique spécialisée

**amount to:** se monter à
**arm:** branche
**asset:** actif
**average:** faire en moyenne
**bulk purchase:** achat en gros
**bulky:** encombrant
**car park:** parking
**cash register:** caisse enregistreuse
**central buying office:** centrale d'achat
**channel of distribution:** canal de distribution
**cheap:** bon marché, pas cher
**checkout:** caisse de sortie
**chore:** corvée
**compete:** concurrencer
**computer chip:** puce informatique
**core:** essential, principal
**crammed with:** bourré de
**customer:** client
**data:** données
**deliver:** livrer
**delivery boy:** livreur
**delivery delay:** retard de livraison
**department:** rayon
**department store:** grand magasin
**direct selling:** vente directe
**display (on):** à l'étalage
**distributor:** distributeur
**doorstep/home delivery:** livraison au pas de la porte/à domicile
**door-to-door:** porte à porte
**downtown:** centre ville
**draw (drew, drawn):** attirer
**end of range:** fin de gamme
**entertainment:** loisir
**eye-catching:** qui attire l'œil
**factory outlet:** magasin d'usine
**fad:** mode, engouement
**flagship (adj.):** phare
**franchise:** franchise
**franchisee:** franchisé
**franchising:** système de franchises
**franchiser :** franchiseur
**free-of-charge:** gratuit
**furniture:** ameublement
**generics:** produits génériques
**gross:** brut
**handset:** combiné
**hard discounter:** magasin discount

'Look!. It really is heaven'

**high street:** rue commerçante
**hip:** à la mode, branché
**home party:** vente à domicile
**impulse buying:** achats d'impulsion
**layout:** disposition (dans un magasin)
**licensed dealer:** revendeur agréé
**lose (lost, lost) ground:** perdre du terrain
**mail order:** vente par correspondance
**mall:** centre commercial
**manufacturer:** fabricant
**margin:** marge
**market share:** part de marché
**mass consumption:** consommation de masse
**merchandise:** marchandise
**middleman:** intermédiaire
**mushroom:** pousser comme des champignons
**opening hours:** heures d'ouverture
**order:** commande, commander
**outlet:** point de vente
**pedestrian:** piéton
**place an order:** passer une commande
**point of sales:** point de vente
**purchase:** achat
**quality price ratio:** rapport qualité-prix
**range:** gamme
**regulation:** réglementation
**retailer:** revendeur
**rush hour:** heure de pointe
**sale:** vente
**sales representative:** représentant, commercial
**sales target:** objectif de vente
**sample:** échantillon
**savings:** économies
**second-hand:** d'occasion, de seconde main
**sell (sold, sold):** vendre
**shelf (*pl.*: shelves):** rayonnage
**shelf storage:** mise en rayon
**shop/store:** magasin, boutique
**shrink (shrank, shrunk):** rapetisser, diminuer
**sports apparel:** articles de sports
**staff:** personnel
**stem:** enrayer, juguler
**stock *(V)*:** vendre
**store *(V)*:** avoir en stock
**subcontractor:** sous-traitant
**subscribe:** s'abonner
**suburb:** banlieue
**supplier:** fournisseur
**supply:** fournir
**swipe:** passer (une carte magnétique)
**take (took, taken) over:** racheter
**target:** cibler
**theme park:** parc à thème
**trade:** vendre, faire du commerce
**trendy:** à la mode
**upfront:** à payer d'avance
**upscale:** haut de gamme
**vending machine:** distributeur automatique
**warehouse:** entrepôt
**wholesaler:** grossiste

## Charts and tables

**1.** Study the following bar charts which give you information about the places where affluent Americans shopped for clothing and accessories in the year preceding the survey.

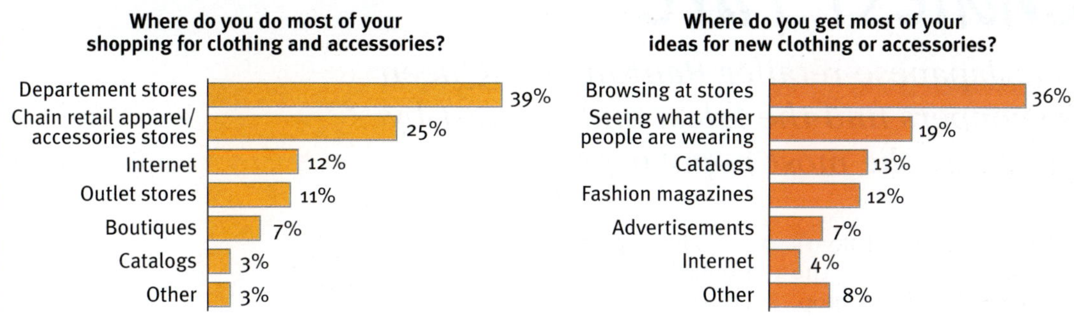


From *Time*, March 8, 2006

**2.** Compare the various means of distribution. →**Tools 11, p. 244**

**3.** Do a similar bar chart for your own shopping habits.

## Online tasks

**Do you know about Macy's?**

Learn about Macy's and their famous Thanksgiving parade. Visit **www1.macys.com/store/about/history/index.jsp** to find out about the store's history and report to the class.

## Communication tasks

**Roleplay: Shopping**

Go on **www.retailowner.com/Articles/H6all/tabid/88/Default.aspx**. Read about the various points which are crucial in providing a customer with an attractive shopping experience.

**A:** You are a customer.
Use what you have learnt about an attractive shopping experience to criticize B's store.

**B:** You are a retailer.
A is critical of your store. Defend your choices or agree to make changes.

# For sale: Only the trendiest fare

*Eclectic Japanese retailer RanKing RanQueen helps shoppers find the latest and greatest by stocking only the most popular products.*

At rush hour in Tokyo's Shinjuku Station, the world's busiest train stop, a tiny shop near the exit is crammed with commuters. They're browsing the latest CDs, magazines, and novels, as well as teeth whiteners, nose hair removers, and mineral waters.

Welcome to the bizarre world of RanKing RanQueen, where hundreds of products in more than 250 categories pack the interior of what at first glance is little more than a glorified convenience store.

Yet beneath the shop's neon glow, RanKing has given a simple marketing concept a new twist: The retailer's eight stores stock only the latest goods and assign each item a ranking based on its current popularity in Japan.

Owned by Tokyu, a $12 billion conglomerate that runs railways, department stores, and supermarkets, RanKing was launched in 2001 to add some spice to the sea of newsstands and noodle shops its parent company typically operates at high-volume hubs[1].

Tokyu manager Kazuyuki Tada hit upon the idea of a shop that would reflect current fads – a place, he says, where social trends could be grasped in three minutes.

The approach is a particularly clever way to exploit consumers' need to feel that they're part of the latest trend – even if it's just a toothbrush, says Masahiro Yotsumoto, a director at the Dentsu Center for Consumer Studies. It's no surprise that when an item is ranked tops, its sales tend to double.

RanKing relies on data from firms inside and outside the Tokyu group, particularly its own Tokyu Hands, a hip retailer of lifestyle products. RanKing also updates its ratings on a weekly or monthly basis, ensuring frequent visits from its clientele of mostly 20-something women.

While it won't release exact sales figures, RanKing says its monthly per-store revenue is up 10 to 20 percent over the past year, and its flagship store in Tokyo's Shibuya district now draws nearly 20,000 customers on weekends.

Although total sales at Tokyu's retail operations are expected to remain flat at $6 billion this year, the company plans to expand the RanKing chain to 15 stores by 2008.

*Business 2.0 Magazine*, July 21 2006

1. *hub*: centre

## References

You can find relevant information by reading various pages in your book and memorising a few facts and ideas.

→ **Companies, p. 28**
→ **Consumers, p. 70**
→ **Distribution, p. 130**

ACTIVITY **Practise giving an account of this article.**

## Introduction

You should explain where the article comes from, when it was published and what it is about.
→Tools 4, p. 236

This article appeared in *Business 2.0 Magazine* in July 2006. It relates the success of a new type of store which has opened in Japan and describes how it sells hundreds of products in more than 250 categories within a very small space.

## Development

Once you have understood the article, organise your ideas into two or three different parts, using set phrases and link-words. →Tools 4, p. 236

1. The new store: description
2. The new store: concept
3. The new store: success

You should also use the information given in *Info* and what you have learnt, for example by referring to the various pages indicated in *References*.

### 1. The new store: description

• **The company**: RanKing RanQueen was launched in 2001. It is owned by Tokyu, a $12 billion conglomerate that runs railways, department stores and supermarkets. It also operates newspaper stands and noodle shops (fast-food outlets in Japan) in high-volume hubs, i.e. airports, stations, etc., where there are a lot of people.

• **Location**: Shinjuku Station in Tokyo, Japan, which is the world's busiest train station.

• **Number of stores**: 8

• **Type of store**: very small; the stores are packed with products. At first glance they look like convenience stores.

• **Type of products**: one can find virtually everything, from the latest CDs and magazines, to teeth whiteners and mineral waters. There are hundreds of products in more than 250 categories.

### 2. The new store: concept

The parent company's manager wanted to create a shop that would reflect current fads. His idea was to launch a place where customers would be able to understand what was fashionable in three minutes. Customers get the feeling the retailer helps them choose what they want by offering only the latest products, and selling only the trendiest. This approach exploits consumers' need to feel that they're part of the latest trend, even for such a trivial object as a toothbrush.

• **How it works**: RanKing uses data from firms inside and outside the parent company, for instance Tokyu Hands, a hip retailer of lifestyle products. Then, thanks to the data collected, it is able to choose the items it wants to offer by assigning each of them a ranking based on its current popularity.
It also updates its products every week or every month, thus ensuring that customers visit the stores frequently.

### 3. The new store: success

At rush hour the tiny shop near the exit of Tokyo's station is packed with commuters. The increase in sales is normal, since the store offers only the products that everyone wants to buy. No exact sales figures have been released. However, RanKing says its monthly per-store revenue is up 10 to 20% over the past year and RanKing's flagship store in Tokyo's Shibuya district now attracts nearly 20,000 customers over weekends.
**Prospects**: Tokyu is planning to expand the RanKing chain to 15 stores by 2008.

## Conclusion

You should sum up the main ideas and try to open out in a new direction.

This article shows how new concepts can be found in distribution, especially by relying on today's time-pressed, fashion-crazy consumers. The parent company has used its knowledge of outlets in high-volume places to launch a new type of store. Even if points of sales are expensive in such places, the surface area is so small that it is bound to be profitable. However, a lot of market research must be done for the store to remain successful since its sales are based on ever-changing fads.

## Branching out

Now, you should move away from the article and develop more ideas. The following questions can help you.

**1** To what extent does this sort of retail outlet cater to today's consumers?

**2** Do you think RanKing RanQueen's success can last? Why/Why not?

## 7. Brands

# For Your Eyes Only

## *Mini Cooper's campaign, aimed just at owners, looks to enhance the car's cachet.*

Why would an automaker spend hundreds of thousands of dollars in advertising to reach people who already bought the car? Go ask Mini USA. In the next few weeks, the company will launch a series of ads in magazines ranging from Maxim to The New Yorker aimed just at their current 150,000 U.S. owners. Potential customers won't even be able to read what's on the page.

That's because the ads will be encrypted, decipherable only by the cognoscenti[1]. Mini is sending owners a "covert" kit – looking like a wizened-looking book – that will include special glasses, a decoder, and a "magic window decryptor." Using those, owners will be able to find Web addresses in the ads that lead them to free prizes and invitations to events. Non-owners will just have to feel slightly jealous that they're out of the loop[2].

The strategy is to get owners buzzing about the brand while piquing the curiosity of potential buyers. "It's a covert and an overt campaign almost simultaneously," says John Butler, a creative director at Mini's new ad agency. "If you get the kit, you're rewarded. If not, you get the gist that owning a Mini is like being in a club."

The prizes perpetuate that clubbiness. The first will be an invitation to join Mini's upcoming "Mini Takes the States" event, a cross-country rally where hundreds of Mini Coopers will drive from Monterey, Calif., to Lakeville, Conn. Another, following the spy motif, will be joke switch covers for the Mini's dashboard, like one that labels the fog-light switch "ejector seat".

Luxury carmakers have dangled perks in front of their drivers for some time, of course. Infiniti owners receive invitations to panel discussions from noted designers and architects. New buyers of BMW's high-powered models can attend the BMW Performance Center for daylong advanced driving classes. Jeep does something similar with "Camp Jeep". Mini's approach is more wacky than posh – in keeping with the owners of the eccentric, $18,000 Mini Cooper.

*Business Week*, July 31, 2006

1. *cognoscenti*: les spécialistes, les connaisseurs
2. *out of the loop*: pas au courant

### Compréhension

**1.** **Rédigez en anglais un compte rendu de ce document ; tenez compte de tous les éléments fournis. (150 mots)**
**2.** **Traduisez le titre et le premier paragraphe de l'article.**

### Expression

**Répondez en anglais aux questions suivantes.**

1 How is Mini exploiting the idea that owners belong to a select club? (150 words)
2 Do you think such brand strategies can work? Why/Why not? (100 words)

(N.B. L'usage du dictionnaire bilingue est autorisé.)

## The key points of the article

### 1 Social turmoil
**a.** Reasons for the strike.
**b.** Different kinds of protests.
**c.** Consequences.

### 2 The agreement
**a.** The players.
**b.** Deal they reached.

## Branching out

**1** Why is it important to avoid strikes in the transport industry?

**2** Are trade unions still powerful enough to stand up for the rights of workers/ employees? Why/why not? →*Key data*, p. 58

## {Methods}

### ■ Speaking practice

**1 Watch out for the right pronunciation.**
The following words are close to their French equivalents: *rail* – *chaos* – *maritime* – *union* – *stoppage* – *passengers* – *generous* – *inflation*.
Read them aloud, paying attention to the pronunciation and the stressed syllable.

**2 Read figures aloud.** →Tools 10, p.243
**a.** a 24-hour walkout
**b.** a 35-hour working week
**c.** 3.2 per cent
**d.** 0.75 per cent
**e.** April 2007

### ■ Writing practice

**1 Collective nouns**
• *This* ***is*** *good* ***news*** *for passengers and freight customers.*
The word "news" looks like a plural but is followed by a verb in the singular.
Other nouns are also singular in their form but plurals in their meanings: abstract nouns (*advice, experience, information, work*, etc.) and nouns that are uncountable in English (*luggage, furniture*, etc.).
All those nouns can be preceded by *some, any, no, a little, a bit of, a piece of*, etc. (*a piece of news/information*).

**Complete with the correct verbal form.**
**a.** The most important news of the day (*is / are*) the agreement between the RMT and Network Rail.
**b.** There (*was/were*) many people who were happy about the deal, as strikes cause too much disturbance.
**c.** The information according to which rail workers strikes were called off (*was / were*) of paramount importance.
**d.** The advice that (*was / were*) given to the RMT members was to maintain the 24-hour walkout.

**2 Prepare a short account in English.**
Use the sentences in part **1**: combine sentences **a** and **b** to explain what the news is.
Add a sentence to sum up the advantages workers will gain thanks to the deal that was reached.
→Tools 4, p. 236

## LISTENING PRACTICE

CD TRACK 48-49

*Trevor Coleman and Doris Ratting are talking airlines.*

**1 Comprehension**
Listen to the recording to find the following information.

**Part 1**
**a.** Where does Doris come from? How did she travel?
**b.** Name and type of company she used.
**c.** Company Trevor likes, and why.
**d.** Important assets for Doris.

**Part 2**
**a.** Why is frequency an important benefit to Trevor?
**b.** Second major benefit in Trevor's eyes.
**c.** Third major benefit in Trevor's eyes.

**2 Expression**
Give an oral account, or write a 100-word paragraph, summing up what you have heard.

# Go green, Miliband tells supermarket bosses

Environment secretary David Miliband yesterday summoned[1] bosses from the big four supermarkets to demand they work harder to make their businesses more environmentally friendly.

The meeting, at the Department for Environment, Food and Rural Affairs, was attended by Sir Ken Morrison, chairman of Wm Morrison; Justin King, chief executive of Sainsbury's; David Cheesewright, Asda chief operating officer; and Lucy Neville-Rolfe, Tesco company secretary. Mr Miliband said: "The food industry has the potential to significantly affect our fragile environment, but it is also in the unique position of being able to make a major positive contribution to reducing our environmental footprint[2]." He told the supermarket chiefs he wanted them to meet targets for reducing carbon emissions and asked how they could increase their uptake of locally produced seasonal food.

Tesco recently launched a 10-point "community plan" which includes a pledge to source more food from local suppliers and encourage shoppers to buy locally produced goods. The company has also announced plans to start moving non-food products by rail. Asda already moves some goods by train.

Yesterday's meeting took place as Defra released new figures showing an increase in $CO_2$ emissions caused by food transport for the UK. Road and air "food miles" generated nearly 18m metric tons[3] of carbon dioxide in 2004 – up 6% on the previous year. No figures are available beyond[4] 2004. The increase followed a 15% rise in emissions over the decade to 2002. Food transported by air – mainly fresh fruit and vegetables – accounted for only 0.1% of total food miles, but generated 13% of total food transport $CO_2$ emissions.

The supermarkets insist they are making progress. Sainsbury's said: "The mileage our lorries make has reduced by 5% in the last year." Liberal Democrat environment spokesman Chris Huhne called for government action to encourage more local supply. "Our own research has revealed that supermarket lorries travel the equivalent of almost four return trips to the moon every day. The big chains have a duty to provide environmentally friendly alternatives by supporting local producers."

Julia Finch and Andrew Clark,
*The Guardian*, July 21, 2006

1. *summon*: convoquer
2. *footprint:* empreinte (sens figuré ici)
3. *metric ton*: tonne (=1000 kg)
4. *beyond*: au-delà de

CD TRACK 50

## Work on words

### 1 | Find their equivalents in English

**Headline** passer au vert
**§1** exiger – respectueux de l'environnement
**§2** directeur général – secrétaire général(e) – de manière significative – émissions de gaz carbonique – augmenter – consommation – de saison
**§3** lancer – fournisseur
**§4** chiffres – précédent – disponible
**§5** kilométrage – camion – réclamer – recherche – voyage aller retour – devoir – fournir – soutenir

### 2 | Find their synonyms

**§2** president – very important – goal
**§3** promise (N) – find supplier for – customer – transport (V) – product
**§4** make public – produce – ten years – represent

## Info

***Department for Environment*** (or ***Defra***) UK government department headed by the ***Environment secretary*** → p. 54

***Wm Morrison, Sainsbury's, Asda, Tesco*** → p. 76 & 128.

***Liberal Democrat*** Someone left of centre, who favours state intervention but also free enterprise.

## Headlines

**1** Develop reflexes! You don't know who "Miliband" is: read the first words of the article to find the answer.

**2** Anticipate the contents of the article from the headline.

## The key points of the article

### 1 Read §1

**a.** Reason why the government and supermarkets have met.
**b.** Number of supermarkets concerned.

■ Complete this summary of §1 with: *environmentally – formerly – government – make – major – required.*
The British ... has ... the four ... supermarkets, that is to say Tesco, Asda, Wm Morrison (... Safeway) and Sainsbury's, to ... more efforts so as to become more ... friendly.

### 2 Read §2 and §3

**a.** Reason why the government wants the supermarkets to make efforts.
**b.** Name two things the supermarkets can do.
**c.** Explain Tesco's action.
**d.** Which supermarket is also making efforts?

### 3 Read §4 and §5

**a.** Major problem of food transport by road and air in the UK.
**b.** Compare 2002, 2003 and 2004 for "food miles" carbon emissions.
**c.** Is there a lot of food transported by air?
**d.** Progress made by Sainsbury's.
**e.** Comparison made about road transport.
**f.** One possible solution.

## {Methods}

### ■ Speaking practice

**1 Read figures aloud.** →Tools 10, p. 243

Read §4 aloud. If necessary, start by writing the following figures down. Then practise reading the groups of words in parentheses with the figures.
**a.** $CO_2$ (emissions)
**b.** 18m (metric tons)
**c.** (in) 2004
**d.** (up) 6% (on the previous year)
**e.** (beyond) 2004
**f.** (a) 15% (rise)
**g.** (over the decade to) 2002
**h.** (only) 0.1% (of total food miles)
**i.** 13% (of total food transport $CO_2$ emissions)

**2 Prepare an oral introduction.**
- Identify the source.
- Explain what the article is about (who, what, where, when).

### ■ Writing practice

**1 Translate §4.**
Pay attention to the figures and the prepositions.

**2 Write an account of the article in French (120 words).** →Tools 4, p. 236

## Branching out

**1** How can the supermarkets encourage shoppers to buy locally produced goods?

**2** Can you think of other points in Tesco's 10-point "community plan" that may be more environmentally friendly?
→*Key data*, p. 177

## Language

- *The environment secretary* ***wants the supermarkets to reduce*** *carbon emissions.*
- *He* ***asked them to increase*** *their uptake of locally produced seasonal food.*

Les verbes *want (like/love), ask, tell, advise, enable, allow, offer, teach* (entre autres) sont suivis de ***to*** + **infinitif**. Quand le sujet du second verbe est différent de celui du premier, comme dans les deux exemples, et s'il s'agit d'un pronom personnel (cf. second exemple), il est à la forme complément.
Attention à la place de la négation, avant *to* : *He asked them* ***not to increase*** *carbon emissions.*

**Translate into English**

**1.** Le ministre de l'environnement a conseillé aux supermarchés de rechercher des producteurs locaux.
**2.** Les supermarchés ont proposé au gouvernement de transporter tous les produits non alimentaires par rail.
**3.** Cette décision leur permettra de ne pas produire autant d'émissions de dioxyde de carbone. Elle devrait aussi leur permettre de faire des économies de carburant.
**4.** Les consommateurs veulent qu'ils leur proposent des produits plus écologiques. Le gouvernement va demander aux producteurs locaux de faire des efforts sur les prix.

**With free trade, transport has known a spectacular increase in many areas, entailing environmental problems.**

## 1-Definitions

There are four main means of transport: road, air, rail and water (sea, rivers, canals).
The word "hub" refers to a place where traffic is exchanged through several modes of transport.

### Transports of goods, or freight

The choice of the appropriate means of transport varies with the types and weights of products, the distance, the deadline, and whether their departing and arriving places are located near a railway network, an airport, a motorway network, a harbour, etc.

## 2-Road transport/hauling

In France, as in most countries, road transport carries up to 80% of all freight as it is the only one enabling door-to-door deliveries.
Different types of trucks (US)/lorries (GB) are used:
- lorries with a maximum capacity of 19 tons for lighter loads,
- articulated lorries are used for heavy loads (up to 40 tons).

High-added-value products, such as computers, are transported more safely by road carriers who also supply supermarkets with FMCGs. "Food miles" indicate the distance food is transported from source to store shelf.

### Advantages and drawbacks

Road transport is the most adapted to satisfy customers who expect their orders to be delivered within an increasingly shorter period of time in the just-in-time economic context.
However road transport has drawbacks.
- Many lorries go half empty, with an impact on the environment.
- Lorry drivers can be requested to ignore the regulations and drive too many hours, causing many road casualties.
- Social conflicts can affect road transport, with road blockades. Yet, they are limited in France as the sector is mostly shared by small and medium sized companies.

## 3-Rail transport

Transport of goods by train has been on the decline ever since World War I. Unlike lorries, trains cannot go everywhere, and rail is not a flexible means of transport. It is used for heavy loads (1,200 tonnes of goods per train).

### Combining rail and road: ferroutage

Since 2002, the French and Swiss have been using ferroutage (the transport of trucks or containers on trains) in an attempt to curb road traffic on the roads linking Northern and Southern Europe. This type of railway shuttle is already used in the Channel Tunnel. →**Chapter 13, *Landmark*, p. 209**

**Road trains**

Australian trucks are famous for being the largest trucks in the world. They are so huge that they are called "road trains" or "road monsters". They can have up to 32 wheels and weigh up to 115 tonnes (the largest European truck weighs 40 tonnes). Road trains can drag up to 4 trailers with a maximum length of 53.5 metres. They are not allowed in densely populated areas.

**The Mont Blanc tunnel tragedy**

In March 1999, a lorry caught fire in the middle of the tunnel linking France and Italy, killing 39 people. The tunnel was closed for improvement and repairs for 3 years. The re-opening of the Mont Blanc tunnel in 2003 was considered a serious mistake by environment activists who believe that the tunnel is still not safe enough.

The challenge over the next few decades is to build or enlarge rail tunnels through the Alps and Pyrenees. →*Exam*, p. 168

### The success of high-speed trains

Many tourists and business travellers are attracted by fast, comfortable high-speed trains throughout Europe. First launched in France and commercialized in 1981, they can reach 350 km per hour, soon expected to reach 400. Today, the SNCF operates 1,500 km of high-speed railway and is the second largest European railway company after the Deutsche Bahn (Germany).
→*Exam*, p. 168

## 4-Water transport

### Sea transport /shipping

Shipping is widely used to transport liquid in bulk in tankers or super tankers (above 250,000 tonnes). The world's largest tanker is the Knock Nevis (Norway), up to 648,000 tonnes when fully loaded. Their major drawback is causing oil spills and chemical poisoning, with disastrous consequences on the environment. To try to avoid such disasters, doubled-hulled tankers will be replacing single-hulled ones by 2015.

### Container ships, or "box boats"

Containers were invented after World War II. The first container ship could transport 58 containers. Today the usual quantity amounts to 15,000. Containers are used to transport "dry" goods. Containerization has revolutionized ship transport as it allows no waste of space.
Since 9/11, harbours have had to meet very strict safety standards. New regulations are always popping up, generating delays and slowing down economic activity.

### Merroutage

Similar to ferroutage, merroutage consists of transporting lorries and trains by ship. The aim is to cut down air pollution, as ships emit 2.5 times less carbon dioxide than lorries.

### Canals and rivers

Fluvial transport is considered an eco-friendly alternative to road transport. Barges can transport huge amounts of dry goods such as crops. Some rivers are already in full economic boom, such as the Seine which has recently become a water motorway. Paris harbour (in Gennevilliers) is in full growth, soon expecting to deal with half a million containers a year.

## 5-Air transport

Air transport is mostly used by business travellers or tourists on long and medium hauls. It is also used for freight, as the significant number of air cargo companies shows. However, as it is costly and used for perishable goods which must travel long distance. Companies such as UPS called "integrators", specialize in international door-to-door deliveries and resort to air transport.

Bright container ships

**The worst oil spills**
**1967** Torrey Canyon, UK – 119,000 tonnes
**1978** Amoco Cadiz, Brittany – 220,000 tonnes
**1989** Exxon Valdez, Alaska – 38,000 tonnes
**1999** Erika, Brittany – 13,000 tonnes

### Milestones
Before air traffic deregulation (1978 in the USA, 1993 in Europe) airlines were state-controlled. National air-carriers such as British Aiways or Air France held a monopoly in their own countries. Now, with globalisation and rising oil prices, airlines compete with a growing number of low-cost carriers.
The air industry has had difficult times, the worst being the 9/11 attacks. The combination of deregulation, 9/11 and the skyrocketing price of oil led many airlines to bankruptcy.

### The rise of no-frills airlines
Two main types of carriers are competing.
- Traditional airlines offer business class and first class, with various kinds of facilities to passengers paying a high fare.
- Low-cost carriers fly "no frills": passengers pay for the seat and the flight; food is not included, there is no business class and no comfort.

### Big airliners fight back
National airlines have adopted different strategies.
- Mergers, such as Air France and the Dutch company KLM; KLM now holds 47% of the group's shares.
- Global alliances: Sky Team regroups ten partners, including Air France/ KLM, Alitalia and Continental Airlines.
- The medical argument: big airlines offer more leg room. This is a major argument, as deep vein thrombosis (DVT), also called economy-class syndrome, is liable to affect 12% of the passengers taking a long haul flight once a year.

### Safety measures
After the British secret services foiled a major terrorist attack in August 2006, safety measures have become even more drastic. Passengers' check-ins can last several hours; hand-luggage is emptied or scanned; liquids are strictly banned. The new measures have resulted in many delays, especially for US destinations.

### A new airline breed
A number of small carriers have found new niches in lesser travelled routes. These carriers, among which Cityjet, Fly BE or VLM, have adopted a high quality and comfort strategy; the key to their success: punctuality and frequency. →*In brief*, **p. 143**

**Air France's nightmare**
The most famous European low-cost air carriers are **Ryanair** and **easyJet**, which operate an impressive number of daily regular flights from and to most big European cities. Ryanair, an Irish based company led by the very famous Michael O'Leary, has succeeded in obtaining new air routes in 19 French airports, in what used to be Air France's exclusive hunting ground. Mr O'Leary's aim is to transport over 5 million passengers in 2007.

## Question time

**1** What are the four means of transport?
**2** Which one is the most widely used and why?
**3** What are the drawbacks of road transport?
**4** What does ferroutage consist of?
**5** What happened in the Mont Blanc Tunnel in 1999?
**6** What do tankers and super tankers transport?
**7** Why has containerization revolutionized water transport?
**8** Why do environment activists wish to develop fluvial transport?
**9** What are the different types of air carriers on the market?
**10** What were the consequences of deregulation, terrorism and the price of oil on airlines?

LANDMARK

# Airbus

## In the beginning

**In the 1960s** European aircraft manufacturers did not only compete with the American giants (Boeing and McDonnell Douglas) but also with each other. However, in the mid-1960s negotiations started over a European project.

**1962** The Concorde is the first major European joint aircraft programme.

**1967** The British, French and German governments sign a Memorandum of Understanding (MoU) in September to start development of the 300-seat Airbus A300.

Thus, Airbus Industrie began as a consortium of plane companies to compete with the Americans.

## First agreement, first success

Airbus Industrie was set up in 1970 between Sud-Aviation (France) and Deutsche Airbus (Germany). CASA (Spain) joined in 1971. Following engine problems, the British government withdrew from the project from 1969 until 1978 when British Aerospace purchased a 20% share of the company. In 1972 the A300 made its maiden flight and the A300B2 entered service in 1974. At first the consortium was not very successful but by 1979 there were 81 aircraft in service. The launch of the A320 in 1981 made Airbus a major player on the aircraft market – it had over 400 orders before it first flew, compared to 15 for the A300 in 1972.

## Delayed new projects

**2000** DaimlerChrysler Aerospace (successor to Deutsche Airbus), Aérospatiale (successor to Sud-Aviation) and CASA merged to form EADS.

**2001** BAE Systems (formerly British Aerospace) and EADS formed the Airbus Integrated Company to develop the new Airbus A380. Seating 555 passengers, it should be the world's largest commercial passenger jet when it enters service. However, its schedule has been delayed. There are four final Airbus assembly lines, two in Toulouse (France), one in Hamburg (Germany) and the most recent one in Seville (Spain).

## Competition with Boeing

Airbus and Boeing compete fiercely for aircraft orders. Airbus products are still outnumbered 6 to 1 by Boeings. There are over 5,000 Boeing 737s alone in service, compared with around 3,850 Airbus aircraft. Airbus made a late entry into the modern jet airliner market (1972 vs. 1958 for Boeing): it won more than 50% of aircraft orders recently and delivered more aircraft in 2003 and 2004. However, in 2005, Boeing was the world's largest civil aircraft manufacturer with 49% of orders and 45% of deliveries, overtaking Airbus for the first time since 2000. Each company offers models a bit smaller or a bit bigger than the other. Airlines see this as a benefit since they get a more complete product range than if both companies offered identical planes.

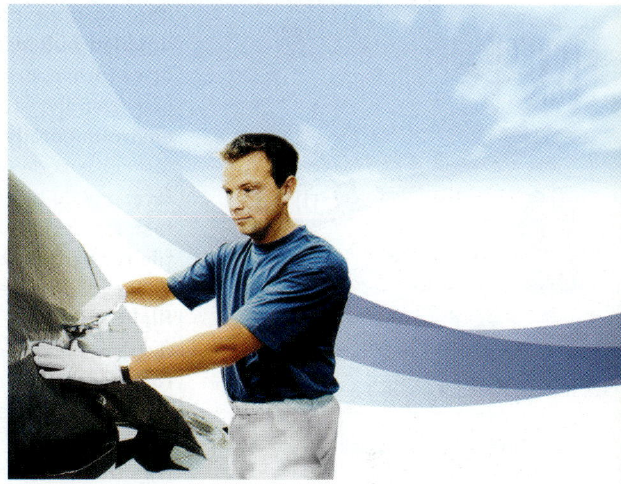

Airbus: a world of innovation

## Trade war

Trade disputes have broken out between the US and the EU over the subsidies that the two sides pay to the aircraft industry. The US claims that the financial support European governments – loans with advantageous terms – provided to Airbus is in breach of world trade rules. The EU argues the same is true of Washington's subsidies for Boeing through military and research contracts and tax breaks. The US claims Airbus has received the equivalent of $40bn in subsidies since 1967 while the EU says Boeing has pocketed some $18bn in subsidies since 1992.

The US says that Airbus is no longer a young company and that it should not receive subsidies. The EU retorts that Airbus' success reflects a steady decline at Boeing rather than regular injections of public money.

Each side also claims that a large chunk of the other's subsidies has been used towards developing new-generation super sized passenger jets – Boeing's 7E7 "Dreamliner" and Airbus' A380. Their success is critical to both companies' future performance.

**Online t@sk**

Visit Airbus website on
www.airbus.com/en/worldwide/
to analyse the company's presence worldwide. Report to the class.

"It's the last time I fly with a no-frills airline!"

**aircraft:** avion, appareil
**airliner:** avion de ligne
**airport:** aéroport
**articulated lorry:** semi-remorque
**assembly:** montage
**assembly line:** chaîne de montage
**ban:** interdire
**bankruptcy:** faillite
**barge:** péniche
**book:** réserver
**booking:** réservation
**-bound:** en partance pour, à destination de
**bridge:** pont
**business class:** classe affaires
**business traveller:** voyageur d'affaires
**car park:** parking
**car rental:** location de voitures
**carbon dioxide:** gaz carbonique
**carbon emission:** émission de gaz carbonique
**carrier:** transporteur
**casualty:** victime (d'accident)
**check-in:** embarquement
**compete:** concurrencer
**competitor:** concurrent
**complaint:** réclamation
**container:** conteneur
**container ship:** porte-conteneurs
**containerisation:** conteneurisation
**costly:** cher, coûteux
**curb:** limiter
**cut-throat:** acharné (concurrence, etc.)
**deep vein thrombosis (DVT):** thrombose veineuse profonde (TVP)
**delay:** retard
**delivery:** livraison
**departing place:** point de départ
**deregulation:** déréglementation
**detain:** retenir
**door-to-door:** porte à porte
**doubled-hulled:** à double coque
**drive (drove, driven):** conduire
**eco-friendly:** écologique
**environmentally friendly:** respectueux de l'environnement
**fare:** prix du billet
**fast:** rapide
**file for bankruptcy:** se déclarer en faillite, déposer le bilan
**flight:** vol
**fly (flew, flown):** voler, voyager en avion
**food miles:** distance parcourue par les aliments du lieu de production au lieu de vente
**free trade:** libre échange
**freight:** fret
**hand-luggage:** bagages à main
**harbour:** port
**haul:** voyage
**haulier:** transporteur (routier)
**high-added-value:** à forte valeur ajoutée
**high-speed train:** train à grande vitesse
**highway:** autoroute
**hub:** plate-forme de correspondances, hub
**in bulk:** par grosses quantités
**just-in-time:** juste à temps
**legroom:** place pour les jambes
**level crossing:** passage à niveau
**link:** relier
**load:** charge
**lorry (GB):** camion
**lorry driver:** (chauffeur) routier, camionneur
**lounge:** salon, salle d'attente
**low-cost company:** compagnie aérienne à bas prix
**maiden flight:** premier vol, vol inaugural
**means of transport:** moyen de transport
**merger:** fusion
**metric ton:** tonne (= 1,000 kg)
**mileage:** kilométrage
**monopoly:** monopole
**motorway:** autoroute
**network:** réseau
**no frills:** avec service minimum
**non-stop flight:** vol sans escale
**oil spill:** marée noire
**on board:** à bord
**one-way:** aller simple
**order:** commande
**passenger:** passager
**perishable goods:** biens périssables
**plane:** avion
**rail worker:** employé du rail
**railway network:** réseau ferroviaire
**railway track:** voie de chemin de fer
**reclining:** inclinable
**regulation:** réglementation
**reliable:** fiable
**repayment terms:** conditions de remboursement
**return trip:** voyage aller retour
**road blockade:** barrage routier
**route:** trajet
**safely:** en sécurité
**safety measures:** mesures de sécurité
**safety standards:** normes de sécurité
**schedule:** planning, calendrier
**seat:** siège
**ship:** navire
**shipping:** navigation
**shipwreck:** naufrage
**shuttle:** navette
**signal:** aiguillage
**signalman:** aiguilleur
**single-hulled:** à une seule coque
**small-and medium-sized companies/firms:** petites et moyennes entreprises
**state-controlled:** sous contrôle de l'État
**station:** gare
**stream:** cours d'eau
**strike:** grève
**subsidy:** subvention
**supertanker:** pétrolier géant, supertanker
**support:** (N) soutien ; (V) soutenir
**tanker:** pétrolier, tanker
**tax break:** réduction d'impôt, avantage fiscal
**tourist:** touriste
**traffic:** circulation
**trailer:** remorque
**truck (US):** camion
**tunnel:** tunnel
**weigh:** peser
**weight:** poids

## Charts and tables

**1.** Study the following chart displaying the main complaints made by airplane customers.

WRITTEN COMPLAINTS 2005-2006

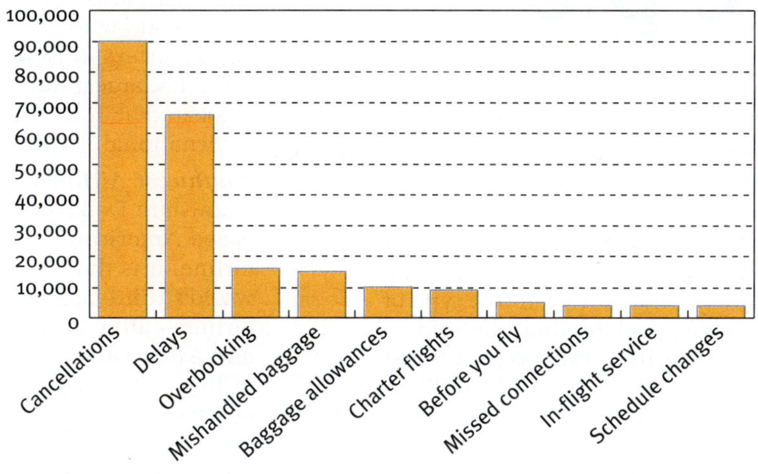


Air Transport Users

**2.** Give an oral presentation of this chart. →Tools 11, p. 244

## Communication tasks

### Role play

**A: You are a customer.**
You were very disappointed by several services and shocked by many annoying events during your last flight. You phone the airline customer assistance number to complain.

**B: You work at the customer assistance hotline for a famous airline company.**
An angry customer phones you. You have to provide reassuring answers and calm him/her down. You can prepare a list of useful advice to answer the customer's request. Don't forget to "smile" on the phone!

You can find help and inspiration on the Air Transport Users Council website at
www.caa.co.uk/default.aspx?categoryid = 306
→Tools 9, p. 242

### Letter of complaint about planes

You are **A.** The hotline was not very helpful. Write a letter to the head office to complain.
→Tools 7, p. 240

# Low-cost airlines seek more pie

Low-cost carriers are extending their push into the territory of their bigger competitors, with JetBlue Airlines Corp. announcing Thursday that it will expand to Ohio, and Southwest Airlines Co. ready to debut in Washington, D.C.

The New York-based JetBlue said it will begin providing daily non-stop flights in October between Port Columbus International Airport and New York and Boston, offering introductory one-way fares as low as $69. Dallas-based Southwest on Thursday announced one-way fares as low as $79 for new daily non-stop flights between Washington Dulles International Airport and four cities.

The carriers are leading the way toward a low-cost model in an industry in which several major airlines have filed for bankruptcy in recent years, said Frank Werner, a finance professor in New York. "In the last five years, since 9/11 and Iraq and the price of oil going through the ceiling, the major carriers have found out they have to become low-cost carriers," Werner said. "This is the natural evolution of the industry."

Defining low-cost airlines has become more difficult because there are times when the traditional carriers have lower prices for some flights than the low-cost airlines, said the chief economist at the Air Transport Association trade organization. "I think the lines have been blurred and there's no longer a very meaningful distinction between one type of carrier and another," he said.

Airline industry analyst Terry Trippler said JetBlue, Southwest and other low-cost airlines are filling the gap left when major airlines reduced flights to cut costs. However, he said, too many planes can mean excess capacity and a drop in fares that could damage the industry across the board. "In the long term, we must have a stable air transportation system. If these airlines continue to bleed red ink[1], we're not going to have that," he said. "I'm not saying anyone is expanding irresponsibly, but we are in a situation where we have to be very careful."

JetBlue spokeswoman Jenny Dervin said that by focusing on shorter flights, the airline stimulates the economy and tourism at new sites, while driving fares down by 50 percent in some locations.

*Business Week*, July 2006

1. *bleed red ink*: battre de l'aile

## Info

***JetBlue Airlines***
American low-cost airline with headquarters in New York. Its largest hub is located at JFK International Airport.

***Southwest Airlines***
A low-fare Dallas-based American airline. It is the world's third-largest airline – after Delta and American airlines – by number of passengers carried and the largest in the US by number of passengers carried domestically. Low-cost easyJet and Ryanair have repeated its business model.

## References

You can find relevant information by reading various pages in your book and memorising a few facts and ideas.

→ **Companies, p. 28**
→ **Consumers, p. 70**
→ **Transport, p. 147**
→ **Tourism, p. 191**

ACTIVITY **Practise giving an account of this article.**

## Introduction

You should explain where the article comes from, when it was published and what it is about. →Tools 4, p. 236

This article, which was published in *Business Week*, an American weekly, in July 2006, reports on low-cost airlines and their expansion over the past five years.

## Development

Once you have understood the article, organise your ideas into two or three different parts, using set phrases and link-words. →Tools 4, p. 236

1. The expansion of low-cost airlines
2. Reasons for their expansion
3. Risks of the expansion

You should also use the information given in *Info* and what you have learnt, for example by referring to the various pages indicated in *References*.

### 1. The expansion of low-cost airlines

Low-cost carriers with a limited number of flights to limited destinations are expanding.

- JetBlue Airlines Corp., a New York-based no-frills carrier, and Southwest Airlines Co., another low-fare US airline and the world's third-largest airline after Delta and American airlines by number of passengers carried, both announced that they would expand and provide new non-stop flights to various destinations.
- JetBlue provides daily non-stop flights starting October 2006 between Port Columbus International Airport and New York and Boston. Southwest offers new daily non-stop flights between Washington Dulles International Airport and four cities.

Both companies offer very low one-way fares at $69 and $79.

### 2. Reasons for their expansion

- **The problems of major carriers**: Several major airlines have filed for bankruptcy in recent years. Those big companies are not as profitable as they used to be, due to various reasons. 9/11, of course, entailed a downturn in the economy, all the more so for airline companies. Another factor for the problems encountered by airlines is the price of oil which has skyrocketed.
- **Consequences**: The problems they encountered have driven the major carriers' profits down. Therefore they have had to cut costs and to do so, they reduced their flights. The low-cost airlines then decided to offer their services on those destinations. Thanks to their low prices (sometimes 50% cheaper), no-frills carriers boost consumer spending, local economies and tourism at their new destinations.

### 3. Risks of the expansion

- **Dilution of the companies' identities**: It is becoming more and more difficult for consumers to make a clear distinction between no-frills and traditional airlines. On the one hand, some of the traditional airlines have reduced the price of their tickets so much that their fares are lower than low-cost airlines. On the other hand, low-cost carriers are tapping the market which used to belong to the traditional airlines.
- **Loss of stability**: Having both traditional carriers and no-frills airlines might lead to excess capacity, i.e. too many planes. This in turn would lead to even lower prices, which no company would be able to cope with, especially as fuel costs are on the rise. Therefore analysts say that all airline companies have to be careful to remain profitable one way or another.

## Conclusion

You should sum up the main ideas and try to open out in a new direction.

This article shows that the airline industry has undergone a radical change over the past decade with the rise of low-cost carriers. Major traditional carriers can no longer ignore their cheaper rivals which benefit customers and have allowed the economy to develop at smaller places where they did not go. However, no-frills airlines have to become fully reliable if they want to remain attractive to consumers who expect improved services while retaining good value for money.

## Branching out

Now, you should move away from the article and develop more ideas. The following questions can help you.

**1** Have you ever travelled with a low-cost carrier? Why/Why not?

**2** What could major carriers do to regain passengers?

## Case study: dealing with an unexpected problem

You are the manager of a mountain-resort hotel in the Pennines.
You have ordered 12 bedside tables and 48 chairs with white plastic cushions for your hotel as a seminar with 50 people is expected in two days. You agreed on a 10% discount with the company who sells and delivers the items. You have just received the following fax.

**The Decor Furniture Company**
99 Thorn Avenue
Oxford OX4 3XH

Dear Mr Stark,

We confirm your telephone order of last Friday, for 15 bedside tables and 48 chairs with beige plastic cushions to be delivered immediately.
However, our driver was unable to leave our warehouse this morning for deliveries because of heavy fog and unexpected road works. As a result, all our scheduled deliveries will be held for the next 72 hours. Please let us know a suitable delivery date for you.
We are enclosing our invoice for the amount of £600. As agreed, our terms are 5% discount for cash payment or 30 days net.

Yours sincerely,

*Sophie Barton*

Sophie Barton

**Roleplay** →Tools 9, p. 242

**A:** You are Sophie Barton. You receive a phone call from Joe Stark.

**B:** You are Joe Stark. You call Sophie Barton.

## PERSONAL TASK

After the phone conversation, Sophie Barton sends Joe Stark another letter, confirming the new agreement.
→Tools 7, p. 240

# IN THIS UNIT...

- Companies: Amazon, Google, Kazaa, YouTube...
- Learn about online advertising & video sharing
- Introduce video conferencing & other technologies

# 10
## New technologies

**→ Before you START**

*In brief:* **Selling books and groceries online**
*Front page:* **Would you pay with your fingerprints?**

## Do you think one can do real business in a virtual world?

### Words

- **Nouns:** real life, online game, avatar, creation, business
- **Adjectives:** fictional, real, onscreen, graphic, imaginary, popular

### LISTENING PRACTICE

CD TRACK 51

Listen to the recording.
**1.** What are the people talking about?
**2.** Explain their opinions.

# Have some cereal with your Proust, says Amazon

Readers will be able to pick up some Corn Flakes along with the complete works of Proust at the world's biggest online bookshop, Amazon.com, which is branching out into groceries.

The American company's new food arm has begun offering 14,000 non-perishable groceries to its US customers, though sceptics have asked how the company can hope to compete with the far broader range available at supermarkets. Amazon is emphasising the depth, rather than the breadth, of its mix: it says that when it sells a brand it will carry every flavour available including cult favourites that can be tricky to find. The company is also offering a large organic range.

Jeff Bezos, the founder of Amazon, described the venture as "a store filled with stuff you need and stuff you love; everyday staples[1] and fun new snacks."

While online shopping is growing in popularity, it still represents a small proportion of overall sales. About 0.7% of grocery sales in the United States are online. In Britain, shopping of all types on the internet grew by 32% last year to £19bn.

Critics wonder whether Amazon is in danger of losing its cachet as a vendor of books, music and DVDs – the specialities on which it has built its popularity since its foundation in 1995.

Andrew Clark, *The Guardian*, 25 July 2006

1. *staples:* produits de base

CD TRACK 52

## Work on words

### 1 I Find their equivalents in English

**§1** librairie
**§2** épicerie – concurrencer – gamme – que l'on peut se procurer – mettre l'accent sur – profondeur – étendue – marque – biologique
**§3** entreprise
**§4** l'ensemble des ventes

### 2 I Find their synonyms

**§1** obtain – expand
**§2** branch (N) – sell – large – difficult
**§3** products
**§5** creation

## Headlines

**1** What company is concerned? What do you know about this company?

**2** The headline is funny and intriguing. Explain why.

**3** Read **§1** and rephrase this headline to make it more explicit. Start with "Amazon..."

## The key points of the article

### 1 The new venture
**a.** The company (§1).
**b.** The market and the new items offered (§2).
**c.** The target.

### 2 The marketing strategy
**a.** Products chosen.
**b.** Reasons for this choice.

### 3 Limits
**a.** Competition.
**b.** Risk.

## Branching out

**1** Online shopping has been growing steadily. Do you think this trend will go on? Why/Why not? →*Key data*, p. 132

**2** What kind of products do people buy online? Do you think cultural products are declining? Why/Why not? →*Key data*, p. 162

## {Methods}

### Speaking practice

**1 Slogans and catchphrases**

"A store filled with stuff you need and stuff you love!" Slogans and catchphrases are meant to be remembered easily.

**Write slogans and catchphrases.**

Example: ... offering 14,000 non-perishable groceries to its US customers > *14,000 new products available on our new grocery page!*

**a.** Amazon is emphasising the depth, rather than the breadth, of its mix.
**b.** ... when it sells a brand it will carry every flavour available including cult favourites.
**c.** The company is also offering a large organic range.

**2 Read figures aloud.** →Tools 10, p. 243

If necessary, start by writing the following figures down. Then practise reading the groups of words in parentheses with the figures.

**a.** 14,000 (non-perishable groceries)
**b.** 0.7% (of grocery sales)
**c.** 32% (last year)
**d.** £19bn
**e.** (In) 1995

### Writing practice

**1 Expressing probability with modal verbs**

Modal verbs can express the probability of a situation or event: the event can be considered almost impossible (*might*), very likely (*must*), certain (*will*), etc.

| Degree of probability | 4 certain | > 3 | > 2 | > 1 | > 0 impossible |
|---|---|---|---|---|---|
| | *will* | *must* *should* | *may* *might* | *could* | *can't* |

**Complete the following sentences with a modal verb to express probability.**

**a.** Online shoppers ... be able to buy groceries along with books and CDs.
**b.** Fourteen thousand non-perishable groceries ... be offered to US customers.
**c.** Experts wonder if the company ... compete with supermarkets.
**d.** Online shopping ... skyrocket in the coming decade.

**2 Prepare a short account in English.**

Use the sentences in part **1** to sum up the consequences of Amazon's new strategy. Choose among the following link words: *as a matter of fact – what is more – even though – actually.* →Tools 4, p. 236

## LISTENING PRACTICE

CD TRACK 53-54

*Jack Miles and Brett Osterfeld are discussing new hi-tech systems.*

**1 Comprehension**

Listen to the recording to find the following information.

**Part 1**
**a.** Topic of conversation.
**b.** Problem for stores.
**c.** Give details about Gatekeeper's Video Investigator.

**Part 2**
**a.** Explain what a "push out" is.
**b.** Gatekeeper's solution to push outs.
**c.** What are EAS tags? Describe them.
**d.** Reason for replacing them with RFID tags.
**e.** Current problem.

**2 Expression**

Give an oral account, or write a 100-word paragraph, summing up what you have heard.

# Can your fingers pay for you?

Wal-Mart and other retailers are testing whether customers can pay by scanning fingerprints.

You could soon be making purchases with the touch of a finger, according to new research promoting the benefits of biometric payment for discount giants like Wal-Mart, Target, and Costco.

The study, by a Sanford Bernstein analyst, claims that the use of so-called "electronic wallets" reduces the potential for fraud and identity theft, speeds up the checkout process, and most importantly, lowers transaction processing fees for retailers, improving their bottom line. The report estimated that a 20% reduction in processing costs at large retailers like Wal-Mart over the next several years could result in a 3% to 4% increase in earnings per share by 2009. Wal-Mart and Costco are said to be studying the possibility but both companies declined to comment.

Retailers are currently experimenting with several other emerging payment technologies such as self-checkout (widely used at Home Depot), and "near field communication," that involves waving your mobile phone near a reader.

How does biometric payment work? Customers first set up an account by scanning their fingerprint at an in-store kiosk and entering their phone number and their checking and credit card account information. When they want to make a purchase, they just place their finger on a scanner at the checkout, enter their phone number and pay.

The benefits to customers are twofold. Firstly, checkout is faster – 70% speedier than traditional forms of payment. Secondly, security is improved. There are around 10 million cases of identity theft annually, 13% of which occurred during a purchase transaction.

But it's the benefit to retailers that could really drive adoption. Transaction fees that the retailers have to pay for credit and debit card payments have skyrocketed, and can account for about 20% of pre-tax profits for low margin retailers. Retailers hate these fees and biometric access is one way to lower them. An expert estimates that switching to fingerprints could slash the net cost of a transaction by anywhere from 40 to 70 cents.

*The London News*, June 25, 2006

CD TRACK 55

## Work on words

### 1 | Find their equivalents in English

**Subhead** empreinte digitale
**§1** promouvoir
**§2** portefeuille – vol – accélérer – caisse (de sortie) – baisser – frais de traitement – revenus – action
**§3** largement, beaucoup – impliquer – bouger, manipuler – lecteur
**§4** fonctionner – compte
**§5** double
**§6** avant impôt – marge

### 2 | Find their synonyms

**§1** advantages
**§2** make ... better – financial result – rise (N)
**§3** at the present time – try (V)
**§5** quicker – happen
**§6** increase a lot – represent – changing – cut (V)

## Info

***Wal-Mart***
American supermarket and the world's largest company, Wal-Mart is famous for its low-price policy. The chain has developed in numerous foreign countries and owns UK's Asda.

→Chapter 8, p. 133

***Cotsco*** and ***Target*** are two other US low margin supermarket chains.

***Home Depot***
The world's largest retailer of home improvement products. The Home Depot is the third largest retailer in the world, behind Wal-Mart and Carrefour.

## Headlines

**1** Develop reflexes! Read the subhead to have more information. How is "fingers" developed in the subhead?

**2** Anticipate the contents of the article from the headline and the subhead.

## The key points of the article

### 1 Read §1

**a.** A modern way customers may use to pay in supermarkets.
**b.** Which supermarkets are concerned?

■ Complete this summary of §1 with:
*allowing – payment – profitable – research – retail – shoppers.*
New ... has established that ... to use biometric ... could be ... for American ... giants such as Wal-Mart, Target and Costco.

### 2 Read §2 and §3

**a.** The advantages of electronic payment.
**b.** Which advantage does the journalist consider the most important?
**c.** Who would benefit in the end?
**d.** Other technological forms of payment.

### 3 Read §4, §5 and §6

**a.** What customers have to do before they can use the technology.
**b.** What happens when they check out.
**c.** Compare traditional and technological means of payment as far as speed is concerned.
**d.** Why is safety important for shoppers?
**e.** Reason why retailers want to reduce the transaction fees.

## {Methods}

### ■ Speaking practice

**1 Read figures aloud.** →Tools 10, p. 243
Read the second part of §2 and §5 aloud. Practise reading the groups of words in parentheses with the figures.
**a.** (a) 20% (reduction)
**b.** (a) 3% (increase)
**c.** (a) 3% to 4% (increase)
**d.** (by) 2009
**e.** 70% (faster)
**f.** (the) 10 million (cases)
**g.** 13%

**2 Prepare an oral introduction.**
• Identify the source.
• Explain what the article is about (who, what, where, when).

### ■ Writing practice

**1 Translate §5 and §6.**
Pay attention to the figures and the prepositions.

**2 Write a summary of the article in French (120 words).**
→Tools 3, p. 234

## Branching out

**1** Would you like to pay by scanning your fingerprints? Why/Why not?

**2** What other technological devices do, or could, supermarkets use? →*Key data*, p. 132 & 162

## Language

• *Scott Langdoc estimates that switching could shave the cost of a transaction by anywhere **from 40 to 70 cents**.*
• *A 20% reduction in processing costs at retailers like Wal-Mart could result in a 3% **to** 4% **increase in** earnings.*
Pour exprimer une variation (augmentation, baisse, etc.), ou une étendue, on utilise les prépositions ***from*** (point de départ) et ***to*** (point d'arrivée). Notez que *from* est parfois omis, et la préposition ***in***.

**Translate into English**
**1.** Les gens qui font leurs courses dépensent de 150 à 200 dollars à chaque passage en caisse.
**2.** Les frais de transaction que paient les commerçants représentent de 1 à 2 % du montant total des achats.
**3.** Le fait de scanner les empreintes digitales des clients permettrait aux commerçants une diminution des coûts de transactions de 40 à 70 cents.
**4.** Il y a une nette (*sharp*) augmentation du nombre de cas de vols liés à l'identité qui se produisent pendant les achats.

tions. Its growth rate has been estimated at 31% a year since 2004. Millions of collectibles, computers, furniture, vehicles and other items are listed, bought and sold daily through the internet. Anyone can sell anything as long as it is not illegal. Moreover, payment on e-Bay is considered safe thanks to PayPal, a site specialized in secure online payment worldwide.
In 2005, e-Bay bought Skype, the world's fastest growing internet communication website, allowing users around the world to communicate through voice and video for free.

### Blogging, the expansion of a new fad

The word "blog" is a contraction of "Web log", a website designed like a diary, providing comments and images on any possible topic the blogger chooses to tackle.
Computer programming requires a certain amount of know-how, but computer literacy is not necessary to create blogs which use blog software, such as WordPress or LiveJournal and can be hosted by dedicated blog hosting services.
Fifty million blogs worldwide were registered in July 2006, a figure which has been multiplied by 100 in 3 years. Among them 20% were French.
Blogging has brought about new legal issues: workers have been fired because their blogs was deemed slanderous, or allegedly leaked confidential information.

### MMORPGs (massive multiplayer online role playing games)

Online video games with very sophisticated video software now compete with video game consoles such as Nintendo and Sony which are not designed to operate online yet.
MMORPGs, such as *Second Life* (SL) or *World of Warcraft* (WoW), are parallel virtual worlds where players play, invest, work, learn, etc. There were more than 15m MMORPG players in 2006.
Many companies use the games as demo platforms to test their products or services virtually before releasing them on the real market, which is cheaper than advertising campaigns. NGOs such as the American Cancer Society or Save the Children have also understood their impact to raise funds.

**A corporate tool**

Politicians, political parties and CEOs are increasingly entering the blogging world as they found it was a free and useful tool to establish direct discussions with voters or consumers. In France Michel Edouard **Leclerc**, CEO of the eponymous supermarket, pioneered blogging in the corporate world; he says that although writing and updating a blog is very demanding and not without risks as you are necessarily confronted with embarrassing issues, it remains a fantastic tool to communicate with people. Leclerc's blog is visited by 2,500 to 10,000 visitors a year.

## Question time

1 How long did it take for the Internet to become part of our daily lives?
2 Explain two areas in which high technology plays a major part.
3 What are the advantages of a Wi-Fi connexion?
4 What can people do on e-Bay?
5 What is a blog?
6 Why are mobile phones considered as high tech items?
7 Would/Do you like to watch TV on your mobile? Why/Why not?
8 What makes mobile phones a controversial issue?
9 How do you understand the fact that mobile phones used to be chief American love/hate objects?
10 Why are massive multiplayer online games attractive for brands?

LANDMARK

# Google

**Google is the world's most popular web-based search engine with millions of requests every day. It has had a major impact on online culture and is now so famous that its brand name has become a verb.** **→Chapter 7, Brands, *Prep Page*, p. 122**
**The name "Google" came from a misspelling of "googol" which refers to 10100 (a 1 followed by one-hundred zeros). Google, Inc. had 9,378 full-time employees as of September 2006.**

## Early history

**1996** Google begins as a research project by two Stanford students, Larry Page and Sergey Brin. Original address of the domain: *google.stanford.edu*.
**1997** The domain *google.com* is registered.
**1999** The company moves into Silicon Valley, home to many technology start-ups. Growing numbers of internet users like Google's simple, clean design.

## Growth

**2000** Google develops the automation of online advertising. A company selling sneakers can bid to have a link to its website appear in the sponsored area whenever someone does a Google search for "tennis" or "Michael Jordan", etc. Its link is shown according to how much it pays and how many people click on the link.
**2001** Google patents its ranking mechanism ("PageRank").
**2004** Initial public offering (IPO). 19,605,052 shares at $85 each. The sale raises $1.2bn and many employees become instant millionaires. Launching of Google Earth.
**2006** Numerous new services, such as Google Page Creator (an easy-to-use webpage creator) and Google Notebook – a tool permitting users to clip text, images and links from web pages, save them online and share them with others. Purchase of the popular online video site YouTube.
Google has turned in a profit every year since 2001.

## Corporate culture

Google is known for its relaxed corporate culture, including "You can be serious without a suit". Brin and Page wear black T-shirts, jeans and sneakers (and white lab coats for special occasions).

- Each employee has access to the corporate recreation centre and workout rooms, washers and dryers, a massage room, assorted video games, a piano, a pool table, etc.
- Engineers are encouraged to spend 20% of their time on projects that interest them. That's how services such as Gmail started.
- The company's site often offers cartoon "Google Doodles" logos with drawings or humorous font designs.

- Google is famous for its April fool's Day events. As a result, many people thought the announcement of Gmail in April 2004 was a joke!

## "Don't be evil?"

Google's code of conduct is "Don't Be Evil". However, it has been criticised.

- Google's cooperation with the French and German governments to remove Nazi sites from search results has led to claims of censorship. Far worse, in 2006, Google agreed to a censored version of their website to please the Chinese government. Google argues it has to obey local laws.
- Google's cookies worry a lot of individuals, corporations and governments about privacy.
- Google Book Search's effort to digitise millions of books has led to copyright disputes.
- A number of governments are worried about the security risks posed by geographic details provided by Google Earth.

## Future prospects

Google has to face more and more competition from mainstream technology companies. For example Microsoft offers similar services, such as webmail (Gmail vs. Hotmail), search and other applications (Microsoft's Windows Live Local vs. Google Maps).

Can Google maintain its success – a company worth $100 billion – and remain true to the ideals that made it so popular? In 2004 *Wired* magazine had "GOOGLEMANIA!" on the cover. The 2006 cover, by contrast, says "GOOGLEPHOBIA", with an article about the enemies Google is making as it expands.

**Online t@sk**

Log on to Google's website and report on the latest developments.

### COMPUTERS AND COMPOUNDS

**computer:** ordinateur
**computer-aided:** assisté par ordinateur
**computer crime:** délit informatique
**computer file:** fichier informatique
**computer game:** jeu électronique
**computer graphics:** infographie
**computer literacy:** compétence en informatique
**computer literate:** initié en informatique
**computer nerd/geek:** surdoué/cinglé en informatique
**computer programming:** programmation informatique
**computer virus:** virus informatique
**laptop (computer):** (ordinateur) portable
**personal computer (PC):** ordinateur

**access point:** point d'accès
**account:** compte
**addiction:** accoutumance
**auction:** vente aux enchères
**available:** accessible, disponible
**biometric:** biométrique
**branch out:** étendre ses activités, se diversifier
**broadband:** ADSL
**broadcast:** émettre
**browse:** surfer
**built-in:** intégré
**CCTV (closed circuit television):** télévision en circuit fermé
**cell phone:** téléphone portable
**censorship:** censure
**charge:** faire payer
**checkout:** caisse de sortie
**chip:** puce (électronique)
**click:** cliquer
**clip:** attacher
**conference call:** audioconférence, téléconférence
**copyright:** droits de reproduction
**copy and paste:** copier-coller
**crack:** déchiffrer
**damage:** endommager
**data:** données
**demo platform:** plate-forme de démonstration
**device:** mécanisme
**digital:** numérique
**digitise:** numériser
**domain:** domaine
**download:** (N) téléchargement ; (V) télécharger
**downloadable:** téléchargeable
**download-to-own service:** service d'achat en téléchargement
**electronic surveillance tag:** étiquette de surveillance électronique
**electronic wallet:** porte-feuille électronique
**email box:** (boîte de) messagerie
**embedded:** gravé, inséré
**enhance:** améliorer
**enter:** entrer, saisir
**entertainment:** loisir
**extra-flat:** extra-plat
**extra-light:** ultra-léger
**fad:** engouement, mode
**fee:** coût, charge
**fibre-optic:** à fibre optique
**file:** fichier
**file-sharing:** partage de fichiers
**fingerprint:** empreinte digitale
**font:** police de caractères
**game console:** console de jeux
**hack:** pirater
**handheld:** tenu à la main
**handset:** combiné
**hard disk :** disque dur
**harmless:** sans risque
**host:** héberger
**information superhighway:** autoroute de l'information
**instant message:** SMS
**know-how:** savoir-faire
**lock (up):** verrouiller
**login:** identification
**mainstream:** principal, dominant
**microwave oven:** four à micro-ondes
**multiplayer:** multi-joueurs
**network:** réseau
**obsolete:** dépassé
**online:** en ligne
**online payment:** paiement en ligne
**online shopping:** courses en ligne
**P2P/peer to peer:** P2P, d'utilisateur à utilisateur
**password:** mot de passe
**pastime:** passe-temps
**phishing:** aller à la pêche aux numéros de cartes de crédit

'IT'S A GADGET FOR BUYING GADGETS OVER THE NET'

**privacy:** vie privée
**processing:** traitement
**publisher:** éditeur
**radio frequency:** fréquence radio
**reader:** lecteur
**register:** enregistrer
**release:** sortir, publier
**remote control:** télécommande
**remove:** supprimer
**robotics:** robotique
**safety:** sécurité
**saturate:** saturer
**scan:** scanner
**screen:** écran
**search engine:** moteur de recherche
**secure:** sans risque
**service provider:** fournisseur d'accès
**share:** partager
**shoplifter:** voleur (à l'étalage)
**slanderous:** diffamatoire
**slide show:** diaporama
**smart:** intelligent
**software:** logiciel
**spam:** courriel indésirable
**state-of-the-art:** dernier cri
**switch:** changer
**theft:** vol, cambriolage
**tool:** outil
**Trojan horse:** cheval de Troie
**USB key/bar:** clé USB
**user:** utilisateur
**videoconference:** visioconférence
**webaholic:** drogué du net
**website:** site internet
**wireless:** sans fil
**World Wide Web ("www"):** toile
**worm:** ver

## Charts and tables

**1.** Study the following pie charts on music and technology.

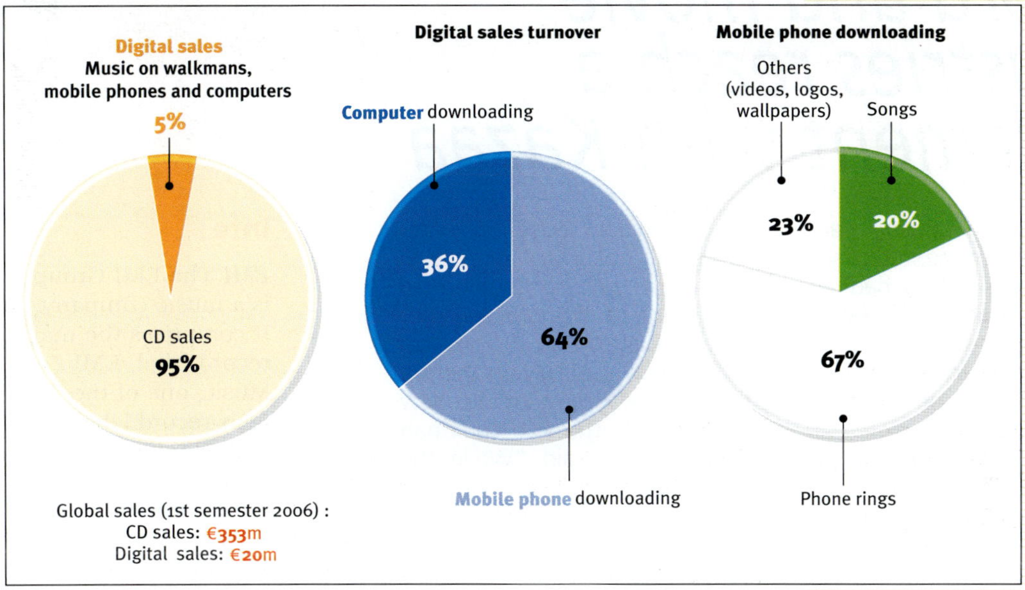


**2.** Give an oral presentation of each pie chart to show how deeply new technologies have affected music sales. →**Tools 11, p. 244**

## Online tasks

### Presenting a service

Visit the website of the University of Cambridge to discover useful tips for videoconferencing: **www-tus.csx.cam.ac.uk/videoconf/vctips.html** .

**1.** Introduce some other technologies that can be useful in meetings, such as PowerPoint slide shows and conference calls.

**2.** Give concrete examples and show the assets and drawbacks of these new technologies in business meetings.

### Do you know about video sharing?

Visit **www.youtube.com/t/fact_sheet** to learn about this consumer media company designed for people to watch and share videos worldwide through the internet.
Choose one topic and report to the class.

## Communication tasks

### Roleplay: Buying/selling MP3 readers

**A:** You are a product manager at Virgin Megastore.
You are interested in buying MP3 readers.
**B:** You are a sales manager at an MP3 manufacturer.
You want to sell a range of MP3 readers.
Prepare your arguments and act out the conversation.
→**Tools 13, p. 246**

# Record and movie industries reach a settlement with Kazaa

The music industry and Hollywood movie studios said Thursday that they had settled lawsuits[1] against the owner of the digital file-sharing network Kazaa, which will try to transform itself into a legitimate online distributor of films and music.

Sharman Networks, a privately held company that operates Kazaa from Australia, agreed to pay $115 million to the major record companies and movie studios, which had accused Kazaa of aiding the illegal copying of music on the Internet. The chief executive of Sharman, Nikki Hemming, said, "We are looking forward to collaborating with the music and motion picture companies to make P2P an integral part of the future of online digital entertainment."

Peer-to-peer network technology, or P2P, allows users to share computer files over the Internet, including music and movies stored in digital form. Kazaa was a pioneer of peer-to-peer network software.

Under the settlement, Sharman will pay the major record companies "in excess of[2] $100 million," said John Kennedy, chief executive of the International Federation of the Phonographic Industry in London. "We are under no illusion that this solves everything, but this is very encouraging."

The major recording companies will not invest directly in Kazaa but will be entitled to 20 percent of the proceeds[3] of any eventual sale of the service, Mr. Kennedy said, giving them a stake in the success of the new arrangement. The vice chairman of EMI Music, said "While the award may seem like a vast pot of money, it will merely offset[4] the millions we have invested – and will continue to invest – in fighting illegal pirate operations around the world and protecting the works that our artists create."

Kazaa has been earning revenue primarily from advertising, and Mr. Kennedy said the recording industry would not object if it persisted with an advertiser-supported model, rather than charging users, as long as it pays royalties. The movie industry has also begun to embrace peer-to-peer technology as a way to distribute material. Several download-to-own services, which allow users to buy digital files of films on the Internet, have also been started.

E. Pfanner, *The New York Times*, 28 July 2006

1. *lawsuit*: procès
2. *in excess of*: supérieur à
3. *proceed(s)*: montant des recettes
4. *offset*: compenser

## Info

***EMI*** The EMI Group is a music company. It comprises the major record label, EMI Music, one of the Big Four record labels – with Universal Music Group, Sony Music Entertainment and Warner Music Group – and EMI Music Publishing, the largest music publisher in the world.

## References

You can find relevant information by reading various pages in your book and memorising a few facts and ideas.

→ **Companies, p. 28**
→ **Marketing, p. 87**
→ **New technologies, p. 161**

ACTIVITY **Practise giving an account of this article.**

## Introduction

You should explain where the article comes from, when it was published and what it is about. →Tools 4, p. 236

This article comes from *The New York Times*, an American daily and was published in July 2006. It reports on the arrangements made between Kazaa, the most famous free downloading site, and the music industry.

## Development

Once you have understood the article, organise your ideas into two or three different parts, using set phrases and link-words. →Tools 4, p. 236

1. What Kazaa is
2. Consequences on traditional businesses
3. A necessary agreement

You should also use the information given in *Info* and what you have learnt, for example by referring to the various pages indicated in *References*.

### 1. What Kazaa is

Kazaa is operated by Sharman Networks from Australia.

• **Peer-to-peer network software**: Kazaa was one of the first companies to develop peer-to-peer network software. P2P allows computer users to share computer files over the internet. Users can upload and download various data on a site: thus the data stored on the site are available to anyone. The data can be work files that workers can share at the office, but it can also mean music and movies stored in digital form which the public can access freely and exchange in MP3 format, for instance.

• **Kazaa's business model**: Kazaa did not charge users for uploading and downloading but made money thanks to advertising.

### 2. Consequences on traditional businesses

• **Loss of money**: Major record companies and movie studios accused Kazaa of resorting to illegal copying of music on the internet. Therefore they lost huge sums of money as Kazaa and its users did not pay any royalties on the films or records they downloaded.

• **Copyright protection**: Companies invested millions to try and fight illegal pirate operations and protect the works of artists.

• **Embracing new technologies**: The movie and music industries have started using the same peer-to-peer technology as a way to distribute material over the internet. Thus they have developed the same type of service except that customers pay to buy digital files of films on the internet.

### 3. A necessary agreement

• **The agreement**: The major companies have filed lawsuits against Kazaa, which has agreed to pay $115 m to the major record companies and movie studios. Even though this does not compensate the losses of the film and music industries it is a positive move.

• **Working together**: Kazaa will try to transform itself into a legitimate online distributor of films and music. It can probably help other companies thanks to its expertise in P2P which could become an integral part of the future of online digital entertainment. The major recording companies will not invest directly in Kazaa. However, they will be entitled to 20% of the money of any eventual sale of the service.

## Conclusion

You should sum up the main ideas and try to open out in a new direction.

This article deals with the development of downloading goods from the internet and the new business models this trend has entailed. By favouring P2P sharing, companies such as Kazaa have been able to attract a huge audience who want to profit from free films and music. However, in the long run, such ventures can endanger creation: when artists don't get royalty money for the art they make, they can't survive. Therefore, finding an agreement with this type of company was an emergency. Now that things seem to be on the right track, one may consider the positive side of things, namely that traditional companies have had to embrace new technologies and find solutions to cater to new consuming habits.

## Branching out

Now, you should move away from the article and develop more ideas. The following questions can help you.

**1** Are you in favour of peer-to-peer technology? Why/Why not?

**2** Why is it necessary for companies to adapt to new technologies?

## 9. Transport

# Shortfall threatens EU transport plans

*Some of Europe's biggest transport projects are under threat because of a shortfall in funding.*

Only five or six of 30 European Union showcase infrastructure projects are likely to receive sufficient EU funding, it emerged yesterday.

The European parliament's transport committee warned yesterday there was a gap between politicians' pledges to upgrade transport networks and the willingness of governments to finance their construction. The gap is widening because of the decision by EU leaders last December to set a more stringent budget for the period from 2007 to 2013. That removed about two-thirds of the €20bn EU funding earmarked for the 30 projects to be completed by 2020. Together with funding from national governments and the private sector, they are forecast to cost €225bn.

Jacques Barrot, the EU's transport commissioner, said the shortfall could force the EU to rethink its priorities, to ensure that at least the most important infrastructure projects were built soon.

**Projects: Most projects concern rail but there are also plans to improve transport on inland waterways and upgrade ports. Some have been controversial and derided as white elephant projects driven by pork barrel politics, such as the Messina Bridge that would link the Italian mainland to Sicily, which Italy wants to start building this autumn.**

The six priority European rail projects most likely to go ahead are Berlin to Palermo in Sicily, possibly via a new bridge across the strait of Messina; a line between Spain and France across the Pyrenees; the Paris-Strasbourg-Munich-Bratislava route; Lyons to Budapest; and a route through the Baltic states from Warsaw to Helsinki. There will also be efforts to improve rail signalling and management, with a new system to be tested on the route between Rotterdam and Genoa. These six projects alone are expected to require at least €8bn of EU funding. The transport committee said yesterday that the EU urgently needed to find a further €4bn to cover at least the cross-border sections of some of the other 24 projects.

Big transport projects have been the subject of lengthy European political debate. National rivalries have emerged as governments have pushed for their pet projects to be included on the list, such as the bridge linking Sicily to Italian mainland.

D. R.

### Compréhension

**1.** **Rédigez en anglais un compte rendu de ce document. (150 mots, +/– 10%)**
**2.** **Traduisez le sous-titre et le deuxième paragraphe de l'article.**

### Expression

**Répondez en anglais aux questions suivantes.**

1 Why are some transport projects controversial? (100 words)
2 Do you think rail networks should be a priority for the EU? Why/Why not? (150 words)

(N.B. L'usage du dictionnaire bilingue est autorisé.)

## 10. New technologies

# Warner Bros. To Cut Link With Adware Firm Zango

## "Inappropriate Material" Could Reach Children.

Warner Bros. Studios, home to Bugs Bunny, Scooby Doo and Harry Potter, said yesterday that it plans to terminate a business relationship with Zango Inc., an adware company that has been offering free games on the Warner Bros. website in exchange for permission to install a computer program that could push advertisements and pornography.

Zango is offering free downloads of games on a Warner Bros. webpage called "Fun Stuff" that appears to be for children. But when users click on the game, they're directed to a page that asks for permission to install on the computer a program called Zango Search Assistant. Hidden in the terms of agreement is the disclosure that users may receive adult-oriented ads through it.

It's unknown how long the link was on the site. However, consumer groups that work to protect children from the dangers of the Web began to speak out. The issue also revived the debate over mainstream corporations that support, through business relationships, the seedier side of the Web.

Companies such as Zango are best known for installing intrusive computer programs called adware, which deliver pop-up advertisements while computer users surf the Internet. Adware companies have built their businesses by serving online advertising for some of America's top corporations.

Consumer groups said yesterday that this sort of controversy highlights the importance of mainstream companies policing their own websites.

"The Web doesn't get the same level of protection that these big companies dedicate to their offline properties," said the executive director of WiredSafety, an organization dedicated to protecting kids online. "Too often they trust their sites to techies and marketing people. If you are in the kids' space, you have a heightened obligation for doing things right, and you have to think before you engage with these kinds of partners."

The Children's Online Privacy Protection Act bars website operators from collecting personal information about children under age 14 without parental consent. Zango notes that the person who agrees to install the software must be over 18. But the box that confirms the user's age on the Warner Bros. site is already checked, by default.

*The Washington Post*, July 28, 2006

### Compréhension

**1.** **Rédigez en français un résumé de ce document. (150 mots, +/– 10%)**
**2.** **Traduisez le titre, le sous-titre et le premier paragraphe de l'article.**

### Expression

**Répondez en anglais aux questions suivantes.**

1 What is the difference between online and offline properties, as far as protection is concerned? (100 words)

2 Which industries should be particularly careful to protect children, and why? (150 words)

(N.B. L'usage du dictionnaire bilingue est autorisé.)

## Case study: reporting on the Internet

You work for a multimedia company. You have to report to your boss about the various prospects of the internet. Read the following information and report.

### Online ad revenues set to soar, says Zenith

The internet will take more than one-fifth of all UK advertising revenues by 2009, according to a leading media forecaster. ZenithOptimedia predicted that advertisers' spending on the internet will jump from £1.6bn in 2006 to £3bn in 2009.

### Internet sales power 25% surge in John Lewis profits

The John Lewis Partnership revealed a 25% surge in half-year profits yesterday, powered by a big jump in internet sales and continued appetite for flat-screen televisions.

### Cyberbullying: how to protect the children

Any parent who has ever picked up a newspaper will be aware that paedophiles use the internet to groom potential victims. It is estimated "several hundred" children have been assaulted or raped as a result of an initial contact made via the internet. The most important defence is to educate children about how to use internet, e-mail and chat rooms safely.

### *When the internet is a mixed blessing*

The internet has transformed the relationship between patients and their doctors. By transferring knowledge from the latter to the former, it has allowed patients to become experts in their illnesses and negotiate their treatment with doctors on a more equal footing.

## PERSONAL TASK

Match the following words to the corresponding definitions.

1. ezine
2. B2B (business-to-business)
3. B2C (business-to-consumers)
4. blog
5. forum
6. moderator
7. upload
8. netiquette
9. home page
10. bookmark
11. shopping cart
12. download

**a.** A frequent, chronological publication of personal thoughts
**b.** Place where customers can see what they have ordered before paying for it
**c.** An electronic magazine (delivered via a website or an email newsletter)
**d.** A link stored in a browser for future reference
**e.** At a forum, someone who helps discussions stay productive and within the guidelines
**f.** An online community where visitors may read and post topics of common interest
**g.** The main page of a website
**h.** Transfer data from the internet to a personal computer
**i.** Business that sells products or provides services to other businesses
**j.** The code of conduct regarding acceptable online behaviour
**k.** Business that sells products or provides services to end-user consumers
**l.** Transfer data from a personal computer to the internet

Answers: 1c, 2i, 3k, 4a, 5f, 6e, 7l, 8j, 9g, 10d, 11b, 12h

# IN THIS UNIT...

- Companies: Co-op, Body Shop, HSBC...
- Learn about eco design & carbon emissions
- Sell rice to Amazon
- Introduce a company's involvement in environment-friendly actions
- Consumer electronics: write a questionnaire

# 11
## Sustainable development

## → Before you START

*In brief:* **Biodiesel**
*Front page:* **How can you make a bank greener?**

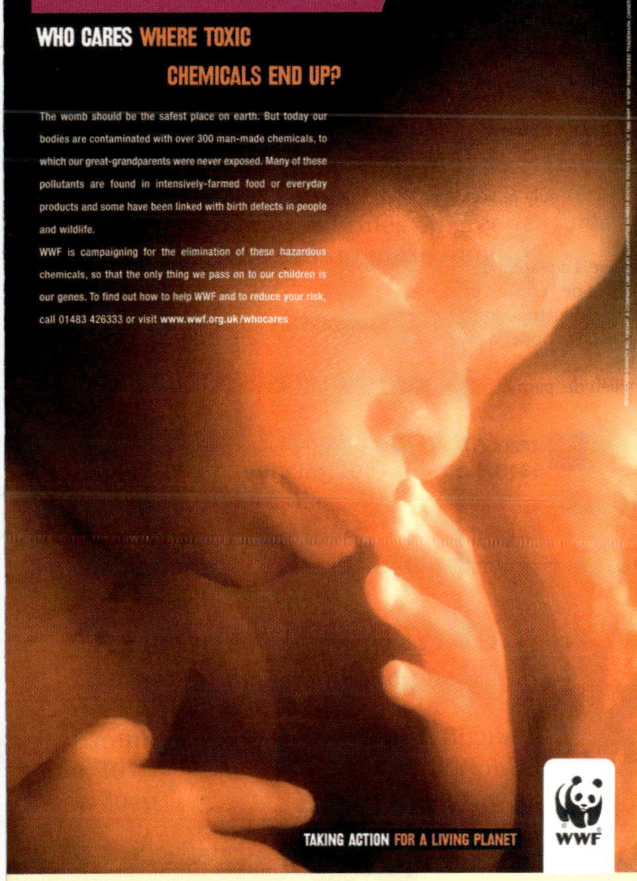


## What does the WWF mean with such a campaign?

### Words

- **Nouns:** planet, chemicals, future, generation, children, legacy
- **Adjectives:** dangerous, toxic, worrying, future, damaged

### LISTENING PRACTICE

CD TRACK 56

Listen to the recording.
**1.** What are the people talking about?
**2.** Explain their opinions.

# We can go green and grow profits, says HSBC

HSBC will tell staff to recycle more and stop printing out emails as part of a £100m investment in "green" measures over the next five years. The bank will spend £35m in the first year on making its buildings more environmentally efficient and encouraging its 280,000 employees to change their behaviour.

Stephen Green, HSBC's chairman, said promoting sustainability would benefit the bank. "Our commitment to sustainability is not some philanthropic agent or incompatible with our strategy of growing profits. On the contrary, it's intrinsic to it," he told reporters.

But Greenpeace said the bank, which made £12bn profit last year, could afford to spend more on green initiatives to offset its carbon emissions. It also warned HSBC customers that the bank was likely to invest in companies that harmed the environment. Craig Bennett, the charity's head of corporate accountability, said HSBC, along with all banks, needed to make greater efforts to restrict climate change. The bank was criticised three years ago for investments in Indonesian logging companies. Greenpeace and other campaigners targeted its annual meeting to highlight how large areas of rainforest were under attack from loggers.

HSBC said a Sustainability Leaders Fund would also be part of the initiative. It will mostly invest in 40 large European companies that are at the forefront of sustainable development, with 25% invested in smaller European firms that are developing new technologies to support sustainable development. Mr Green also announced a push to advise clients on how to tackle climate change, while the bank's own efforts would range from investing in solar and wind power to encouraging staff not to print out emails.

It removed all personal waste bins from its global headquarters in Canary Wharf, east London, this month, and the 8,000 staff there now use communal bins for recyclable dry waste and other bins for wet waste.

Phillip Inman, *The Guardian*, June 30, 2006

CD TRACK 60

## Info

***Canary Wharf***
Central district in the new urban development of London.

## Work on words

### 1 | Find their equivalents in English

**Headline** faire des bénéfices
**§1** personnel – imprimer – investissement – efficace – employés – comportement
**§2** durabilité – être dans l'intérêt de – engagement
**§3** compenser – prévenir – responsabilité des entreprises – changement climatique – exploitation du bois – cibler – assemblée générale annuelle – forêt tropicale
**§4** à la pointe – développement durable – soutenir – conseiller – s'attaquer à – aller de … à … – énergie éolienne
**§5** poubelle – siège social – déchets

### 2 | Find their synonyms

**Headline** become environmentally friendly
**§3** have enough money to – hurt – strategies
**§5** ban – shared

## Headlines

**1** Develop reflexes! If you don't know what HSBC is, look for an explanation in the first lines of the article. Look at the subjects of the first two sentences (**§1**). What is HSBC?

**2** Anticipate the contents of the article from the headline.

## The key points of the article

### 1 Read §1

**a.** The company: name, and number of employees.
**b.** Investment: what, when and how much.
**c.** What the employees will have to do.
**d.** What the company will do.

■ Complete this summary of §1 with: *bank – friendly – greener – printing – recycling – spend – staff.*
A British ..., HSBC, has decided to invest £100m over the next five years to become .... During the first year, it will ... £38m to make its buildings more environmentally ... and to incite its ... to change their habits by ... more and ... less.

### 2 Read §2 and §3

**a.** According to the bank's chairman, what are the advantages of becoming more environmentally friendly?
**b.** Profits of the company in 2005.
**c.** Greenpeace's opinion about HSBC and banks in general.
**d.** Example given by Greenpeace.

### 3 Read §4 and §5

**a.** HSBC's initiatives regarding its investment.
**b.** HSBC's campaign towards its clients.
**c.** HSBC's initiatives with its staff.

## {Methods}

### ■ Speaking practice

**1 Read figures aloud.** →Tools 10, p. 243
Read §1 and the first part of §4 aloud. If necessary, start by writing the following figures down.
Then practise reading the groups of words in parentheses with the figures.
**a.** (part of a) £100m (investment)
**b.** £35m (in the first year)
**c.** (its) 280,000 (employees)
**d.** (invest in) 40 large European companies
**e.** (with) 25% (invested in smaller European firms)

**2 Money, money**
Get used to dollars and pounds. Change all the money data into euros.

**3 Prepare an oral introduction.**
• Identify the source.
• Explain what the article is about (who, what, where, when).

### ■ Writing practice

**1 Translate §3.**

**2 Write an account of the article in English (120 words).** →Tools 4, p. 236

## Branching out

**1** How can HSBC advise its customers on how to tackle climate change?
**2** Does the fact that a company is green influence your attitude as a consumer?
→*Key data*, p. 27

## Language

• ***The bank****, which made £12bn profit last year, could afford to spend more on green initiatives.*
• *HSBC, along with* ***all banks****, needs to make greater efforts to restrict climate change.*
Exemple 1 : ***bank*** est précédé du déterminant ***the*** : c'est une banque précise (HSBC) dont on a déjà parlé.
Exemple 2 : ***banks*** est précédé du déterminant ***Ø*** : il s'agit de toutes les banques, sans précision.
Au singulier, le déterminant ***Ø*** renvoie à la notion : *promoting* ***Ø*** *sustainability.*
Attention, dans les deux cas, le français utilise le déterminant « le/la/les ».

**Translate into English**
**1.** Les entreprises ne font pas toujours attention à leurs investissements.
**2.** La banque a prévenu ses clients qu'elle ne leur enverrait plus de relevé (*statement*) afin d'économiser le papier.
**3.** Les efforts iront des investissements dans l'énergie solaire et éolienne aux campagnes pour que les employés gâchent moins et recyclent davantage.
**4.** La banque a supprimé les poubelles personnelles de son siège social et les employés doivent maintenant trier les déchets recyclables.

In Britain, food and garden waste is recycled to make compost. Pesticides, chemicals and the burning of waste which produces a huge amount of $CO_2$ are avoided.

## 3-Sustainable business

### Corporate ethics

Many brands are talking today about sustainable development, especially car and oil companies which are the most involved in $CO_2$ emissions. BP, the British oil company, encourages its customers to donate money for the development of recyclable energy by providing them with the tools to calculate the pollution produced by their cars and the money it costs to neutralize this pollution. Car manufacturers are developing hybrid cars.
→Chapter 1, *Front page*, p. 24

### Micro-credit: a sustainable enterprise

- **Definition**

Micro-credit was launched in developing countries to encourage the poor to support themselves. It consists of granting very small loans to small entrepreneurs lacking disposable income, and people considered as not "bankable".

- **How it works**

Borrowers buy their own tools and equipment, cutting out the middlemen and transforming their lives through self-employment. The Grameen Bank now has 6.5 million borrowers, among whom a majority are women. Studies show that when women gain economic autonomy, the health, nutrition and education of the whole household, especially children, improve at the same time. Moreover, women have been estimated more reliable to pay back their loans.

Thanks to their pioneering role in micro-credit, Bangladeshi economists Muhammad Yunus and Grameen Bank won the 2006 Peace Nobel Prize. The chairman of the Nobel Committee said: "Lasting peace cannot be achieved unless large population groups find ways in which to break out of poverty. Micro-credit is one such means." Yunus said he would use the money to fund a project to produce low-cost, nutritious food for the poor, an eye hospital, a drinking water project and a health care scheme.

**Sweden: an example to follow**

The Swedish minister for sustainable development has announced a plan to completely give up oil dependency by 2020. It is possible thanks to Sweden's large amounts of biomass, hydropower and wind power. Laws that would be unthinkable elsewhere have been passed: taxes on fuel and carbon dioxide emissions, tax exemptions for home owners switching to renewable energies, the converting of cars from gas to ethanol and biogas from plant waste, plus a number of eco-friendly measures, such as the building of geo thermal plants and solar-powered health centres.

## Question time

1 What are the areas in which sustainable development can play a role?
2 What is environment degradation due to?
3 What is at the origin of global warming?
4 What are the consequences of global warming?
5 Why is water considered a key issue?
6 What is the WBCSD?
7 What is the Kyoto Protocol? Who was it not ratified by?
8 Name some measures taken to curb pollution.
9 Explain what GMOs are and why they are controversial.
10 What does micro-credit consist of?

LANDMARK

# The Body Shop

**Founded by Anita Roddick, The Body Shop International plc, known as The Body Shop, is a British chain of cosmetics stores. It became famous for its line of products not tested on animals and produced in an ecologically sustainable manner.**

## The brand

In 1970, two Britons, Anita Perella and Gordon Roddick (who married the same year) saw a San Francisco shop called "The Body Shop" selling shampoos and lotions. It claimed environmental concerns and offered customers discounts for bringing in their own bottles instead of using new ones. The shop sold Roddick the rights to the "Body Shop" name in the early 1980s.

## From a Brighton corner shop to a worldwide franchise

The first shop opened in 1976 in Brighton, Sussex, England with just 25 hand-mixed homemade skin care lotions advertised to be made with natural ingredients.

**The marketing mix**

- simple descriptive names: Tea Tree Oil Facial Wash, Mango Dry Mist, etc.
- exotic ingredients such as jojoba oil and rhassoul mud
- details about ingredients and their properties on the packaging
- price: more expensive than supermarket cosmetics but cheaper than exclusive brands

Customers could refill containers for a 15% discount.

These revolutionary ideas attracted a loyal clientele. Roddick made her company famous with original campaigns and social and environmental activism.

The Body Shop expanded at a rate of 50% annually. It went public in 1984. By 2004, 1,980 stores served over 77 million customers in 50 different markets in 25 different languages and across 12 time zones.

One of Body Shop's original campaigns

## Franchising and direct selling

**1978** A kiosk in Brussels became the first overseas franchise.

**1982** Two new shops every month.

**1990** Shops in 39 countries; 2,500 people wanted to open a franchised shop in the USA.

**1994** "The Body Shop At Home" started direct selling in the UK; then in Canada (1995), Australia (1997), and Ireland and the USA in 2001.

## Campaigns: Business as Unusual

From early on, Roddick criticized the "environmental insensitivity" of the industry. The book she wrote about the success of her company is called *Business as Unusual*. She put posters on shop windows and sponsored local charity and community events claiming that the power of public pressure can create change.

**1986** "Save the Whales", with Greenpeace.

**1989** "Stop The Burning" asked the Brazilian Government to stop burning the tropical rainforests. One million customers signed the petition.

**1990** Establishment of The Body Shop Foundation and alliance with Friends of the Earth.

**1991** The "Trade Not Aid" initiative aimed at favouring fair labour practices, safe working environments and pay equality. It started a paper factory in Nepal employing 37 people producing bags, notebooks and scented drawer liners.

**1993** International campaign to protest against the exploitation of Nigeria by Shell.

**1996** "Against Animal Testing", the largest petition (four million signatures) ever delivered to the European Commission.

**August 2002** 1.6m customers and cyber activists signed the petition to make renewable energy more accessible to 2bn people without access to energy.

## Betrayal?

In March 2006, The Body Shop International agreed to a £652 million takeover offer by L'Oréal. This started a controversy as the Body Shop has always had a policy of not using any animal-tested ingredients in its cosmetics while L'Oréal is famous for its animal testing policy. Ethical Consumer and animal welfare group Naturewatch began a number of protests and boycotts.

However, L'Oréal executives have said that they would maintain the image of The Body Shop.

**Online t@sk**

Visit The Body Shop's website to read about their values and campaigns on www.thebodyshopinternational.com/Values+and+Campaigns/.
Choose one and report.

# Vocabulary

**alternative:** alternative
**appalling:** épouvantable
**average:** moyenne
**aware:** conscient
**ban:** interdire
**behaviour:** comportement
**benefit:** être dans l'intérêt de
**biodiversity:** biodiversité
**borrower:** emprunteur
**bury:** enterrer
**campaigner:** militant
**carbon (dioxide):** gaz carbonique
**cattle:** bétail
**chemicals:** produits chimiques
**climate change:** changement climatique
**commitment:** engagement
**consumption:** consommation
**consumption pattern:** habitude de consommation
**core:** principal
**corporate:** d'entreprise
**corporate accountability:** responsabilité des entreprises
**cosmetics:** produits de beauté
**counterpart:** homologue
**crop:** récolte
**crude oil:** pétrole brut
**dam:** barrage
**damage:** endommager
**desertification:** désertification
**destroy:** détruire
**disposable income:** revenu disponible
**donate:** faire un don
**drought:** sécheresse
**dry waste:** déchets secs
**dump:** (N) décharge ; (V) jeter
**efficient:** efficace
**emergency:** urgence
**energy efficiency:** efficacité énergétique
**energy policy:** politique énergétique
**exporter:** exportateur
**facility:** installation
**factory:** usine
**fair trade:** commerce équitable
**farmer:** agriculteur
**fertilizer:** fertilisant
**fleet:** flotte (de véhicules)
**flood:** inondation
**fossil fuel:** combustible fossile
**fuel:** carburant
**genetically engineered:** génétiquement manipulé

**genetically modified:** génétiquement modifié
**global trade:** commerce mondial
**global warming:** réchauffement de la planète
**grant:** accorder
**green:** vert, écolo
**greenhouse effect:** effet de serre
**growth:** croissance
**harm:** endommager
**harmful:** dangereux
**hazard:** risque, danger
**heat wave:** vague de chaleur
**highlight:** souligner, mettre l'accent sur
**household appliance:** appareil ménager
**hunger bout:** famine
**hurricane:** ouragan
**innovative:** innovant, novateur
**investment:** investissement
**lack:** manque
**landfill:** décharge
**living standard:** niveau de vie
**loan:** prêt
**logger:** bûcheron
**logging:** exploitation du bois
**mandatory:** obligatoire
**manufacturer:** fabricant
**material:** matériau
**melt:** fondre
**middleman:** intermédiaire
**natural gas:** gaz naturel
**nuclear waste:** déchets nucléaires
**offset:** compenser
**overpopulation:** surpopulation
**ozone layer:** couche d'ozone
**packaging:** emballage
**pest:** animal nuisible
**plant:** usine
**print out:** imprimer
**radioactivity:** radioactivité
**rainforest:** forêt tropicale
**recycling bin:** poubelle de recyclage
**refinery:** raffinerie
**renewable:** renouvelable
**revamp:** réorganiser
**save:** économiser
**sea level:** niveau de la mer
**seed:** graine
**shortage:** pénurie
**soil:** sol
**solar panel:** panneau solaire
**solar power:** énergie solaire
**sort:** trier
**spare:** économiser
**species:** espèce
**spray:** aérosol
**sprinkle:** arroser
**sustainability:** durabilité
**sustainable development:** développement durable
**switch to:** passer à
**tackle:** s'attaquer à
**target:** objectif
**toilet tissue:** papier toilette
**unsustainable:** non durable
**urban sprawl:** villes tentaculaires
**vehicle emissions:** gaz d'échappement
**warn:** prévenir
**waste:** gâcher
**waste bin:** poubelle
**water supplies:** réserves d'eau
**weigh:** peser
**wet waste:** déchets humides
**wind farm:** éolienne
**wind power:** énergie éolienne

## Charts and tables

**1.** Study and compare the following charts on carbon dioxide emissions.

CARBON EMISSIONS WORLDWIDE 1800-2000

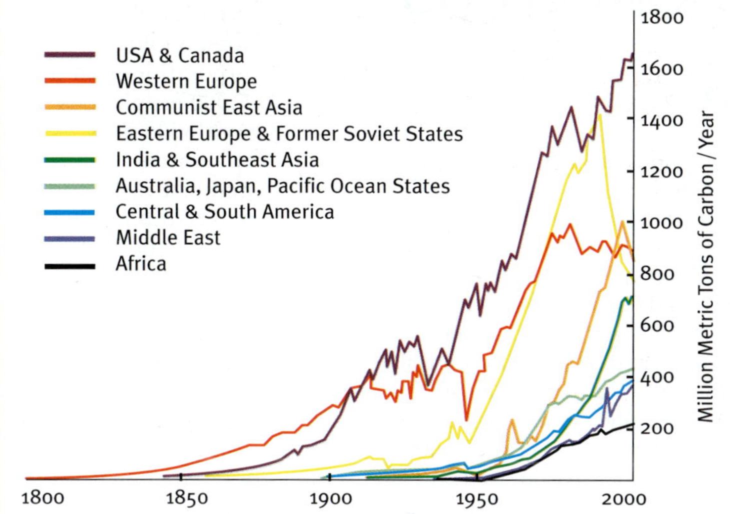


From *The Carbon Dioxide Information Analysis Center*

ANNUAL CARBON DIOXIDE EMISSIONS

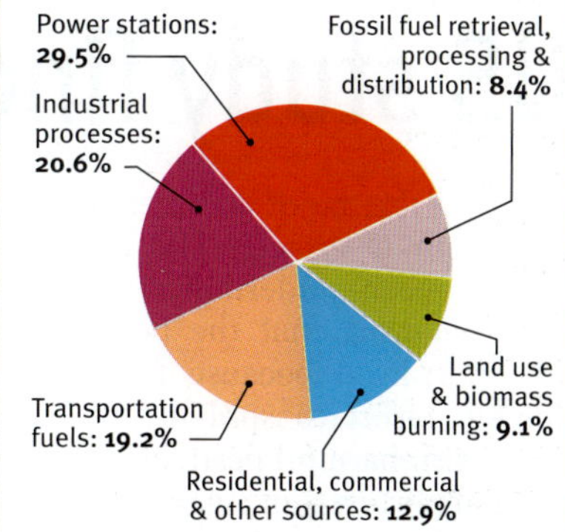


From *The Emission Database for Global Atmospheric Research*

**2.** Give an oral presentation of both charts. →**Tools 11, p. 244**

## Online tasks

### Presenting a company

Visit the website set up by the French car company Peugeot-Citroën: **www.sustainability.psa-peugeot-citroen.com**

**1.** Introduce the company's involvement in environmentally-friendly actions. What is "eco-design"? How can cars become more environmentally-friendly?

**2.** Report orally on the presentation dedicated to carbon dioxide emissions: **www.sustainability.psa-peugeot-citroen.com/environment/greenhouse-effect/picture-today.htm.**

**3.** Give examples of possible changes in the car industry in the long run. →**Chapter 1, *Front page*, p. 24**

### Do you know about the WBCSD?

Visit **www.wbcsd.ch** to learn about the World Business Council for Sustainable Development (WBCSD). →***Key data*, p. 177**
Visit the page showing various projects and initiatives: energy efficiency in buildings, water and sustainable development, sustaining ecosystems and ecosystem services, etc.
Choose the initiative that appeals to you most and report to the class.

# Farmers use as much pesticide with GM crops, US study finds

One of the major arguments in favour of growing GM crops has been undermined by a study showing that the benefits are short-lived because farmers quickly resort to spraying their fields with harmful pesticides.

Supporters of genetically modified crops claim the technique saves money and provides environmental benefits because farmers need to spray their fields fewer times with chemicals.

However, a detailed survey of cotton growers in China found that, although they did use fewer pesticides in the first few years of adopting GM plants, after seven years they had to use just as much pesticide as they did with conventional crops. After three years, the GM farmers had cut pesticide use by 70 per cent and were earning over a third more than conventional farmers. But, by 2004, the GM cotton farmers were using just as much pesticide as their conventional counterparts[1] and were spending far more because GM cotton seed is three times the price of conventional cotton seed.

Hundreds of Chinese farmers had switched to cotton that had been genetically modified with a gene for a bacterial toxin. Bt[2], the toxin, is secreted by the GM cotton plant and is highly effective at stopping the growth of bollworm[3], a major pest that can cause millions of pounds worth of damage. Major cotton producers, the US, China, India and Argentina, adopted Bt cotton after it was introduced in 1996 by Monsanto, the American biotechnology company. Today, more than a third of the global cultivation of cotton is accounted for by Bt cotton. Before the introduction of the GM crop into China, farmers in the country had to spray 20 times each growing season to control bollworm but, with Bt cotton, the average number of treatments fell to below seven.

The study found that all those benefits have since been lost due to the rise of other pests. Bt farmers in 2004 on the average have to spray pesticide 18.22 times, which is more than three times higher compared with 1999. Secondary pests are not normally a problem in cotton fields because sprays against bollworm tend to keep them in check. However, because Bt cotton is targeted mainly against bollworm, other pests are able to exploit the relatively low use of pesticide that such fields need.

Steve Connor, *The Independent*, 27 July 2006

1. *counterparts*: homologues
2. *Bt (Bacillus thuringiensis)*: nom de la bactérie
3. *bollworm*: ver du cotonnier

## Info

***Monsanto***
A multinational agricultural biotechnology corporation with over 15,000 employees worldwide, it is the world's leading producer of Roundup, its flagship product, and of genetically engineered seeds. The company's marketing of GE seed and its aggressive lobbying practices have made Monsanto a primary target of the anti-globalisation movement and environmental activists who refer to its products as "frankenfoods" and to the company itself as "Monsatan".

## References

You can find relevant information by reading various pages in your book and memorising a few facts and ideas.

→ **Companies, p. 27**
→ **Consumers, p. 70**
→ **Sustainable development, p. 177**
→ **Globalisation, p. 221**

**Activity** **Practise giving an account of this article.**

## Introduction

You should explain where the article comes from, when it was published and what it is about. →Tools 4, p. 236

This article, published in *The Independent*, a British daily, in July 2006, reports on the results of a new study which has shown that the benefits of GM crops could be reduced to nothing in the very short term.

## Development

Once you have understood the article, organise your ideas into two or three different parts, using set phrases and link-words. →Tools 4, p. 236

1. The advantages of GM crops in the first years
2. The findings of a new study

You should also use the information given in *Info* and what you have learnt, for example by referring to the various pages indicated in *References*.

### 1. The advantages of GM crops in the first years

Genetically modified crops enable farmers to use less pesticide because they don't need to spray their fields with chemicals so often. Therefore, people who favour their use generally claim that the technique is economical, as farmers spend less money on pesticides, as well as more environmentally friendly with fewer pesticides in the fields.

- **The Chinese example**: Hundreds of Chinese cotton growers had to treat their fields by spraying 20 times each growing season to control bollworm, a pest that destroys cotton. Then they switched to cotton that had been genetically modified with a gene for a bacterial toxin.
- **The toxin**: Bt was introduced in 1996 by Monsanto, the American biotechnology company. The Bt toxin is secreted by the GM cotton plant and is highly effective at stopping the growth of bollworm, a major pest that can cause millions of pounds worth of damage. Major cotton producers, such as the US, China, India and Argentina, adopted Bt cotton after 1996. Today more than a third of the cultivation of cotton worldwide is accounted for by Bt cotton.
- **Results**: In the first three years of adopting GM plants, the Chinese farmers had reduced their use of pesticides by 70% and the farmers had to spray their fields seven times each season, instead of the previous 20. Thanks to the money saved, they were also earning over a third more than conventional farmers.

### 2. The findings of a new study

A detailed survey studied the same cotton growers in China. It has shown that the benefits – less pesticide and more money – don't last long.

- **The pesticides**: The study found that after seven years the farmers had to use just as much pesticide as they did before using Bt cotton. New pests appeared in the cotton fields. Before, they were not a problem because the sprays against bollworm kept them away. However, Bt cotton is designed against bollworm only, which means that other pests can develop if no pesticides are used. As a result, the farmers had to spray three times more than before.
- **The savings**: The study also found that the GM cotton farmers were spending far more than the farmers who did not use Bt cotton because GM cotton seed is three times as expensive as conventional cotton seed.

## Conclusion

You should sum up the main ideas and try to open out in a new direction.

This article reports on a study which is likely to lead to new developments in the already controversial use of GM crops. One of the main arguments of GM products is that they allow less pesticide to be used. Supporters of GM food have always claimed this benefit. However, the new study shows that, even though the farmers did spray fewer pesticides in the first few years, the benefits did not last long. New pests developed and forced a renewed use of pesticide. Consequently, opponents of GM crops are likely to be even more opposed to their use.

## Branching out

Now, you should move away from the article and develop more ideas. The following questions can help you.

**1** Does the term "Frankenfood" seem suitable to you to describe GM products? Explain and give examples.

**2** Do you think European consumers are right when they demand to know the content and origin of the food they consume? Why/Why not?

## Case study: selling Fair Trade rice

FAIR TRADE RICE PRODUCT INFORMATION

| | | |
|---|---|---|
| **Name and type of rice** | White, Red, Coral & Purple Jasmine | White & Brown Basmati |
| **Supplier/Brand** | AlterEco | Woodstock Farms |
| **Availability** | Andronico's, Giant Eagle, New Leaf, Village Market, Whole Foods, Wild Oats, Amazon.com | Numerous natural food grocers |
| **Organic?** | Yes | Yes |
| **Fair Trade Label?** | Yes | Yes |
| **Bulk?** | Yes (11 lb bags) | Yes (25 lb bags) |
| **Other packaging** | 1 lb boxes | 2 lb boxes |

**How much does Fair Trade rice cost?**
Though prices vary by type, store and quantity, Fair Trade rice prices generally run $1.25 - $4.00 per pound.
**Is Fair Trade rice organic?**
Jasmine rice from Thailand and Basmati rice from India are USDA certified organic.
**Is it certified Fair Trade? Is it labeled?**
Fair Trade rice carries the Fair Trade Certified label accredited by TransFair USA.
**Who are the producers of fair trade rice?**
Fair trade rice is grown by small-scale farming families in Thailand and India.

### Roleplay

**A:** You are a member of Woodstock Farms salesforce.
You want to convince Amazon to sell another brand of fair trade rice.

**B:** You are Amazon's product manager.
You meet for an appointment.

## PERSONAL TASK

A research about consumer electronics in the UK took place in July 2006 on behalf of the Energy Saving Trust (**www.est.org.uk**). It has shown that consumers are planning to buy around 30 million electrical items over a six month period (that's more than one new item per household in the UK).
The list of new items now thought of as essential by consumers includes:
- a cordless telephone (two thirds of people about to buy one say it is essential),
- an electric toothbrush (50% say it is essential),
- a juice maker (25% say it is essential),
- a coffee machine (25% say it is essential),
- a bread maker (20% say it is essential).

The Chief Executive of the Energy Saving Trust said: "Householders are increasingly adding new electrical gadgets to their homes. This is having a significant impact on our energy bills and on the environment. Over the past 10 years electricity consumption from consumer electronics has increased by 47%. And over the next 5 years it is expected to rise by 82%. It would result in greater carbon dioxide emissions, one of the main causes of climate change."

Work in groups to prepare a questionnaire. Then interview three people and report to the class, comparing French and British consumers.

# IN THIS UNIT...

- Companies: Iberia, Thomas Cook...
- Learn about ethical tourism & extreme tourism
- Negotiate a honeymoon trip
- Report on the way Americans travel
- Write to confirm a reservation

# 12
## Tourism

**→ Before you START**

*In brief:* **A plane strike**
*Front page:* **Travel insurance**

## What are the pros and cons of booking a trip online?

## Words

- **Nouns:** trip, destination, (package) holiday, availability, booking, reservation
- **Adjectives:** cheap, quick, convenient, (un)reliable, online

## LISTENING PRACTICE

CD TRACK 61

Listen to the recording.

**1.** What are the people talking about?
**2.** Explain their opinions.

# Iberia pilots' strike hits British holidaymakers

The travel plans of hundreds of passengers flying between the UK and Spain were thrown into disarray today as a Spanish pilots' union called a seven-day strike.

Spanish carrier Iberia, which jointly markets some flights with British Airways under a code-sharing agreement, cancelled three flights between London and Madrid, and two connecting the capital with Barcelona. Some 240 Iberia flights are likely to be cancelled daily until Sunday, due to the strike action over feared job losses.

A BA spokesman said today: "We are working on contingency plans to ensure that as many British Airways customers who are booked on Iberia flights can get to their destinations. We would urge any BA customer who has booked a flight between Heathrow and Madrid or Barcelona on July 10, 11 and 12 to contact BA if they booked their ticket direct from the airline or their travel agent to see if their flight is affected and how they can be re-accommodated[1]."

A statement on the British Airways website informed affected passengers that they could make changes to their booked journeys, obtain a refund or re-route with no penalty, regardless of fare type. New tickets would be valid for travel until the end of the year.

*The Guardian,* 10 July 2006

1. *re-accomodated:* (ici) satisfait par un nouveau billet

CD TRACK 62

## Info

***Iberia***
Spain's largest airline, based in Madrid. The company was privatized in April 2001.

***British Airways***
The UK's largest airline, also one of the largest in Europe.

## Work on words

### 1 | Find their equivalents in English

**Headline** grève – frapper – vacancier
**§1** passager – confusion
**§2** vol – annuler – assurer une correspondance avec
**§3** plan d'urgence – réserver – agent de voyage
**§4** voyage – remboursement – pénalité – prix du billet

### 2 | Find their synonyms

**§2** airline – offer something for sale
**§4** change the itinerary – not taking into account

## Headlines

**1** Read the headline and the topic sentence (**§1**) to anticipate the contents of the article.

**2** Match the key-words in the headline to the corresponding expressions in the article.

## The key points of the article

### 1 Iberia pilots on strike
**a.** Link between Iberia and British Airways.
**b.** Details about the strike.
**c.** Reasons for the action.

### 2 Attitude of the company
**a.** Main concern for British Airways.
**b.** How the information was transmitted.

### 3 Consequences for BA customers
**a.** What passengers flying on July 10, 11 or 12 have to do.
**b.** The two possibilities for passengers with affected flights.

## Branching out

**1** What guarantees can air travel companies offer to their customers?
→*Key data*, p. 191

**2** To what extent are strikes unfair on passengers?

## {Methods}

### ■ Speaking practice

**1 Practise your pronunciation of "th".**
The letters "th" can be pronounced either [θ] as in *thirty*, or [ð] as in *then*.
Choose the right pronunciation for the following words from the article.
*the – thrown – three – that – their – Heathrow*

**2 Read figures aloud.** →Tools 10, p. 243
**a.** a seven-day strike **b.** 240 Iberia flights
**c.** July 10, 11 and 12.

### ■ Writing practice

**1 Nationalities**
***the*** *UK*, **Ø** *Spain*: "the" is used before certain names of regions or countries: *the United Kingdom, the United States, the Netherlands*. However, most of the time, there is no article before the name of a country: *France, Belgium, China*, etc. Adjectives of nationality generally end in *-(i)an, -ese*, or *-ish*. They begin with a capital letter and do not change in the plural: *Italy* > *the Italians, Great Britain* > *the British, Vietnam* > *the Vietnamese*, etc.

**Complete the following sentences with the right adjective of nationality and/or the right determiner before the name of the country.**
**a.** Hundreds of (*Great Britain*) and (*Spain*) passengers were thrown into disarray.
**b.** The (*Spain*) carrier Iberia cancelled three flights between London and Madrid.
**c.** Customers, whether coming from (*the* – *Ø*) United Kingdom or from (*the* – *Ø*) Iberian Peninsula, can check their flight.
**d.** All passengers, including the ones coming from (*the* – *Ø*) Spain, will easily get refunds or new tickets.

**2 Prepare a short account in English.**
Use the sentences you made in part 1.
• Mix sentences **a** and **b** together, using a link-word expressing cause.
• Mix sentences **c** and **d** together, using proper link-words.
→Tools 4, p. 236

## LISTENING PRACTICE

CD TRACK 63-64

*Tim Bingman and Christina Norton are talking.*

**1 Comprehension**
Listen to the recording to find the following information.

**Part 1**
**a.** Topic of conversation.
**b.** Christina's decision.
**c.** Example she gives:
- The problem.
- What accounts for the problem.
- Consequences for the local population.

**Part 2**
**a.** The size of the industry.
**b.** Christina's opinion.
**c.** The book she's got (title, contents).
**d.** Problem issue she mentions.

**2 Expression**
Give an oral account, or write a 100-word paragraph, summing up what you have heard.

# Consumer protection: Be safe not sorry

*Have you booked your holiday online? Beware, it may not be protected.*

Buy a holiday, or a flight and a room, and if a company involved goes bust, you would hope to get your money back. And if you're away when it happens, or if there is a disaster, you would hope to be flown home. For the past 30 years, that is generally what has happened. But for increasing numbers of holidaymakers today, it would not.

The explosion in online booking and low-cost flights is having a side effect: more than 11 million Britons will buy foreign holidays this summer without consumer protection. And because the numbers travelling unprotected are growing, the system which offers a guarantee to everyone else is crumbling.

When EUjet, the Kent[1]-based airline, ceased trading last July, it left 12,000 people stranded[2] abroad and 27,000 with worthless tickets. Only the 130 who had bought a flight as part of a package holiday completed their trip or were given a refund. The Civil Aviation Authority (CAA) found that two-thirds thought their purchase was protected when it was not. Those abroad paid between £50 and £300 to get home. Those buying a package benefited from the Atol (Air Travel Organiser's Licence) system, overseen by the CAA.

So if an advert, brochure or website displays the Atol logo, you're covered. Holidays are often bought months in advance and can involve more than one airline, hotel, car hire and so on. An Atol-protected purchase covers you if there is a problem at any of them. You can also expect to be looked after if a hurricane strikes or a bomb explodes.

Where does that leave you? Buy a holiday from a traditional tour operator – online, over the phone or through a travel agent – and you're covered. Buy a holiday put together by a travel agent and you probably will be covered, but should ask. Buy online from one or more firms and, unless you see the Atol logo in each case, you probably won't be. Don't rely on travel insurance – many policies will not cover you, so do study the small print[3].

*The Independent*, 28 May 2006

1. *Kent*: comté au sud-est de Londres
2. *stranded*: en rade
3. *the small print*: (contrats) toutes les clauses

CD TRACK 65

## Work on words

### 1 | Find their equivalents in English

**Headline** en sécurité
**Subhead** réserver
**§1** vol – impliqué – faire faillite
**§2** effet secondaire – à l'étranger – s'écrouler
**§3** voyage organisé – voyage – remboursement – achat – surveiller
**§4** publicité – afficher – location de voiture – ouragan – frapper
**§5** à moins que – compter sur – assurance – police (assurance)

### 2 | Find their synonyms

**Subhead** pay attention/be careful
**§1** people on holiday
**§2** not expensive – British people – increasing
**§3** stop (V) – overseas – without any value – finish (V)

## Headlines

**1** Proverbs…
The headline sounds very much like a famous proverb: "Better safe than sorry". Choose the meaning you think is right:
**a.** Mieux vaut des remords que des regrets.
**b.** Deux précautions valent mieux qu'une.
**c.** À quelque chose malheur est bon.

**2** Anticipate the contents of the article from the headline and the subhead.

## The key points of the article

### 1 Read §1

**a.** Industry. Find four words related to this industry in §1.
**b.** Possible problems for customers.
**c.** Possible solutions in case of a problem.
**d.** Tendency nowadays.

■ Complete this summary of §1 with:
*bankrupt – customers – disaster – flight – flown – holidaymakers – more – refund.*
... used to get a ... or to be ... home when they had bought a ... , or a hotel, or a holiday and a ... occurred or a company went .... However, ... and more ... are having problems nowadays.

### 2 Read §2 and §3

**a.** Trend in the industry.
**b.** Consequence on consumers.
**c.** Explain what happened to EUjet in July 2005.
**d.** Explain what happened to the people who had an EUjet ticket.
**e.** Explain what the Atol is.

### 3 Read §4 and §5

**a.** What does the Atol logo indicate?
**b.** The risk factor: compare holidays bought from traditional tour operators, travel agents and online purchases.
**c.** Problem with travel insurance.

## Branching out

**1** Explain why tourism is a fragile industry.
**2** To what extent has the internet altered the tourism industry? →*Key data*, p. 191

## {Methods}

### ■ Speaking practice

**1 Read figures aloud.** →Tools 10, p. 243
Read §1 and §3 aloud. If necessary, start by writing the following figures down. Then practise reading the groups of words in parentheses with the figures.
**a.** 12,000 (people stranded abroad)
**b.** 27,000 (with worthless tickets)
**c.** (the) 130 (who had bought a flight)
**d.** (between) £50 and £300

**2 Money, money**
Get used to dollars and pounds. Change all the money data into euros.

**3 Prepare an oral introduction.**
• Identify the source.
• Explain what the article is about (who, what, where, when).

### ■ Writing practice

**1 Translate §2 and §3.**
Pay attention to figures and verbal forms.

**2 Write an account of the article in French (120 words).**
→Tools 4, p. 236

## Language

• *You **can** also expect to be looked after if a hurricane strikes or a bomb explodes.*
• *You probably **will** be covered, but **should** ask.*

Il y a cinq modaux principaux : ***can, may, must, will*** et ***shall*** (et leurs formes passées *could, might, would, should*).

Ce sont des auxiliaires : la négation se place après, ils sont suivis d'un verbe (sans *to*) et ne prennent pas de terminaison en *–s* à la 3e personne du singulier du présent.

**Translate into English**
**1.** Vous devriez vous assurer que vos vacances sont couvertes si une catastrophe se produit pendant que vous êtes à l'étranger.
**2.** Il se peut que l'agence de voyage fasse faillite et que vous n'ayez plus d'interlocuteur.
**3.** On ne peut pas simplement compter sur les assureurs : tu devrais étudier toutes les clauses pour vérifier ce qui se passe en cas de bombe, par exemple.
**4.** Il se pourrait que vous soyez rapatriés en avion en cas de problème ; mais il se peut que vous ayez un billet à payer.

# Key data

**Unlike business travel, tourism involves travelling for leisure. It also refers to a booming industry which is thriving and providing tourists with always more services and facilities related to transport, accommodation, catering, sightseeing, etc. Tourism has become global, and is vital for many countries.**

## 1-British pioneers

### History

Leisure travel can be traced back to the Antiquity: holiday resorts were built to accommodate the richest Roman citizens.
In more recent times, the British pioneered leisure travel; they were particularly keen on the sunny climate of southern Europe where there are still many reminders of their presence such as the *Promenade des Anglais* in Nice on the French Riviera, or famous hotel names like Bristol, Carlton, Majestic, etc. Thomas Cook, the first "tour operator" was British and has been on the travel market ever since 1841. →***Landmark*, p. 193**

### Mass tourism

The expansion of mass tourism took place when technology had made sufficient progress, that is to say in the 19th century (Industrial Revolution), when railways were replacing horse carts and coaches, allowing a much greater number of people to travel longer distances in a shorter period of time.
Social progress can also account for the boom in tourism: since the mid 1930s, most workers from developed European countries have received paid holidays.
Mass tourism saw another boom with air travel, after World War II. The increase in foreign travel was monitored by tour operators whose activities have never stopped growing since.

**La Costa Brava: a sacrificed landscape**

From the 1960s to the 1980s the most popular place in Europe was the Spanish Costa Brava which attracted French, German, Dutch, Belgian and British tourists by the thousands. To accommodate the mass of sun-seekers, the Spanish authorities did not hesitate to spoil their sea front by erecting monstrous concrete tower blocks.

## 2-Modern tourism

The traditional destinations such as seaside and mountain resorts are still popular, but they are much more sophisticated than they used to be a few decades ago: today's resorts offer all kinds of sports facilities, day and night entertainment, excursions, different types of accommodation, from full boarding to self-catering, etc. Every age group can find something to suit their tastes and abilities.

### Package holidays

Package holidays became a fad in the mid 60s; in France Club Méditerranée revolutionized tourism by offering all-inclusive package holidays, where money was replaced by tokens or wooden pearls inside the holiday camp, which was called the "village". This type of holiday has multiplied since with a great number of travel agencies worldwide, most of them offering all-inclusive club packages for all types of destinations. Most travel agencies are operated by a few large tour operators, mainly European and American.

### Facts and figures

Tourism is still a growing industry representing 15% of sales in the service sector. Europe represents a little over 50% of world tourism. According to the World Tourism Organization, international tourism will keep growing by 4% annually until 2020. Although Europe will still be the number one destination, its share will drop by 14% as long hauls are expected to increase faster than internal travels.
Today, many budget-oriented tourists prefer to fly with low-cost carriers and book their own accommodation without the help of a travel agent. Because of the growing number of budget airlines, there is a significant decrease in the demand for all-inclusive package travels. →**Chapter 9, Transport, p. 148**

### Today's tourists

The average tourist is from an urban area, preferably young or senior. Both ends of the age span are keen travellers, the young because they travel with their families, friends, schools or associations, and seniors because they have more free time, are in good health and have more disposable income.
→**Chapter 4, Consumers, p. 68**

### Online booking

Thanks to the internet, online travel booking has been developing at an extraordinary pace: in France, one traveller out of ten booked their holidays online in 2004, a figure that doubled in 2005. Many travellers are becoming experts in holiday booking and planning.
As a result, a great number of traditional travel agents rightly feel threatened by this new trend and the number of travel agent jobs has already started to drop. Another problem of online booking is uninsured travellers. →***Front Page*, p. 188**

## 3-New trends

To get a piece of the enormous cake global tourism represents, tour operators keep looking for new niches.

### Sustainable tourism

Tourism poses a threat to the environment as it means more pollution (from cars, planes, etc.), and the destruction of natural landscapes to build resorts and all kinds of facilities to accommodate and entertain tourists; hence the rise of eco-tourism over the past 20 years. While the mainstream tourism industry has doubted that tourists care about destinations or local people, research has shown that travellers increasingly want to meet local people on equitable terms and care about the environment, rather than just visiting places and sitting in resorts all day. →***Prep Page*, p. 196**

### Extreme tourism

- Adventurous tourism, which is associated with high risk, consists of travelling to difficult, hostile places, such as mountains, jungles, deserts and caves, or participating in dangerous events.

**A hot destination**

In 2005, 76 million foreign tourists chose to come to France, making it the top tourist destination before Spain and the United States with revenues reaching €34bn. The new phenomenon was the growing number of travellers from Asia and Oceania who accounted for 26% of foreign tourists. The British were by far the best represented with 14.9m tourists (Germans: 13.2m; Dutch: 11.6m).

**In the wake of the tsunami**

After the December 2004 tsunami, Thai authorities became aware of the necessity for sustainable tourism, which would also profit the locals and not just be gilded ghettoes for well-off foreigners. The environment will also benefit from this shift in mass tourism.

**Disaster tours**

After Hurricane Katrina had struck New Orleans, Louisiana in September 2005, one of the biggest attractions was storm damage. Isabelle Cossart's local travel agency was hit during this period and has hit back by offering travellers a tour of the damaged quarters of the city.

• Extreme tourism is a growing business in the former Soviet Union and in South American countries such as Peru, Chile and Argentina. The mountainous and rugged terrain of Northern Pakistan has also developed into a popular extreme tourism location. Other unusual attractions are offered, such as adrenaline-boosting trips in former warplanes at twice the speed of sound (2.5 Mach)!

• Finally, space tourism is one of the new destinations for extreme travellers, although it remains extremely... expensive!

**Lost in Space**

Together with the SpaceShipOne designer, Burt Rutan, Virgin's founder Sir Richard Branson launched Virgin Galactic, the first space transport company in the world: 7,000 people are already registered to travel 70 miles above the Earth for €166,000. The trip is programmed for 2008.

→ **Chapter 2, New Entrepreneurs, *Landmark* p. 43.**

### Agritourism

• Agritourism is another new form of tourism, with wine tourism and life on a farm coming first. Wine tourism is a profitable niche with wine tours, wine festivals and other special events around oenology (the science of wine). Farms attract country-life lovers. Travellers are accommodated in farms and can help with farming tasks such as fruit and vegetable picking, or practise any other activity related to farming, such as horse riding. In addition, agritourism helps to support many producers and can contribute to the new development of a region, as in Italy.

• In the same line, industrial tourism involves visits to operational industrial sites where the core activity of the site is "non-tourism" oriented. It can include food processing factories, wineries, mining operations, port operations, etc.

### Cruising

Although cruising has been part of the traditional tourist landscape for a century with the sinking of the Titanic in 1912 as a tragic landmark, it is now a major part of the tourism industry, with millions of passengers each year. One of the world's leaders is Carnival Cruise Lines which has pioneered the concept of cheaper, shorter cruises. The line calls its ships *The Fun Ships*: they have become famous for their Las Vegas internal design and entertainment, with a wide range of activities offered on board. The Carnival Liberty, housing 2,974 passengers and 1,100 crew members, is Carnival's first ship to be based in Europe.

## Question time

**1** When did mass tourism start developing?
**2** Explain the reasons for this development.
**3** In what ways was Club Méditerranée innovative?
**4** How do more and more people book their travels?
**5** What happened to the Costa Brava and why?
**6** What does eco-tourism consist of?
**7** Give examples of new trends in tourism.
**8** What is your opinion about disaster tours?
**9** Can you account for the new success of cruising?

LANDMARK

# Thomas Cook and Son

**Thomas Cook, who organised the first package tour in history in July 1841, can be considered the father of modern mass tourism. First, technological progress allowed large numbers of people to be transported in a relatively short time; secondly more people began to enjoy the benefits of leisure time.**

## The first package tour

Thomas Cook was a member of a Temperance Society – wanting to limit the drinking of alcohol – and a Baptist minister. In 1841, a group of 570 British people from Leicester wanted to have a Temperance rally eleven miles away. Thomas Cook arranged for the rail company to charge one shilling (1/20 of a pound) per person. The price paid included the return ticket, entrance to a show and food for the train journey. Cook received a share of the passengers' fares. He understood the potential of offering holidays in which all the costs were included and he organised outings for Temperance societies and Sunday-school children during the following three summers. This led him to start his own business offering rail excursions for pleasure, in which he took a percentage of the money made from the sale of the railway tickets.

A 1890 brochure cover for round-the-world tours

## Getting down to business

**1845** Cook arranged accommodation for a party to travel from Leicester to Liverpool.

**1846** He took 350 people on a tour of Scotland.

**1851** He arranged for over 165,000 people to attend the London Great Exhibition.

**1855** First excursion abroad: grand circular tour of Brussels, Cologne, the Rhine, Heidelberg, Baden-Baden, Strasbourg and Paris.

**1860s** Cook took parties to Switzerland, Italy, Egypt and the USA. He invented "inclusive independent travel": travellers went independently but his agency charged for travel, food and accommodation.

**1872** A 222-day round-the-world tour for 200 guineas (a little more than £20) with a steamship across the Atlantic, a stage coach across America, a paddle steamer to Japan and an overland journey across China and India.

**1888** Company offices around the world, including 3 in Australia and 1 in Auckland, New Zealand.

**1890** Over 3.25 million tickets sold.

## Thomas Cook and Son

With his only son, John Mason Cook, Thomas Cook formed a partnership. *Thomas Cook and Son* acquired premises on Fleet Street, London with an office and a shop which sold guide books, luggage, telescopes and footwear. Their business model was improved with the introduction of the "hotel coupon" in 1866: detachable coupons could be used in restaurant or hotels as long as they were on Cook's list.

## Holidays for workers

The tourist industry developed rapidly in late Victorian Britain. The growing middle classes had time off from their work and could afford the luxury of travel.

**1871** The Bank Holiday Act introduced a statutory right for workers to take (unpaid) holidays. Most went to the seaside resorts, such as Brighton, Blackpool and Bournemouth, helped by the expansion of the railway network. Domestic tourism was the norm, while the rich went overseas.

**1925** 1.5 million manual workers in Britain had paid holidays (11 million by 1939).

## The firm today

**2002** Thomas Cook was acquired by a German company which changed its name to Thomas Cook AG. Today it is one of the UK's largest travel companies, employing around 11,000 people and offering holidays to more than 1,000 locations. The company operates 615 high street shops selling travel and foreign exchange, 121 separate bureaux de change, 7 Thomas Cook travel warehouses, 3 call centres, Thomas Cook TV and thomascook.com. In addition, Thomas Cook has more than 10 tour operating brands and operates Thomas Cook Airlines, the UK's second largest leisure airline.

Brochure cover from the 2005 summer season

**Online t@sk**

Visit Thomas Cook's corporate site on www.thomascook.com/corporate/home.asp. Find information about the company's attitude to sustainable tourism and report to the class.

## TOUR, TOURISM, TRAVEL AND COMPOUNDS

- **tour:** voyage, périple, excursion
**package tour:** voyage organisé
**tour operator:** voyagiste
- **agritourism:** agritourisme
**eco-tourism:** écotourisme
**extreme tourism:** tourisme extrême
**mass tourism:** tourisme de masse
**space tourism:** tourisme de l'espace
**sustainable tourism:** tourisme durable
**wine tourism:** tourisme du vine
- **air travel:** voyages par avion
**business travel:** voyage d'affaires
**travel company:** entreprise de voyage
**travel guide:** guide de voyage
**travel insurance:** assurance de voyage
**traveller:** voyageur

**abroad:** à l'étranger
**accommodate:** loger
**accommodation:** logement
**airline:** companie aérienne
**all-inclusive:** tout compris
**book:** réserver
**brochure:** brochure
**budget:** économique, pas cher
**cancel:** annuler
**car hire:** location de voiture
**carrier:** transporteur
**catering:** restauration
**charge *(V)*:** facturer
**climate:** climat
**coach:** bus, car
**coast:** côte
**complete:** finir
**concrete:** béton
**connecting (flight):** (vol en) correspondance
**consumer protection:** protection du consommateur
**crew:** équipage
**cruising:** croisières
**customer:** client
**desert:** désert (N)
**developing country:** pays en voie de développement
**disposable income:** revenu disponible
**domestic:** intérieur
**entertain:** distraire
**entertainment:** distraction, loisirs
**entrance:** entrée
**environmentally aware:** conscient de l'environnement
**explode:** exploser
**facilities:** équipements, installations
**fad:** engouement, mode
**fare:** prix du billet, tarif
**flight:** vol
**fly:** prendre l'avion
**foreign:** étranger (adj.)
**foreigner:** étranger (N)
**four-wheel-drive:** 4X4
**full boarding:** pension complète
**guarantee:** garantie
**guide book:** guide de voyage
**holiday:** vacances
**holidaymaker:** vacancier
**hurricane:** ouragan
**impressive:** impressionnant
**insurance policy:** police d'assurance
**journey:** voyage
**lack:** manquer de

"On behalf of Charter Airlines may I apologise again for the delay while the plane is being built."

**landmark:** point de repère ; grand monument
**landscape:** paysage
**leisure:** loisir
**location:** lieu, emplacement
**low-cost flight:** vol pas cher
**luggage:** bagage
**mainstream:** grand public, dominant
**niche:** créneau
**order:** commander
**outing:** sortie, excursion
**overseas:** à l'étranger
**package holiday:** voyage organisé
**paid holidays:** congés payés
**party:** groupe
**passenger:** passager
**penalty:** pénalité
**pioneer:** pionnier
**railway network:** réseau ferroviaire
**railways:** chemins de fer
**recycling plant:** usine de recyclage
**refund:** remboursement
**remote:** lointain
**reroute:** dérouter
**resort:** lieu de vacances, station
**return ticket:** aller-retour
**route:** trajet
**safe:** en sécurité
**seaside resort:** station balnéaire
**senior:** personne du 3e âge
**shift:** changement
**ship:** navire
**side effect:** effet secondaire
**sightseeing:** visites
**small print:** (contrats) toutes les clauses
**spoil:** abîmer, endommager
**spot:** lieu, coin
**steamship:** bateau à vapeur
**storm:** tempête
**strike (struck, struck):** frapper
**strike:** grève
**suit:** convenir
**threaten:** menacer
**thrive:** prospérer
**time off:** congé
**tip:** pourboire ; tuyau, astuce
**token:** jeton
**toll:** péage
**tourist trap:** piège à touriste
**trip:** voyage
**valid:** valide
**wilderness:** état sauvage
**winery:** établissement vinicole

## Charts and tables

**1.** Study the following charts to determine what customers need when they travel.

WHO DO AMERICAN TOURISTS LIKE TRAVELLING WITH?

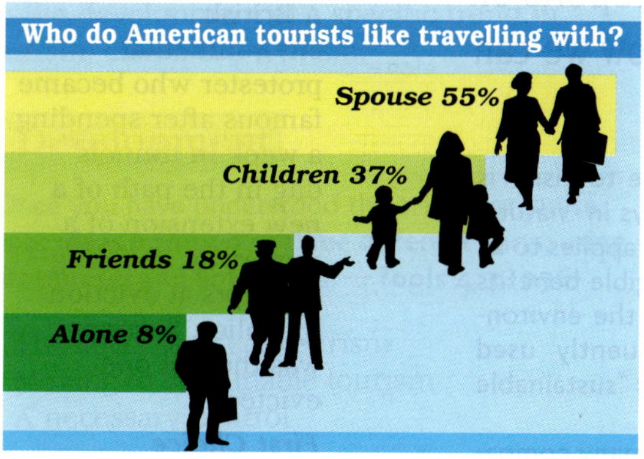


From *tia.org*

WHAT HELPS AMERICAN TRAVELLERS RELAX ON A TRIP?

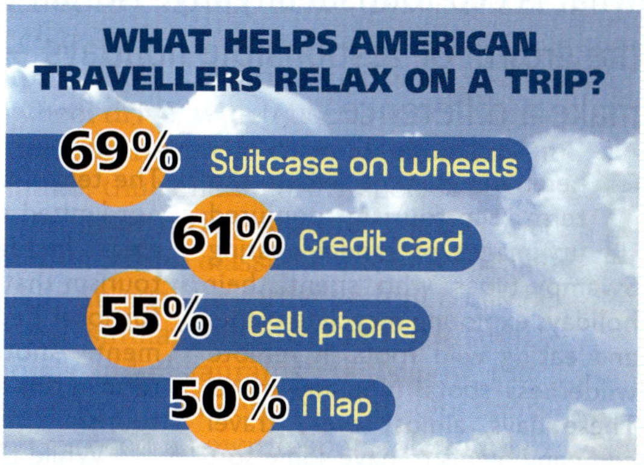


Adapted from *cheaptickets.com*

**2.** Give an oral presentation of these charts. →**Tools 11, p. 244**

## Communication tasks

**Roleplay: an ideal honeymoon trip**

**A:** You are a customer.
You want to book two tickets, a car and a hotel room for your honeymoon.
You have a precise idea of what you want and you want to pay as little as possible.
**B:** You work for a travel agency.
You have to satisfy your customer's request. But you also have to reach your sales goals for this month.
Be polite and persuasive enough to make your customer change his/her mind.
→**Tools 13, p. 246**

## Online tasks

**Do you know about tour operators?**

Visit Easyjet's and Thomas Cook's websites to discover their different approach to tourism.

- **www.thomascook.com/corporate/press.asp?page = businesspolicy**
- **www.easyjet.com/EN/Book/**

Compare their business strategies (goals, target, etc.) and report to the class.

## 11. Sustainable development

# Food waste is buried treasure, charity tells firms

Food charity FareShare is setting up a scheme it hopes will reduce the estimated 7 million tonnes of food dumped in landfill sites in Britain every year. A quarter of the food buried in the ground is perfectly edible, says FareShare chief executive Tony Lowe. "It's just that companies don't know what else to do with it."

Tomorrow sees the launch of FareShare 1st, a business that aims to offer the food and drink industry a cheaper, greener alternative to landfill. It will take the surplus product off the manufacturers' hands, distribute what is edible through its existing network, which fed more than 12,000 people last year, and then dispose of the rest by the greenest means possible, such as composting or animal feed.

The government is committed to reducing the amount of waste that goes into landfill, and FareShare 1st says that not only will its solution be more environmentally sustainable, it will also be cheaper for manufacturers.

Mr Lowe reckons the venture will break even in the first year but is aiming for profits of £250,000 by the fourth year.

"We will offer the food industry a one-stop solution," he said. At the moment, FareShare takes only the food that can be eaten. It works with companies, including Sainsbury's, Tesco, Marks & Spencer, Pret A Manger and Starbucks, redistributing surplus fresh food to homeless and vulnerable people. Last year it delivered food to 250 organisations, contributing towards more than 3.3 million meals for 12,000 people each day.

FareShare 1st has held trials for the venture, which guarantees to dispose of all a company's food waste, through Nestlé and Kellogg's for the past 12 months. It hopes to get a number of other leading manufacturers on board, including Kraft and Northern Foods.

"It's a tragedy that so much food goes straight into the ground," said Mr Lowe. "Now companies can not only help their communities, but they will also get a green alternative to landfill and make a saving on their disposal costs."

A former Marks & Spencer store manager, Mr Lowe explained "the potential for FareShare 1st is huge and could provide a model of ensuring resources can be managed in a responsible, equitable but still profitable way in the future."

Fiona Walsh, *The Guardian*, July 24, 2006

## Compréhension

**1.** **Rédigez en français un compte rendu de ce document. (130 mots, +/– 10%)**
**2.** **Traduisez les deux premiers paragraphes de l'article.**

## Expression

**Répondez en anglais aux questions suivantes.**

1 To what extent could FareShare 1st be both an answer to the government's requirements and a profitable business? (100 words)

2 Do you think companies should use the concept of solidarity? Why/Why not? (150 words)

(N.B. L'usage du dictionnaire bilingue est autorisé.)

## 12. Tourism

# Marriot hotels go smoke-free in the USA and Canada

Marriott International announced this week that as from September all the hotels it operates in the United States and Canada will be smoke-free.

William Crow, an analyst working for Raymond James & Associates, sees this decision as part of a trend within the hotel industry. In February the Westin Hotel chain brought in a smoke-free policy. In March the Disneyland Resort in Anaheim, California followed suit. Other hotels have been gradually cutting down on their quota of smoking rooms over the last few years. Crow sees this as a sign of the times. "Given where we are as a country, the no-smoking laws that have been put in place, we'll probably see other chains jump on board," he said.

The Marriott empire is gigantic, comprising the Marriott, JW Marriott, Ritz-Carlton, Renaissance, Courtyard, Residence Inn, SpringHill Suites, Fairfield Inn, TownePlace Suites and Marriott ExecuStay brands. All in all, more than 2,300 hotels and corporate apartments and nearly 400,000 guest rooms will be involved in the smoke-free switch, making the move, according to Marriott, the most significant in the business.

"Creating a smoke-free environment demonstrates a new level of service and care for our guests and associates," Chairman and Chief Executive J.W. Marriott Jr. said in a statement. The new policy will outlaw smoking in all guest rooms, restaurants, lounges, meeting rooms, public spaces or employee work areas. Moreover, above 90% of Marriott guest rooms are already non-smoking, and smoking is banned in many public spaces due to local laws, according to Marriott International.

Explaining its decision to become smoke-free, Westin said an average of 92% of its customers had been requesting non-smoking rooms. The switch cost the chain about $200 a room, mostly in costs associated with deep cleaning and treating hard surfaces, walls and carpets to eliminate allergens, replacing air filters, and cleaning air conditioning units.

However, smoke-free hotels recover these costs thanks to lower maintenance expenses while getting rid of the non-smoking option facilitates the inventory of rooms, Crow pointed out.

*California News*, 19 July 2006

## Compréhension

**1.** **Rédigez en anglais un compte rendu de ce document. (100 mots, +/– 10%)**
**2.** **Traduisez le titre et le cinquième paragraphe de l'article.**

## Expression

**Write a letter.**

You work at Nestlé's chocolate department where you are in charge of organising seminars. You would like to book a week for 30 employees. Ask about the possibilities and state/explain what you expect/would like.

(N.B. L'usage du dictionnaire bilingue est autorisé.)

## Case study: making an offer

You work for a tourist agency. A famous phone company wants to invite its ten best employees to a seven-day trip. You have to make an offer.

Prepare a leaflet describing a seven-day offer to one of the following destinations: Jamaica, Kenya or China.

Your leaflet should include details about:

- Accommodation: type of room, comfort, air-conditioning, etc.
- Transport: companies, airports, taxes, check-in times, etc.
- Meals and activities: included or not, type of meals, sports, visits, etc.
- Conditions: cancellation, open tickets, refunds, lost baggage
- Formalities: passports, visas, etc.
- Habits: clothes, weather, tips, etc.

## PERSONAL TASK

You work for a hotel in Kenya. You have received the letter below from a tourist agency. Answer the letter to confirm the reservation. →Tools 7, p. 240

**Hotel Travel**
58 W. Seventh Street
Cincinnati, OH 45202
Phone: 513-621-6345
Fax: 513-621-2732

Papillon Lagoon Reef Hotel
Diani Beach
Mombasa, Kenya

24 May 2007

Dear Sir
I would like to book ten rooms for seven days starting October 10 for the best employees of a global phone company.
As this trip has been arranged to thank them for their superb results, I require ten of your deluxe rooms, with balconies, each with private bathroom, telephone, television, room service plus every meal included.
My customers will certainly make the most of your beach-side location but we would like to have information as to what is included (water sports including windsurfing, snorkelling and beach fishing, diving trips to explore the nearby coral reefs).
Also, could you let us know whether safaris or day trips are available from your hotel, and include the rates for what you offer?
We need to book the airline tickets as soon as possible and would be grateful for a reply by return of post.

Yours faithfully

*Rosa Carleton*

Rosa Carlton
Travel manager

# IN THIS UNIT...

- EU Institutions: the Commission, the Parliament...
- Learn about Eurotunnel & new EU members
- Visit Europe Direct website
- Interview people on cross-border shopping
- Report on European opinions about the EU

# 13
## Europeans

**→ Before you START**

*In brief:* **Smoking at work**
*Front page:* **European migrants and working habits**

# Why can languages be a problem in Europe?

## Words

- **Nouns:** language, barrier, translation, misunderstanding
- **Adjectives:** official, difficult, rare, bilingual, slow

## LISTENING PRACTICE

CD TRACK 66

Listen to the recording.
**1.** What are the people talking about?
**2.** Explain their opinions.

# *Smokers need not apply*

Fancy a quick cigarette with your coffee? Not if the boss can stop you. But is it the boss's business? The European Commission was asked to answer this question after an Irish job ad specified that smokers were not welcome. Brussels decided that employers who refuse to hire smokers are not in breach of Europe's anti-discrimination laws.

"Age, disability, religion, race, gender and sexual orientation are all areas the Commission can legislate on," says Commission spokesperson Katharina von Schnurbein. "Anything else is the member state's responsibility." In some countries, such as France and Belgium, it is illegal to hire on any basis other than qualifications. But there has been outrage that the Commission is not acting to halt the growing trend which sees employers sticking their noses into[1] applicants' lifestyles. For instance, the World Health Organisation, based in Geneva, launched a hiring ban on smokers in December 2005, the same month that Sophie Blinham was sacked within minutes of starting her new job at an English communications firm after admitting she smoked.

The Commission's decision is not "a green light for employers to discriminate," insists von Schnurbein. But Tom Jenkins of the European Trade Union Confederation disagrees. "This opens the possibility for all kinds of discrimination," he says, citing the obese and alcoholics. Philip Tobin, the Irish Internet entrepreneur who placed the ad, accused smokers of "stinking." "If you eat a pungent lunch, you might stink, too," retorted Jenkins.

*The Cork Times,* August 21, 2006

1. *stick one's nose into*: fouiner, mettre son nez dans...

CD TRACK 67

## Work on words

### 1 | Find their equivalents in English

**Headline** poser sa candidature
**§1** petite annonce
**§2** handicap – sexe – état membre – virer
**§3** sentir mauvais

### 2 | Find their synonyms

**§1** recruit (V) – violate
**§2** anger – tendency – prohibition
**§3** spicy

## Headlines

Which words in the headline outline the issue tackled in the article? Develop each of them to anticipate the contents of the article.

## The key points of the article

### 1 Discrimination
**a.** What ad started the debate in Ireland?
**b.** The British employee's experience.
**c.** Decision made by the WHO.

### 2 The European Commission and member states
**a.** The European Commission's judgement.
**b.** Reason put forward.
**c.** Laws enforced in France and Belgium.

### 3 The arguments against the hiring ban
**a.** First argument denouncing anti-smoker employers (§2).
**b.** Counter-argument about smokers who "stink" (§3).
**c.** The risk of the hiring ban (§3).

## {Methods}

### Speaking practice
**Practise pronouncing adjectives of nationality and names of cities or countries.**
Irish – France – Belgium – Geneva – English – Dublin.

### Writing practice
**1 Expressing possession with *'s***
- *the boss**'s** business*
- *the member state**'s** responsibility*
- *the Commission**'s** decision*

The structure of the possessive case (*Y's* **...**) is used with singular nouns and plural nouns not ending in *s*. When a name ends in *s*, it takes *'s* or just an apostrophe. The possessive case is chiefly used with people, countries or animals (in the two examples from the article, a group of people).
Otherwise, the structure is *the* **...** *of* + *Y* (*the rooms of the building*).

**Complete the following sentences with the proper structure (*Y's* ... or ... *of Y*).**
**a.** The (responsibility / company) is at stake if smokers are discriminated against in Ireland.
**b.** It is not the (duty / Commission) to legislate on such matters.
**c.** The (aim / authorities) is to legislate on other forms of discrimination.
**d.** The (decision / EU) gives more freedom to employers.
**e.** The (attitude / the Irish manager) mentioned in the article is openly discriminating.

**2 Prepare a short account in English.**
Use sentences in part **1** and link-words.
→Tools 4, p. 236

## Branching out

**1** How can people be discriminated against at work? How can it be avoided?
→*Key data*, p. 58

**2** Do you think European institutions should protect workers and employees in the workplace? Why/why not?

## LISTENING PRACTICE

CD TRACK 68-69

*George Garrett and Emma O'Reilly are discussing the EU.*

### 1 Comprehension
Listen to the recording to find the following information.

**Part 1**
**a.** Country where the conversation is taking place.
**b.** Nationality of the two speakers.
**c.** What Emma explains about the development of tourism.
**d.** Explain George's reaction.

**Part 2**
**a.** Compare Emma's country in 1973 and in 1990.
**b.** George gives two counter examples. Explain.
**c.** What Emma explains about international trade.
**d.** Two reasons why George doesn't agree with Emma about international trade.
**e.** George's conclusion.

### 2 Expression
Give an oral account, or write a 100-word paragraph, summing up what you have heard.

# UK migrants fuelling Spanish boom

A study published yesterday by Caixa Catalunya, the Spanish savings bank, found that without immigrants, Spain's economy would not have flourished. In fact, instead of growing at a yearly rate of 2.6 per cent per capita, it would have declined at an annual rate of 0.6 per cent. Foreigners have proved crucial in boosting domestic demand and raising productivity, the report said.

Another report has shown Britons and other foreigners have played a dynamic role by starting small-businesses at a faster rate than Spaniards. Whether they are running their own bars on the Costa del Sol, teaching English or earning their living in more unusual ways, Britons have set up more companies than any other nationality.

Latest figures showed in 2005, of all the 1.6 million foreigners in Spain, 140,882 ran their own small businesses. The Spanish Business Institute said there was a 15 per cent rise in the number of foreigners opening businesses, compared with a 3 per cent increase in Spanish-run firms. More than 21,000 Britons have registered their own small business in Spain, followed by 13,579 Germans, and 13,293 Chinese.

Nic Alderton, 34, who runs his own film company, Simplicity Films, from his home in Catalonia, is typical of the "new breed[1]" of foreigners. He came to Spain from London three years ago to start his company, which shoots advertisements and promotional films. John Woodward, 50, whose firm Voyages Orsom provides team-building courses on his catamaran from Barcelona, said: "It has got much easier in recent years in Spain. I employ 15 Spaniards and some have worked for me for years. Perhaps they like a different style of management. Instead of having a boss who smokes a cigar and shouts at you all the time, they say we are easier to work with."

Of a total population of 45 million, immigrants now number nearly two million. The rate of immigration to Spain has been the second highest in Europe, after Italy. Raquel Váquez, head of analysis at Caixa Catalunya, said: "Immigrants have a direct influence on the increase in consumer spending and demand for housing, the two factors which have resulted in Spain's GDP growth."

Graham Keeley, *The Independent*, 31 August 2006

1. *breed*: espèce

CD TRACK 70

## Work on words

### 1 | Find their equivalents in English

**§1** caisse d'épargne – étranger (N)
**§2** créer
**§3** enregistrer
**§4** filmer – publicité – offrir – équipe
**§5** dépenses de consommation – PIB

### 2 | Find their synonyms

**Headline** feed – quick growth
**§1** annual – decrease (V) – essential – increase (3 verbs)
**§2** people from Britain – launch (V) – quick – people from Spain
**§3** the most recent – manage

## Headlines

Anticipate the contents of the article from the headline.

## The key points of the article

### 1 Read §1
**a.** Economic trend in Spain.
**b.** Annual growth rate.
**c.** Reason for this trend.

■ Add information to the following sentences using the following words in the proper form: *boost – capita – cent – foreign – foreigner – fuel – raise – rate – Spain's.*
• UK migrants have ... the Spanish boom.
• Thanks to ... immigrants, ... economy has grown at an annual ... of 2.6 per ... per ....
• ... have both ... demand and ... productivity.

### 2 Read §2 and §3
**a.** Type of businesses foreigners have started.
**b.** Number of foreigners living in Spain.
**c.** Number of foreigners who run their own businesses.
**d.** Compare immigrants and Spaniards as far as opening businesses is concerned.
**e.** Compare Britons and other immigrants.

### 3 Read §4 and §5
**a.** Two examples of Britons who have set up their companies in Spain.
**b.** One reason that may account for the number of foreign firms.
**c.** Relations with employees.
**d.** Proportion of immigrants in Spain.
**e.** Compare with the rest of Europe.
**f.** Reason why immigrants boost the economy.

## Branching out

**1** Would you like to work in another European country? Why/Why not?
→ ***Key data*, p. 207**

**2** Why do you think British immigrants are more dynamic than Spanish small business-owners in Spain?

## {Methods}

### ■ Speaking practice

**1 Read figures aloud.** **→ Tools 10, p. 243**
Read §3 aloud. If necessary, start by writing the following figures down. Then practise reading the groups of words in parentheses with the figures.
**a.** (in) 2005
**b.** (all the) 1.6 million (foreigners)
**c.** 140,882
**d.** (a) 15 (per cent rise)
**e.** (a) 3 (per cent increase)
**f.** (more than) 21,000 (Britons)
**g.** 13,579 (Germans)
**h.** 13,293 (Chinese)

**2 Prepare an oral introduction.**
• Identify the source.
• Explain what the article is about (who, what, where, when).

### ■ Writing practice

**Write a summary of this article in English (around 150 words).**
**→ Tools 3, p. 234**

## Language

• *Britons have set up **more** companies **than** any other nationality.*
• *Britons and other foreigners have played a dynamic role by starting small-businesses at a **faster** rate **than** Spaniards.*
• *They are running their own bars on the Costa del Sol, teaching English or earning their living in **more unusual** ways.*

Le comparatif de supériorité sert à comparer deux éléments.
- Quand il s'agit de quantité, on utilise ***more***... (exemple 1). Le second élément de la comparaison (quand il est explicite) est introduit par ***than***.
- Quand on compare à l'aide d'un adjectif, la structure est la même pour un adjectif long. Quand il s'agit d'un adjectif court (une syllabe, ou deux syllabes terminé par *-y*), on ajoute ***-er*** à l'adjectif ; la terminaison *–y* devient *i* : *It has got much easier in recent years in Spain.*
Comme dans ce dernier exemple, on peut augmenter le comparatif avec *much*, ou *far* (beaucoup plus...).

**Translate into English**
**1.** Les immigrants ont souvent été plus dynamiques que les Espagnols.
**2.** Les Britanniques ont démarré davantage de petites entreprises que les Chinois ou les Allemands.
**3.** Les employés espagnols semblent trouver qu'il est plus facile de travailler avec un patron anglais qu'avec un Espagnol.
**4.** La demande pour les logements a été beaucoup plus significative (*significant*) au cours de ces dernières années grâce à l'arrivée de nombreux étrangers.

**Europe is the second smallest continent in the world, covering only 2% of the globe's surface. 710m people live in Europe, accounting for 11% of the world's population.**
**The European Union's 27 member states cover an area of 4,336,790 sq km with approximately 487m inhabitants (December 2006). It has land borders with 21 nations and describes itself as "a family of democratic European countries". It represents the world's largest economy.**

## 1-The European Union: a few landmarks

### Milestones

**1951** Foundation of the European Union (Treaty of Paris).
**1957** The European Economic Community (EEC), Treaties of Rome.
**1962** The Common Agricultural Policy (CAP) allows Europe to become the second largest exporter of agricultural products, just behind the USA.
**1992** European Monetary Union (EMU) and European citizenship (Maastricht Treaty).
**1995** Free circulation of people within the Schengen zone (Schengen Agreement, except the UK).
**2001** The Nice Treaty (institutional changes necessary to make Europe a political entity).
**2004** The new Constitutional Treaty is submitted to ratification by the 25 members of the EU.
**2005** France and the Netherlands reject the Constitutional Treaty in referendums. The other countries choose not to submit the treaty to their voters in order to avoid possible rejection.

### Members: 27 countries, and more to come

Twenty-five countries joined the European Union between 1958 and 2004 (in chronological order): Belgium, France, Italy, Luxembourg, the Netherlands, Germany, Denmark, Ireland, the UK, Greece, Portugal, Spain, Austria, Finland, Sweden, Cyprus, Czech Republic, Estonia, Hungary, Latvia, Lithuania, Malta, Poland, Slovakia, Slovenia.
**January 2007**: Bulgaria and Romania joined the Union. Seven more countries are on the waiting list: Turkey, Republic of Macedonia, Albania, Bosnia and Herzegovina, Montenegro and Serbia.

### EU institutions

The three major institutions of the EU are the Council of the European Union, the European Parliament, directly elected every five years, and the European Commission.
The latest Parliament was elected in 2004 and has 732 MEPs (Members of the European Parliament) who are organised into parties according to their political inclinations: Group of the Party of European Socialists for the left, European People's Party/European Democrats for the right.

### Europe's humanitarian aid

The EU is present in media-forgotten zones, post-conflict and post-natural disaster areas through ECHO – European Commission Humanitarian aid Organisation. Its yearly budget tops €500m.

Celebrating European Job Mobility

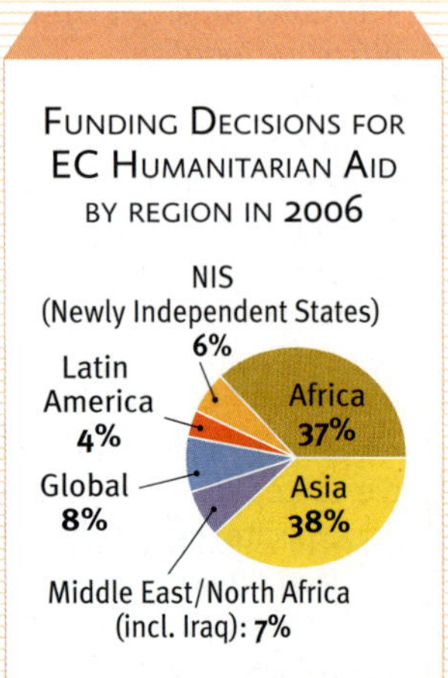

## 2-An economic Union

### The euro

The euro came into circulation in 2001 in the Eurozone/Euro Area/Eurosystem, i.e. the 12 countries which had met the convergence criteria. They are (in alphabetical order) Austria, Belgium, Finland, France, Germany, Greece, Ireland, Italy, Luxembourg, the Netherlands, Portugal and Spain. The European Central Bank is responsible for the monetary policy within the Eurozone. Although the new currency makes internal trade and travel easier, the change boosted prices, which in turn had negative repercussions on most Europeans' purchasing power.
Slovenia adopted the euro in January 2007. The other EU members do not belong to the Eurozone, because they do not want to (the UK) or because their monetary situation is not sound enough. Eleven more member states are to adopt the euro in 2009 at the latest.

Britans want Europe but not the euro! (2000)

### The EU's economy

The EU has the world's largest economy by GDP, a little above the USA but with 180m more inhabitants. It should maintain an annual growth rate of 3% until 2020, thanks to the new members such as the Baltic Republics, Slovenia and Poland, whose impressive growth compensates for the older members – France, Germany, Italy, etc. The most impressive result: Latvia, with an 8% annual growth, nearly the same as China (the world leader at 9% for the past 25 years). Europe is the world's largest exporter and the second largest importer.
The main source of revenue for the EU is the service sector, which accounts for 69% of the GNP whereas agriculture accounts for a mere 2.3%. Tourism is another important source of income. →**Chapter 12, Tourism**
However, many problems affect the Union:
- demographics (low birth rate and an aging population)
- unemployment over 9%; 17% of the population live below the poverty line (2004).

### Mobility

The suppression of borders has allowed people to move freely from one country to the other, either for leisure or for work. European citizens can live and work anywhere in the EU. However a lot of obstacles remain because living standards vary from one country to the other.
In order to facilitate workers' mobility, the EU countries have tried to harmonize their university systems. Programmes such as Erasmus and Leonardo da Vinci encourage students to study or find work placements in other EU countries. However, red tape remains an obstacle.

**Job Days: encouraging job mobility within the Union**

Since 2006, the European Commission has organized Job Days in more than 300 EU cities. The aim of these European Job fairs is to open the job market to all EU citizens, in order to encourage them to choose job mobility which so far has not met a real success. Job Days allow companies and applicants to meet one another in a more effective way. The success of these Job Days (500 events in 2006) has surprised the organizers who have decided to extend and multiply them from 2007 onward.

## 3-Fears and problems

### One country versus one union

The growing power of the European Commission over foreign policy, tax, economic and social policies is meant so that the EU can play an increasing role on the world stage.
Many young people today willingly identify themselves as Europeans but most citizens fear the loss of their cultural identities, languages, habits, jobs and social benefits.

### Pro-Europeans and eurosceptics

Many pro-Europeans believe that a strong, united Europe at all levels (economic, political, cultural, military, etc.) is the only viable response in today's highly divided world. Although pro-Europeans do not always agree with the EU's economic or political decisions, they still believe that there is no going back. Eurosceptics oppose the process of European integration, with a balanced proportion of right wingers – who fear the loss of national sovereignty – and left wingers, who disapprove of an economically liberal Europe which would widen the gap between the haves and the have nots.

### Labour fears

The fact that labour costs vary from one European country to the other have made citizens of the most "developed" countries fear the arrival of a cheaper labour force from eastern countries. The new members suffer from a massive exodus of their workforce to the western part of the EU. Poland and Romania have trouble finding the basic manpower they need, especially in this period of growth. In the EU itself, the rights of workers can be threatened by organized crime: as many as 1,000 Poles might live in forced work camps in the south of Italy.

### Language barriers

The 23 official languages for the 27 states of the EU remain a barrier, all the more so as only 3 working languages are used in the European Commision (English, French and German). A lot of time and money is spent on the translations of all the statements into all the EU languages: 4,000 interpreters work in the European Parliament. Translations delay information; certain languages find no interpreters, which leads to information gaps, or worse, to misunderstandings. To avoid these drawbacks, some Commission Members have suggested English as the official language of the EU. However this would deprive ordinary people of the access to the information they are legally entitled to and favour some countries over others.

### Success or failure?

Europe's most famous achievements are its space programme with the Ariane spaceship, and its air carrier industry Airbus, Boeing's (US) main challenger. But Airbus has found itself in trouble lately because it was unable to meet its clients' delivery deadlines. →**Chapter 9, Transport, *Landmark*, p. 149**

**Eurosceptics**

In 2004, only 3 out of 10 citizens in both the UK and Sweden felt their countries had benefited from their EU membership. The French and Dutch rejected the European Constitution in 2005. The Norwegians rejected EU membership twice. The Swiss rejected membership in the European Economic Area. The Danes and the Swedes rejected the euro. Iceland never applied for membership. Greenland left the EU (then the EEC) when it became independent from Denmark in 1979. The UK refused to be a part of the Schengen Agreement or the Economic and Monetary Union.

## Question time

1 What was the first European treaty?
2 Name the countries belonging to the EU.
3 What is referred to as Euroland?
4 What does the Schengen agreement allow the European citizens to do?
5 What do some Europeans fear about Europe?
6 What initiatives have been taken by the European Commission to encourage job mobility?
7 What is Europe's position in the world economy?
8 Is the EU involved in humanitarian aid? How?
9 What are the problems related to job mobility within the Union?

LANDMARK

# The Channel Tunnel

**The Channel Tunnel, operated by Eurotunnel, is a 50.5km-long rail tunnel beneath the English Channel. By connecting Folkestone, Kent, to Coquelles, near Calais, it has made Britain more "European".**

Before and during construction it was known as the "Chunnel" (portmanteau word: *Channel* + *tunnel*). It offers three principal services: Eurostar passenger service linking London, Paris and Brussels, a shuttle for vehicles, and freight trains. In 2004, more than 7m passengers travelled through the tunnel on Eurostar while Eurotunnel carried more than 2m cars, 1,281,207 trucks and 63,467 coaches.

## The history of a mega project

A link between Britain and the continent had been suggested on various occasions since a French engineer imagined a tunnel in 1802. Passengers would travel through the tunnel in horse-drawn coaches while a mid-tunnel island would provide a fresh-air respite for the horses. Various trials were unsuccessful because of insufficient funds, military or political objections, the last one after Britain's entry into the Common Market in 1974-75.

When the two ends of the service tunnel met in December 1990, walking on dry land from Britain to the continent was possible for the first time since the last ice age 8,500 years ago. The tunnel was officially opened by Queen Elizabeth II and President François Mitterrand on 6 May 1994. It is the second-longest rail tunnel in the world, and the 39km undersea section is the longest in the world.

## Construction

Digging the tunnel took 15,000 workers over 7 years. Operations were conducted simultaneously from both ends. Engineers used 11 large tunnel boring machines (TBMs), which combined drilling, material removal and consolidation of the walls with concrete. Almost 8 million $m^3$ of soil was removed.

## Features

The Channel Tunnel is in fact 3 parallel tunnels. Two rail tunnels, measuring 7.6 m in diameter and about 30m apart, carry trains. In between them a 4.8m in diameter service tunnel is connected to the main tunnels at intervals of 375m. It allows maintenance workers access to the rail tunnels and provides a safe escape route during emergencies.

## Financial trouble

Eurotunnel, the company that built and funded the project and currently runs the shuttle services, has been in financial difficulties almost from the start. The estimated cost of the project reached £10bn, including a cost overrun of 80%. Shares that funded the project lost 90% of their value between 1989 and 1998. Eurotunnel blames high interest payments and a lower traffic than was expected. Possible solutions could include cutting the number of trains per hour on a normal day from four to two, reducing staff and streamlining the business.

A British cliché about France? (2000)

## Borders and immigration

The official border between France and the UK is a painted line halfway through the tunnel. Border controls are handled at boarding or on the train. The two governments agreed to provide immigration staff at opposite ends of the tunnel: French immigration is located in the UK while the British one is in France.

Illegal immigrants and asylum seekers have used the tunnel to attempt to enter Britain. The French Red Cross opened a refugee centre at Sangatte in 1999, which housed up to 1,500 people, most of them trying to get to the UK. Some rode freight trains, others simply walked. Some were injured and more than a dozen died. In 2002, a double fence was built at a cost of £5m, reducing the numbers of refugees detected each week from 250 to almost none. Other measures included CCTV cameras and increased police patrols. At the end of 2002, the Sangatte centre was closed.

**Online t@sk**

Visit Eurostar's corporate site and go to www.eurostar.com/UK/uk/leisure/about_eurostar.jsp.
Choose one theme and report to the class.

## COUNTRIES AND NATIONALITIES

**Austria/Austrian**
**Belgium/Belgian**
**(Great) Britain/British/Briton (a)**
**Bulgaria/Bulgarian**
**Cyprus/Cypriot**
**Denmark/Danish**
**Estonia/Estonian**
**Finland/Finnish**
**France/French**
**Germany/German**
**Greece/Greek**
**Hungary/Hungarian**
**Ireland/Irish**
**Italy/Italian**
**Latvia/Latvian**
**Lithuania/Lithuanian**
**Luxembourg/from Luxembourg**
**Malta/Maltese**
**Poland/Polish**
**Portugal/Portuguese**
**Romania/Romanian**
**Slovakia/Slovakian**
**Slovenia/Slovenian**
**Spain/Spanish/Spaniard (a)**
**Sweden/Swedish**
**the Czech Republic/Czech**
**the Netherlands/Dutch**
**the United Kingdom (UK)/British**

**achievement:** réussite
**aging:** vieillissant
**agreement:** accord
**applicant:** candidat
**apply:** poser sa candidature
**asylum seeker:** demandeur d'asile
**barrier:** barrière
**be entitled to:** avoir droit à
**belong to:** appartenir à
**birth rate:** taux de natalité
**border:** frontière
**breach:** enfreindre
**Channel:** la Manche
**citizen:** citoyen
**coach:** autocar
**Common Agricultural Policy (CAP):** politique agricole commune (PAC)
**Common Market:** marché commun
**connect:** relier
**convergence criteria:** critères de convergence
**cost overrun:** dépassement des coûts
**costly:** coûteux, cher
**Council:** Conseil
**crossing:** traversée
**currency:** devise
**domestic:** intérieur
**EEC (the):** la CEE
**emergency:** urgence
**enlargement:** élargissement
**European Union (EU):** Union européenne (UE)
**European Commission:** Commission européenne
**Eurosceptic:** eurosceptique
**exporter:** exportateur
**extra:** supplémentaire
**failure:** échec
**fear:** peur
**finance:** financer
**foreign:** étranger (adj.)
**foreign policy:** politique étrangère
**foreigner:** étranger (N)
**former:** ancient
**founding principle:** principe fondateur
**free movement:** libre circulation
**freight:** fret
**fund:** financer
**funding:** financement
**GDP (gross domestic product):** PIB (produit intérieur brut)
**gender:** sexe
**grant:** bourse
**growth rate:** taux de croissance
**haves and the have nots (the):** les riches et les pauvres
**immigrant:** immigré

**importer:** importateur
**information gap:** déficit d'information
**inhabitant:** habitant
**interpreter:** interprète
**investment:** investissement
**IT (information technology):** informatique
**job market:** marché de l'emploi
**join:** adhérer à
**legislate:** légiférer
**living standard:** niveau de vie
**maintenance:** entretien
**member state:** état membre
**membership:** appartenance
**MEP (Member of the European Parliament):** député européen
**migrant:** immigré
**monetary policy:** politique monétaire
**national sovereignty:** souveraineté nationale
**non-EU:** qui n'appartient pas à l'UE
**official language:** langue officielle
**Parliament:** Parlement
**pillar:** pilier
**policy:** politique
**Polish plumber:** plombier polonais
**poverty line:** seuil de pauvreté
**red tape:** paperasserie
**refugee:** réfugié
**regulation:** réglementation
**rejection:** rejet
**scheme:** projet, dispositif
**set up:** créer
**shuttle:** navette
**small business:** petite entreprise
**social gap:** écart social
**space programme:** programme spatial
**spaceship:** vaisseau
**statement:** déclaration
**step:** étape
**streamline:** rationaliser
**subsidiary:** filiale
**support:** (V) soutenir ; (N) soutien, aide
**trade:** (V) commercer avec ; (N) échanges (commerciaux)
**training:** formation
**translation:** traduction
**treaty:** traité
**trial:** essai
**World Health Organization (WHO):** Organisation Mondiale de la Santé (OMS)
**world stage:** scène mondiale

## Charts and tables

**1.** Study and compare the following charts reflecting the opinions of Europeans on the European Union.

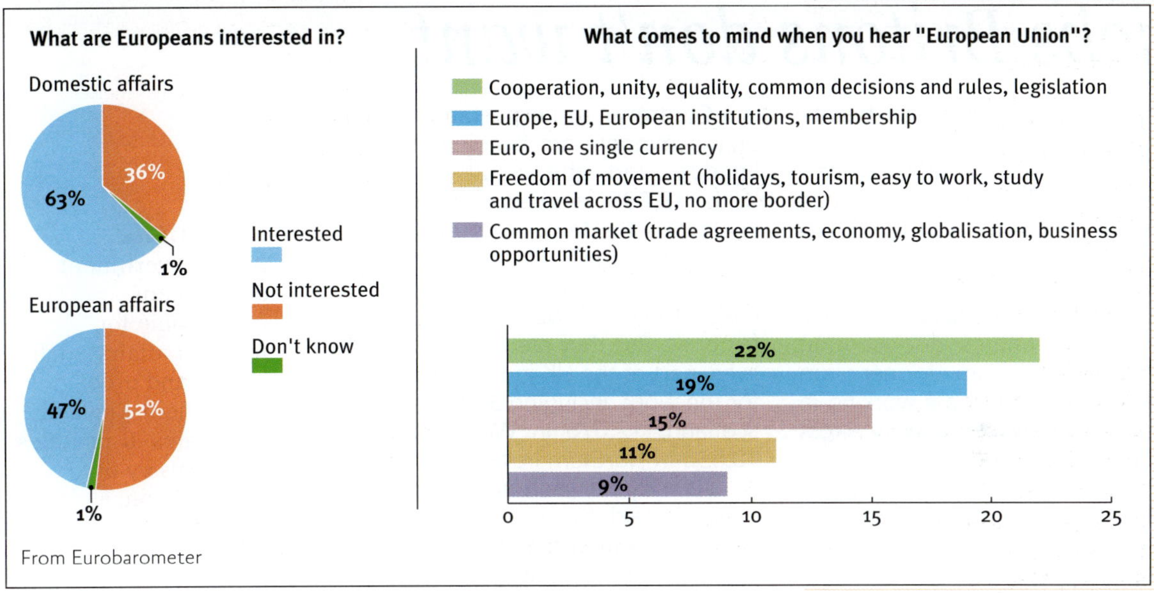


**2.** Give an oral presentation of each chart. →**Tools 11, p. 244**

## Online tasks

You want to open your business in another EU country? Visit "Your Europe – Business" on **ec.europa.eu/youreurope/nav/en/business/index.html** to get practical information and advice.
Choose one topic and report to the class.

## Communication tasks

### Role play

Visit the Europe Direct website on
**ec.europa.eu/europedirect/index_en.htm**

**A: You are a manager.**
You have many questions about job opportunities in the EU, for instance how to get your qualifications recognised. You have already completed your European CV.

**B: You work for the Europe Direct calling centre.**
You provide people with practical information on job opportunities in Europe.
→**Tools 14, p. 248**

# Eastern Europeans take jobs Britons don't want

From bus drivers to beauticians and from clowns to civil engineers, the influx of east and central Europeans has had a dramatic impact on the British jobs market.

Everyone has heard of Polish plumbers and Slovak nannies, but new figures disclose that newcomers from former Iron Curtain countries are working in every conceivable capacity across the United Kingdom.

The number of immigrants from the EU's new member states registering to work in this country has reached half a million for the first time since the EU expanded in May 2004.

By far the biggest group are Poles, who make up 307,660 of the new arrivals, followed by 54,640 Lithuanians and 50,230 Slovakians.

Office and business jobs were the most popular, with east Europeans filling 169,130 such posts and just over 100,000 are working in restaurants, bars and catering. Agricultural work – the vast majority in seasonal employment – and factory jobs also had high numbers registering. But a detailed breakdown[1] by the Home Office of the figures demonstrates the extraordinary variety of jobs filled by the newcomers, many of whom stay for a year or two before returning home.

Contrary to expectations, only a minority are heading for London and the South-east. With 73,035 workers, eastern England is the favourite destination, reflecting its large amount of agricultural land and heavy concentration of food processing factories. But they are moving to every part of the UK in the search for the work, including 37,570 in Scotland, 12,670 in Wales and 18,530 in Northern Ireland.

Liam Byrne, the Immigration minister, said the new workers were "benefiting the UK, by filling skills and labour gaps that cannot be met from the UK-born population".

Ministers were initially advised that only up to 13,000 east European workers would head to the UK after the EU's expansion and were taken by surprise by the scale of the influx. But they will be relieved by data showing only 3 per cent of the newcomers are out of work, with only a few hundred given help for homelessness or being considered for jobseeker's allowance payments.

Nigel Morris, *The Independent*,
22 November 2006

1. *breakdown*: analyse

## Info

***Home Office***
A UK government department, responsible for internal affairs, such as law and order, throughout England and Wales. It includes the Ministry of Immigration.

## References

You can find relevant information by reading various pages in your book and memorising a few facts and ideas.

→ **Work, p. 57**
→ **Europeans, p. 208**

**ACTIVITY** **Practise giving an account of this article.**

## Introduction

You should explain where the article comes from, when it was published and what it is about. →Tools 4, p. 236

This article was published in *The Independent*, a British daily, in November 2006, after new figures were analysed by the Home Office. It reports on the arrival of workers from new EU member states to the UK and the consequences on the UK job market.

## Development

Once you have understood the article, organise your ideas into two or three different parts, using set phrases and link-words. →Tools 4, p. 236

1. Who the newcomers are
2. The jobs they take
3. Reactions

You should also use the information given in *Info* and what you have learnt, for example by referring to the various pages indicated in *References*.

### 1. Who the newcomers are

• Immigrants seeking work in the UK come from the countries of eastern and central Europe such as Poland, Lithuania and Slovakia which joined the EU in May 2004.
• The numbers of immigrants reached 500,000 in 2006. The biggest group are Poles, with over 300,000 people. Lithuanians and Slovakians both account for over 50,000 people.
• Many newcomers stay for a year or two before returning to their home country.

### 2. The jobs they take

• Even though Polish plumbers and Slovak nannies have become famous, the new study shows that the newcomers have very varied jobs, from bus drivers to beauticians and from clowns to civil engineers.
However, they mainly take the jobs Britons don't want.
• The majority of the new immigrants – almost 170,000 – fill office and business jobs. Another 100,000 are working in restaurants, bars and catering. East and central Europeans also work in agricultural, essentially in seasonal employment – and in factories.
• Place: here again, the key word is variety and the immigrants are moving to every part of the UK, including 37,570 in Scotland, 12,670 in Wales and 18,530 in Northern Ireland. It was thought the majority would settle in London and the South-east. However, eastern England with its large amount of agricultural land and food processing factories is the favourite destination.

### 3. Reactions

• At first reactions were very negative. As a matter of fact, only up to 13,000 east European workers were expected in the UK after the EU's expansion. Everyone was taken by surprise by the scale of the influx.
• However, the situation is far more positive. Firstly, the new workers have had a major impact on the British jobs market and have benefited the UK, by filling skills and labour gaps.
Secondly, the figures show that only 3% of the newcomers are jobless, and that only a few hundred are given help for homelessness or being considered for jobseeker's allowance payments. Therefore they don't claim social benefits.

## Conclusion

You should sum up the main ideas and try to open out in a new direction.

This article aims at reassuring Britons about the workers who arrive from the EU new member states and who have sometimes fuelled negative reactions because of unemployment and the fact that they are paid lower wages. New figures released by the Home Office should help dispel those negative attitudes. However, one may wonder whether figures will be enough to change people's minds. The entry of more members into the EU in January 2007 might trigger new reactions.

## Branching out

Now, you should move away from the article and develop more ideas. The following questions can help you.

**1** Do you think an enlarged Europe will be stronger and more profitable for its members? Why/Why not?

**2** Do you think Europe can catch up with faster-growing economies such as China and India? Why/Why not?

## Case study: Cross-border shopping in the EU

**Definition:** Cross-border shopping includes any purchases made from retailers or providers located in other European Union countries, either in person or via distance shopping (during a business trip or holidays, or through distance shopping, via internet, by phone or by post from suppliers situated in other EU member states). It does not include purchases of foreign-made products bought in one's own country. Interviews were conducted face-to-face in people's homes in their national language between February 20 and March 24, 2006. The countries surveyed include the twenty-five member states of the European Union.

People were asked "To what extent do you agree with the following statements, regarding purchasing from retailers or providers located in other EU countries?"

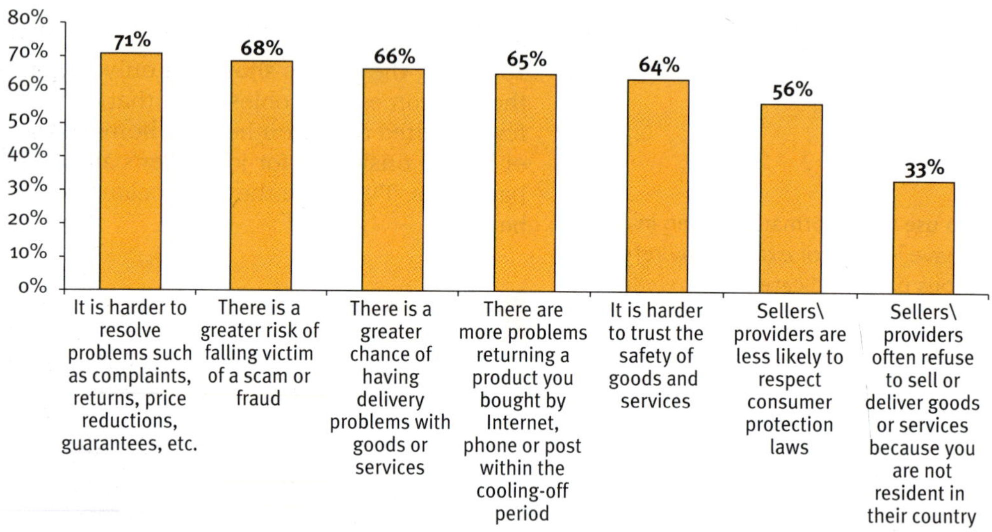


From European Commission, Public Opinion Analysis

**1.** Analyse the chart and report to the class.

**2.** Group work

Draw up a questionnaire about various aspects of cross-border shopping in the EU. Make at least ten questions. You can use the questions above as inspiration.

Then interview three people and report to the class.

## PERSONAL TASK

You have been asked what your main reasons for learning a new language would be. Here are a few reasons to inspire you:

- to be able to study in another country,
- to meet people from other countries,
- to know a language that is widely spoken around the world,
- to be able to understand people from other cultures,
- to get a better job in France or to be able to work in another country.

Give an oral presentation to explain your reasons.

# IN THIS UNIT...

- Companies: Wal-Mart, McDonald's, HSBC...
- Learn about fair trade & young Chinese people
- Report on the WTO & trade disputes
- Write a letter of apology to an old-established customer

# 14
## Globalisation

**→ Before you START**

*In brief:* **Shopping habits from one country to another**
*Front page:* **Helping farmers in developing countries**

## Who is campaigning for what on this poster? Which countries favour GM foods?

### Words

- **Nouns:** export/import (N), export/import (V), precaution, farmer, ban
- **Adjectives:** genetically modified, safe ≠ unsafe, dangerous, funny

### LISTENING PRACTICE

CD TRACK 71

Listen to the recording.
**1.** What are the people talking about?
**2.** Explain their opinions.

# Wal-Mart to Abandon Germany

Wal-Mart Stores, admitting defeat in Germany's giant but cutthroat retail market, announced Friday that it would sell its 85 stores here to a German retailer, incurring[1] a loss of $1 billion.

Wal-Mart is retreating from the German retail market by selling out to the Metro Group. The decision came two months after Wal-Mart sold out in South Korea and amounts to a marked retreat by the world's largest retailer from its breakneck global expansion.

In Germany the market is characterized by unrelenting price competition, well-established discounters and the cultural resistance of German shoppers to hypermarkets – sprawling stores where the fresh vegetables may be a few aisles away from the shirts or the lawn mowers.

When it broke into the German market in 1998, Wal-Mart acquired the outlets of two second-tier[2] retailers – geographically dispersed and often in poor locations.

The company initially installed American managers, who made some cultural gaffes, like offering to bag groceries for customers (Germans prefer to bag their own groceries) or instructing clerks to smile (Germans, used to brusque service, were put off).

Beyond the competitive pressures, there is the reality of the German consumer – one of the most price-conscious in Europe. "Wal-Mart has tried, for the better part of a decade, to adapt to this market," an analyst said. "I think they've looked at the situation and come to the conclusion, 'how long is it going to take?' "

Mark Landler, *The New York Times*, 29 July 2006

1. *incur*: encourir
2. *second-tier*: de second rang

CD TRACK 72

### Info

***Germany*** There are many discount supermarket chains in Germany, such as SPAR, Lidl, or ALDI that is said to have been Germany's first real discount supermarket.

***Wal-Mart*** → **Chapter 8, Distribution, *Landmark*, p. 133**

## Work on words

### 1 | Find their equivalents in English

**§1** au détail – impitoyable – revendeur – perte
**§2** à folle allure
**§3** allée
**§4** emplacement
**§5** mettre dans des sacs – employé

### 2 | Find their synonyms

**§2** sell all – be equivalent to
**§3** constant – rivalry – huge
**§4** make its entrance – store (N)
**§5** at the beginning – disconcerted
**§6** for the major part of – ten years

### Headlines

**1** Headlines are often short. What words are missing here? Write the full sentence.

**2** Compare the headline and the first sentence of the article. What similarities and differences are there? Why?

## The key points of the article

### 1 Wal-Mart in Germany

**a.** Number of Wal-Mart stores in Germany.
**b.** How long has the company owned stores in this country?
**c.** What was the problem of the stores?
**d.** Amount of money lost in Germany.
**e.** Name of the new store owner.

### 2 An inadequate marketing strategy

**a.** Pick out adjectives and expressions used to define the German retail market.
**b.** German cultural specificities.
**c.** Reasons why Wal-Mart could not adapt.
**d.** What other country was a failure for Wal-Mart? What can be concluded in terms of marketing strategy?

## Branching out

**1** Are American brands easily adaptable to any market? →*Key data*, p. 118

**2** How can global chains of stores adapt to the specificities of local markets?

## {Methods}

### ■ Speaking practice

**Read figures aloud.** →Tools 10, p. 243
Then practise reading the groups of words in parentheses with the figures.
**a.** 85 (stores) **b.** ($)1 billion **c.** (in) 1998

### ■ Writing practice

**1 Expressing the idea of progression**

Comparative forms can be used:
• to emphasize the idea of a progression.
Short adjectives: adj.*-er and* adj.*-er*
Long adjectives: *more and more* + adj.
*Wal-Mart products are* ***cheaper and cheaper***.
• to express a parallel progression.
Short adjectives: *the* adj. + *-er* ..., *the* adj. + *-er*
Long adjectives: *the more (less)* + adj. ..., *the more (less)* + adj.
***The more*** *they try,* ***the more*** *money they lose.*
• to express "d'autant plus ... que ...":
Short adjectives: *all the* adj. + *-er*
Long adjectives : *all the more / less* + adj. ... *as/since...*
*They are* ***all the more*** *disappointed* ***as*** *they were hoping to make a lot of profits.*

**Translate the following sentences with the proper comparative form.**
**a.** Wal-Mart a de plus en plus de difficultés avec ses magasins en Europe.
**b.** Wal-Mart perd de plus en plus d'argent sur le marché allemand.
**c.** Plus Wal-Mart grossit, plus il lui devient difficile de s'adapter aux marchés locaux.
**d.** Plus les clients sont soucieux des prix, plus la concurrence est féroce.
**e.** Les managers locaux sont d'autant plus recherchés qu'ils connaissent les besoins spécifiques de leurs clients.

**2 Prepare a short account in English.**
Use the sentences in part **1**.
• Mix sentences **a** and **b** together, using *according to the article.*
• Mix sentences **c** and **d** together, using *on the one hand ...on the other hand.*
• Find a link word to use sentence **e** as a possible solution.
→Tools 4, p. 236

## LISTENING PRACTICE

CD TRACK 73-74

*Roberto Medina and Faye Cardinal are discussing a new case.*

**1 Comprehension**
Listen to the recording to find the following information.

**Part 1**
**a.** Product (type, origin).
**b.** What happened the day before.
**c.** Where the products came from, and why.
**d.** How the authorities managed.

**Part 2**
**a.** Total number of products concerned.
**b.** Give details about the guilty people.
**c.** Give details about the products of the day before.
**d.** Roberto's conclusion.

**2 Expression**
Give an oral account, or write a 100-word paragraph, summing up what you have heard.

# Supermarket chain's scheme to help African growers bears fruit

Fruit growers in South Africa have seen more than £330,000 ploughed back[1] into their communities over the past year by the supermarket group Waitrose, which is hoping to raise a further £500,000 to fund educational projects over the next six months.

The cash has been raised as part of the food retailer's initiative to return a sizeable proportion of profits it earns on sales of citrus fruits to the farmers who grow them. The scheme has proved more successful than had been hoped, and now the Waitrose Foundation, which operates as a partnership between the supermarket and members of the supply chain, is adding avocados to the grapefruits, lemons and clementines on offer.

Some 25 educational schemes have already been launched on 10 citrus farms across South Africa, including training in literacy and IT[2], as well as classes in craft work to enable farm workers to earn an income out of season. The citrus season is only six months long so it is vital to teach new skills to the growers.

Waitrose's managing director, Steven Esom, who was in South Africa last month visiting some of the projects, said: "I was 100% convinced this is the right thing to do before I went; now I'm 110% convinced. It is absolutely clear that it's trade not aid that will work."

Waitrose, part of the John Lewis Partnership, had initially expected to raise £250,000 in the first year. Now it hopes to raise £500,000 in the next six months. Mr Esom is delighted with the response of customers who "feel a strong link" with those who produce the food they buy.

The Waitrose Foundation was set up as a long-term response to South Africa's social and economic problems and its work has been welcomed by the South African authorities.

Mr Esom is keen to see the scheme extended. "There's an opportunity in grapes and maybe in processed products. And it could be extended to wine."

Fiona Walsh, *The Guardian*, May 29, 2006

1. *ploughed back*: réinvestis
2. *IT*: abréviation de *information technology* (= informatique)

CD TRACK 75

to sensitize customers to growers' living conditions.

Addition

### Info

***South Africa***
The Republic of South Africa is a net exporter of farming products and foodstuffs, the largest number of exported items being sugar, grapes, citrus fruit and wine. It is the eighth largest wine producer in the world.

***Waitrose*** → p. 128
The Waitrose Foundation is a fair trade initiative. Waitrose sells both Fairtrade products and Waitrose Foundation products with another specific logo.

## Work on words

### 1 | Find their equivalents in English

**Headline** porter ses fruits
**§1** rassembler (des fonds) – financer
**§2** bénéfice – gagner – ventes – agrumes – agriculteur – partenariat – ajouter
**§3** lancer – savoir lire et écrire – artisanat – revenu – compétences
**§5** lien
**§6** bien accueilli
**§7** tenir à – raisins – (produits) transformés

### 2 | Find their synonyms

**Headline** project – producer
**§1** more – finance
**§2** money – give back – considerable
**§3** essential
**§4** business – help
**§5** at the beginning – very happy
**§6** create

## Headlines

**1** Develop reflexes! Look for more information in **§1**.
**a.** Name of the supermarket chain.
**b.** Africa is a continent. Which country is concerned?

**2** Anticipate the contents of the article from the headline.

**3** There's a pun in the headline with "fruit". Can you explain it?

## The key points of the article

**1 Read §1**
**a.** Name of supermarket.
**b.** Country.
**c.** What the supermarket did.
**d.** What the supermarket wants to do.

■ Complete this summary of §1 with:
*British – chain – finance – growers – invested – over – projects – raise – South.*
Waitrose, a ... supermarket ..., has already ... more than £330,000 into ... African fruit ...' communities. It wants to ... another £500,000 to ... educational ... ... the next six months.

**2 Read §2 and §3**
**a.** Origin of the money.
**b.** The supermarket's initiative.
**c.** New fruit concerned.
**d.** What the money helped to do.
**e.** What the farmers learned.
**f.** Reason for learning craft work.

**3 Read §4, §5, §6 and §7**
**a.** Waitrose's managing director's reaction.
**b.** Customer's response to the project.
**c.** The Foundation's mission.
**d.** Waitrose's future projects.

## {Methods}

■ **Speaking practice**

**1 Read figures aloud.** →Tools 10, p. 243
Read §4 and §5 aloud. If necessary, start by writing the following figures down. Then practise reading the groups of words in parentheses with the figures.
**a.** (I was) 100% (convinced)
**b.** (now) I'm 110% (convinced)
**c.** (raise) £250,000 (in the first year)
**d.** (raise) £500,000 (in the next six months)

**2 Money, money**
Get used to dollars and pounds. Change all the money data into euros.

**3 Prepare an oral introduction.**
• Identify the source.
• Explain what the article is about (who, what, where, when).

■ **Writing practice**

**1 Translate §1 and §2.**
Pay attention to the figures, the prepositions and the verbal forms.

**2 Write an account of the article in English (120 words).**
→Tools 4, p. 236

## Branching out

**1** Do you, as a customer, "feel a strong link" with the people who produce the food you buy? Are you for or against fair trade? Why/Why not? →*Key data*, p. 222

**2** Do you think "trade not aid" is the right way to do things, and why/why not?

## Language

• *We are most pleased about this initiative and support it with **much** anticipation.*
***Much*** équivaut à « beaucoup de » devant un nom indénombrable (qu'on ne peut pas compter). ***Many*** a le même sens devant un dénombrable au pluriel. ***A lot of*** est employé dans les deux cas.
Souvenez-vous : on utilise également ***much***, ou ***far***, devant un comparatif (beaucoup plus...).
***Few*** (peu de) et ***a few*** (quelques/un peu de) sont utilisés avec un dénombrable pluriel. ***Little*** (peu de) et ***a little*** (un peu de) sont utilisés avec un nom indénombrable.
Tous ces quantifieurs peuvent être utilisés après ***too*** (trop...) et ***so*** (tellement...).

**Translate into English**
**1.** Le supermarché a réinvesti beaucoup de bénéfices dans les fermes sud-africaines.
**2.** Beaucoup d'agriculteurs ont profité des cours et ils peuvent maintenant gagner un peu d'argent quand ce n'est pas la saison des agrumes.
**3.** Ce n'est pas très intelligent de leur apporter beaucoup d'aide : il vaut mieux développer les affaires et faire du commerce, c'est beaucoup plus utile.
**4.** Au départ, ils pensaient que ce projet rapporterait peu d'argent, mais ils ont rencontré tellement de succès qu'ils vont développer de nouveaux produits.

# 14 Globalisation

*Key data*

**Globalisation is a term which started being used in the 1980s; it refers to the growing economic interdependence of countries worldwide through exchanges of goods and services. The trend increased with the boom of technology.**

## 1-Definitions

### Globalisation everywhere

Globalization concerns various sectors.
- Industrial globalisation: expansion of multinational companies around the world.
- Financial globalisation allows the free circulation of capital.
- Informational globalisation: wherever people live they can access the same information, watch the same TV programmes, etc.
- Cultural globalisation refers to increasing cross-cultural contacts.

All ultimately favour the globalisation of trade, also called free trade. This is done thanks to:
- reducing or eliminating tariffs,
- reducing transportation costs,
- reducing capital controls.

### Free trade areas (FTAs)

FTAs are areas where there are no tariffs or barriers preventing trade and exchanges. Several countries agree to belong to an unrestricted trading zone in most sectors: the North American Free Trade Agreement (NAFTA) includes Canada, the USA and Mexico. There are many other FTAs, in Asia for example.
On the contrary, quotas can limit trade: they consist of limiting the quantity of goods that can be imported into a country during a given period of time. If a country uses them, the other country tends to retaliate, leading to trade disputes.

### Multinationals or MNCs (Multi National Corporations)

A multinational is a company managing production in at least two countries. Some of the most famous MNCs are BP, Shell, HSBC, HP, Microsoft, Wal-Mart, Walt Disney, Monsanto, etc. Fifty of them have a budget exceeding that of many countries: therefore they play an essential role in globalisation. Many countries compete to attract multinationals by offering them various incentives such as tax breaks, or by letting them have lax environmental and labour standards. Multinationals profit from the situation by underpaying an already cheap labour force, sometimes triggering waves of protests. Another issue for MNCs is counterfeiting, which is expanding despite the increasing crack-down. →**Chapter 3, Work, *Prep Page*, p. 62 & Chapter 7, Brands**

## 2-A controversial issue

Globalisation has its supporters and its detractors. Supporters believe that globalization is economically and socially positive: by boosting trade, it increases the living standards of developing countries while making developed ones even more prosperous. Its detractors, also called alter-globalists, consider globalisation

**The Chinese textile crisis**

Chinese textile goods attract consumers because of their rock bottom prices. However, in 2005, the quotas of Chinese ready-to-wear products were reached in Europe, and shiploads of Chinese clothes remained stuck in harbours. China and the EU started negotiations which ended up in the lowering of quotas for future years. However, the whole European textile sector feels threatened by Chinese imports. According to the WTO agreements, the EU should not be allowed to impose quotas on foreign imports.

McDonald's in Saudi Arabia

a war machine: they argue it aims at imposing corporate imperialism and cultural assimilation while crushing human rights, destroying the environment and stealing resources from developing countries. The World Trade Organization and the World Social Fund represent each side.

### The World Trade Organization (WTO)

The Geneva-based WTO establishes the rules for global trading and resolves disputes between its 149 member states. Before its formation in 1995, the GATT (General Agreement on Tariffs and Trade) was in charge of international trade. The WTO's main aim is to increase world trade by erasing or lowering trade barriers. Here are some of its principles on what a good trading system should be.

- It should tend toward fewer trade barriers.
- It should be predictable: companies and governments should rest assured that trade barriers will not be raised and that markets will remain open.
- It should tend toward greater competition.
- It should be more accommodating for less developed countries, giving them more time to adjust, greater flexibility and more privileges.

The WTO operates on consensus between the member states. This makes the process more democratic but also very long. It works with the International Monetary Fund and with the World Bank. The IMF's purpose is to check the global financing system and to give financial aid when needed. The World Bank is responsible for providing finance and advice to countries for the purposes of economic development and eliminating poverty.
WTO members meet every one or two years and the meetings are now marked by gatherings of anti-globalisation protesters which have attracted public attention about the issues raised by globalisation.

### The World Social Forum (WSF)

The World Social Forum first met in 2001 in Porto Alegre in Brazil. Alternative globalisation movements from around the world meet in January at the same time as the WTO, but not in the same place. The WSF has been criticized for not taking any practical decisions, but it is supposed to be a place of discussion. It launched the slogan "Another World is Possible". Members have led spectacular actions such as the destruction of plantations of transgenic crops belonging to Monsanto. The WSF also questions the legitimacy and the role of the IMF and the World Bank.

### The GMO (Genetically Modified Organism) dispute

The USA markets and exports genetically modified crops without particular precautions. Many European countries, among which France, believe that genetic modification could be unsafe and they are strongly opposed to the unregulated spreading of GMOs. This precaution principle prevents them from accepting the US exports of genetically modified soya beans and corn. The French ban on US genetically modified crops is considered illegal by the US which claims that it is totally against the principles of free trade.

### Another controversial issue: the AoA (Agreement on Agriculture)

The AoA allows Europe and the USA to spend $380 billion a year on agricultural subsidies which are supposed to protect small

**The largest global bank, the HSBC**

The Honk Kong and Shanghai Banking Corporation (HSBC) is referred to as "the bank that ate the world". Created in Hong Kong and Shanghai in 1865, the London-based giant bank, which has expanded in all mature markets such as the US and Europe, is returning to China. HSBC has succeeded in establishing global brand awareness with its multicultural and multilingual advertising campaigns which aim to highlight the bank's adaptability around the world. In China, HSBC is in harsh competition with Citigroup to impose its leadership and win the world's newly rich and its untapped credit card market.

farmers. However, most subsidies go to a minority of big farmers who flood the global market with cheap agricultural products, making it impossible for small producers, especially those in poor countries, to survive. Moreover, the AoA tends to reduce tariff protections for small farmers, making their development even more difficult.

## 3-Fair trade: a sustainable alternative?

The idea of fair trade was born in Europe in the 1960s. The aim of fair trade, which at the time was referred to as "Trade not Aid", was to give all producers around the world a fair and equal access to the markets. The movement has become increasingly popular and given rise to the idea of solidarity.

### Guidelines

Fair trade's guidelines are simple and appeal to the average consumer.

- Small producers from developing countries must be paid a fair price for their products.
- Fair trade companies must not resort to child labour and unfair labour practices.
- The consumer should be ready to pay a premium for fair trade products which follow superior quality standards (hand-picked coffee beans, fertilizer-free rice, etc.).
- Fair trade encourages better environmental practices and responsible methods of production.

Most fair trade activities are operated by ATOs (Alternative Trading Organizations) which work with partners in poor countries. They help them build their businesses and sell their products directly to consumers in developed countries. Some of the largest and most efficient ATOs are Oxfam and Traidcraft in the UK, or Alter Eco in France. Fair trade sales have increased by 20% every year since 2000. In 2005, the number of sales of fair trade goods amounted to €660 million.

### Fair trade labelling

In order to guarantee to the consumers the fair trade origins of the products they bought, Dutch ATOs activists launched the Max Havelaar label in 1988. Today, there are other fair trade labels, such as Transfair, and Fair Trade Mark.

**Global solidarity**

The French government passed a law in July 2006 to charge each passenger departing from a French airport a "solidarity tax" collected for the benefit of poor countries. The idea is that globalization should work both ways and help the developing world instead of always making profits out of its weaknesses. The tax ranges from €1 to €40 depending on the journey. Airlines strongly disapprove of the law, but other countries have already decided to follow France's example.

## Question time

**1** When was the word globalisation first used?
**2** Define three areas in which globalisation plays an important part.
**3** What are the advantages of globalisation?
**4** What are its drawbacks?
**5** What is the WTO? What is its purpose?
**6** What are FTAs? Name one, giving details on its members.
**7** What international organisations does the WTO work with?
**8** What is the WSF?
**9** Explain what fair trade consists of.

LANDMARK

# McDonald's

**The first McDonald's opened abroad was in Canada in 1967. Now, McDonald's has 30,000 restaurants in 119 countries worldwide, serving 50 million people each day. *The Economist* uses a "Big Mac index", i.e. the comparison of a Big Mac's cost in various world currencies to judge their purchasing power parity.**

## The All-American Meal

**1940** The McDonald brothers created a restaurant where people could eat a burger and have a drink in their cars. The first drive-thru restaurant was born!
**1948** Opening of their first restaurant in San Bernardino, California, serving hamburgers and milkshakes. Quick, cheap burgers were produced with an assembly line, "Speedee Service System."
**1955** Ray Kroc, who understood the concept could be profitable, invested all his money in "McDonald's Corporation". He opened his first franchise in Chicago, with the advertising slogan "The All American Meal"; it consisted of a 15¢ hamburger (4¢ extra for cheese), 10¢ fries, and a 20¢ shake. It could be served to families at a speedy 25 seconds. Eventually, Kroc bought the entire company.
**1962** The famous Golden Arches were created. McDonald's celebrated 2bn hamburgers served.

## Appealing to children

**1979** The "Happy Meal" for children was created by an advertising manager: specially tailored for children, sold in a small box or a paper bag, the meal also contains a toy, such as McDonaldland characters, McWrist wallets, etc. This greatly contributed to promote McDonald's as a family restaurant. It also turned many children into addicts of both the sugary meal and the toy. The toys could not be bought separately, thus encouraging children to ask for more. Happy Meals also started promoting movies with *Star Trek*. While initially Happy Meal toys were cheap plastic objects – a frisbee or a ball – they are now far more sophisticated. Many are related to a film, or an existing toy line, such as Barbie. However, Disney has announced it will stop its alliance with McDonald's.

→Chapter 4, Consumers, *In brief*, p. 66

A 1995 magazine advert

## A global empire

A new outlet opens every 3 hours somewhere in the world. McDonald's gives its food a local touch: Maharaja Macs and vegetable nuggets in India, McHuevos – a hamburger with a poached egg on top – in Uruguay, Kiwiburgers in New Zealand and Chicken Tatsuta (a fried chicken sandwich spiced with soy sauce and ginger) in Japan. In Islamic countries, McDonald's restaurants offer a "Halal" menu. McDonald's has often been credited with increasing the standards of hygiene and service in many of the markets it has entered.

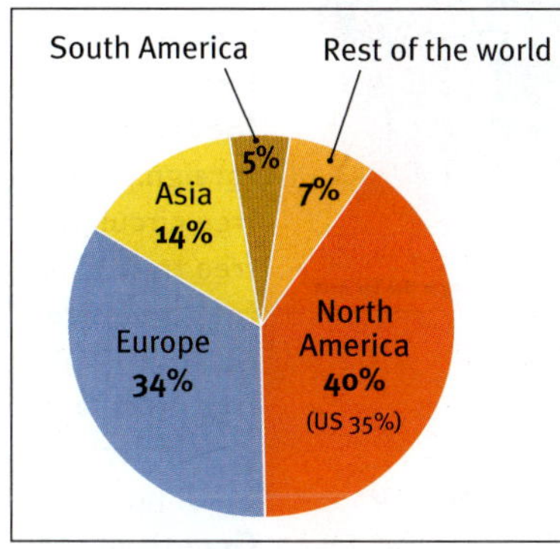


McDonald's market share

## Criticism

McDonald's most vocal critics, such as Morgan Spurlock's documentary, *Super Size Me* (2004), argue increasing numbers of overweight people over-consume junk food. Critics have also focused on McDonald's business practices. Eric Schloesser's book, *Fast Food Nation* (2001), now a film, criticizes working conditions and the company's demands from its suppliers, which may disrupt food-industry practices, for example potato crops or meat.

→Chapter 4, Consumers, *In brief*, p. 66

Locations near cultural monuments, such as the restaurant next to the Spanish Steps in Rome, have been opposed.
Finally, because of its standardized products and procedures, McDonald's is assimilated to cheap culture. "McWords" have appeared, such as McJob – low-paying jobs for interchangeable employees in a corporate machine –, or McMedicine – over-prescribing medication for profit or convenience. They have a very negative connotation.

**Online t@sk**

Visit McDonald's corporate site and go to www.mcdonalds.com/corp/about/factsheets.html.
Choose one theme and report to the class.

# 14 Globalisation

## Vocabulary

"Sorry lads.I'm closing this workshop down,and relocating in the far east."

**abroad:** à l'étranger
**agreement:** accord
**aid:** aide, soutien
**alter-globalist:** alter mondialiste
**alternative:** alternatif
**assembly line:** chaîne de montage
**availability:** accessibilité
**ban:** interdiction
**barrier:** barrière
**brand:** marque
**break into (a market):** faire son entrée sur
**breakneck (adj.):** à folle allure
**bribe:** corrompre
**cargo:** cargaison, chargement
**ceiling:** plafond
**challenge:** défi
**check:** vérifier
**child labour:** travail des enfants
**competition:** concurrence
**consumer goods:** produits de consommation
**container:** conteneur
**contest:** concours
**controversial:** sujet à controverses
**controversy:** polémique
**corn:** maïs
**counterfeit:** contrefait
**counterfeiting:** contrefaçon
**counterpart:** homologue
**crackdown (on):** mesures de répression (contre)
**craft work:** artisanat
**crop:** culture, récolte
**currency:** devise
**customs:** douane
**cutthroat:** impitoyable
**defeat:** défaite
**developing:** en voie de développement
**dispute:** conflit
**earn:** gagner
**erase:** supprimer
**exchange:** échange
**export *(N)*:** exportation
**export *(V)*:** exporter
**exporter:** exportateur
**fair trade:** commerce équitable
**farmer:** agriculteur
**flood:** inonder
**foodstuff:** produits alimentaires
**foreign:** étranger
**free circulation:** libre circulation
**free trade:** libre échange
**free trade area (FTA):** zone de libre-échange
**free-trade agreement (FTA):** accord de libre-échange
**fund:** financer
**Genetically Modified Organism (GMO):** organisme génétiquement modifié (OGM)
**precaution principle:** principe de précaution
**genuine:** authentique
**global:** mondial
**guarantee:** garantir ; garantie
**guideline:** directive
**hand-picked:** cueilli à la main
**harbour:** port
**import:** (N) importation ; (V) importer
**importer:** importateur
**incentive:** incitation
**income:** revenu
**innovative:** novateur
**interdependence:** interdépendance
**International Monetary Fund (IMF):** Fonds monétaire international (FMI)
**item:** article
**label:** label, étiquette
**labelling:** étiquetage
**lax:** souple, laxiste
**legitimacy:** légitimité
**living standards:** niveau de vie
**lobby:** groupe de pression
**located:** situé
**location:** emplacement, lieu
**market share:** part de marché
**negotiation:** négociation
**parity:** parité
**partnership:** partenariat
**phon(e)y:** faux
**piracy:** contrefaçon
**poverty:** pauvreté
**predictable:** prévisible
**premium price:** prix fort
**prevent ... from V-*ing*:** empêcher ... de ...
**price-conscious:** attentif aux prix
**protester:** manifestant
**purchasing power:** pouvoir d'achat
**question:** remettre en question
**raise (funds):** rassembler (des fonds)
**range from ... to...:** aller de... à...
**ready-to-wear:** prêt à porter
**retaliation:** représailles
**retaliate:** user de représailles
**rock bottom price:** prix défiant toute concurrence
**sales:** ventes
**scheme:** plan, projet
**seize:** saisir
**sell out:** vendre tout le stock
**shipload:** cargaison
**smuggler:** contrebandier
**solve:** résoudre
**soya beans:** soja
**spending power:** pouvoir d'achat
**standard:** norme
**subsidiary:** filiale
**subsidies:** subventions
**support:** soutenir, aider
**survey:** étude
**tariff:** droits de douane, barrière douanière
**tax break:** réduction d'impôt, avantage fiscal
**threaten:** menacer
**trade:** échanges (commerciaux)
**trade barrier:** barrière douanière
**trigger:** déclencher
**underpay:** sous-payer
**unfair:** inéquitable
**untapped:** inexploité
**upmarket:** haut de gamme
**World Bank:** banque mondiale
**World Social Forum (WSF):** Forum social mondial
**World Trade Organisation (WTO):** Organisation Mondiale du Commerce (OMC)
**worldwide:** dans le monde entier

## Charts and tables

**1.** Study the following charts which give you information about the France Telecom group worldwide for 2005.

NUMBER OF CUSTOMERS PER COUNTRY

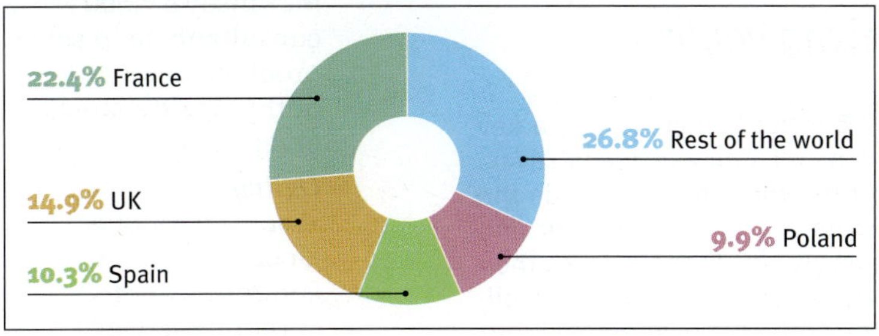


A WORLDWIDE OPERATOR

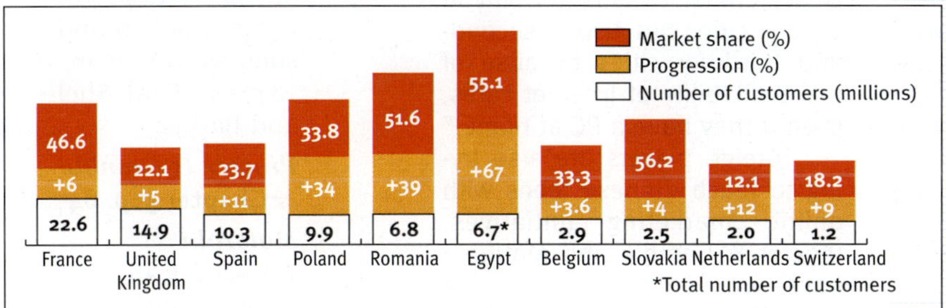


From France Telecom website

**2.** Give an oral presentation of these charts. →**Tools 11, p. 244**

## Online tasks

### Presenting the WTO

Visit the World Trade Organisation website: **www.wto.org/**

**1.** Introduce the WTO's mission around the world.

**2.** Report on the principles of the trading system:
**www.wto.org/english/thewto_e/whatis_e/tif_e/fact2_e.htm**

**3.** Choose a trade dispute on
**www.wto.org/english/tratop_e/dispu_e/dispu_e.htm**
and report to the class.

### Do you know about fair trade at work?

Visit the Fair Trade foundation website on
**www.fairtrade.org.uk/index.htm**
and learn about fair trade at work. Choose one topic and report to the class.
→*Key data*, p. 222

# China's surprising teen consumers

*Creators of consumer products need to understand the unusual mindset of mainland youth.*

Chinese teens are fashion crazy, and spend an obscene amount of time watching TV, surfing the Internet, and playing online games. In short, they are pretty much like kids in Tokyo, London, and New York City, though perhaps with less spending power – right?

Well, not exactly. A survey released by McKinsey & Co. suggests Chinese teen spirit is unique in key respects that complicate the efforts of multinational consumer-goods companies. One striking observation from the survey of nearly 800 youths aged 12 to 17, in both flashy urban centers such as Beijing and Shanghai and rural towns, is the strong nationalist streak among young teens. Many say they prefer and trust mainland brands over foreign ones. Another un-teen like characteristic: they generally want to save money.

Salting money away[1] is seen as a key value, along with a heavy sense of familial obligation to support aging parents. In fact, 96% of respondents cite this as a crucial responsibility. Eighty-eight per cent trust Chinese brands, while only 65% say the same about foreign brands.

Chinese teens collectively represent a market of about $36 billion a year. Chinese parents, who tend to dote on their kids, spend $28.75 billion on them, and $7.5 billion comes directly out of the pockets of the young.

The Net is increasingly a key part of all Chinese teens' lives. "The big thing to use now is the Internet and to provide music and gaming for the teens, making their favorite leisure activities available through the Internet," says Chak, Beijing-based planner at Ogilvy China. "This is not only in coastal cities but also in second- and third-tier cities because of the availability of Internet cafés, even if they have a PC at home."

Foreign players are also trying to reach Chinese teens with online marketing initiatives. Procter & Gamble and Motorola have sponsored online dancing and lip-synching[2] contests to sell Crest toothpaste and lower-end mobile phones, respectively.

Connecting with Chinese teens will take some very clever marketing approaches, ones that recognize this group's diversity and values. And with $36 billion in spending up for grabs[3], plenty of mainland and foreign companies are trying to crack the code of teen buying habits.

*Business Week*, 31 July 2006

1. *salt money away*: mettre de l'argent de côté
2. *lip-synching*: chanter en playback (de "*synchronisation*")
3. *up for grabs*: à gagner

## Info

***McKinsey & Co***
McKinsey's 7,500 consultants help solve problems for some of the world's largest organisations.

***Ogilvy***
A subsidiary of a global marketing communications corporation, Ogilvy has helped build some of the world's most recognisable brands, such as American Express, Ford, Shell and Barbie.

***Procter & Gamble***
→ **Chapter 5, p. 84**

***Motorola***
An American international communications company, Motorola started in 1928.

***Crest***
A brand of toothpaste made by P&G.

## References

You can find relevant information by reading various pages in your book and memorising a few facts and ideas.


→ **Companies, p. 27**
→ **Consumers, p. 71**
→ **Marketing, p. 87**
→ **New technologies, p. 161**
→ **Globalisation, p. 220**


**ACTIVITY** **Practise giving an account of this article.**

## Introduction

You should explain where the article comes from, when it was published and what it is about.
→Tools 4, p. 236

This article from *Business Week*, an American business weekly, was published in July 2006. It reports on Chinese teenagers, a very attractive segment for multinationals who wish to attract new consumers worldwide.

## Development

Once you have understood the article, organise your ideas into two or three different parts, using set phrases and link-words. →Tools 4, p. 236

1. A huge, rich market
2. Chinese teenagers are just... teenagers
3. A specific market

You should also use the information given in *Info* and what you have learnt, for example by referring to the various pages indicated in *References*.

### 1. A huge, rich market

Chinese teenagers represent a huge market, which is likely to be profitable for the companies who know how to reach them. It amounts to about $36bn a year.
Because of the single child policy, which has been implemented in China since the 1980s, those children, also called "Generation Y", are said to be "little emperors". Their parents and grandparents are said to spoil the family's only child. Chinese parents spend $28.75bn on teenagers, who themselves spend another $7.5bn.
As a result, even though Chinese teenagers' spending power is slightly inferior to that of teenagers in western countries, many Chinese and foreign companies want to know and understand their buying habits.

### 2. Chinese teenagers are just... teenagers

Chinese teens are very similar to teens worldwide, in capital cities such as Tokyo, London, and New York City. They love fashion, spend a huge amount of time watching TV, surf the internet and play online games. As a matter of fact, even if some have a computer at home, many spend a lot of time in cyber cafés, whether they live in the most developed cities such as Shanghai and Beijing or in less developed places.
Therefore, one of the most profitable segments is to provide Chinese teens with internet music and games, like everywhere else in the world. Thus, foreign companies such as P&G and Motorola have been trying to sell them Crest toothpaste and lower-end mobile phones through online marketing initiatives, such as online dancing and lip-synching contests.

### 3. A specific market

However, studies have shown that Chinese teenagers also represent a very specific target, which may make the work of consumer-goods multinationals more difficult.
• First, many Chinese teens prefer and trust mainland brands over foreign ones: 88% trust Chinese brands, while only 65% say the same about foreign brands.
• Then, Chinese teens see saving money as an essential value, with a heavy sense of familial obligation to support their aging parents. Almost all the surveyed kids (96%) said this was crucial. Thus, attracting Chinese teens to western branded consumer goods may turn out more difficult as they want to save their money or spend it preferably on Chinese brands. Consequently, companies who want to reach them have to develop clever marketing approaches that recognise their diversity and values.

## Conclusion

You should sum up the main ideas and try to open out in a new direction.

By reporting on a specific market segment, Chinese teenagers, this article highlights the difficulties multinational companies may encounter with foreign markets. Although these teens can be compared to other kids across the planet, their market has specific features which marketers have to take into account if they want to succeed.

## Branching out

Now, you should move away from the article and develop more ideas. The following questions can help you.

**1** Why is it essential for multinational companies to carry out surveys on foreign markets? Explain and give examples.

**2** Do you think the internet is a clever marketing initiative to reach teenagers worldwide? Why/Why not?

## 13. Europeans

# Crackdown planned for transit drivers who flout EU rules

Drivers who flout traffic regulations while travelling across Europe face a crackdown from Brussels under plans to tackle road offences in the EU.

Jacques Barrot, European Union transport commissioner, yesterday pledged to draft legislation to clamp down on motorists and lorry drivers who break speed limits and flout other traffic laws as they make their way across the 25-nation bloc.

The move followed publication of the latest EU road safety report which showed that motorists travelling outside their home country accounted for as much as 35 per cent of traffic violations. The problem was particularly acute for those countries at the geographical heart of the EU, such as Germany and the Benelux states, which were on the key transit routes for truckers and other drivers crossing the continent, Mr Barrot said. Their apparent failure to stick to local traffic laws contributed to a very dangerous lowering of road safety standards in transit countries. "These transit countries really suffer from the fact that a large number of drivers cross these countries without showing any respect for the rules and are then not properly sanctioned," Mr Barrot said.

The issue will be on the agenda of a meeting of EU transport ministers next month. Brussels wants governments not only to toughen fines for offences such as speeding but also to co-operate more closely to ensure such fines are collected and potential offenders face prosecution when the incident occurs on a foreign road.

Separately, the report showed a drop in the number of road deaths in the EU but a worrying trend in many of the former communist countries that joined the EU in 2004, which Mr Barrot said was due to infrastructure factors, such as the poorer condition of roads in Eastern Europe, but also more driving under the influence of alcohol. The highest number of deaths per population was in Latvia followed by Lithuania. The eight former communist member states formed a group of laggards which in 2004 saw no improvement or even a worsening of efforts to tackle road fatalities. In the same year, nine countries – including Germany, France and Italy – saw road deaths fall by more than 14 per cent.

*Financial Times*, February 23, 2006

### Compréhension

**1.** **Rédigez en anglais un résumé de ce document. (120 mots, +/– 10%)**
**2.** **Traduisez le troisième paragraphe de l'article.**

### Expression

**Répondez en anglais aux questions suivantes.**

**1** Why are transit drivers particularly targeted as far as road safety is concerned? (100 words)
**2** Do you think European traffic laws can be implemented? Why/Why not? (150 words)

(N.B. L'usage du dictionnaire bilingue est autorisé.)

## 14. Globalisation

# *M&S aims to open 150 new stores overseas*

Marks & Spencer is understood to be planning an ambitious international expansion programme that will see it opening an overseas store every week for the next three years.

The scale of the expansion scheme – some 150 new outlets – is substantially greater that the group had so far indicated. At the time of the store chain's recent annual profits announcement chief executive Stuart Rose said he had plans for 25 to 30 new overseas stores.

The programme will take the total number of M&S international outlets to more than 350. The vast majority of the new stores will be franchised operations, where M&S sets out how the stores should look and sells its branded goods, but accepts no responsibility for the running of each store. M&S operates in 29 countries and Hong Kong. It has 198 franchised outlets together with 19 directly owned stores in Hong Kong, Gibraltar and Ireland.

UK retailers have a chequered history in their attempts to export UK high street brands abroad. Among those to have tried to expand overseas and failed are Next, Dixons, J Sainsbury and Boots. But in recent years an increasing number of retailers have turned to franchises to extend their brand without risking shareholders' cash. Among those using franchises are Debenhams and Mothercare, which have both opened stores in India with local partners.

Of the M&S franchised stores 65 are in the Asia-Pacific region, 60 in Europe, 45 in Central Europe with the balance in central Asia and the Middle East. The new expansion scheme includes more stores in India and Russia. There are no plans to open in mainland China, although M&S is considering following other retailers, such as B&Q and Tesco, which are established there.

This summer M&S will open its largest international franchise outlet yet – in Dubai. The outlet, operated by partner Al Futtaim, will be 52,000 sq ft – about twice the size of a standard British supermarket – and will stock a wider range of M&S goods than other franchises, which focus on adult clothing. The Dubai store will include children's wear and home furnishings.

Some of the new overseas outlets could include M&S's food ranges. After a store opened recently in Geneva, the group was inundated with requests for the store to include food.

Julia Finch, *The Guardian,* June 21, 2006

### Compréhension

**1.** **Rédigez en anglais un compte rendu de ce document. (125 mots)**

**2.** **Traduisez les paragraphes 4 et 5, de *UK retailers have a chequered history* à *are established there.***

### Expression

**Répondez en anglais aux questions suivantes.**

1 What are the advantages of franchising for companies wishing to expand abroad? (150 words)

2 How can you explain that some companies fail to break into foreign markets? (100 words)

(N.B. L'usage du dictionnaire bilingue est autorisé.)

## Case study: writing a letter

Your company has received the following letter.

**Platinum Co**
33 North Lane
Manchester MP 3 2 DT

La Béarnaise
130 av. du Château d'Este
64140 Billère

15 September 2007

Dear Mr Larraut,

Subj: Our invoice PC756 (15/7), reminder 15/8

It has come to our attention that the quoted invoice has remained without payment.
According to our records, you ordered 50 packs of organic flour on 30 June. They were delivered to your premises on 15 July and our invoice was issued the same day for payment within 30 days as usual. A reminder was automatically issued one month later since no payment had been received and we have had no explanation for this delay. Our phone calls have been met with repeated misunderstandings.
I regret I have no alternative but to send this final request before putting the matter in the hands of our lawyers.
I do regret to have to resort to such measures with a long-established customer, but we are faced with no other choice.

Yours sincerely,

Paul Soames
Finance Manager

You have been asked to write the answer in English.

Your manager has left a list of points to mention in the letter: *accuser réception ; étonné par ton et contenu ; erreur (dernière commande le 31/5, livraison le 7/6, règlement le 15/6) ; pas de commande ensuite ; factures rejetées par notre informatique ; standardiste pas bilingue ; nouvelle commande à passer ; mais attendons réponse ; conclusion optimiste.*

→Tools 7, p. 240

## PERSONAL TASK

In December 2006, The Institute for Public Policy Research published a report showing that at least 5.5m (almost 1 in 10) British citizens live overseas permanently. Study the pie-chart and report to the class.

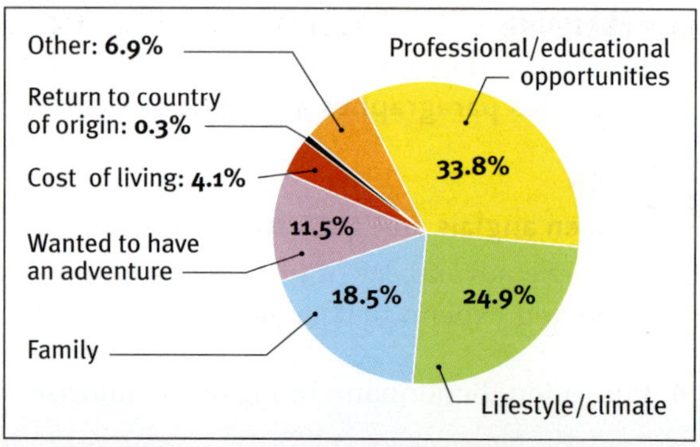


WHY BRITONS MOVE OUT
From IPPR, 2006

# Tools

# 1. Comprendre un document

Dans votre vie professionnelle, vous serez amené à consulter toutes sortes de documents, à les lire pour les analyser, les comparer, et en tirer des conclusions pour faire une synthèse.

## 1 | Identifier le document

• Regardez d'abord les éléments périphériques susceptibles de vous aider : illustrations, sources du document, date de publication, type de publication.
→Tools 15, Revue de presse, p. 250
• Repérez le nombre de paragraphes. Si le texte est bien écrit, il respecte la règle « une idée par paragraphe, un paragraphe par idée ».
• Ne vous concentrez pas sur les mots que vous ignorez : identifiez avant tout les mots-clés contenus dans le paragraphe, qui sont d'ailleurs peut-être dans le titre du document.

## 2 | Interroger le document

Un article de presse est construit de la manière suivante :
• **le titre/*headline*** (qui peut être explicité par un **sous-titre/*subhead***) : voir ci-dessous les différents types de titres que l'on peut rencontrer.
• **le premier paragraphe** qui peut avoir deux fonctions différentes :
- l'introduction au sujet ; dans ce cas, il comporte l'essentiel des informations dans ce qu'on appelle une *topic sentence* (*topic:* sujet abordé), c'est-à-dire une phrase qui résume le reste de l'article ;
- un exemple qui illustre le sujet de l'article.
• **le reste de l'article** qui apporte des précisions et complète l'information.

Lire un article, ce n'est donc pas avoir une attitude passive. Il faut poser des questions pour que l'article (y compris son titre) révèle les informations qu'il contient.
- **De quoi** parle-t-il ?
- **Quand** et **où** cela s'est-il passé ? **Depuis** quand ?
- **Qui** est concerné ?
- **Pourquoi et comment** cette situation / ce problème (que je viens d'identifier) s'est développé(e) / a évolué ?
Il s'agit donc de repérer les phrases de l'article qui répondent aux questions en *Wh-* : *Who? What? Where? When? Why?* Vous pouvez utiliser un surligneur de couleur différente pour chacune de ces questions, y compris dans le titre et le sous-titre.

## 3 | Analyser les titres

Les titres sont dans la presse anglo-saxonne une arme à double tranchant : ils sont utiles pour comprendre l'article, mais certains peuvent être difficiles à comprendre. Ne vous laissez pas dérouter : en cas de problème, passez à la lecture de l'article.
On distingue différents types de titres.

### a. Les titres classiques

Ils ne disent rien sur le contenu de l'article : il faut continuer à lire pour savoir de quoi il traite.
> *Pick me up* (The Economist, *19 December 2006*). L'article évoque une commande record pour Rolls Royce à Hong-Kong.

### b. Les titres parlants

Ils permettent d'anticiper le contenu de l'article.
> *'Drastic' shrinkage in Arctic ice* (BBC News website, *14 September 2006*) : cet article aborde le réchauffement de la planète.
Notez que s'ils sont explicites, les titres sont souvent elliptiques : certains mots grammaticaux, comme les verbes ou les articles, sont supprimés afin que le titre soit plus bref.
> *Hamleys to expand into Middle East*, The Guardian, *July 10, 2006* ( = *Hamley is about to expand…*)
> *Dairy Crest in £33m doorstep milk deal* (p. 126)

### c. Les titres astucieux

Les titres peuvent comporter un jeu de mots en référence à un film, un livre, un slogan publicitaire, un proverbe, etc. Vous ne les comprendrez pas toujours. Posez-vous par exemple des questions sur les sons que comporte le titre (les jeux avec les sons sont fréquents en anglais), et lisez attentivement les informations données.
> *Heinz means friends* (p. 22)
> *Making big bucks with beer and burgers* (p. 38)
> *Big pharma's bad karma* (The Guardian, *2 January 2007*)
Le journaliste s'est amusé de l'association courante de *pharma* et *karma* pour proposer un titre accrocheur qui "rime". Il faut dans ce cas lire le sous-titre de l'article (*The drug giants will protest at being undercut by cheap medicines made in the developing world, but it's time they faced some competition.*) pour comprendre qu'il aborde les médicaments bon marché fabriqués dans les pays en voie de développement qui vont concurrencer ceux des grandes entreprises pharmaceutiques.

> *A bigger bang* (The Guardian, *4 November 2006*) Le titre joue avec l'expression *big bang*, et ce n'est qu'en lisant le sous-titre que l'on comprend que l'article parle de l'internet (*The second internet goldrush is in full swing, …*)

## 4 | Classer et organiser les informations

Toutes les informations du document ne sont pas essentielles : apprenez à les classer.
Quelle est l'information principale ? Quelles sont les informations secondaires (= que je pourrais ne pas mentionner, qui ne répondent pas aux questions essentielles) ?
Par ailleurs, le journaliste envisage peut-être plusieurs points de vue. Vous pouvez donc les classer, par exemple dans un tableau à deux colonnes des arguments « pour » et des arguments « contre ».

# 2. Présenter un document à l'oral

Le temps de préparation et le temps de passage devant l'examinateur varient selon les sections. Une première partie de l'oral est en général consacrée à la présentation du document préparé, la seconde partie à un entretien avec l'examinateur. Dans tous les cas, vous devrez vous entretenir avec l'examinateur. N'oubliez pas que les entraînements sont essentiels : exposés, entraînement à la prise de parole en continu en classe ou en groupe, jeux de rôle, activités proposées dans la rubrique ***Speaking pratice***, lecture des textes à voix haute, etc.
Graphiques : →Tools 11, p. 244 et nombreux entraînements des pages ***Be professional***.

## 1 I Le temps de préparation

### a. Créez des repères dans l'article

Vous pouvez par exemple numéroter les paragraphes, noter dans la marge du lexique que vous ne voulez pas oublier, ou encore surligner les informations de base (nom de l'entreprise, pays, etc.). Ainsi vous les retrouverez rapidement.

### b. Ne rédigez pas tout !

Vous pouvez rédiger une phrase, par exemple votre introduction ou votre conclusion, qui sont des moments importants de votre exposé. Mais les examinateurs ne souhaitent jamais entendre un commentaire récité « par cœur », ni avoir en face d'eux quelqu'un qui lit sans lever les yeux. Utilisez la préparation pour réfléchir aux articulations de votre exposé (introduction, annonce du plan...).

## 2 I L'introduction

### a. Identifiez le document

Utilisez les sources du document : origine et date.
• Son origine : *This article was published in..., This document dated... comes from...*
La Revue de presse →Tools 15, p. 250 vous informe sur les principales publications en langue anglaise. Vous n'êtes bien sûr pas censé connaître les gazettes locales, mais il serait ennuyeux de confondre le quotidien britannique *The Times* avec l'hebdomadaire américain *Time*. Un journaliste américain et un journaliste britannique expriment des points de vue différents sur de nombreux sujets, par exemple l'Europe.
Le nom du journaliste qui a écrit l'article n'a pas d'intérêt, sauf s'il s'agit d'un auteur connu (personnalité politique, économique, acteur de renom, etc.) ou de quelqu'un qui est impliqué dans le processus qu'il décrit (chef d'entreprise, DRH, etc.).
• Sa date : le contexte de la publication donne du sens à votre présentation.
Comment dire la date : si vous n'indiquez que le mois, utilisez la préposition *in* : *This article was published in March 2007.* En revanche, si vous indiquez le jour, vous devez utiliser *on* : *This article was published on 22 March 2007.*
Attention : on dit à haute voix *on the twenty-second of March* même si ne figure à l'écrit que *22 March*.

### b. Exprimez l'idée générale

*The article deals with/reports on/studies...*
*This article tackles a controversial/topical issue...*

## 3 I Le plan

Il doit être annoncé clairement dès la fin de votre introduction. Soyez logique : parlez des raisons avant d'évoquer des conséquences, du passé avant les perspectives d'avenir, etc.
*In the first part/Firstly/To begin with*
*In the second part/Then...* →Tools 18, p. 253
Rappelez de temps en temps votre plan pour dire à votre examinateur où vous en êtes. Utilisez les mots de liaison appropriés.

## 4 I Le développement

Reformulez ! Construisez votre compte rendu sans répéter l'article mot pour mot. Il est impératif de dire les choses autrement pour montrer que vous avez compris. Utilisez la rubrique ***Work on words*** pour vous constituer un stock de synonymes sur des mots courants. Par exemple, pour parler d'une entreprise, vous pouvez varier en utilisant *firm, company, business*, et selon les cas, *start-up, store, outlet, venture*. Pour exprimer une augmentation, utilisez *grow* mais aussi *increase, rise, soar, skyrocket...*

## 5 I La conclusion et l'ouverture

• Concluez : *In a word, to conclude...*Vous pouvez rappeler les idées clés de votre exposé.
• Vous aurez ensuite un entretien avec votre examinateur. Il peut s'agir d'un élargissement de l'article à un contexte personnel ou plus général. À vous de lancer des idées à la fin de votre conclusion afin d'ouvrir le débat dans le sens que vous estimez opportun. Les questions de ***Branching out*** vous entraînent à ce type de démarche.

## Communiquez !

• Variez le ton de votre voix. Veillez aux intonations.
• Levez les yeux : vos notes sont un tremplin pour l'expression, pas un texte que vous lisez.
• Faites des pauses, vérifiez que ce que vous dites passe bien.
• Si on vous demande de lire un passage, votre lecture doit montrer que vous comprenez ce que vous lisez. Respectez accents de mot et de phrase.
• Si vous citez le texte, précisez à quel endroit de l'article la citation se trouve (*line...*).
• Si vous n'avez pas bien compris la question de votre examinateur, demandez-lui poliment de répéter : *I'm afraid I didn't understand, could you repeat that, please?*
• Montrez-vous souriant(e) et naturel(le).

# 3. Rédiger un résumé

Différents examens écrits de BTS tertiaires comportent des exercices variés :
- un résumé (parfois appelé « contraction de texte »),
- un compte rendu (parfois appelé « présentation »).

Ces exercices peuvent être demandés à partir d'articles en anglais ou en français.
Il est donc essentiel que vous distinguiez résumé et compte rendu. Le jour de l'examen, il est également essentiel de prêter attention à ce qui vous est demandé avant de commencer à rédiger : tous les ans, des candidats se trompent d'exercice, ou de langue, et perdent ainsi les points de l'épreuve !

## 1 | Définition du résumé

Un résumé est la réduction objective d'un document, en général au tiers. Par exemple, un article de 450 mots devra être réduit à 150.

### a. Neutralité

Rester neutre vis-à-vis d'un texte est crucial quand il s'agit de le résumer : ne prenez aucun recul, et limitez les exemples à ceux qui sont indispensables à la compréhension du texte.

### b. Ordre

Suivez l'ordre du texte : n'ajoutez ni introduction ni conclusion. Ne citez pas les sources du document. (En revanche, la date peut avoir son importance pour le sens de l'article, cf. exemple.)

## 2 | Identifier le thème général de l'article

### a. Les paragraphes

Numéroter les paragraphes vous aide à respecter l'ordre de présentation en vue de votre résumé.

### b. L'idée principale

Lisez l'article une fois en entier pour trouver son thème général. Formulez-la par écrit, dans la langue dans laquelle vous devrez rédiger votre résumé.

### c. Le titre (le sous-titre et le premier paragraphe)

- Repérez les mots clés du titre. S'il n'est pas explicite, ne perdez pas de temps à tenter de le déchiffrer, et passez au sous-titre, s'il y en a un, ou sinon, à la première *topic sentence*. →**Tools 1, p. 232.**
- Posez-vous les questions en *Wh-*. →**Tools 1, p. 232.**

## 3 | Hiérarchiser les idées

Établissez une liste des informations repérées chronologiquement, paragraphe par paragraphe. Vous devrez ensuite respecter cet ordre.
Pensez que vous êtes limité dans le nombre de mots : il faut donc éliminer ce qui n'est pas essentiel, pour ne conserver que les idées principales.

## 4 | Travailler le lexique

Un résumé nécessite de chercher des mots.
- Si vous devez résumer en anglais (à partir d'un article en anglais ou en français), il est nécessaire de trouver des synonymes ou des équivalents pour les mots et expressions clés de l'article, afin de ne pas paraphraser l'article, c'est-à-dire de ne pas le répéter à l'identique quand vous rédigerez.
- Si vous devez résumer en français (à partir d'un article en anglais), concentrez-vous sur les mots à utiliser, le vocabulaire spécifique que vous devez connaître. Attention au nombre de mots demandés : ne traduisez pas l'article mot à mot ! Vous devez trouver des équivalents plus brefs.

## 5 | Rédiger

- N'oubliez pas les mots de liaison qui doivent articuler ce que vous écrivez.
- Pensez à indiquer le nombre de mots utilisés en fin de travail.

## 6 | Relire le résumé

### a. La fidélité à l'article

- Demandez-vous si votre résumé est fidèle à l'article proposé : si quelqu'un le lit, aura-t-il une idée exacte du contenu de l'article ?
- Vérifiez que vous avez évité la paraphrase, et que vous n'avez pas recopié de phrases de l'article d'origine.

### b. La qualité de la langue

- Si vous avez rédigé en anglais, consacrez une relecture à vérifier les points sur lesquels on trouve souvent des erreurs : les formes verbales (prétérit, *present perfect*, *s* à la 3e personne du singulier du présent simple, etc.), comparatifs et superlatifs, etc.
- Si vous avez rédigé en français, vérifiez votre orthographe, ainsi que les temps et les accords des verbes.

### Exemple

**Consigne :** Rédigez en anglais un résumé de l'article situé sur la page de droite en 120 mots (+/- 10 %).

**Trouver le thème général du texte proposé**

**• L'idée principale**

*Numerous consumers are shopping for bargains after Christmas.*

**• Le titre (le sous-titre et le premier paragraphe)**

- ***Who?*** *Bargain hunters*
- ***Does what?*** *...are coming out in force*
- ***Why?*** *The retail sector is offering hefty price cuts*

**Hiérarchiser les idées**

Repérez les idées chronologiquement, paragraphe par paragraphe.

**§1** *brisk trade – bargain hunters come out in force – hefty price cuts*
**§2** *visits yesterday were up 6.9% on Boxing Day 2005*
**§3** *more stores open – promotional activity – consumer back to shop – consumers were waiting*

# Bargain hunters out in force

The retail sector is doing a brisk trade as bargain hunters come out in force, lured by the hefty[1] price cuts on offer.

Figures from FootFall, which measures shopper numbers, showed visits yesterday were up 6.9% on Boxing Day[2] 2005.

FootFall marketing director, Natasha Burton said: "The promise of more stores being open and the promotional activity showcasing[3] available deals has certainly helped entice the consumer back to shop. This year, the steady build-up and the quiet Christmas Eve seem to suggest that consumers were waiting for the post-Christmas sales and that the savvy shopper is now back out shopping with a vengeance. This has given retailers a welcome boost and with many of the high profile sales starting today, this has hopefully set the tone for a prosperous sales period ahead."

Retail analysts said stores were determined to make up ground[4] after the predicted high street frenzy in the final weekend before Christmas largely failed to materialise. Richard Ratner, a retail analyst at Seymour Pierce, said: "We are expecting some really savage discounting. There is an awful lot of stock to shift and a very short window to sell it. Last year the sales were dead, in terms of numbers of shoppers, after the first week or so. Retailers hope they will be able to keep people coming in for longer this year."

HSBC has forecast as much as £1.3bn in cash and vouchers has been given as presents in recent days, leaving shoppers well resourced even after a costly Christmas. Bluewater shopping centre in Kent expects to welcome 175,000 bargain hunters today. A spokeswoman said many stores were cutting prices by between 50% and 70%, with winter wear high among the most deeply discounted items. On Tyneside, Barry Turnbull, general manager of the Metro Centre, said Boxing Day had seen thousands of people queuing ahead of the 10am opening time. In London, more than 2,000 shoppers had gathered at Selfridges before the doors opened at 9am. In Birmingham, about 27,500 people arrived at the Bullring shopping centre in the first hour of trading. A spokesman said the average spend had increased by about 10%.

Fiona Walsh, *The Guardian Unlimited*, December 27, 2006.

1. *hefty*: gros
2. *Boxing Day*: lendemain de Noël, férié au Royaume-Uni
3. *showcasing*: présentant, mettant en vitrine
4. *make up ground*: compenser, regagner le temps perdu

*for the post-Christmas sales – the savvy shopper is now back out shopping – given retailers a welcome boost – prosperous sales period ahead."*

**§4** *make up ground after Christmas – expecting some really savage discounting – awful lot of stock to shift and a very short window to sell it – keep people coming in for longer this year.*

**§5** *cash and vouchers given as presents – shoppers well resourced even after a costly Christmas – Bluewater shopping centre in Kent – cutting prices by between 50% and 70%, with winter wear high among the most deeply discounted items – On Tyneside, Metro Centre, thousands of people queuing ahead of the 10am opening time London, Selfridges – Birmingham, Bullring shopping centre*

## Travailler le lexique

Trouvez des synonymes et équivalents pour les mots et expressions clés de l'article.

**§1** *buyer – good business – looking for bargains – numerous – attractive discounts*

**§2** *shoppers on the increase*

**§3** *more outlets open – advertising the price cuts – lure shoppers – possible that consumers were waiting for the after-Christmas sales – smart consumers – run-up to Christmas – retailers expecting an increase and a successful sales period*

**§4** *low/slack business before Christmas – hefty price cuts – few days – many goods to sell*

**§5** *Christmas gifts of money and vouchers – consumers are affluent – expensive Christmas – winter clothes – lines of shoppers – average spend on the rise*

## Rédiger

**Proposition de résumé**

*Enticed by big discounts, consumers have been rushing to the shops in the after-Christmas period, accounting for almost 7% more shoppers as compared to last year on the same day.* ***As a matter of fact****, the rather disappointing run-up to Christmas may mean that buyers were smart enough to wait for the sales. The spending spree is likely to bring retailers an appreciated business increase,* ***but*** *the huge amount of goods to sell means that the retail sector will need to attract people after the first few days of heavy shopping. Gifts of money or vouchers mean that people are affluent even if Christmas was expensive.* ***Indeed****, various examples across the UK confirm the trend, with thousands of people lining up outside the shops before they opened.*

*(127 mots)*

# 4. Rédiger un compte rendu

## 1 | Définition du compte rendu

Un compte rendu est la restitution construite d'un document, en général au tiers. Par exemple, un article de 450 mots devra être réduit à 150.

### a. Plan

Proposez un plan structuré : vous n'êtes pas obligé de suivre l'ordre de l'article. En revanche, vous devez regrouper les idées qui vont ensemble.

### b. Commentaire

- Introduire en citant les sources du document.
- Conclure puis ajouter un rapide commentaire.

Apprenez les formules pour introduire et dater un article, pour conclure. →**Tools 18, p. 253**

## 2 | Identifier le thème général de l'article

Voir page 234.

## 3 | Travailler le lexique

Voir page 234.

## 4 | Hiérarchiser les idées

Établissez une liste des informations repérées chronologiquement, paragraphe par paragraphe. Puis regroupez-les en fonction de votre plan.
Pensez que vous êtes limité dans le nombre de mots : il faudra donc éliminer ce qui n'est pas essentiel, pour ne conserver que les idées principales.

## 5 | Rédiger

- Réfléchissez à un plan en fonction des idées listées dans l'article. Basez-vous sur les idées essentielles (les réponses aux questions en *Wh-*).
- Pensez à la logique de votre plan : traitez d'abord les causes puis les conséquences ; le passé puis l'avenir ; les perspectives puis leurs limites.
- N'oubliez pas les mots de liaison.
- Pensez à indiquer le nombre de mots utilisés.

## 6 | Relire le compte rendu

Voir page 234.

### Exemple

**Consigne :** Rédigez en français un compte rendu de l'article en page de droite en 135 mots (+/- 10 %).

**Trouver le thème général du texte proposé**

**• L'idée principale**

*A Briton is making money with a caviar farm in France*

**• Le titre (sous-titre et le 1^er^ §)**

- ***Who?*** *A Briton, a British marine biologist*
- ***Does what?*** *... will strike gold / register record sales of 7 million (£4.7 million) with a caviar farm*
- ***When?*** *this year, following a ban on international trade in wild sturgeon eggs*

**Hiérarchiser les idées**

Repérez les idées paragraphe par paragraphe.

**§1** *A British marine biologist opened a caviar farm in France in 1995 – record sales of 7 million (£4.7 million) this year – a ban on international trade in wild sturgeon eggs*

**§2** *business booming – global market estimated to be worth £270 million – 4 French producers have all witnessed a sharp rise in demand this Christmas – a UN agency to limit exports of wild Caspian Sea caviar – Mr Jones's company will sell up to 11 tonnes this year, more than half of France's total production, making it the second largest supplier of farmed caviar in the world.*

**§3** *Fortnum & Mason agreed to stock his product, which has a retail price of about £1,000 a kilo – about a quarter of the price of the wild variety of "black gold" – Cathay Pacific also a customer – few investors in France 11 years ago – funded by his business partner – "Now we've got banks knocking on our door every week."*

**§4** *plans to expand its annual production to 15 T and eventually to 20 T – introduced sturgeon into two new sites – have to be patient, fish do not produce eggs until they are seven years old – worthwhile if the global market for farmed caviar doubles to 120 T by 2010, as Mr Jones predicts.*

**§5** *With the UN seeking to halt overfishing of sturgeon in the Caspian Sea, Iran is allowed to export only 44.3 T of caviar this year and its neighbours none at all – black market flourishing to supply the world's gastronomes, who consume 250 T of caviar a year – sturgeon farms are gaining ground, projects under way in Italy, California, Germany, Uruguay, Bulgaria, Canada, China & Israel.*

**Travailler le lexique**

Trouvez des synonymes et équivalents pour les mots et expressions clés de l'article. Vous devez ici rédiger en français. Pensez à transposer les sommes en euros, notamment si elles sont en £.

**§1** biologiste – suscité l'incrédulité – élevage d'esturgeons – ventes record de 7 millions d'euros – interdiction d'exporter le caviar sauvage – 11 ans

**§2** AJ, 60 ans, entreprise florissante – marché mondial estimé à plus de 400 millions d'euros. Se place parmi 4 producteurs français – augmentation considérable de la demande aux fêtes de fin d'année. Conséquence d'une décision des Nations Unies pour limiter exportations de la mer Caspienne – ventes pourraient grimper jusqu'à 11 tonnes – 2^e^ fournisseur mondial de caviar d'élevage.

**§3** Fortnum & Mason (Londres) va distribuer – prix de détail 1500 euros/kg, soit environ 1/4 du prix de « l'or noir » sauvage – Cathay Pacific également client – Rares investisseurs disposés à le soutenir en 1995 – Aujourd'hui, les banques se bousculent.

# Briton strikes black gold on his caviar farm in France

A British marine biologist who was met with incredulity when he opened a caviar farm in southwest France in 1995 will register record sales of €7 million (£4.7 million) this year following a ban on international trade in wild sturgeon eggs.

Alan Jones, 60, from Lutterworth in Leicestershire, is at the forefront[1] of a business that is booming in a global market estimated to be worth £270 million. The firm he co-founded in the Bordeaux region, Sturgeon, is among four French producers, which have all witnessed a sharp rise in demand this Christmas as a result of moves by a United Nations agency to limit exports of wild Caspian Sea caviar. Mr Jones's company will sell up to 11 tonnes this year, more than half of France's total production, making it the second largest supplier of farmed caviar in the world, he says.

He was in London this week after Fortnum & Mason agreed to stock his product, which has a retail price of about £1,000 a kilo – about a quarter of the price of the wild variety of "black gold". The airline Cathay Pacific is also a customer. But Mr Jones said there were few investors in France willing to back him 11 years ago. "When we wanted to start up, the bank looked at our brochure and said: 'We don't believe in your project'," he remembers. The project was subsequently funded by his business partner, Jean Boucher. "Now we've got banks knocking on our door every week."

The firm, which plans to expand its annual production to 15 tonnes and eventually to 20 tonnes, has introduced sturgeon into two new sites in southwest France. "But this is not a business in which you can just increase production when you want," said Mr Jones. "You just have to be patient." The fish do not produce eggs until they are seven years old, he explains. However, the wait will be worthwhile if the global market for farmed caviar doubles to 120 tonnes by 2010, as Mr Jones predicts.

With the UN seeking to halt overfishing of sturgeon in the Caspian Sea, Iran is allowed to export only 44.3 tonnes of caviar this year and its neighbours none at all. A black market is flourishing to supply the world's gastronomes, who consume 250 tonnes of caviar a year. And sturgeon farms are gaining ground, with projects under way in Italy, California, Germany, Uruguay, Bulgaria, Canada, China and Israel.

*The Times*, December 27, 2006

1. *forefront*: à la pointe de

**§4** Projet : augmenter la production annuelle à 15 t puis 20 t, deux nouveaux sites dans le Sud-Ouest de la France – patience indispensable (7 ans nécessaires pour que le poisson produise des œufs) – rentable si le marché mondial du caviar d'élevage double pour atteindre 120 t d'ici 2010, selon les prédictions de M. Jones.

**§5** Les Nations Unies cherchent à interrompre la surpêche en mer Caspienne – exportations de l'Iran limitées à 44,3 t caviar cette année, pas d'autre pays autorisé à exporter – marché noir pour fournir la consommation (250 t/an) – caviar d'élevage se développe (Italie, Californie, Allemagne, Uruguay, Bulgarie, Canada, Chine et Israël).

**Rédiger**

**Proposition de plan**

1. L'entreprise d'Alan Jones
2. Les raisons du succès
3. Les perspectives du marché

**Proposition de compte rendu**

Cet article, publié dans *The Times* fin décembre 2006, fait le point sur le caviar.

En 1995, Alan Jones fonda une entreprise de caviar d'élevage avec un partenaire. Aujourd'hui, Fortnum & Mason distribue son caviar au quart du prix de « l'or noir » sauvage et l'entreprise s'apprête à réaliser des ventes record de 7 millions d'euros.

La demande mondiale annuelle est de 250 tonnes. Mais les Nations Unies veulent interrompre la surpêche de l'esturgeon en mer Caspienne : cette année, seul l'Iran a pu exporter environ 45 tonnes de caviar sauvage.

M. Jones a ouvert deux nouveaux sites dans le Sud-Ouest de la France pour augmenter sa production. Patience indispensable (il faut 7 ans pour obtenir des œufs) ! Mais le marché mondial du caviar d'élevage devrait doubler pour atteindre 120 tonnes d'ici 2010.

Cet article illustre la part de risque inhérent au lancement d'une entreprise, et le succès qui peut en découler si le contexte est positif.

*(144 mots)*

# 5. Savoir utiliser le dictionnaire

Le jour de l'examen écrit, le dictionnaire bilingue est autorisé. Pour en tirer le plus grand avantage, apprenez à utiliser cet outil précieux qui, mal utilisé, risque de vous faire perdre du temps.

## 1 I Quelques principes de bon sens

### a. Savoir utiliser le dictionnaire c'est aussi savoir s'en passer.

Ne regardez pas systématiquement tous les mots que vous ne connaissez pas, ne vérifiez pas ceux que vous connaissez déjà.

### b. Travailler la matière

Pour traduire un mot, une expression ou une phrase entière, il faut travailler le(s) mot(s) que vous avez sous les yeux comme un matériau : on traduit une première fois, on retravaille sa phrase, on cherche des synonymes, etc. →**Tools 6, p. 239**

### c. Délimiter aux mots inconnus

Si un mot inconnu bloque vraiment la compréhension ou la traduction, vous pouvez alors ouvrir le dictionnaire.

## 2 I La démarche de recherche

Repérez la nature et la fonction du mot dans la phrase : est-ce un nom, un adjectif, un adverbe, un verbe, une particule, etc. ? Souvenez-vous qu'un même « mot-racine » peut fonctionner comme nom ou verbe. Repérer la catégorie grammaticale du mot vous permettra d'éviter une lourde erreur de traduction.

> *range* (N): gamme – *range from... to...*(V): aller de ... à ...

> *import* (N): importation – *import* (V): importer

Vous pouvez aussi utiliser le dictionnaire pour vérifier la construction d'un verbe : dans l'exemple qui suit, vous pouvez trouver les différentes constructions du mot *profit*.

## Exemple : *profit*

Voici l'extrait de la page du dictionnaire *Robert & Collins Super Senior* concernant le mot *profit*. Les différentes informations qui y sont contenues vous sont expliquées.

Le mot que vous cherchez est écrit en caractères gras.

La prononciation est indiquée en caractères phonétiques.

Un autre sens proche existe, rangé plus loin dans le dictionnaire.

Abréviations à connaître : *sth* = something, *sso* = someone, *qch* = quelque chose, etc.

Ces sigles sont expliqués au début ou à la fin de votre dictionnaire : †† = archaïque.

**profit** ['prɒfɪt] [→ SYN] [1] n (Comm) profit m, bénéfice m ; (fig) profit m, avantage m ◆ **profit and loss** profits mpl et pertes fpl ; see also 4 ◆ **gross/net profit** bénéfice m brut/net ◆ **to make** or **turn a profit** faire un bénéfice or des bénéfices ◆ **to make a profit of $100** faire un bénéfice de 100 dollars (*on sth* sur qch) ◆ **to sell sth at a profit** vendre qch à profit ◆ **to show** or **yield a profit** rapporter (un bénéfice) ◆ **there's not much profit in doing that** (lit, fig) on ne gagne pas grand-chose à faire cela ◆ **with profits policy** (Insurance) police f (d'assurance) avec participation aux bénéfices ◆ **with profit** (fig) avec profit, avec fruit ◆ **to turn sth to profit** (fig) mettre à profit qch, tirer parti de qch
[2] vi (fig) tirer un profit or un avantage ◆ **to profit by** or **from sth** tirer avantage or profit de qch, bien profiter de qch ◆ **I can't see how he hopes to profit (by it)** je ne vois pas ce qu'il espère en retirer or y gagner
[3] vt (†† or liter) profiter à ◆ **it will profit him nothing** cela ne lui profitera en rien

Ce chiffre encadré correspond aux catégories grammaticales : 3 pour ce mot (*N* = noun, *vi* = verbe intransitif, *vt* = verbe transitif).

Cette lettre précise le genre du mot : *m* = masculin, *f* = féminin, *n*= neutre.

Deux traductions sont possibles pour le mot *profit* : « profit », la traduction la plus immédiate pour un francophone, mais aussi et surtout « bénéfice », la traduction la plus courante. Au sens figuré, le mot *profit* peut signifier « avantage ».

Certaines expressions sont données en abrégé : *comm* = sens commun, *lit, liter* = sens littéraire, *fig* = sens figuré.

Le mot entre parenthèses précise le champ d'application : *profit* a un sens spécifique dans le domaine de l'assurance, par exemple.

## Entraînements

### a. Quiz

1. Combien d'expressions figurées trouvez-vous dans l'entrée *profit* ?
2. Le mot *profit* est-il un nom ou un verbe ?
3. L'expression *profit and loss* se traduit-elle par « profit et perte » ?
4. Dit-on *make a profit* ou *turn a profit* pour traduire « faire un bénéfice » ?

### b. Comment traduit-on... ?

1. *gross profit*
2. *with profit*
3. *to profit from something* (Avec quelle autre préposition le verbe peut-il se construire dans ce cas ?)

### c. Traduisez les exemples suivants.

Ils proviennent de pages de votre manuel.

1. Sega said its **profit** fell 93 percent.
2. [After the tsunami], Thai authorities became aware of the necessity for sustainable tourism, which would also **profit** the locals.
4. Nader started a variety of **non-profit** organizations, among which Commercial Alert, founded in 1999.

# 6. Traduire de l'anglais au français

Cet exercice permet d'évaluer votre capacité à comprendre un document dans le but de le restituer dans une autre langue. Il teste donc votre connaissance de l'anglais, mais aussi votre maîtrise du français.

## 1 I Identification et repérage

- Lisez le document une fois en entier permet de le situer dans un contexte et d'éviter de gros contresens. Faites attention au ton (purement informatif, polémique, etc.) et au niveau de langue (familier, formel, administratif, etc.)
- Repérez le passage à traduire pour ne pas oublier de passage et ne pas vous tromper de ligne (un passage même bien traduit vaut 0 si ce n'est pas le passage demandé).
- Repérez les articulations : mots de liaison, formes verbales, ou encore ponctuation.

## 2 I Résolution des problèmes

- Ne vous attardez pas d'emblée sur les mots que vous ne connaissez pas : quand vous travaillerez dans le détail, vous pourrez certainement approcher le sens de ce mot en vous aidant du contexte.
- Analysez la fonction du mot dans la phrase : verbe, nom, adverbe, adjectif, etc. ? Attention aux pronoms : à qui font référence *he, she* ou *they* ?
- Isolez les mots composés (ou enchaînements) par des traits. Commencez par le dernier mot et remontez vers la gauche.
> *The eight former communist member states*: les huit États-membres anciennement communistes – *greenhouse gases emissions restriction laws:* lois visant à restreindre les émissions de gaz à effets de serre
- N'abusez pas du dictionnaire : voir p. 238.

## 3 I Les procédés de traduction

### a. La traduction littérale

La traduction mot à mot est le procédé le plus simple et le plus fidèle au texte de départ. Utilisez-la chaque fois que vous le pouvez.
> *The UK's biggest retailer is paying £72m for the stores.* (p. 128) Le plus grand détaillant britannique va débourser 72 millions de livres pour les magasins.

### b. L'emprunt

- Certains mots sont entrés dans la langue française et n'ont pas besoin d'être traduits.
> bulldozer, jean, senior, week-end, milk-shake (parfois orthographiés différemment, par exemple *weekend* s'écrit sans trait d'union en anglais).
- Lorsque le terme existe en français, traduisez-le.
> *hotline:* assistance en ligne ; *garden-centre*: jardinerie ; *fast food*: restauration rapide
- On ne traduit pas certains noms de lieux ou d'organismes qui sont entrés dans la langue française (les tours du World Trade Center, la NASA, etc.). Vérifiez la signification des abréviations et acronymes pour voir s'il existe un équivalent en français.
> *WTO (World Trade Organisation):* OMC (Organisation Mondiale du Commerce)

### c. La transposition

Ce procédé très courant consiste à changer la catégorie grammaticale du mot que l'on traduit. Ainsi, un adjectif ou un verbe peuvent devenir un nom, etc.
> *Business is very* ***slack*** *at the moment:* Les affaires **ne marchent pas** en ce moment. (adj. → verbe)
> *Immigrants now* ***number*** *nearly two million* (p. 204): Le **nombre** d'immigrants se monte maintenant à presque deux millions. (verbe → nom)
> *Beyond the* ***competitive*** *pressure...* (p. 216): Au-delà de la pression de la **concurrence**... (adj. → nom)

### d. L'étoffement

- Quand le texte anglais est très concis, il faut développer la traduction pour tout traduire.
> *There has been outrage that the Commission is not acting...* (p. 202): Le fait que la Commission n'agisse pas... a suscité l'indignation
- Parfois des noms propres qui ont déjà été donnés sont répétés sans *Mr/Mrs/Ms* : il est impératif de les rétablir en français.
> *Nichols set out...* (p. 36) > Susan Nichols s'est mise à...

### e. L'équivalence

On l'utilise pour des expressions idiomatiques (typiques d'une langue), les proverbes ou des structures grammaticales qui diffèrent d'une langue à l'autre. Soyez vigilants quand vous traduisez des expressions toutes faites ou des titres.
> *Closer to home in the grocery business,...* (p. 128) : Plus près de la Grande-Bretagne dans le marché de l'alimentation,...
> *The fast and the furious*, titre d'un article consacré aux constructeurs automobiles chinois, dans *The Economist 19 December 2006* : *fast and furious* est une expression qui signifie « à un rythme endiablé, qui bat son plein ». Traduire mot à mot n'aurait aucun sens, tandis que l'expression équivalente « À un rythme endiablé » pourrait convenir.

## 4 I La rédaction

Votre traduction doit rester fidèle au texte anglais. Quelques erreurs à ne pas commettre :
- broder autour du texte : n'expliquez pas ce que vous traduisez ;
- proposer plusieurs traductions : vous devez choisir une traduction ;
- laisser des blancs : proposez toujours une traduction.

Relisez-vous, et demandez-vous si votre traduction a du sens, si vous pourriez la lire dans un article de presse en français. Dernière recommandation : vérifiez orthographe et grammaire en français !

# 7. Écrire une lettre commerciale

Il existe plusieurs types de lettres : commande, relance, réclamation, etc.

## 1 | Présentation

Autrefois, les règles de mise en page et la ponctuation étaient très strictes. Aujourd'hui, avec l'informatique, on a tendance à utiliser un type simplifié : ne sont indiqués que les signes de ponctuation indispensables (*open punctuation*).

La lettre peut être justifiée à droite et à gauche avec des retraits à chaque paragraphe, mais on se contente souvent de la justifier à gauche, comme dans l'exemple ci-dessous.

**Référence et objet**
Vous pouvez avoir à indiquer une référence à un courrier précédent. Elle vient tout en haut de la lettre, au-dessus de la date.
L'objet d'une lettre indique en un mot ou deux son contenu, et permet au destinataire de connaître le contenu d'un coup d'œil. Ici, l'objet serait par exemple *Glossgold samples*. Cet objet est indiqué le plus souvent après la salutation de début de lettre.

**Glosshair Cosmetics**
3 Stacey Avenue
London, N18 3PS
NOM DE L'ENTREPRISE QUI ENVOIE LE COURRIER

16 August 2007 DATE

Ms Pamela Hornton DESTINATAIRE
Sales manager
Hitone Hairdressers
151 Fulwood Road
Nether Green
Sheffield S10 3QA

Les salutations de début et de fin se correspondent.
- Si vous connaissez le nom du destinataire
Début : *Dear Mr/Mrs/Ms X...*
Fin : *Yours sincerely, Best regards*
- Si vous ne le connaissez pas
Début : *Dear Sir/Madam...*
Fin : *Yours faithfully*

Dear Ms Hornton SALUTATION

Following our phone conversation yesterday, I'm happy to send you a few samples of our new shampoo.
Glossgold has just been launched on the market and we are confident it will meet the success it deserves. It has been created by our team of in-house researchers who have all attended medical school and it therefore offers all the necessary guarantees to meet your customers' expectations. Not only does it make hair soft and shiny, but it also makes it stronger and more pollution-resistant. We feel this should make for a strong sales argument. Moreover, ten different original fragrances are available, which makes it attractive to men, women and young people alike.
Please find enclosed with the samples our list of prices and terms of sales. Bulk orders are always sent with samples to hand out to your faithful customers.
We do hope that you will find Glossgold meets your expectations and that we will have the opportunity of working together.
Should you require more information, do not hesitate to contact me.

Looking forward to doing business with you,

Yours sincerely,
Adrian Laird
Adrian Laird NOM
Marketing manager FONCTION DANS L'ENTREPRISE

Enc.: 30 samples, list of prices and terms of sales

**La signature**
Une lettre comporte une signature manuscrite, suivi du nom typographié et de la fonction du signataire dans l'entreprise.

**Pièces jointes**
On fait figurer en bas d'une lettre la liste des pièces jointes au courrier, précédée de la mention *Enc.* ou *Encs.* (= *enclosed*).

## 2 | Expressions utiles

1. Looking forward to meeting you next week.
2. I would appreciate an answer at your earliest convenience.
3. I look forward to hearing from you.
4. In reply to your inquiry, please find enclosed...
5. Please accept our apologies for the delay.
6. With reference to your letter, I regret that I must...
7. I am pleased to confirm that your order...
8. I hope we will work together in the very near future.
9. Thanking you in advance for your understanding in this matter...
10. Further to your request, we wish to draw it to your attention that...
11. Thanking you in advance for your kind cooperation, ...
12. Could you let me have our answer as soon as possible?

## 3 | Les messages électroniques

• **Le destinataire** figure sur la ligne *To*.

• On peut envoyer des **copies visibles** avec la ligne *Cc* (*Carbon copy*), ou des copies dont certains destinataires resteront invisibles avec la ligne *Bcc* (*Blind carbon copy*).

• **L'objet** (ligne *Subject*) doit être indiqué avec précision et clarté (ce qui permet au destinataire de savoir pourquoi on lui écrit, puis de retrouver les courriers facilement).

• **Les formules de politesse** sont abrégées (mais présentes !). On conclut souvent par *Best regards*, ou simplement *Regards*.

• Comme dans les SMS, **les abréviations** peuvent être utilisées dans les courriels.

# 8. Parler de son expérience professionnelle

Vous devez être en mesure de rendre compte de vos stages (ou autres expériences) en milieu professionnel. Pour cela vous devrez suivre un ordre logique et utiliser un vocabulaire adéquat.

## Ce que vous devez exposer

**En introduction** : à quelles périodes de vos études vous avez effectué ces stages, leur durée.
**1. L'entreprise** dans laquelle vous avez travaillé
Ajoutez bien sûr des informations sur son activité, sa taille, son emplacement.
Expliquez comment vous avez trouvé ce stage.
**2. Les tâches** qui vous ont été confiées
Décrivez ce que vous deviez faire, et ce que vous avez accompli, ainsi que les problèmes éventuels auxquels vous avez été confrontés et les satisfactions que vous en avez retirées.
**En conclusion** : évaluez cette expérience sur le terrain en relation avec votre formation.

## Exemple

During my two-year course, I followed a 14-week work placement in a mobile phone company called Vodaphone.
I found this placement by myself, by sending an application letter and a CV. →**The rules of the game, p. 14** Among all the applications I sent to 20 companies, Vodaphone was the first to give me a positive answer/reply. The company's headquarters are located in the suburbs of Lyons and I had a half hour commute to and from work. The working hours were the usual 9 to 5 ones.
I shared an office with the sales manager who was my supervisor. He/she showed me how to use and update a customer file, how to write invoices, bills of order, etc. I was able to create my own phoning guidebook under his/her supervision. I learned how to answer customers' complaints and I attended some of his/her customers' appointments.
After the first week, I was able to work on my own: I took initiatives and prospected new clients; I was in charge of customers' follow-ups, I wrote letters, sent e-mails and did some phoning. I was able to carry out all these tasks thanks to the computer skills I had acquired during my course.
My supervisor manages a team of four sales reps; I realised how important it was to have good interpersonal skills in order to motivate a team. At the end, I was able to instruct a new trainee; it allowed me to put into practice the skills I had learned.
I believe this work placement was a success as it allowed me first to realise I had chosen the right studies, and secondly to better understand how the working world operated. I now feel ready to be part of it.

# 9. Parler au téléphone

Voici une activité qui deviendra peut-être quotidienne et que vous devrez maîtriser parfaitement.

## 1 I Les techniques de base

- Lorsque vous avez un interlocuteur au téléphone, identifiez d'abord clairement sa demande.
- Apprenez à repérer les mots importants pour pouvoir répondre de manière précise.
- N'hésitez pas à lui demander poliment de répéter ou de parler plus lentement si vous n'êtes pas sûr.
- Vous devez avoir en tête des formules de salutations pour terminer votre conversation.
- Une dernière recommandation : souriez ! On repère facilement si quelqu'un sourit juste au ton de sa voix.

## 2 I Les structures de base

### a. Answering the phone

Hello
X Company, YY (your name), good morning / afternoon / evening.
Who's calling?
Can I help you?
Hold on a minute / just a moment, please.
I'll connect you to Mr/Mrs/Ms Z.
I'll put you through.
YY speaking.
Mr/Mrs/Miss/Ms Z is not here / is out of his/her office for the moment.
I'm afraid there's no answer.
The line/the extension is engaged.
Can I take a message?
Would you like to leave a message?
Would you like him/her to call you back?

### Répondre au téléphone

Allô
(Entreprise) X, YY (votre nom), bonjour / bonsoir.
Qui est à l'appareil ?
Que puis-je faire pour vous ?
Ne quittez pas / veuillez patienter, s'il vous plaît.
Je vous passe M./Mme/Mlle Z.
Je vous le/la passe.
YY à l'appareil.
M./Mme/Mlle Z n'est pas là / n'est pas dans son bureau pour le moment.
Ça ne répond pas.
La ligne / le poste est occupée.
Puis-je prendre un message ?
Souhaitez-vous laisser un message ?
Voulez-vous que il/elle vous rappelle ?

### b. Asking for information

Can I have your name / phone number / e-mail address, please?
Who's calling, please?
Could you please spell it?
Could you tell me what it's about?
Could you give me a few details?

### Demander des renseignements

Puis-je prendre votre nom / numéro de téléphone / adresse mail, s'il vous plaît ?
C'est de la part de qui ?
Pourriez-vous l'épeler, s'il vous plaît ?
C'est à quel sujet ?
Pourriez-vous me donner quelques détails ?

### c. Making a call

Good morning/afternoon, YY, from X Company.
Can / could I talk to..., please?
Am I speaking to...?
I'd like to speak to the person in charge of...
The reason I'm calling is... / I'm calling about...
Could you tell him/her that I rang?
Could you ask him/her to call me back?
To call France, dial 00 33 →Tools 10, p. 243

### Appeler

Bonjour, YY, de (l'entreprise) X.
Puis-je parler à..., s'il vous plaît ?
Je parle bien à... ?
J'aimerais parler à la personne qui s'occupe de...
La raison de mon appel est la suivante...
Pourriez-vous lui dire que j'ai appelé ?
Pourriez-vous lui demander de me rappeler ?
Pour appeler la France, composez le 00 33.

### d. Problems of understanding

I'm sorry, you've got a wrong number.
Would you mind repeating that, please?
I'm not sure I have quite understood your name.
Sorry, did you say that...?
Sorry, I didn't catch that.
Let me read this back to you.

### Problèmes de compréhension

Désolé(e), vous vous êtes trompé de numéro.
Pourriez-vous répéter, s'il vous plaît ?
Je ne suis pas sûr(e) d'avoir bien saisi votre nom.
Avez-vous dit que...
Désolé, je n'ai pas bien saisi cela.
Permettez-moi de vous relire...

### e. Ending the call

Mr/Mrs/Ms Z will call you back this afternoon / evening.
Thanks for calling.
You're welcome. Good bye.

### Terminer la conversation

M./Mme/Mlle vous rappellera cet après-midi / ce soir.
Merci d'avoir appelé.
Je vous en prie, au revoir.

# 10. Réviser les chiffres

Vous allez rencontrer des chiffres (*figures*) sans arrêt : dans votre entreprise, bien sûr, et pendant vos années d'étude, qu'il s'agisse de numéros de téléphone, de résultats financiers, de ventes, de surfaces, de pourcentages, etc.
Vous trouverez dans la plupart des pages ***In brief*** et ***Front page*** des activités pour vous entraîner : profitez de ces occasions pour les revoir systématiquement, et n'hésitez pas à revenir sur cette double page aussi souvent que nécessaire.

## 1 | Chiffres de base et grands nombres

**• De 13 à 19 : suffixe *-teen* (cf. *a teenager*)**
> *thirteen, fourteen, fifteen, eighteen, nineteen.*
Attention aux modifications soulignées.

**• Les dizaines : suffixe *-ty.***
> *twenty, thirty, forty, fifty, sixty, seventy, ninety.*
On ajoute un trait d'union entre les dizaines et les unités : *94: ninety-four. 52: fifty-two. 44: forty-four.*

**• Dizaines et centaines**
On ajoute *and* entre les centaines et les dizaines, sauf en anglais américain.
> *128: one hundred and twenty-eight*

**• La virgule**
On utilise la virgule en anglais pour marquer les milliers, mais on ne la lit pas à voix haute.
> six mille quatre cent s'écrit *6,400* et s'énonce *six thousand four hundred*
Attention, on ne met pas de virgule aux années !
> 1995 : *nineteen ninety-five* ; 2007 : *two thousand and seven*

**• *hundred, thousand, million, billion***
L'abréviation de *million* est *M* ou *m*, celle de *billion* est *bn.* Elles sont fréquemment utilisées dans la presse.
Ces mots sont invariables quand on compte précisément.
> *6,543: six thousand five hundred and forty-three*
Ils ne prennent de *s* de pluriel que dans des expressions indéterminées comme « des centaines », « des milliers », etc.).
> Il y avait des milliers de clients. *There were thousands of customers.*

## 2 | Mathématiques

**• Les décimales**
En anglais, elles sont indiquées par un point.
> 4,5 (quatre virgule cinq) s'écrit en anglais *4.5* et s'énonce *four point five.*
Les décimales sont prononcées l'une après l'autre.
> *15.32* se dit *fifteen point three two*

**• Les ordinaux**
Ils servent pour la date (*the eleventh of October*), mais aussi pour les fractions : 1/3 (un tiers) : *one third.*
C'est toujours le deuxième mot qui prend la marque du pluriel : *two fifths.*
Les seules fractions où l'on n'utilise pas les ordinaux sont 1/2 (*one half*) et 1/4 (*a/one quarter*).

**• Les pourcentages (%)**
Ils se lisent *per cent.*

**• Le zéro**
Il est prononcé comme la lettre *O* dans les numéros de téléphone, de chambre, de carte bancaire, de vol, d'immatriculation, etc.
Toutefois, si le nombre est inférieur à 1, le zéro qui se trouve avant la virgule se dit *nought.*
> 0,001 (zéro virgule zéro zéro un) s'écrit en anglais *0.001* et s'énonce *nought point oh oh one.*

**• Les proportions**
On utilise les prépositions *in* ou *out of.*
> Un sur quatre : *one in four / one out of four.*

## 3 | Cas particuliers

**• Les monnaies (ou les prix)**
Quand une somme d'argent est écrite en chiffres, la devise est toujours inscrite avant la somme.
> *£100* : cent livres sterling, 100 £
Attention, la devise est dite en dernier à haute voix, ou écrite en dernier en toutes lettres.
> *£300: three hundred pounds*

Par ailleurs, il est important de savoir à quelle valeur correspondent quelques monnaies étrangères, essentiellement la livre sterling (le dollar est suffisamment proche de l'euro pour avoir un ordre d'idée).

**• Les mesures**
Les Britanniques ont officiellement adopté le même système que nous (métrique) depuis 1971. Mais on trouve encore la plupart du temps des surfaces exprimées en *square yards* et non en mètres carrés, des *miles* et non des kilomètres, etc. Les Américains utilisent toujours quant à eux le système impérial.
Il est donc important de savoir à quoi correspondent quelques mesures, afin de pouvoir convertir dans des unités qui aient du sens pour vous, comme pour les monnaies.

**- Longueur / *length***
1 inch (in.) = 0,0254 mètre
1 foot (ft.) = 12 inches = 0,30 mètre
1 yard (yd.) = 36 inches = 3 yards = 0,91 mètre
1 mile (mi.) = 1 609 mètres = 1,6 km

**- Liquide / *capacity***
1 pint (pt.) (GB) = 1,2 pints (US) = 0,5 litre
1 gallon (gal.) = 4,54 litres (GB) ; 3,8 litres (US)

**- Superficie / *area***
1 square foot (sq. ft.) ≈ 0.1 $m^2$
1 square mile (sq. mi.) ≈ 2.5 $km^2$ > 2 sq.mi. ≈ 5 $km^2$

**• Les adjectifs composés**
Attention au singulier de l'adjectif.
> Un chèque de 50 £ : *a £50 cheque, a fifty-pound cheque*
> Un vol de dix heures : *a 10-hour flight*

**• Les numéros de téléphone, de carte, etc.**
On les lit en énumérant les chiffres les uns après les autres. Quand deux chiffres identiques se suivent, on utilise *double.* Le zéro se lit comme la lettre *O.*
4985 5589 3502 4401 : *four nine eight five / double five eight nine / three five O two / double four O one*
Les pauses se font en fonction des espaces.

TOOLS

# 11. Utiliser des graphiques, diagrammes ou tableaux

## 1 | Décrire

Dans un premier temps, identifiez le document.
camembert : *pie chart*
courbe : *line-chart, flow chart*
graphique : *graph/chart*
histogramme : *bar chart*
organigramme : *organisation chart*
statistiques : *statistics*
tableau : *table*

Définissez sa source, son objet, la date et le contexte géographique ou social de l'étude.
*This chart covers the period from…to…; it measures…; it traces the growth of…*

## 2 | Donner du sens

Les chiffres donnés aboutissent à des constatations sur des évolutions (*trend, tendency*).

• augmenter : *rise, increase, go up, climb*
atteindre un sommet : *reach a peak, peak, climax*
monter en flèche : *skyrocket*
s'envoler : *soar, jump*
se redresser : *to pick up*
dépasser : *to top*
une augmentation : *an increase, a rise, a climb, a jump, a boom, growth*

• diminuer : *fall, decrease, go down*
chuter : *drop*
décliner : *decline*
dégringoler : *plummet, plunge*
s'effondrer : *nosedive, collapse*
atteindre un creux : *reach a trough/a bottom low*
une diminution : *a decrease, a decline, a fall, a drop*

•stagner : *stagnate, remain stable*
atteindre un palier, se stabiliser : *level out/off*
varier, fluctuer : *fluctuate*
être au même niveau que : *be level with*

•Attention aux prépositions que vous utilisez !
augmenter/diminuer de : *rise/fall by*
augmenter de … à … : *rise from … to …*
augmenter/diminuer jusqu'à : *rise/fall to*
se monter à : *stand at*
une augmentation/chute de : *rise/fall of*
fluctuer entre … et … : *fluctuate between … and …*

Vous pouvez nuancer les tendances avec des adjectifs ou des adverbes (en ajoutant *-ly* à l'adjectif).

| | |
|---|---|
| brutal : *sharp* | spectaculaire : *dramatic* |
| en flèche : *steep* | beaucoup : *a lot, a great deal* |
| important : *considerable, substantial* | environ : *approximately, roughly* |
| léger : *slight, marginal* | régulier : *regular, steady (steadily)* |
| petit à petit : *gradual* | |
| soudain : *sudden* | |

Utilisez des chiffres, des comparatifs et des superlatifs. →**Tools 10, p. 243**

*the highest/lowest figures, more/less …than…, were higher in… than in…*
Vous pouvez être amené à classer : *rank first, come last, an all-time high/low*, etc.
Les verbes utilisés sont en général au prétérit (passé daté et révolu), sauf si on décrit une tendance qui se poursuit au moment où l'on parle (dans ce cas là, on utilise le *present perfect*).

## 3 | Interpréter

Mettez les données en perspective : les statistiques décrivent un phénomène mais n'en donnent pas l'analyse. À vous de formuler une interprétation : *It seems to indicate…, Judging from…, It would/could mean that…, we may infer that…*
Utilisez des mots de liaison exprimant cause et conséquence et des formes passives : *therefore, because of…; the trend can be explained/accounted for/by…*

### Exemple INTERNET SHOPPING

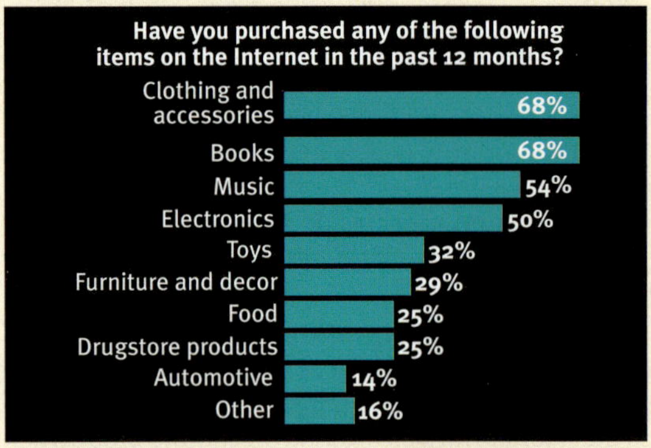


From *Time*, March 2006

*This bar-chart shows the various products American consumers have bought on the internet over a year, between March 2005 and March 2006.*
*The vast majority, almost 70%, bought books and clothing accessories. Another considerable proportion of consumers purchased music (54%) while one in two/50% bought electronics. One third bought toys and another third bought furniture and decor products. One quarter of internet shoppers acquired food and drugstore products. Finally, 14% people purchased car-related products while another 16% gave no indications as to what they bought.*
*This chart reflects the current trends where shoppers tend to choose books, music and electronics on the internet, which allows them both a wider choice and home delivery. On the other hand, the fact that consumers purchase clothes on the internet shows that online retailers have adapted well to this channel of distribution and that people feel safe enough to buy even though they can't try. The trend can also be accounted for as more and more consumers are time-pressed and appreciate the comfort of home shopping.*

# 12. Analyser une publicité

La présence d'un document iconographique dans certaines sections, et notamment bien sûr en « Communication des entreprises », est le reflet d'un aspect fort de notre société. Il est devenu une des formes essentielles de communication et un langage qui donne à voir et à penser. C'est donc un support incontournable qu'il est essentiel d'apprendre à voir et à décoder, dont il faut dégager l'implicite et apprécier l'humour, etc.
Un document publicitaire est toujours porteur d'un message qui vise à vendre (un produit, une marque) ou à convaincre (campagne de sensibilisation). Gardez toujours ceci à l'esprit !
Un certain nombre de termes doivent être utilisés à bon escient (reportez-vous aux pages de lexique 104 et 120, chapitres 6 et 7 et à la banque de mots ci-dessous).

La démarche se fait toujours en trois temps.

## 1 | Identifier et décrire

Ce sont les réponses aux *Wh-* questions (*who, what, where, when*) que vous devez toujours vous poser et que vous pouvez enrichir de détails qui vous semblent pertinents.

• Cherchez **le logo** qui vous permettra d'identifier l'auteur (le payeur) de la campagne, puis le slogan qui met en mots le message que l'on veut faire passer.
> *Who had this ad made? Who is the advertiser? (brand, company, advertise, awareness campaign, what product or service is advertised)*

• Observez également **la disposition** des différents éléments dans la page, la prédominance du visuel ou du texte (publicité informative par exemple, *infomercial*).
> *The different elements, what the picture represents, its layout, the slogan and/or catch phrase*
Rappel :
- *IN the middle*
- *AT the top/bottom*
- *ON the left/right*
- *IN the foreground/background*

Vous pourrez parfois déterminer où le support était visible (affichage dans la rue, magazine, etc.).

## 2 | Analyser

Dégagez du sens en analysant l'intention / le message du document. Vos connaissances dans le domaine de l'entreprise peuvent éclairer votre commentaire.
> *The aim of the campaign is to move/shock/inform, let the public know*, etc.

**Essayez de définir :**
• **le lien entre les différents éléments :** partie visuelle (choix des documents, effets des couleurs, texte (information contenue), et slogan.
• **la cible**, en vous posant la question : à qui cette publicité s'adresse-t-elle ? Une certaine catégorie de personnes, une tranche d'âge, tout le monde ?
> *target, social/age group, housewives, teenagers, their parents, family men, married couples, middle-aged people, businessmen*, etc.
• **la tactique** utilisée pour convaincre : l'humour ou le sérieux, le choquant, la complicité, etc.
Vérifiez s'il n'y a pas de jeu de mots (*pun*) dont les publicitaires (*advertising agency*) sont friands.

## 3 | Interpréter

Vous pouvez interpréter et réagir en fonction de votre personnalité et vos goûts.
Demandez-vous si la publicité sera efficace.
> *the key arguments used to convince the target, influence, be convincing/effective*, etc.
Vous a-t-elle plu, amusé, choqué ?
> *humorous, informative, shocking, colourful, dull, sinister, eye-catching, old-fashioned, clever.*
N'oubliez pas que ce qui amuse ou fait prendre conscience dans un pays laissera indifférent dans un autre. Partez de votre propre culture ou jugement pour vous identifier à celui qui reçoit le message.

## Banque de mots utiles

| | |
|---|---|
| faire de la publicité (pour un produit, etc.) | *advertise* |
| une publicité | *advertisement* |
| publicitaire (profession) | *advertiser* |
| la publicité (en général) | *advertising* |
| publicité informative | *infomercial* |
| agence de publicité | *advertising agency* |
| campagne | *campaign* |
| campagne de sensibilisation | *awareness campaign* |
| reconnaissance de la marque | *brand awareness* |
| marque | *brand* |
| image de marque | *brand image* |
| tranche d'âge | *age group* |
| cible, cibler | *target* (N, V) |
| consommateur | *consumer* |
| panneau publicitaire | *billboard* |
| texte publicitaire | *copy* |
| maquette | *layout* |
| produit | *product* |
| transmettre | *convey* |
| efficace | *effective* |
| qui attire l'œil, accrocheur | *eye-catching* |
| direct | *straightforward* |

# 13. Le sketch de vente (NRC)

## 1 | Le principe de l'épreuve

Durée de préparation 15 minutes, durée de passage devant l'examinateur 15 minutes.

Cette épreuve en anglais n'a rien à voir avec l'épreuve professionnelle de négociation : en effet, vous n'êtes pas obligé de conclure la vente, cela ne conditionne pas la réussite de l'épreuve. Vous avez en anglais une marge de liberté infinie, à condition de ne pas faire de contresens manifeste sur le document de départ.

**Critères de réussite :**
- votre anglais de spécialité,
- votre capacité à comprendre l'examinateur et à rebondir sur des situations inattendues,
- votre capacité à n'oublier aucune des étapes obligatoires : caractéristiques du produit, avantages comparatifs, prix, délais de livraison, moyens de paiement, service après vente, devis, offre de ristourne, etc.

## 2 | Le document de départ

- C'est la base à partir de laquelle vous allez renseigner votre client qui n'est pas censé avoir le prospectus en main. Donc n'hésitez pas à lui donner les renseignements dont il a besoin, même s'ils figurent sur le document ! En revanche, il ne faut pas les lire mais les reformuler.
- Vous devez « inventer » tout ce qui ne figure pas dans le document : positionnement de l'entreprise, prix, SAV, livraison, coloris, etc.

## 3 | La situation de communication

- Vous êtes en rendez-vous avec un prospect chaud. Vous n'êtes pas en magasin, vous avez devant vous un particulier ou un professionnel. Vous pouvez choisir le type de vente que vous souhaitez faire, *B to C* (*Business to Customer*, c'est-à-dire la vente au particulier) ou *B to B* (*Business to Business*, c'est-à-dire la vente à une entreprise ou à un commerce), en orientant votre prise de contact avec l'examinateur.

- Si la vente est conclue, la commande se passe auprès de vous. N'oubliez pas de faire remplir le bon de commande, de parler des modalités de paiement et de prendre congé. N'envoyez pas votre client dans un autre lieu (magasin, etc.) pour acheter le produit.

### Exemple : le début de l'entretien

Attention ce qui vous est proposé n'est pas exclusif, c'est un modèle parmi d'autres possibles.

- **Prise de contact**

> *Good morning/ afternoon* (Ne dites jamais *Hi*, ou *Hello*)

- **Vous vous présentez.**

> *I am X, a sales rep for XX* (Inventez le nom de l'entreprise s'il ne figure pas dans le document)

- Vous parlez du **positionnement** de votre entreprise et de ce qu'elle vend.

*Our company is one of the top food/computer/ software company on the market.*

- Vous passez à **la raison de votre présence**.

> *I'm here to give you all the information you need on our new/latest product/service.*

- Vous passez la parole à votre examinateur/ client.

> *Before I explain the advantages/main features of the product/service, have you got any questions?*

Passer la parole à votre examinateur/client lui permet de se sentir libre de réagir comme il le souhaite : cela montre aussi que vous vous sentez capable de répondre à n'importe quelle demande.

Ensuite l'entretien se passera selon le produit et selon le client.

## 4 | Expressions utiles

Elles vous permettront de mener l'entretien à bien, et sont à adapter suivant le produit. À vous de repérer le moment propice où les « placer ».
Les phrases proposées sont simples : à vous de les enrichir en fonction de la situation, sans répéter toujours les mêmes structures. Attention : certaines expressions sont équivalentes, et ne sont pas toutes à utiliser pêle-mêle, sans distinction.
Ces propositions ne tiennent pas compte de la communication : la spontanéité nécessaire au contact n'est pas prise en considération. Pour cela, c'est à vous de jouer !
Utilisez les *gap-fillers* lorsque vous hésitez : *so, well, you know, you see, in fact, actually* (en réalité), etc.
Les mots soulignés sont expliqués dans la banque de mots ci-après.

This product *(le nommer)* offers many advantages.
It is both economical and time-saving.
It was especially designed to make it user-friendly: you just need to plug it in, and press the start button.
Also, its small size allows you to store it very easily.
It is convenient and saves space.
As for cleaning, nothing could be simpler.
It comes with a very complete instruction leaflet.
It is very easy to maintain. It's maintenance-free.
Should you need it, you are entitled to free maintenance.
Its design is particularly trendy.
The latest model is one of our bestsellers.
You have the choice between a wide range of colours.
It comes into several sizes.
It is already assembled.
The price we offer is very competitive: if you buy it in a store, it'll cost you X pounds/dollars more, at least. (Penser à utiliser les chiffres correctement !)
→ **Tools 10, p. 243**

It has an excellent quality-price ratio.
Our price includes the delivery.
The delivery is not included but if you order today, I can offer you free delivery.
The delivery times are very short.
May I remind you that X pounds/dollars is an excellent price for such a quality product?
It is reliable and resistant, that's why we offer a two-year guarantee/warranty. You can extend the guarantee if you wish; it will cost you only X pounds/dollars.
Our offer is limited in time that's why I advise you to take advantage of it /to seize the opportunity.
It is suitable for any type of room.
We can make a free estimate, if you wish.
It will be delivered at your home within x days/ weeks.
Shall we fill in the bill of order?
As for the terms of payment, you will be charged 25% with the order and the rest on delivery.
You can pay in several instalments.
If you order now, I can offer you a x% discount on the price.
If you are not satisfied with our product after the first month/week you can get a full refund.
You can contact our after sales service from Monday to Friday during office hours.
Our after sales service is available around the clock.
Please do not hesitate to contact us even for a minor problem.
It's a good investment; I know you won't regret it.
I congratulate you, you have made the good choice/ a good bargain/purchase and you won't regret it.

En *B to B*, l'entretien sera similaire : seules les quantités seront différentes. Vous devrez établir un tarif dégressif en fonction des quantités commandées.
Vous pouvez aussi proposer une période d'essai de votre produit en magasin.
The more you buy, the less expensive it becomes
We can propose you a xx month/week trial in your store.

## Banque de mots utiles

| | |
|---|---|
| *after sales service* | service après vente |
| *around the clock* | 24 heures sur 24 |
| *assemble* | assembler, monter (*meuble*) |
| *available* | disponible |
| *bargain* | affaire |
| *bestseller* | qui se vend très bien |
| *bill of order* | bon de commande |
| *congratulate* | féliciter |
| *convenient* (adj.) | pratique |
| *deliver* | livrer |
| *delivery* | livraison |
| *delivery times* | délais de livraison |
| *design* | dessiner, concevoir |
| *discount* | ristourne, réduction |
| *economical* | économique |
| *efficient* (adj.) | efficace |
| *estimate* | devis |
| *fill in* | remplir (bon de commande, fiche, etc.) |
| *free maintenance* | entretien gratuit |
| *guarantee* (GB) | garantie |
| *handmade* | fait à la main |
| *hi-tech* | haute technologie |
| *instalment* | mensualité |
| *instruction leaflet* | mode d'emploi |
| *investment* | investissement |
| *latest* | le plus récent, le dernier en date |
| *maintain* | entretenir |
| *maintenance* | entretien |
| *maintenance-free* | sans entretien |
| *office hours* | heures de bureau |
| *order* | commander, commande |
| *plug in* | brancher (prise électrique) |
| *purchase* | achat |
| *quality price ratio* | rapport qualité prix |
| *refund* | remboursement |
| *reliable* | fiable |
| *resistant* | solide |
| *save* | économiser |
| *size* | taille |
| *state-of-the-art* | dernier cri |
| *store* | ranger |
| *suitable* | adapté |
| *terms of payment* | modalités de paiement |
| *time-saving* | qui fait gagner du temps |
| *trendy* | à la mode, tendance |
| *trial* | essai |
| *user-friendly* | facile à utiliser, convivial |
| *warranty* (US) | garantie |
| *wide range* | gamme étendue |
| *within* | d'ici (indique un intervalle de durée) |

# 14. L'entretien d'embauche à l'examen

## 1 | Quelques principes

Les offres d'emplois auxquelles vous pouvez être amenés à postuler concernent des secteurs et des métiers précis : commercial, chef des ventes, ou acquéreur de franchise.

Vous devez montrer la qualité de votre anglais : la meilleure façon de le faire dans ce contexte n'est pas de répéter textuellement ce qu'il y a dans l'annonce (on recherche toujours des personnes dynamiques, compétentes, ayant l'esprit d'initiative).

Vous devez faire la preuve que vous êtes le candidat idéal pour le poste proposé grâce à une expérience professionnelle fictive que vous décrirez.

L'entretien d'embauche est différent des autres sujets dans la mesure où vous allez être amené à questionner l'employeur/examinateur sur :
- **l'entreprise** : cible (*target*), notoriété (*fame*), taille (*size*), positionnement (*place on the market*), etc.
- **ce que cette entreprise vous offre** en échange de vos compétences : salaire de base (*basic salary*), prime (*bonus*), avantages en nature (*perks*), avantages sociaux (*benefits*), formation (*training*)
- **ses exigences** : horaires (*working hours*), lieu (*place*), objectifs de vente (*sales targets*), etc.

## 2 | Méthode

*Ashfield Care, the number one medical care company, is looking for a part time sales representative for the UK.*

***Excellent salary, a company car, social benefits***

Because Ashfield care has been expanding quickly, our company needs a part time sales rep to manage a new team nationwide.

***Requirements***
- A-level is the minimum qualification required;
- Previous medical sales experience will be considered a bonus;
- Highly motivated person with outstanding interpersonal skills: excellent communicator showing confidence, enthusiasm and ability to influence others;
- OTE + bonus + perks+ benefits;
- Excellent salary and a genuine career opportunity;
- A career compatible with your lifestyle: 5 mornings per week;
- Responsibility for the sale of a whole range of products.

***Don't miss a fantastic career opportunity!***

Send your CV with cover letter to Ashfield Care, 15a Outram Street, Sutton in Ashfield, Nottinghamshire NG17 4BA

Vous devez analyser l'annonce proposée pour répondre aux questions élémentaires sur l'entreprise, ce qu'elle souhaite et ce qu'elle offre.
L'emploi proposé : un emploi à temps partiel pour un visiteur médical (*part time medical sales representative*) qui devra couvrir la totalité du territoire national (*nationwide*) avec une équipe nouvelle (*new team*).
Dans le corrigé proposé, vous travaillez déjà dans une entreprise où vous avez a fait vos preuves mais vous désirez changer de secteur, avoir d'autres possibilités de carrière, et travailler à temps partiel.

### a. L'entreprise

Relevez toutes les indications concernant le secteur, le positionnement de l'entreprise, sa cible, etc.
- **Son nom** : Ashfield Care, bien positionné au Royaume-Uni (*the UK's premier contract sales organisation*)
- **Son développement** : se développe + vite que la concurrence (*developing faster*)
- **Sa cible** : les médecins généralistes (*GP*) et les infirmières libérales

### b. Ce que l'entreprise attend des candidats

- **Diplômes universitaires** : le bac suffit (*A level qualifications*)
- **Expérience professionnelle** : une expérience de la vente dans le médical ou le para médical est préférable (*previous medical sales experience*)
- **Qualités** : confiance (*confidence*), communication (*excellent communicator*), enthousiasme (*enthusiasm*), capacité à influencer les autres (*the ability to influence others*)

### c. Ce que l'entreprise offre

- Une activité en accord avec votre mode de vie (*lifestyle*)
- Une opportunité de carrière fantastique (*a fantastic opportunity*)
- Cinq demi-journées de travail par semaine (*working five mornings per week*)
- La responsabilité des ventes de nouveau produit (*responsible for the sale of … products*)
- Un très bon salaire, une voiture de fonction, des avantages sociaux

### Exemple de déroulement

Attention ! Le dialogue qui suit est un exemple possible. Ne vous focalisez pas sur cet exemple, au risque de vous figer et de tomber dans une récitation par cœur : il doit vous servir à réfléchir et à vous entraîner sur d'autres annonces.
Les mots appartenant au lexique spécialisé sont en gras.

*You*: Good morning/afternoon, sir/madam. I am X and I am interested in your **job offer**. / Pleased to meet you.
*Examiner*: Good morning, pleased to meet you. Please sit down.
*You*: Thank you. How shall I start?
*Examiner*: Can you tell me about yourself?
*You*: Well, first I have a **degree in sales and management**, and I have been working as a **sales rep** for Glaxo[1] for 2 years now.
*Examiner*: Why are you interested in our offer, then? Aren't you satisfied at Glaxo? It is a very famous pharmaceutical firm!
*You*: Yes, I know, but I feel that at Glaxo my **career** is blocked. There are too many employees, too many sales reps and showing your qualities is very difficult. I understand your company is smaller but in **full expansion**, and I'm interested in participating in your **success.** Moreover, I wish to **work part time** because I have children to raise / I have other activities, mainly sportive. I coach a football team in my neighbourhood, and with a **full time job** it's almost impossible.
*Examiner*: Ok, but what tells me that you are **the right person for the job**?
*You*: I can give you all the **sales figures** I've **reached** for the past 2 years which show that I've been quite **successful.**
*Examiner*: All right. Do you know about our **target customers?**
*You*: Of course! My **customer file** is made up of GPs, nurses and hospital wards[2]. I have more than one hundred **customers** right now.
*Examiner*: So, I imagine you must be quite a **good communicator**?
*You*: My manager says I have got **excellent interpersonal skills**.
*Examiner*: Would you like to ask us some questions about the job, the firm or anything you may find important?
*You*: What will my **job consist of**? Will I be **part of a team** or work by myself in a **limited sector**?
*Examiner*: Both options are possible. First you'll be part of a team to get familiar with our **know-how**.
*You*: All right... Well, I saw in your job offer that you proposed an attractive **salary**. If you don't mind, I would like to know **what kind of salary I can expect**.
*Examiner*: You'll get 12,000 **pounds** a year as a **basic salary**, plus a **percentage** on each sale. Our **bonus scheme** is very attractive: it can double your salary, and it is easy to enter if you are an experienced sales rep as you seem to be.
*You*: What **perks** do you offer?
*Examiner*: You'll have a **company car**, a laptop computer and a mobile phone.
*You*: As for the **benefits**, what do they consist of?
*Examiner*: You get **health insurance, paid holidays** and **a retirement scheme**.
*You*: That sounds fine. Do you think I've got a chance of **joining** your company? / Do you think I've got a chance of becoming part of your team?
*Examiner*: Well, I can't give you a final answer now as we have two more **applicants** to see. If you're **hired,** how long will it take before you can start with us?
*You*: One month, at most, time for me to **give my notice** to Glaxo.
*Examiner*: All right, then, we'll send you an answer **within** the next 3 or 4 days.
*You***:** Thank you very much, good-bye.
*Examiner*: Good-bye.

1. Glaxo est une grosse entreprise pharmaceutique ; si aucun nom ne vous vient à l'esprit, inventez-en un.
2. *hospital ward* : service hospitalier

**Dans le même esprit, 90% des candidats sont amenés à parler de leur stage en entreprise.**

I've done three five-week work placements.
J'ai effectué 3 stages de 5 semaines.
One of my work placements was carried out in a computer firm.
Un de mes stages a été effectué dans une entreprise d'informatique.
I learned how to put into practise the theoretical knowledge I got at school.
J'ai appris comment mettre en pratique le savoir théorique appris à l'école.
I was able to establish a customer file, to visit/meet customers.
J'ai pu établir un fichier client, faire des visites clients, rencontrer les clients.
I did a lot of phoning / door-to-door canvassing.
J'ai fait beaucoup de phoning, de prospection porte à porte.
I enjoyed the contact with customers even if it wasn't always easy.
J'ai apprécié le contact avec les clients, même si parfois ce n'était pas facile.
I was in charge of customer follow up.
J'étais chargé du suivi client.
I had a really good supervisor.
J'ai eu un excellent formateur / responsable de stage.
I enjoyed the atmosphere in the company.
J'ai apprécié l'atmosphère de l'entreprise.
The employees were very helpful.
Les employés/salariés étaient très serviables, prêts à m'aider.

# 15. Revue de presse

## 1 I Les grands titres

Les titres qui suivent sont parmi les plus connus du monde anglophone. Tous ou presque peuvent être consultés et lus sur internet.

| **Titre et pays** | **Caractéristiques** ***characteristics*** |
|---|---|
| **MAGAZINES** | |
| *The Economist – GB*<br>• créé en 1843<br>• tirage : 785 000 exemplaires (*copies*) | En dépit de son nom, le magazine propose bon nombre d'articles qui touchent à d'autres sujets (culture, science, technologie, etc.). |
| *Time – USA*<br>• créé en 1923<br>• tirage : 6 millions | Le précurseur qui touche à tous les domaines. Ligne éditoriale proche des Républicains. |
| *Newsweek – USA*<br>• créé en 1933<br>• tirage : 4 millions | À sa création, il s'est inscrit dans la lignée de *Time* sans parvenir à obtenir le même nombre de lecteurs. Ligne éditoriale proche des Démocrates. |
| **NEWSPAPERS** | |
| *The Times – GB*<br>• créé en 1785<br>• tirage : 700 000 | Un journal noble par son âge. Tendance « conservateur ». |
| *The Independent – GB*<br>• créé en 1986<br>• tirage : 250 000 | Un journal récent, qui, comme son nom l'indique, revendique… son indépendance. |
| *The Guardian – GB*<br>• créé en 1821<br>• tirage : 400 000 | Tendance centre-gauche. L'*Observer*, publié le dimanche, appartient au même groupe depuis 1993. |
| *The New York Times – USA*<br>• créé en 1851<br>• tirage : 1,1 million en semaine | Réputation de sérieux, transcription de tous les discours. L'édition du dimanche monte à 1,6 million d'exemplaires. |
| *Washington Post – USA*<br>• créé en 1877<br>• tirage : 730 000 | Tendance libérale, il a remporté le prix Pulitzer pour son enquête lors du scandale du Watergate. |
| *USA Today – USA*<br>• créé en 1982<br>• tirage : 2,3 millions | N'a pas la réputation des autres grands quotidiens nationaux américains, peu d'articles de fond. |
| *International Herald Tribune – USA*<br>• créé en 1887<br>• tirage : 235 000 | Publié à Paris, il vise surtout les Américains résidant en Europe (on peut maintenant l'acheter aux États-Unis). Ses articles et éditoriaux proviennent du *New York Times* et du *Washington Post*. |

## 2 I Les types de quotidien

Il existe deux formats de journaux :

• ***broadsheet*, ou grand format**

On les associe à la presse de qualité.
Titres : *Times*, *Guardian*, *Independent*, *Daily Telegraph* pour le Royaume-Uni ; édition nationale du *New York Times* pour les États-Unis.

• ***tabloids*, ou presse à sensation**

Ils se distinguent par leurs gros titres accrocheurs, des articles abondamment illustrés de photographies et leur goût pour les histoires à scandale.
Exemples : *Sun*, *Daily Mirror*, *Daily Express* et *Daily Mail* pour le Royaume-Uni, *New York Daily News* et *Chicago Sun-Times* pour les États-Unis.
Depuis de nombreuses années, les lecteurs du *Sun* trouvent en page 3 une photo pleine page de jeune femme posant seins nus. L'expression *page three* s'applique aujourd'hui à toutes les photos de femmes aux seins nus publiées dans les *tabloids*.

## 3 I Les journaux du dimanche (*Sunday papers*)

Un *Sunday paper* s'accompagne d'un ou de plusieurs suppléments magazines en couleurs et contient des rubriques très variées (arts, sports, voyages, etc.). Sa lecture occupe souvent une place de choix dans l'esprit des anglophones, qui peuvent en acheter plusieurs et y consacrer une partie de la journée.

• Journaux paraissant uniquement le dimanche : *Observer*, *News of the World*.
• Éditions du dimanche de quotidiens : *Independent on Sunday*, *Sunday Times*, *Sunday Telegraph*, etc.).

## 4 I Banque de mots utiles

| | |
|---|---|
| journaliste d'agence | *syndicated journalist* |
| pigiste | *freelance journalist* |
| chroniqueur | *columnist* |
| quotidien | *daily* |
| hebdomadaire | *weekly* |
| mensuel | *monthly* |
| trimestriel | *quarterly* |
| la une | *front cover* |
| (gros) titre | *headline* |
| gros titres criards | *screaming headlines* |
| faire la une | *make the headlines* |
| faits divers, brèves | *news in brief* |
| sous-titre | *subhead* |
| mise en page | *layout* |
| dernière page | *back page* |
| texte | *body copy/text* |
| légende | *caption* |
| encadré | *box* |
| caractères gras | *bold type* |
| italiques | *italics* |

TOOLS

# 16. Anglais britannique et anglais américain

Les différences entre l'anglais « britannique » (GB) et l'anglais « américain » (US) portent sur la prononciation, le vocabulaire et quelques points de grammaire. Cette page vous permet d'apprendre les principales différences de vocabulaire. Pour la prononciation, reportez-vous à votre dictionnaire si nécessaire.

## 1 | Mots différents

| anglais GB | anglais US | français |
|---|---|---|
| *autumn* | *fall* | automne |
| *bill* | *check* | addition (restaurant) |
| *biscuit* | *cookie* | gâteau sec |
| *bonnet* | *hood* | capot (voiture) |
| *boot* | *trunk* | coffre (voiture) |
| *car park* | *parking lot* | parking |
| *chemist's* | *drugstore* | pharmacie |
| *chips* | *French fries* | frites |
| *cinema* | *(movie) theater* | cinéma |
| *engaged* | *busy* | occupé (téléphone) |
| *film* | *movie* | film |
| *fireman* | *firefighter* | pompier |
| *flat* | *apartment* | appartement |
| *garden* | *yard* | jardin |
| *ground floor* | *first floor* | rez-de-chaussée |
| *handbag* | *purse* | sac à main |
| *holiday* | *vacation* | vacances |
| *junction* | *intersection* | croisement |
| *letter box* | *mail box* | boîte à lettres |
| *lift* | *elevator* | ascenseur |
| *lorry* | *truck* | camion |
| *motorway* | *freeway* | autoroute |
| *number plate* | *license plate* | plaque d'immatriculation |
| *pavement* | *sidewalk* | trottoir |
| *petrol* | *gas* | essence |
| *postcode* | *zip code* | code postal |
| *postman* | *mailman* | facteur |
| *queue* | *line* | file d'attente |
| *rubber* | *eraser* | gomme |
| *rubbish* | *trash, garbage* | ordures |
| *shop* | *store* | magasin |
| *shop assistant* | *clerk* | vendeur |
| *sweets* | *candy* | bonbons |
| *tap* | *faucet* | robinet |
| *toilet* | *restroom* | toilettes |
| *trousers* | *pants* | pantalon |
| *underground* | *subway* | métro |

## 2 | Différences orthographiques

**• Différences systématiques sur les terminaisons**

*-our* et *-er* en anglais GB = *-or* et *-re* en anglais US

> GB *colour, labour, favour, odour* // US *color, labor, favor, odor*

> GB *centre, fibre, litre, theatre* // US *center, fiber, liter, theater*

**• Le « l » final**

Il est doublé devant certains suffixes en anglais GB seulement.

> Le prétérit de *travel* s'écrit *travelled* (GB) ou *traveled* (US).

**• Autres différences orthographiques**

GB *kerb* (bordure de trottoir) – US *curb*
GB *tyre* (pneu) – US *tire*
GB *cheque* (cheque) – US *check*
GB *programme* (programme) – US *program*
GB *through* (à travers) – US *thru*

# 17. Les faux amis

Ces mots peuvent tromper car ils ressemblent à des mots que vous connaissez en français, mais leur sens est différent. Attention aux contresens !
Vous trouverez ci-dessous :
- en colonnes 1 et 2 le mot anglais « faux ami » et sa traduction en français,
- en colonnes 2 et 3 le mot français avec lequel vous ne devez pas confondre et sa traduction en anglais.

| Faux-ami anglais → | Traduction en français | Mot français → | Traduction en anglais |
|---|---|---|---|
| *achieve* | réaliser, mener à bien | achever | *complete* |
| *actual* | réel, concret | actuel | *current, today's, present* |
| *actually* | en fait | actuellement | *currently, at present* |
| *advertisement* | publicité | avertissement | *warning* |
| *affluent* | riche | affluence | *rush* |
| *attend* | assister à | attendre | *wait (for), expect* |
| *balance* | équilibre | balance (une) | *scales* |
| *benefit* | avantage | bénéfice | *profit* |
| *caution* | prudence | caution | *guarantee* |
| *charge* | faire payer | charger | *to load* |
| *check* | contrôle/facture/chèque | chèque | *cheque/check (US)* |
| *close* | proche | clos | *closed* |
| *comprehensive* | complet | compréhensif | *understanding* |
| *copy* | exemplaire | copie | *reproduction* |
| *crime* | criminalité, délit | crime | *murder* |
| *delay* | retard | délai | *time limit* |
| *deliver* | livrer | délivrer | *set free* |
| *deputy* | adjoint | député | *MP, Congressman* |
| *dispose* | se débarrasser | disposer | *to arrange* |
| *engaged* | occupé/fiancé | engagé | *committed* |
| *eventually* | finalement | éventuellement | *possibly* |
| *extra* | supplémentaire | extra | *top, first rate* |
| *figure* | chiffre, silhouette | figure | *face* |
| *fortunate* | chanceux | fortuné | *wealthy, well-off* |
| *global* | mondial | global | *overall* |
| *grand* | grandiose (adj.), 1000 $ | grand | *tall* |
| *habit* | habitude | habit(s) | *clothes, dress* |
| *hazard* | danger | hasard | *chance* |
| *ignore* | refuser de prendre en compte | ignorer | *not to know* |
| *journey* | voyage | journée | *day* |
| *library* | bibliothèque | librairie | *bookshop* |
| *location* | emplacement | location | *renting/hire* |
| *mark* | note | marque | *brand* |
| *mechanic* | mécanicien | mécanique | *engineering* |
| *patron* | client (restaurant) | patron | *boss, chief executive* |
| *petrol* | essence | pétrole | *oil* |
| *photograph* | une photo | photographe | *photographer* |
| *prejudice* | préjugé | préjudice | *harm, wrong* |
| *prevent* | empêcher | prévenir | *to warn* |
| *proper* | correct | propre | *clean, tidy* |
| *refuse* | déchets | refus | *refusal* |
| *regard* | considérer | regarder | *to look at* |
| *relief* | soulagement – aide – relief | relief | *relief* |
| *resume* | recommencer | résumer | *to sum up* |
| *route* | itinéraire | route | *road* |
| *sensible* | raisonnable | sensible | *sensitive* |
| *store* | (grand) magasin | store | *blind* |
| *supply* | fournir | supplier | *to implore* |
| *sympathetic* | compatissant | sympathique | *nice, friendly* |
| *trivial* | insignifiant | trivial | *crude, coarse* |
| *vacancy* | chambre/poste libre | vacances | *holiday GB)/vacation (US)* |
| *valid* | valable | valide | *fit, well* |
| *wagon* | chariot | wagon | *carriage (GB) / car (US)* |

# 18. Expressions utiles

## Expression orale

**Expressing your opinion**
My view is that...
...to my mind...
As far as I'm concerned...
Personally, .../In my opinion, ...

**Expressing agreement (partial or complete)**
Indeed!
I agree with you!
I'm not sure about...
Up to a certain point/extent...
I suppose you're right but...

**Expressing disagreement**
I suppose that's true, but I still think that...
I don't share this point of view.
I highly/strongly disagree on that point.

**Expressing the fact that you are convinced**
I know for a fact that...
You can't deny that...
In actual fact...
It goes without saying that...

**Expressing certainty**
I'm sure/certain/positive that...
It's obvious/clear that...
Undoubtedly, ...
What is quite certain is that...

**Expressing concession**
In spite of + *N*
No matter how...,
However + *adj*...
Unless...

**Expressing contrast**
But.../Unlike..., we...
This is different from/not the same as...
We must weigh up the pros and the cons.
Compared to/with...
Actually, ...
I suppose... is all right, but...
This may be true up to a certain point, but...
You have to acknowledge the fact that...

**Summing up your ideas**
To conclude,.../All in all, ...
It may be concluded that...
To put it in a nutshell, ...

**In case...**
**...you hesitate**
Use *gap fillers*: You know – I mean – Well – Um – Let me think
I'm not a hundred percent certain, but...
From what I know, I can say that...
**...you haven't understood**
I'm sorry, I don't understand.
Could you repeat that, please?
Could you speak more slowly, please?

## Expression écrite

**Expressing agreement**
I could not agree more with...
I am in total/complete agreement with...
I totally approve of.../I'm all in favour of
(*partial agreement*) To a certain extent...

**Expressing certainty**
There is no doubt that...
Doubtless/Undoubtedly, ...
I am convinced that...

**Expressing condition**
Provided/providing that...
As long as...
On (the) condition that...

**Expressing mixed feelings**
I have mixed feelings about...
I am not quite sure about...
I don't really approve of...

**Expressing strong disapproval**
I totally disapprove of...
I wouldn't (exactly) say (that)...
I can't see why...
I resent (+ V-*ING*)

**Expressing cause**
Due to.../Owing to...
On account of.../Because of...
Thanks to...
Considering/Given that...

**Expressing your opinion**
I think/believe...
I find it + *adj.*
I can't help + V-*ING*
What I find most striking/interesting is the fact/idea that...
It makes me think of/It reminds me of...
My point is...
What comes to my mind is...
I agree/disagree with
I would say that...

**Expressing concession**
Despite the fact that...
However + *adj.* this may be...
*Adj.* as it may seem,
Even though.../Though.../Although...
Admittedly, ...
Whatever we/they/people may say, ...

**Expressing contrast**
On the one hand..., on the other hand...
While.../Whereas...
By comparison with...
Contrary/conversely to...

# 19. Verbes irréguliers

| Infinitive | Past simple | Past participle | |
|---|---|---|---|
| **arise** | arose | arisen | *se lever* |
| **awake** | awoke | awoken | *(se) réveiller* |
| **be** | was/were | been | *être* |
| **beat** | beat | beaten | *battre* |
| **become** | became | become | *devenir* |
| **begin** | began | begun | *commencer* |
| **bend** | bent | bent | *courber* |
| **bet** | bet | bet | *parier* |
| **bid** | bade | bidden | *ordonner* |
| **bind** | bound | bound | *lier* |
| **bite** | bit | bitten | *mordre* |
| **bleed** | bled | bled | *saigner* |
| **blow** | blew | blown | *souffler* |
| **break** | broke | broken | *casser* |
| **bring** | brought | brought | *apporter* |
| **build** | built | built | *construire* |
| **burn** | burnt | burnt | *brûler* |
| **burst** | burst | burst | *éclater* |
| **buy** | bought | bought | *acheter* |
| **catch** | caught | caught | *attraper* |
| **choose** | chose | chosen | *choisir* |
| **come** | came | come | *venir* |
| **cost** | cost | cost | *coûter* |
| **creep** | crept | crept | *ramper* |
| **cut** | cut | cut | *couper* |
| **deal** | dealt | dealt | *distribuer* |
| **dig** | dug | dug | *creuser* |
| **do** | did | done | *faire* |
| **draw** | drew | drawn | *dessiner, tirer* |
| **dream** | dreamed/dreamt | dreamed/dreamt | *rêver* |
| **drink** | drank | drunk | *boire* |
| **drive** | drove | driven | *conduire* |
| **eat** | ate | eaten | *manger* |
| **fall** | fell | fallen | *tomber* |
| **feed** | fed | fed | *nourrir* |
| **feel** | felt | felt | *(res)sentir* |
| **fight** | fought | fought | *combattre* |
| **find** | found | found | *trouver* |
| **fly** | flew | flown | *voler* |
| **forbid** | forbade | forbidden | *interdire* |
| **forget** | forgot | forgotten | *oublier* |
| **forgive** | forgave | forgiven | *pardonner* |
| **freeze** | froze | frozen | *geler* |
| **get** | got | got/gotten (US) | *obtenir* |
| **give** | gave | given | *donner* |
| **go** | went | gone | *aller* |
| **grind** | ground | ground | *moudre* |
| **grow** | grew | grown | *pousser* |
| **hang** | hung | hung | *pendre* |
| **have** | had | had | *avoir* |
| **hear** | heard | heard | *entendre* |
| **hide** | hid | hidden | *cacher* |
| **hit** | hit | hit | *frapper* |
| **hold** | held | held | *tenir* |
| **hurt** | hurt | hurt | *blesser* |
| **keep** | kept | kept | *garder* |

| | | | |
|---|---|---|---|
| **know** | knew | known | *savoir* |
| **lay** | laid | laid | *poser* |
| **lead** | led | led | *mener* |
| **lean** | leaned/leant | leaned/leant | *incliner* |
| **leap** | leaped/leapt | leaped/leapt | *sauter* |
| **learn** | learned/learnt | learned/learnt | *apprendre* |
| **leave** | left | left | *quitter* |
| **lend** | lent | lent | *prêter* |
| **let** | let | let | *laisser* |
| **lie** | lay | lain | *être allongé* |
| **lose** | lost | lost | *perdre* |
| **make** | made | made | *faire* |
| **mean** | meant | meant | *vouloir dire* |
| **meet** | met | met | *rencontrer* |
| **mistake** | mistook | mistaken | *se tromper* |
| **pay** | paid | paid | *payer* |
| **put** | put | put | *mettre* |
| **read** [riːd] | read **[red]** | read **[red]** | *lire* |
| **ride** | rode | ridden | *être à vélo/cheval* |
| **ring** | rang | rung | *sonner* |
| **rise** | rose | risen | *se lever* |
| **run** | ran | run | *courir* |
| **say** | said | said | *dire* |
| **see** | saw | seen | *voir* |
| **seek** | sought | sought | *chercher* |
| **sell** | sold | sold | *vendre* |
| **send** | sent | sent | *envoyer* |
| **set** | set | set | *placer* |
| **shake** | shook | shaken | *secouer* |
| **shine** | shone | shone | *briller* |
| **shoot** | shot | shot | *tirer (fusil)* |
| **show** | showed | shown | *montrer* |
| **shrink** | shrank | shrunk | *rétrécir* |
| **shut** | shut | shut | *fermer* |
| **sing** | sang | sung | *chanter* |
| **sink** | sank | sunk | *sombrer, couler* |
| **sit** | sat | sat | *être assis* |
| **sleep** | slept | slept | *dormir* |
| **slide** | slid | slid | *glisser* |
| **smell** | smelt | smelt | *sentir* |
| **speak** | spoke | spoken | *parler* |
| **spell** | spelt | spelt | *épeler* |
| **spend** | spent | spent | *dépenser* |
| **spoil** | spoilt | spoilt | *gâcher* |
| **stand** | stood | stood | *être debout* |
| **steal** | stole | stolen | *dérober* |
| **stick** | stuck | stuck | *coller* |
| **swear** | swore | sworn | *jurer* |
| **swim** | swam | swum | *nager* |
| **take** | took | taken | *prendre* |
| **teach** | taught | taught | *enseigner* |
| **tear** | tore | torn | *déchirer* |
| **tell** | told | told | *dire* |
| **think** | thought | thought | *penser* |
| **throw** | threw | thrown | *lancer* |
| **understand** | understood | understood | *comprendre* |
| **wear** | wore | worn | *porter un vêtement* |
| **weep** | wept | wept | *pleurer* |
| **win** | won | won | *gagner* |
| **withdraw** | withdrew | withdrawn | *retirer* |
| **write** | wrote | written | *écrire* |

## Crédits iconographiques

1ère de couv GETTY IMAGES/Franck Seifert ; 9 COSMOS/Aurora/David Mclain ; 16 © www.CartoonStock.com/ATON1444 ; 21 MAGNUM/Peter Marlow ; 27 GETTY IMAGES/ Time & Life Pictures ; 29 Advertising Archive ; 30 © www.CartoonStock.com/JKN0282 ; 35 CORBIS/Chuck Savage ; 40 ARCHIVES NATHAN/D.R. ; 43 d Advertising Archive ; 43 g Advertising Archive ; 44 © www.CartoonStock.com/JKN0305 ; 51 TUC Library Collections, London Metropolitan University ; 56 TUC Library Collections, London Metropolitan University ; 57 CORBIS/Rick Gayle ; 59 © International Labour Organization ; 60 © www.CartoonStock.com/PTON49 ; 65 CORBIS/Visions of America/Joseph Sohm ; 70 Advertising Archive ; 71 Advertising Archive ; 73 SIPA PRESS/AP/Stephen Chernin ; 74 © www.CartoonStock.com/TBRN13 ; 80 US Consumer Product Safety Commission/D.R. ; 81 Advertising Archive ; 86 Advertising Archive ; 87 REA/Redux/Joshua Lutz ; 89 © Ikea ; 90 © www.CartoonStock.com/SEA0166 ; 95 Advertising Archive ; 100 CORBIS/Zuma/Andrew Faukner ; 101 CORBIS/Tony Arnuza ; 103 © BENETTON/Oliviero Toscani ; 104 © www.CartoonStock.com/HSC0260 ; 105 bas Advertising Archive ; 105 ht © BENETTON/ Oliviero Toscani ; 111 Advertising Archive ; 116 Advertising Archive ; 117 SIPA PRESS/AP/ Dima Gavryski ; 119 bas Advertising Archive ; 119 ht Advertising Archive ; 120 © www.CartoonStock.com/NBA0045 ; 124 ht © National Health Service ; 124 d ADBUSTERS MEDIA FOUNDATION ; 124 g ADBUSTERS MEDIA FOUNDATION ; 125 CORBIS/Historical Picture Archive ; 130 Advertising Archive ; 131 SIPA PRESS/AP/Jae C. Hong ; 133 Advertising Archive ; 134 © www.CartoonStock.com/GRIN81 ; 138 © Mini Marketing Department/Butler Shine Stern ; 141 CORBIS/Christine Osborne ; 147 SIPA PRESS/AP/Fabian Bimmer ; 149 © AIRBUS ; 150 © www.CartoonStock.com/AMC0316 ; 155 © BUSINESS WEEK ; 160 COURRIER INTERNATIONAL/Dessin de Aislin, in The Gazette (Montréal), 12-01-07 ; 161 Advertising Archive ; 163 © GOOGLE ; 164 © www.CartoonStock.com/GRIN95 ; 171 Advertising Archive ; 176 Collection Christophe L. ; 179 Advertising Archive ; 180 © www.CartoonStock.com/SEA0179 ; 185 Advertising Archive ; 190 Advertising Archive ; 193 d THOMAS COOK UK Ltd ; 193 g THOMAS COOK UK Ltd ; 194 © www.CartoonStock.com/ AMC0553 ; 201 © Eurominority ; 206 © EUROPEAN COMMISSION ; 207 Advertising Archive ; 209 Advertising Archive ; 210 © www.CartoonStock.com/CGO0071 ; 215 Advertising Archive ; 220 EDITING/L'Express/Thierry Dudoit ; 221 Advertising Archive ; 223 Advertising Archive ; 224 © www.CartoonStock.com/KSMN81

Coordination éditoriale : Christine Asin
Édition : Sophie Legras
Coordination artistique : Isabelle Jalfre
Conception maquette : Courant d'idées/Rony Turlet
Mise en pages : Nadine Aymard
Couverture : Laurence Durandau
Iconographie : Nadine Gudimard
Schémas : Coredoc/Laurent Blondel et Dany Mourain
Fabrication : Maria Pauliat


ISBN : 978-2-09-160360-5
N° de projet: 10164440 - N AYMARD
Dépôt légal: Octobre 2009
Imprimé en France par MAME Imprimeurs (n°09092131)